D1859813

# THE SIX SYSTEMS
# OF
# INDIAN PHILOSOPHY

# THE SIX SYSTEMS
# OF
# INDIAN PHILOSOPHY

BY

THE RIGHT HON. F. MAX MULLER, K.M.
FOREIGN MEMBER OF THE FRENCH INSTITUTE

GYAN

*Published by*

Gyan Publishing House
5, Ansari Road
Daryaganj, New Delhi-110002
Phone: 011-47034999, 9811692060
E-mail: books@gyanbooks.com

*Distribution Network*
gyanbooks.com
India, USA, Canada, UK, Australia, France

© **Publisher**
All rights reserved. No part of this work may be reproduced, stored, adapted, or transmitted in any form or by any means, electronic, mechanical, photocopying, micro-filming, recording or otherwise, or translated in any language, without the prior written permission of the copyright owner and the publisher.

ISBN : 978-81-212-2275-4 (PB)
First Published, 1899

2nd Impression 2021

*Printed at:* Gyan Press, Delhi.

The book is sold subject to the condition that it shall not, by way of trade or otherwise, be lent, resold, hired out, or otherwise circulated without the prior publisher's written consent.

**The Six Systems of Indian Philosophy**
Author: The Right Hon. F. Max Muller

# THE SIX SYSTEMS

OF

# INDIAN PHILOSOPHY

BY

THE RIGHT HON. F. MAX MÜLLER, K.M.

FOREIGN MEMBER OF THE FRENCH INSTITUTE

NEW YORK

LONGMANS, GREEN, AND CO.

LONDON AND BOMBAY

1899

# PREFACE.

It is not without serious misgivings that I venture at this late hour of life to place before my fellow-workers and all who are interested in the growth of philosophical thought throughout the world, some of the notes on the Six Systems of Indian Philosophy which have accumulated in my note-books for many years. It was as early as 1852 that I published my first contributions to the study of Indian philosophy in the *Zeitschrift der Deutschen Morgenländischen Gesellschaft*. My other occupations, however, and, more particularly, my preparations for a complete edition of the Rig-Veda, and its voluminous commentary, did not allow me at that time to continue these contributions, though my interest in Indian philosophy, as a most important part of the literature of India and of Universal Philosophy, has always remained the same. This interest was kindled afresh when I had to finish for the Sacred Books of the East (vols. I and XV) my translation of the Upanishads, the remote sources of Indian philosophy, and especially of the Vedânta-philosophy, a system in which human speculation seems to me to have reached its very acme. Some of the other systems of Indian philosophy also have from time to time roused the curiosity of scholars and philosophers in Europe and America, and in India itself a revival of philosophic and theosophic studies, though not always well directed, has taken place, which, if it leads to a more active co-operation between European and Indian thinkers, may be productive in the future of most important results. Under these circumstances a general desire has arisen, and has repeatedly been expressed, for the publication of a more general and comprehensive account of the six systems in which the philosophical thought of India has found its full realisation.

More recently the excellent publications of Professors Deussen and Garbe in Germany, and of Dr. G. Thibaut in India, have given a new impulse to these important studies, important not only in the eyes of Sanskrit scholars by profession, but of all who wish to become acquainted with all the solutions which the most highly gifted races of mankind have proposed for the eternal riddles of the world. These studies, to quote the words of a high authority, have indeed ceased to be the hobby of a few individuals, and have become a subject of interest to the whole nation[1]. Professor Deussen's work on the Vedânta-philosophy (1883) and his translation of the Vedânta-Sûtras (1887), Professor Garbe's translation of the Sâ*m*khya-Sûtras (1889) followed by his work on the Sâ*m*khya-philosophy (1894), and, last not least, Dr. G. Thibaut's careful and most useful translation of the Vedânta-Sûtras in vols. XXXIV and XXXVIII of the Sacred Books of the East (1890 and 1896), mark a new era in the

---

[1] Words of the Viceroy of India, see *Times*, Nov. 8, 1898.

study of the two most important philosophical systems of ancient India, and have deservedly placed the names of their authors in the front rank of Sanskrit scholars in Europe.

My object in publishing the results of my own studies in Indian philosophy was not so much to restate the mere tenets of each system, so deliberately and so clearly put forward by the reputed authors of the principal philosophies of India, as to give a more comprehensive account of the philosophical activity of the Indian nation from the earliest times, and to show how intimately not only their religion, but their philosophy also, was connected with the national character of the inhabitants of India, a point of view which has of late been so ably maintained by Professor Knight of St. Andrews University[1].

It was only in a country like India, with all its physical advantages and disadvantages, that such a rich development of philosophical thought as we can watch in the six systems of philosophy, could have taken place. In ancient India there could hardly have been a very severe struggle for life. The necessaries of life were abundantly provided by nature, and people with few tastes could live there like the birds in a forest, and soar like birds towards the fresh air of heaven and the eternal sources of light and truth. What was there to do for those who, in order to escape from the heat of the tropical sun, had taken their abode in the shade of groves or in the caves of mountainous valleys except to meditate on the world in which they found them-

[1] See 'Mind,' vol. v. no. 17.

selves placed, they did not know how or why? There was hardly any political life in ancient India, such as we know it from the Vedas, and in consequence neither political strife nor municipal ambition. Neither art nor science existed as yet, to call forth the energies of this highly gifted race. While we, overwhelmed with newspapers, with parliamentary reports, with daily discoveries and discussions, with new novels and time-killing social functions, have hardly any leisure left to dwell on metaphysical and religious problems, these problems formed almost the only subject on which the old inhabitants of India could spend their intellectual energies. Life in a forest was no impossibility in the warm climate of India, and in the absence of the most ordinary means of communication, what was there to do for the members of the small settlements dotted over the country, but to give expression to that wonder at the world which is the beginning of all philosophy? Literary ambition could hardly exist during a period when even the art of writing was not yet known, and when there was no literature except what could be spread and handed down by memory, developed to an extraordinary and almost incredible extent under a carefully elaborated discipline. But at a time when people could not yet think of public applause or private gain, they thought all the more of truth; and hence the perfectly independent and honest character of most of their philosophy.

It has long been my wish to bring the results of this national Indian philosophy nearer to us, and, if possible, to rouse our sympathies for their honest efforts to throw some rays of light on the dark problems of existence, whether of the objective world at large, or of the subjective spirits, whose knowledge of the world constitutes, after all, the only proof of the existence of an objective world. The mere tenets of each of the six systems of Indian philosophy are by this time well known, or easily accessible, more accessible, I should say, than even those of the leading philosophers of Greece or of modern Europe. Every one of the opinions at which the originators of the six principal schools of Indian philosophy arrived, has been handed down to us in the form of short aphorisms or Sûtras, so as to leave but little room for uncertainty as to the exact position which each of these philosophers occupied on the great battlefield of thought. We know what an enormous amount of labour had to be spent and is still being spent in order to ascertain the exact views of Plato and Aristotle, nay, even of Kant and Hegel, on some of the most important questions of their systems of philosophy. There are even living philosophers whose words often leave us in doubt as to what they mean, whether they are materialists or idealists, monists or dualists, theists or atheists. Hindu philosophers seldom leave us in doubt on such important points, and they certainly never shrink from the consequences of their theories. They never equivocate or try to hide their opinions where they are likely to be unpopular. Kapila, for instance, the author or hero eponymus of the Sâ*m*khya-philosophy, confesses openly that his system is atheistic, an-îsvara, without an active Lord or God, but in spite of that, his system was treated as legitimate by his contemporaries, because it was reasoned out consistently, and admitted, nay, required some transcendent and invisible power, the so-called Purushas. Without them there would be no evolution of Prak*ri*ti, original matter, no objective world, nor any reality in the lookers-on themselves, the Purushas or spirits. Mere names have acquired with us such a power that the authors of systems in which there is clearly no room for an active God, nevertheless shrink from calling themselves atheists, nay, try even by any means to foist an active God into their philosophies, in order to escape the damaging charge of atheism. This leads to philosophical ambiguity, if not dishonesty, and has often delayed the recognition of a Godhead, free from all the trammels of human activity and personality, but yet endowed with wisdom, power, and will. From a philosophical point of view, no theory of evolution, whether ancient or modern (in Sanskrit Pari*n*âma), can provide any room for a creator or governor of the world, and hence the Sâ*m*khya-philosophy declares itself fearlessly as an-î*s*vara, Lord-less, leaving it to another philosophy, the Yoga, to find in the old Sâ*m*khya system some place for an Î*s*vara or a personal God. What is most curious is that a philosopher, such as *S*a*m*kara, the most decided monist, and the upholder of Brahman, as a neuter, as the cause of all things, is reported to have been a worshipper of idols and to have seen in them, despite of all their hideousness, symbols of the Deity, useful, as he thought, for the ignorant, even though they have no eyes as yet to see what is hidden behind the idols, and what was the true meaning of them.

What I admire in Indian philosophers is that

they never try to deceive us as to their principles and the consequences of their theories. If they are idealists, even to the verge of nihilism, they say so, and if they hold that the objective world requires a real, though not necessarily a visible or tangible substratum, they are never afraid to speak out. They are *bona fide* idealists or materialists, monists or dualists, theists or atheists, because their reverence for truth is stronger than their reverence for anything else. The Vedântist, for instance, is a fearless idealist, and, as a monist, denies the reality of anything but the *One* Brahman, the Universal Spirit, which is to account for the whole of the phenomenal world. The followers of the Sâ*m*khya, on the contrary, though likewise idealists and believers in an unseen Purusha (subject), and an unseen Prak*r*iti (objective substance), leave us in no doubt that they are and mean to be atheists, so far as the existence of an active God, a maker and ruler of the world, is concerned. They do not allow themselves to be driven one inch beyond their self-chosen position. They first examine the instruments of knowledge which man possesses. These are sensuous perception, inference, and verbal authority, and as none of these can supply us with the knowledge of a Supreme Being, as a personal creator and ruler of the world, Kapila never refers to Him in his Sûtras. As a careful reasoner, however, he does not go so far as to say that he can prove the non-existence of such a Being, but he is satisfied with stating, like Kant, that he cannot establish His existence by the ordinary channels of evidential knowledge. In neither of these statements can I discover, as others have done, any trace of intellectual cowardice, but simply a desire to abide within the strict limits of knowledge, such as is granted to human beings. He does not argue against the possibility even of the gods of the vulgar, such as *S*iva, Vish*n*u, and all the rest, he simply treats them as *G*anye*s*varas or Kârye*s*varas, produced and temporal gods (Sûtras III, 57, comm.), and he does not allow, even to the Supreme Î*s*vara, the Lord, the creator and ruler of the world, as postulated by other systems of philosophy or religion, more than a phenomenal existence, though we should always remember that with him there is nothing phenomenal, nothing confined in space and time, that does not in the end rest on something real and eternal.

We must distinguish however. Kapila, though he boldly confessed himself an atheist, was by no means a nihilist or Nâstika. He recognised in every man a soul which he called Purusha, literally man, or spirit, or subject, because without such a power, without such endless Purushas, he held that Prak*ri*ti, or primordial matter with its infinite potentialities, would for ever have remained dead, motionless, and thoughtless. Only through the presence of this Purusha and through his temporary interest in Prak*ri*ti could her movements, her evolution, her changes and variety be accounted for, just as the movements of iron have to be accounted for by the presence of a magnet. All this movement, however, is temporary only, and the highest object of Kapila's philosophy is to make Purusha turn his eyes away from Prak*ri*ti, so as to stop her acting and to regain for himself his oneness, his aloneness, his independence, and his perfect bliss.

Whatever we may think of such views of the

world as are put forward by the Sâ*m*khya, the Vedânta, and other systems of Indian philosophy, there is one thing which we cannot help admiring, and that is the straightforwardness and perfect freedom with which they are elaborated. However imperfect the style in which their theories have been clothed may appear from a literary point of view, it seems to me the very perfection for the treatment of philosophy. It never leaves us in any doubt as to the exact opinions held by each philosopher. We may miss the development and the dialectic eloquence with which Plato and Hegel propound their thoughts, but we can always appreciate the perfect freedom, freshness, and downrightness with which each searcher after truth follows his track without ever looking right or left.

It is in the nature of philosophy that every philosopher must be a heretic, in the etymological sense of the word, that is, a free chooser, even if, like the Vedântists, he, for some reason or other, bows before his self-chosen Veda as the seat of a revealed authority.

It has sometimes been said that Hindu philosophy asserts, but does not prove, that it is positive throughout, but not argumentative. This may be true to a certain extent and particularly with regard to the Vedânta-philosophy, but we must remember that almost the first question which every one of the Hindu systems of philosophy tries to settle is, How do we know? In thus giving the Noëtics the first place, the thinkers of the East seem to me again superior to most of the philosophers of the West. Generally speaking, they admitted three legitimate channels by which knowledge can reach us, perception, inference, and authority, but authority freely chosen or freely rejected. In some systems that authority is revelation, *S*ruti, *S*abda, or the Veda, in others it is the word of any recognised authority, Âpta-va*k*ana. Thus it happens that the Sâ*m*khya philosophers, who profess themselves entirely dependent on reasoning (Manana), may nevertheless accept some of the utterances of the Veda as they would accept the opinions of eminent men or *S*ish*t*as, though always with the proviso that even the Veda could never make a false opinion true. The same relative authority is granted to Sm*ri*ti or tradition, but there with the proviso that it must not be in contradiction with *S*ruti or revelation.

Such an examination of the authorities of human knowledge (Pramâ*n*as) ought, of course, to form the introduction to every system of philosophy, and to have clearly seen this is, as it seems to me, a very high distinction of Indian philosophy. How much useless controversy would have been avoided, particularly among Jewish, Mohammedan, and Christian philosophers, if a proper place had been assigned *in limine* to the question of what constitutes our legitimate or our only possible channels of knowledge, whether perception, inference, revelation, or anything else!

Supported by these inquiries into the evidences of truth, Hindu philosophers have built up their various systems of philosophy, or their various conceptions of the world, telling us clearly what they take for granted, and then advancing step by step from the foundations to the highest pinnacles of their systems. The Vedântist, after giving us his reasons why revelation or the Veda stands higher with him than sensuous perception and inference, at least for the discovery of the highest truth (Paramârtha), actually puts *S*ruti in the place of sensuous perception, and allows to perception and inference no more than an authority restricted to the phenomenal (Vyâvahârika) world. The conception of the world as deduced from the Veda, and chiefly from the Upanishads, is indeed astounding. It could hardly have been arrived at by a sudden intuition or inspiration, but presupposes a long preparation of metaphysical thought, undisturbed by any foreign influences. All that exists is taken as One, because if the existence of anything besides the absolute One or the Supreme Being were admitted, whatever the Second by the side of the One might be, it would constitute a limit to what was postulated as limitless, and would have made the concept of the One self-contradictory. But then came the question for Indian philosophers to solve, how it was possible, if there was but the One, that there should be multiplicity in the world, and that there should be constant change in our experience. They knew that the one absolute and undetermined essence, what they called Brahman, could have received no impulse to change, either from itself, for it was perfect, nor from others, for it was Second-less.

Then what is the philosopher to say to this manifold and ever-changing world? There is one thing only that he can say, namely, that it is not and cannot be real, but must be accepted as the result of nescience or Avidyâ, not only of individual ignorance, but of ignorance as inseparable from human nature. That ignorance, though unreal in the highest sense, exists, but it can be destroyed by Vidyâ, knowledge, i. e. the knowledge conveyed by the Vedânta, and as nothing that can at any time be annihilated has a right to be considered as real, it follows that this cosmic ignorance also must be looked upon as not real, but temporary only. It cannot be said to exist, nor can it be said not to exist, just as our own ordinary ignorance, though we suffer from it for a time, can never claim absolute reality and perpetuity. It is impossible to define Avidyâ, as little as it is possible to define Brahman, with this difference, however, that the former can be annihilated, the latter never. The phenomenal world which, according to the Vedânta, is called forth, like the mirage in a desert, has its reality in Brahman alone. Only it must be remembered that what we perceive can never be the absolute Brahman, but a perverted picture only, just as the moon which we see manifold and tremulous in its ever changing reflections on the waving surface of the ocean, is not the real moon, though deriving its phenomenal character from the real moon which remains unaffected in its unapproachable remoteness. Whatever we may think of such a view of the cosmos, a cosmos which, it should be remembered, includes ourselves quite as much as what we call the objective world, it is clear that our name of nihilism would be by no means applicable to it.

The One Real Being is there, the Brahman, only it is not visible, nor perceptible in its true character by any of the senses; but without it, nothing that exists in our knowledge could exist, neither our Self nor what in our knowledge is not our Self.

This is one view of the world, the Vedânta view; another is that of the Sâ*m*khya, which looks upon our perceptions as perceptions of a substantial something, of Prakriti, the potentiality of all things, and treats the individual perceiver as eternally individual, admitting nothing besides these two powers, which by their union or identification cause what we call the world, and by their discrimination or separation produce final bliss or absoluteness.

These two, with some other less important views of the world, as put forward by the other systems of Indian philosophy, constitute the real object of what was originally meant by philosophy, that is an explanation of the world. This determining idea has secured even to the guesses of Thales and Heraclitus their permanent place among the historical representatives of the development of philosophical thought by the side of Plato and Aristotle, of Des Cartes and Spinoza. It is in that Walhalla of real philosophers that I claim a place of honour for the representatives of the Vedânta and Sâmkhya. Of course, it is possible so to define the meaning of philosophy as to exclude men such as even Plato and Spinoza altogether, and to include on the contrary every botanist, entomologist, or bacteriologist. The name itself is of no consequence, but its definition is. And if hitherto no one would have called himself a philosopher who had not read and studied the works of Plato and Aristotle, of Des Cartes and Spinoza, of Locke, Hume, and Kant in the original, I hope that the time will come when no one will claim that name who is not acquainted at least with the two prominent systems of ancient Indian philosophy, the Vedânta and the Sâmkhya. A President, however powerful, does not call himself His Majesty, why should an observer, a collector and analyser, however full of information, claim the name of philosopher?

As a rule, I believe that no one knows so well the defects of his book as the author himself, and I can truly say in my own case that few people can be so conscious of the defects of this History of Indian Philosophy as I myself. It cannot be called a history, because the chronological framework is, as yet, almost entirely absent. It professes to be no more than a description of some of the salient points of each of the six recognised systems of Indian philosophy. It does not claim to be complete; on the contrary, if I can claim any thanks, it is for having endeavoured to omit whatever seemed to me less important and not calculated to appeal to European sympathies. If we want our friends to love our friends, we do not give a full account of every one of their good qualities, but we dwell on one or two of the strong points of their character. This is what I have tried to do for my old friends, Bâdarâya*n*a, Kapila, and all the rest. Even thus it could not well be avoided that in giving an account of each of the six systems, there should be much repetition, for they all share so much in common, with but slight modifications; and the longer I have studied the various systems, the more have I become impressed with the truth of the view taken by Vi*g*ñâna-Bhikshu and others that there is behind the variety of the six systems a common fund of what may be called national or popular philosophy, a large Mânasa lake of philosophical thought and language, far away in the distant North, and in the distant Past, from which each thinker was allowed to draw for his own purposes. Thus, while I should not be surprised, if

Sanskrit scholars were to blame me for having left out too much, students of philosophy may think that there is really too much of the same subject, discussed again and again in the six different schools. I have done my best, little as it may be, and my best reward will be if a new interest shall spring up for a long neglected mine of philosophical thought, and if my own book were soon to be superseded by a more complete and more comprehensive examination of Indian philosophy.

A friend of mine, a native of India, whom I consulted about the various degrees of popularity enjoyed at the present day by different systems of philosophy in his own country, informs me that the only system that can now be said to be living in India is the Vedânta with its branches, the Advaitis, the Madhvas, the Râmânu*g*as, and the Vallabhas. The Vedânta, being mixed with religion, he writes, has become a living faith, and numerous Pandits can be found to-day in all these sects who have learnt at least the principal works by heart and can expound them, such as the Upanishads, the Brahma-Sûtras, the great Commentaries of the Â*k*âryas and the Bhagavad-gîtâ. Some of the less important treatises also are studied, such as the Pañ*k*adas*î* and Yoga-Vâsish*th*a. The Pûrva-Mîmâ*m*sâ is still studied in Southern India, but not much in other parts, although expensive sacrifices are occasionally performed. The Agnish*t*oma was performed last year at Benares.

Of the other systems, the Nyâya only finds devotees, especially in Bengal, but the works studied are generally the later controversial treatises, not the earlier ones.

The Vaiseshika is neglected and so is the Yoga, except in its purely practical and most degenerate form.

It is feared, however, that even this small remnant of philosophical learning will vanish in one or two generations, as the youths of the present day, even if belonging to orthodox Brâhmanic families, do not take to these studies, as there is no encouragement.

But though we may regret that the ancient method of philosophical study is dying out in India, we should welcome all the more a new class of native students who, after studying the history of European philosophy, have devoted themselves to the honorable task of making their own national philosophy better known to the world at large. I hope that my book may prove useful to them by showing them in what direction they may best assist us in our attempts to secure a place to thinkers such as Kapila and Bâdarâya*n*a by the side of the leading philosophers of Greece, Rome, Germany, France, Italy, and England. In some cases the enthusiasm of native students may seem to have carried them too far, and a mixing up of philosophical with religious and theosophic propaganda, inevitable as it is said to be in India, is always dangerous. But such journals as the *Pandit*, the *Brahmavâdin*, the *Light of Truth*, and lately the *Journal of the Buddhist Text Society*, have been doing most valuable service. What we want are texts and translations, and any information that can throw light on the chronology of Indian philosophy. Nor should their labour be restricted to Sanskrit texts. In the South of India there exists a philosophical literature which, though it may show clear traces of Sanskrit influence, contains also original indigenous elements of great beauty and of great importance for historical purposes. Unfortunately few scholars only have taken up, as yet, the study of the Dravidian languages and literature, but young students who complain that there is nothing left to do in Sanskrit literature, would, I believe, find their labours amply rewarded in that field. How much may be done in another direction by students of Tibetan literature in furthering a study of Indian philosophy has lately been proved by the publications of Sarat Chandra Das, C.I.E., and Satis Chandra Acharya Vidyâbhûsha*n*a, M.A., and their friends.

In conclusion I have to thank Mr. A. E. Gough, the translator of the Vaiseshika-Sûtras, and the author of the 'Philosophy of the Upanishads,' for his extreme kindness in reading a revise of my proof-sheets. A man of seventy-six has neither the eyes nor the memory which he had at twenty-six, and he may be allowed to appeal to younger men for such help as he himself in his younger days has often and gladly lent to his Gurus and fellow-labourers.

F. M. M.

OXFORD,
*May* 1, 1899.

# CONTENTS.

## INTRODUCTORY CHAPTER.



## CHAPTER II.

### THE VEDAS.

## CHAPTER III.

### The Systems of Philosophy.

## CHAPTER IV.

### VEDÂNTA OR UTTARA-MÎMÂMSÂ.

## CHAPTER V.

### Pûrva-Mîmâmsâ.



## CHAPTER VI.

### Sâmkhya-Philosophy.

## CHAPTER VII.

### Yoga-Philosophy.

## CHAPTER VIII.

### Nyâya and Vai*s*eshika.

## CHAPTER IX.

### Vai*s*eshika Philosophy.

# INDIAN PHILOSOPHY.

## INTRODUCTORY CHAPTER.

### Philosophy and Philosophers.

WHILE in most countries a history of philosophy is inseparable from a history of philosophers, in India we have indeed ample materials for watching the origin and growth of philosophical ideas, but hardly any for studying the lives or characters of those who founded or supported the philosophical systems of that country. Their work has remained and continues to live to the present day, but of the philosophers themselves hardly anything remains to us beyond their names. Not even their dates can be ascertained with any amount of certainty. In Greece, from the earliest times, the simplest views of the world and of the destinies of man, nay even popular sayings, maxims of morality and worldly wisdom, and wise saws of every kind, even though they contained nothing very original or personal, were generally quoted as the utterances of certain persons or at least ascribed to certain names, such as the Seven Sages, so as to have something like a historical background. We have some idea of who

Thales was, and who was Plato, where and when they lived, and what they did; but of Kapila, the supposed founder of the Sâ*m*khya philosophy, of Patañ*g*ali, the founder of the Yoga, of Gotama and Ka*n*âda, of Bâdarâyana and *G*aimini, we know next to nothing, and what we know hardly ever rests on contemporary and trustworthy evidence. Whether any of these Indian philosophers lived at the same time and in the same place, whether they were friends or enemies, whether some were the pupils and others the teachers, all this is unknown to us, nor do I see any chance of our ever knowing more about them than we do at present. We read that Thales warned King Croesus, we are told that Empedocles finished his days by throwing himself into the flames of Aetna, we know that Socrates drank poison, and that Anaxagoras was the friend of Pericles, but there is nothing to connect the names of the ancient Indian philosophers with any historical events, with any political characters, or with dates before the time of Buddha.

It is quite true that every literary composition, whether in prose or in poetry, presupposes an individual author, that no poem makes itself, and no philosophical system is elaborated by the people at large. But on the other hand, no poet makes himself, no philosopher owes everything to himself. He grows from a soil that is ready made for him, and he breathes an intellectual atmosphere which is not of his own making. The Hindus seem to have felt this indebtedness of the individuals to those before and around them far more strongly than the Greeks, who, if they cannot find a human author, have recourse even to mythological and divine personages in order to have a pedestal, a name, and an authority for every great thought and every great invention of antiquity. The Hindus are satisfied with giving us the thoughts, and leave us to find out their antecedents as best we can.

### Srutam and Smritam.

The Hindus have divided the whole of their ancient literature into two parts, which really mean two periods, Srutam, what was heard, and was not the work of men or any personal being, human or divine, and Smritam, what was remembered, and has always been treated as the work of an individual, whether man or god. Srutam or Sruti came afterwards to mean what has been revealed, exactly as we understand that word, while Smritam or Smriti comprised all that was recognized as possessing human authority only, so that if there ever was a conflict between the two, Smriti or tradition might at once be overruled by what was called Sruti or revelation.

It is curious, however, to observe how the revealed literature of the Hindus, such as the hymns of the Rig-veda, have in later times been ascribed to certain families, nay even to individual poets, though many of the names of these poets are clearly fictitious. Nor are even these fictitious poets supposed to have created or composed their poems, but only to have seen them as they were revealed to them by a higher power, commonly called Brahman, or the Word. What we call philosophy in its systematic form, is, from an Indian point of view, not revealed, *S*rutam, but belongs to Sm*ri*ti or tradition. We possess it in carefully composed and systematically elaborated manuals, in short aphorisms or Sûtras or in metrical Kârikâs, ascribed to authors of whom we hardly know anything, and followed by large commentaries or independent treatises which are supposed to contain the outcome of a continuous tradition going back to very ancient times, to the Sûtra, nay even to the Brâhma*n*a period, though in their present form they are confessedly the work of medieval or modern writers. In the Sûtras each system of philosophy is complete, and elaborated in its minutest details. There is no topic within the sphere of philosophy which does not find a clear or straightforward treatment in these short Sûtras. The Sûtra style, imperfect as it is from a literary point of view, would be invaluable to us in other systems of philosophy, such as Hegel's or Plato's. We should always know where we are, and we should never hear of a philosopher who declared on his deathbed that no one had understood him, nor of antagonistic schools, diverging from and appealing to the same teacher. One thing must be quite clear to every attentive reader of these Sûtras, namely, that they represent the last result of a long continued study of philosophy, carried on for centuries in the forests and hermitages of India. The ideas which are shared by all the systems of Indian philosophy, the large number of technical terms possessed by them in common or peculiar to each system, can leave no doubt on this subject. Nor can we doubt that for a long time the philosophical thoughts of India were embodied in what I call a Mnemonic Literature.

Writing for literary purposes was unknown in India before the rise of Buddhism, and even at the Buddhist Councils when their Sacred Canon, the Tripi*t*aka, was settled, we hear nothing as yet of paper, ink, and reeds, but only of oral and even musical repetition. The very name of a Council was Sa*m*gîti or Mahâsa*m*gîti, i. e. singing together, and the different parts of the Canon were not consigned to writing, but rehearsed by certain individuals. Whenever there arose a dispute as to the true teaching of Buddha, it was not settled by an appeal to any MS., but an invitation was addressed to a member of the Sa*m*gha who knew the text by heart. It is actually mentioned that the Southern Canon was not reduced to writing till the first century B.C., under King Va*tt*âgâmani, about 80 B.C. Nothing can be more explicit than the statement in the chronicles of Ceylon on that point: 'Before this time the wise monks had handed down the texts of the Tipi*t*aka orally; and also the A*tth*akatha (commentary). At this time the monks, perceiving the decay of beings (not MSS.), assembled, and in order that the Law might endure for a long time, they caused it to be written down in books.' Such a state of things is difficult for us to imagine, still if we wish to form a true idea of the intellectual state of India in pre-Buddhistic times, we must accustom ourselves to the idea that all that could be called literature then was mnemonic only, carefully guarded by a peculiar and very strict educational discipline, but of course exposed to all the inevitable chances of oral tradition. That Mnemonic Period existed for philosophy as well as for everything else, and if we have to begin our study of Indian philosophy with the

Sûtras, these Sûtras themselves must be considered as the last outcome of a long continued philosophical activity carried on by memory only.

### Upanishad-period, from about 700 B.C.

But while the Sûtras give us abstracts of the various systems of philosophy, ready made, there must have been, nay there was, one period, previous to the Sûtras, during which we can watch something like growth, like life and strife, in Indian philosophy, and that is the last stage of the Vedic period, as represented to us in the Upanishads.

For gaining an insight into the early growth of Indian philosophic thought, this period is in fact the most valuable; though of systematised philosophy, in our sense of the word, it contains, as yet, little or nothing. As we can feel that there is electricity in the air, and that there will be a storm, we feel, on reading the Upanishads, that there is philosophy in the Indian mind, and that there will be thunder and lightning to follow soon. Nay, I should even go a step further. In order to be able to account for what seem to us mere sparks of thought, mere guesses at truth, we are driven to admit a long familiarity with philosophic problems before the time that gave birth to the Upanishads which we possess.

### Period antecedent to the Upanishads.

The Upanishads contain too many technical terms, such as Brahman, Âtman, Dharma, Vrata, Yoga, Mîmâ*m*sâ, and many more, to allow us to suppose that they were the products of one day or of one generation. Even if the later systems of philosophy did not so often appeal themselves to the Upanishads as their authorities, we could easily see for ourselves that, though flowing in very different directions, like the Ganges and the Indus, these systems of philosophy can all be traced back to the same distant heights from which they took their rise. And as India was fertilised, not only by the Ganges and Indus, but by ever so many rivers and rivulets, all pointing to the Snowy Mountains in the North, we can see the Indian mind also being nourished through ever so many channels, all starting from a vast accumulation of religious and philosophic thought of which we seem to see the last remnants only in our Upanishads, while the original springs are lost to us for ever.

If some of the seeds and germs of philosophy could be discovered, as has been hastily thought, among the savage tribes of to-day, nothing would be more welcome to the historian of philosophy, but until these tribes have been classified according to language, we must leave these dangerous enterprises to others. For the present we must be satisfied with the germs of thought such as we find them in the Upanishads, and in the archives of language which reach back far beyond the Upanishads and even beyond the folklore of Khonds, Bhils, and Koles.

It is true that during that distant period which we can watch in the Upanishads, philosophy was not yet separated from religion; but the earliest religion, at least among the speakers of Aryan languages, seems always to have been not only the first religion, but the first philosophy also, of the races that had taken possession of India, as well as of the best soil of Asia and Europe. If it is the object of philosophy to discover the causes of things, *rerum cognoscere causas*, what was the creation of the earliest mythological gods but an attempt to explain the causes of light, of fire, of dawn, of day and night, of rain and thunder, by postulating agents for every one of them, and calling them Dyaus or Agni, light or fire, Ushas, dawn, the Asvins, day and night, Indra, the sky-god, and calling all of them Devas, the Bright, or *dii*, the gods? Here are the first feeders of the idea of the Godhead, whatever tributaries it may have received afterwards. Of course, that distant period to which we have to assign this earliest growth of language, thought, religion, law, morals, and philosophy, has left us no literary monuments. Here and there we can discover faint traces in language, indicating the footprints left by the strides of former giants. But in India, where we have so little to guide us in our historical researches, it is of great importance to remember that there was such a distant period of nascent thought; and that, if at a later time we meet with the same ideas and words turning up in different systems, whether of religion or philosophy, we should be careful not to conclude at once that they must have been borrowed by one system from the other, forgetting that there was an ancient reservoir of thought from which all could have drawn and drunk.

Considering how small our historical information is as to the intellectual and social life of India at different times of its history, it is essential that we should carefully gather whatever there is, before we attempt to study Indian philosophy in its differentiated and systematised systems. Much of our information may represent a chaos only, but we want such a chaos in order to understand the kosmos that followed.

### Intellectual Life in ancient India.

In certain chapters of the Brâhma*n*as and in the Upanishads we see a picture of the social and intellectual life of India at that early time, which seems fully to justify the saying that India has always been a nation of philosophers. The picture which these sacred books give us of the seething thoughts of that country may at first sight seem fanciful and almost incredible ; but because the men of ancient India, as they are there represented to us, if by tradition only, are different from Greeks and Romans and from ourselves, it does not follow that we have not before us a faithful account of what really existed at one time in the land of the Five or Seven Rivers. Why should these accounts have been invented, unless they contained a certain verisimilitude in the eyes of the people? It is quite clear that they were not composed, as some people seem to imagine, in order to impose after two thousands of years on us, the scholars of Europe, or on anybody else. The idea that the ancient nations of the world wished to impose on us, that they wished to appear more ancient than they were, more heroic, more marvellous, more enlightened, is an absurd fancy. They did not even think of us, and had no word as yet for posterity. Such thoughts belong to much later times, and even then we wonder rather how a local, not to say, provincial poet like Horace should have thought so much of ages to come. We must not allow such ideas of fraud and forgery to spoil our faith and our interest in ancient history. The ancients thought much more of themselves than of the nations of the distant future. If, however, what the ancients tell us about their own times, or about the past which could never have extended very far back, seems incredible to us, we should always try first of all to understand it as possible, before we reject it as impossible and as an intentional fraud. That in very early times kings and nobles and sages in India should have been absorbed in philosophical questions seems no doubt strange to us, because the energies of the people of Europe, as far back as we know anything about them, have always been divided between practical and intellectual pursuits, the former, in ancient times, considerably preponderating over the latter. But why should not a different kind of life have been possible in a country which, without much effort on the part of its cultivators, yielded in abundance all that was necessary for the support of life, which was protected on three sides by the silver streaks of the ocean, and on the fourth by almost impassable mountain barriers, a country which for thousands of years was free from war except the war of extermination directed against barbarous tribes, the so-called sons of the soil? After all, to thoughtful people, finding themselves placed on this planet, they did not know how or why, it was not so very far-fetched a problem, particularly while there was as yet no struggle for life, to ask who they were, whence they came, and what they were intended for here on earth. Thus we read at the beginning of the *S*vetâ*s*vatara-upanishad: 'Whence are we born? Whereby do we live, and whither do we go? O ye who know Brahman, (tell us) at whose command we abide here, whether in pain or in pleasure? Should time or nature, or necessity, or chance, or the elements be considered as the cause, or He who is called Purusha, the man, that is, the Supreme Spirit[1]?'

**Kshatriyas and Brâhmans.**

It might be thought that all this was due to the elevating influence of an intellectual aristocracy, such as we find from very early times to the present day in India, the Brâhmans. But this is by no means the case. The so-called Kshatriyas or military nobility take nearly as active a part in the intellectual life of the country as the Brâhmans themselves. The fact is that we have to deal in the earlier period of ancient India with two rather than with four castes and their numerous subdivisions.

This term *caste* has proved most mischievous and misleading, and the less we avail ourselves of it the better we shall be able to understand the true state of society in the ancient times of India. Caste is, of course, a Portuguese word, and was applied from about the middle of the sixteenth century by rough Portuguese sailors to certain divisions of Indian society which had struck their fancy. It had before been used in the sense of breed or stock, originally in the sense of a pure or unmixed breed. In 1613 Purchas speaks of the thirty and odd several castes of the Banians (Va*ni*g). To ask what caste means in India would be like asking what caste means in England, or what fetish

---

[1] See also Anugîtâ, chap. XX; S. B. E., VIII, p. 311.

(feitiço) means in Portugal. What we really want to know is what was implied by such Indian words as Var*n*a (colour), *G*âti (kith), to say nothing of Sapi*nd*atva or Samânodakatva, Kula (family), Gotra (race), Pravara (lineage); otherwise we shall have once more the same confusion about the social organisation of ancient India as about African fetishism or North American totemism! Each foreign word should always be kept to its own native meaning, or, if generalised for scientific purposes, it should be most carefully defined afresh. Otherwise every social distinction will be called caste, every stick a totem, every idol a fetish.

We have in India the Aryan settlers on one side, and the native inhabitants on the other. The former are named Aryas or Âryas, that is, cultivators of the soil which they had conquered; the latter, if submissive to their conquerors, are the *S*ûdras[1] or Dâsas, slaves, while the races of indigenous origin who remained hostile to the end, were classed as altogether outside the pale of political society. The Âryas in India were naturally differentiated like other people into an intellectual or priestly aristocracy, the Brâhmans, and a fighting or ruling aristocracy, the Kshatriyas, while the great bulk remained simply Vi*s* or Vai*s*yas, that is, householders and cultivators of the soil, and afterwards merchants and mechanics also. To the very last the three great divisions, Brâhmans, Kshatriyas,

---

[1] Thus we read as early as the Mahâbhârata—'The three qualities abide in the three castes thus: darkness in the *S*ûdra, passion in the Kshatriya, and the highest, goodness, in the Brâhma*n*a.' (Anugîtâ, S. B. E., VIII, p. 329.)

and Vaisyas, shared certain privileges and duties in common. Originally they were all of them called twice-born, and not only allowed, but obliged to be educated in Vedic knowledge and to pass through the three or four Âsramas or stages of life. Thus we read in the Mahâbhârata: 'The order of Vânaprasthas, of sages who dwell in forests and live on fruits, roots, and air is prescribed for the three twice-born (classes); the order of householders is prescribed for all.' (Anugîtâ, S. B. E., VIII, p. 316.) While the division into Âryas and Dâsas was due to descent, that into Brâhmans, Kshatriyas, and Vaisyas seems originally to have been due to occupation only, though it may soon have acquired an hereditary character. The Brâhmans had to look after the welfare of souls, the Kshatriyas after the welfare of the body politic, and the Vaisyas represented originally the undifferentiated mass of the people, engaged in the ordinary occupations of an incipient civilisation. The later subdivision of Indian society, as described by Manu, and as preserved under different forms to the present day, does not concern us for our present purpose. The lessons which the names of Varna (colour) and *G*âti (genus) teach us had long been forgotten even in Manu's time, and are buried at present under a heavy heap of rubbish. Still even that rubbish heap deserves to be sifted, as I believe it is now being sifted by scholars like Mr. Risley and others.

In ancient times neither Kshatriyas nor Vaisyas were excluded from taking part in those religious and philosophical struggles, which seem to have occupied India far more than wars of defence or conquest. Nay women also claimed a right to be heard in their philosophical assemblies. The Kshatriyas never surrendered their right to take part in the discussions of the great problems of life and death, and they occasionally asserted it with great force and dignity. Besides, the strong reaction against priestly supremacy came at last from them, for we must not forget that Buddha also was a Kshatriya, a prince of Kapilavâstu, and that his chief opposition, from a social and political point of view, was against the privileges of teaching and sacrificing, claimed by the Brâhmans as their exclusive property, and against the infallible and divine character ascribed by them to their Vedas.

### The Evidence of the Upanishads, *G*anaka, A*g*âtasatru.

If we look back once more to the intellectual life of India in the ancient Vedic times, or at least in the times represented to us in the Upanishads, we read there of an ancient King *G*anaka, whose fame at the time when the Upanishads were composed had already spread far and wide (Kaush. Up. IV, 1; B*ri*h. Âr. Up. II, 1, 1). He was a king of the Videhas, his capital was Mithilâ, and his daughter, Sîtâ, is represented to us in later times as the famous wife of Râma (Râmapûrvatap. Up.). But in the Upanishads he is represented, not as a successful general or conqueror, not so much as a brave knight, victorious in chivalrous tournaments. We read of him as taking part in metaphysical discussions, as presiding over philosophical councils, as bestowing his patronage on the most eminent sages of his kingdom, as the friend of Yâ*g*ñavalkya, one of the most famous philosophical teachers of the Upanishad period. When performing[1] a great sacrifice, this king sets apart a day for a Brahmodyam, a disputation in which philosophers, such as Yâ*gñ*avalkya, A*s*vala, Ârtabhâga, and even women, such as Gârgî, the daughter of Vâ*k*aknu (B*ri*h. Âr. Up. III, 1, 5), take an active part. To the victor in these disputations the king promised a reward of a thousand cows with ten pâdas of gold fixed to their horns. As Yâ*gñ*avalkya claimed these cows on account of his superior knowledge, the other Brâhmans present propounded a number of questions which he was expected to answer in order to prove his superiority. And so he does. The first question is how a man who offers a sacrifice can be freed thereby from the fetters of death. Then follow questions such as, While death swallows the whole world, who is the deity that shall swallow death? What becomes of the vital spirits when a man dies? What is it that does not forsake man in the hour of death? What becomes of man after his speech at death has entered the fire, his breath the wind, his eye the sun, his mind the moon, his ear space, his body the earth, his Âtman the ether, the hairs of his body the herbs, the hair of his head the trees, his blood and seed the waters? Whither did the descendants of King Parikshit go? What is the soul? What contains the worlds? Who rules everything and yet is different from everything? Far be it from me to say that these and other questions were answered by Yâ*gñ*avalkya in a manner that would seem satisfactory to ourselves. What is important

[1] Kaushîtaki Up. IV, 1; B*ri*h. Âr. Up. III, 1.

to us is that such questions should have been asked at all, that they should have formed the staple of public discussion at that early time, a time previous to the establishment of Buddha's religion in India, in the fifth century B.C., and that his answers should have satisfied his contemporaries. There is no other country in the world where in such ancient times such disputations would have been thought of, unless it were in Egypt. Neither Menelaos nor Priam would have presided over them, neither Achilles nor Ulysses would have shone in them. That these disputations took place in public and in the presence of the king we have no reason to doubt. Besides, there is one passage (B*r*ih. Âr. Up. III, 2, 13) where we are told expressly that the two disputants, Yâ*gñ*avalkya and Ârtabhâga, retired into a private place in order to come to an understanding about one question which, as they thought, did not admit of being discussed in public.

Do we know of any other country where at that early time such religious congresses would have been thought of, and royal rewards bestowed on those who were victorious in these philosophical tournaments?

One of the sayings of *G*anaka has remained famous in Indian literature for ever, and deserves to remain so. When his capital, Mithilâ, was destroyed by a conflagration, he turned round and said, 'While Mithilâ is burning, nothing that is mine is burnt.'

Very curious is another feature, that, namely, in these public assemblies not only was a royal reward bestowed on the victor, but the vanquished was sometimes threatened with losing his head[1]. Nor was this a threat only, but it actually happened, we are told, in the case of *S*âkalya (B*ri*h. Âr. Up. III, 9, 26). Must we withhold our belief from such statements, because we have learnt to doubt the burnt hand of Mucius Scaevola and the suicide of Lucretia? I believe not, for the cases are not quite parallel.

Besides these public disputations, we also read of private conferences in which Yâ*gñ*avalkya enlightens his royal patron *G*anaka, and after receiving every kind of present from him is told at last that the king gives him the whole of his kingdom, nay surrenders himself to him as his slave. We may call all this exaggerated, but we have no right to call it mere invention, for such stories would hardly have been invented, if they had sounded as incredible in India itself as they sound to us. (B*ri*h. IV, 4, 23.)

It is true we meet in the Upanishads with philosophical dialogues between gods and men also, such as Kaush. Up. III, 1, between Indra and Pratardana, between Sanatkumâra, the typical warrior deity, and Nârada, the representative of the Brâhmans, between Pra*g*âpati, Indra, and Viro*k*ana, between Yama, the god of death, and Na*k*iketas. But though these are naturally mere inventions, such as we find everywhere in ancient times, it does not follow that the great gatherings of Indian sages presided over by their kings should be equally

[1] I translate vipat by 'to fall off,' not by 'to burst,' and the causative by 'to make fall off,' i.e. to cut off. Would not 'to burst' have been vipa*t*?

imaginary. Even imagination requires a certain foundation in fact.

We have a record of another disputation between a King A*g*âtasatru and the Brâhman Bâlâki, and here again it is the king who has to teach the Brâhman, not *vice versa*.

### A*g*âtasatru[1].

A*g*âtasatru was king of Kâ*s*i (Benares), and must have been later than *G*anaka, as he appeals to his fame as widely established. When he has convinced Bâlâki of the insufficiency of the information which this learned Brâhman had volunteered to impart to him, the proud Brâhman actually declares himself the pupil of the king[2].

I do not mean, however, to deny that originally the relation between the kings and the sages of ancient India was that which we see represented, for instance, in the case of King *G*ânasruti and the Brâhman Raikva, who contemptuously rejects all offers of friendship from the king, till at last the king has to offer him not only gold and land (the Raikvapar*n*a villages in the country of the Mahâv*ri*shas) but his own daughter, in order to secure his amity and his instruction. But though this may have been the original relation between Brâhmans and Kshatriyas, and remained so to the time represented by Manu's Law-book, the warrior class had evidently from a very early time produced a number of independent thinkers who were able to

---

[1] Kaushitaki Up. IV, 2; B*ri*h. Âr. Up. II, 1.

[2] See also the dialogue between Sanatkumâra and Nârada (*Kh*ând. Up. VII, 2, 1).

grapple with and to hold their own against the priests, nay, who were superior to them particularly in one subject, as we are told, namely, in their knowledge of the Âtman, the Self. In the Maitrâyana-upanishad we read of King Brihadratha who gives up his kingdom, retires into the forest, and is instructed by the sage Sâkâyanya, whose name may contain the first allusion to Sâkas and their descendants in India. Such a royal pupil would naturally in the course of his studies become a sage and teacher himself.

Again, in the *Kh*ând. Up. V, 11 we see a number of eminent Brâhmans approaching King Asvapati Kaikeya, and making themselves his pupils. The question which they discuss is, What is our Self and what is Brahman (V, 11, 1)? and this question the king was supposed to be able to answer better than any of the Brâhmans.

### Buddhist Period.

When we leave the period represented by the Upanishads, and turn our eyes to that which follows and which is marked by the rise and growth of Buddhism, we find no very sudden change in the intellectual life of the country, as represented to us in the Sacred writings of the Buddhists. Though there is every reason to suppose that their sacred code, the original text of the Tripitaka, belongs to the third century B.C., and was settled and recited, though not written down, during the reign of Asoka, we know at all events that it was reduced to writing in the first century before our era, and we may therefore safely accept its descriptions as giving us a true picture of what took place in India while Buddhism was slowly but surely supplanting the religion of the Veda, even in its latest offshoots, the Upanishads. It seems to me a fact of the highest importance that the Buddhists at the time when their Suttas were composed, were acquainted with the Upanishads and the Sûtras, at all events with the very peculiar names of these literary compositions. We must not, however, suppose that as soon as Buddhism arose Vedism disappeared from the soil of India. India is a large country, and Vedism may have continued to flourish in the West while Buddhism was gaining its wonderful triumphs in the East and the South. We have no reason to doubt that some of the later Upanishads were composed long after King Asoka had extended his patronage to the Buddhist fraternity. Nay, if we consider that Buddha died about 477 B.C., we are probably not far wrong if we look upon the doctrines to which he gave form and life, as represented originally by one of the many schools of thought which were springing up in India during the period of the Upanishads, and which became later on the feeders of what are called in India the six great systems of philosophy. Buddha, however, if we may retain that name for the young prince of Kapilavâstu, who actually gave up his palace and made himself a beggar, was not satisfied with teaching a philosophy, his ambition was to found a new society. His object was to induce people to withdraw from the world and to live a life of abstinence and meditation in hermitages or monasteries. The description of the daily life of these Buddhist monks, and even of the Buddhist laity, including kings and nobles, may seem to us at first sight as incredible as what we saw before in the Upanishads.

### Prasenagit and Bimbisâra.

We read in the Tripitaka, the sacred code of the Buddhists, of King Prasenagit, of Kosala, drawing near to Buddha and sitting down respectfully at one side before venturing to ask him a question (Samyutta Nikâya III, 1, 4). We read likewise of King Bimbisâra, of Magadha, showing the same respect and veneration to this poor monk before asking him any questions or making any suggestions to him. Bânte or Lord is the title by which the paramount sovereigns of India address these mendicants, the followers of Buddha.

### Brahma-gâla-sutta.

If we want to get an idea of the immense wealth and variety of philosophic thought by which Buddha found himself surrounded on every side, we cannot do better than consult one of the many Suttas or sermons, supposed to have been preached by Buddha himself, and now forming part of the Buddhist canon, such as, for instance, the Brahma-gâla-sutta[1].

We are too apt to imagine that both the believers in the Veda and the followers of Buddha formed compact bodies, each being held together by generally recognised articles of faith. But this can hardly have been so, as we read in the Brahma-gâla-sutta that even among the disciples who

[1] We possess now an excellent translation of this Sutta by Rhys Davids. The earlier translations by Gogerly, by Grimblot (Sept Suttas Pâlis, 1876), were very creditable for the time when they were made, but have now been superseded.

followed Buddha, some, such as Brahmadatta, spoke in support of Buddha, in support of his doctrines and his disciples, while others, such as Suppiya, spoke openly against all the three. Though there was a clear line of demarcation between Brâhmans and Samanas or Buddhists, as far as their daily life and outward ceremonial were concerned, the two are constantly addressed together by Buddha, particularly when philosophical questions are discussed. Brâhma*n*a is often used by him as a mere expression of high social rank, and he who is most eminent in knowledge and virtue is even by Buddha himself called 'a true Brâhma*n*a.' Brâhman with us is often used in two senses which should be kept distinct, meaning either a member of the first caste, or one belonging to the three castes of the twice-born Âryas, who are under the spiritual sway of the Brâhmans.

We must try to get rid of the idea that Brâhmans and Buddhists were always at daggers drawn, and divided the whole of India between themselves. Their relation was not originally very different from that between different systems of philosophy, such as the Vedânta and Sâ*m*khya, which, though they differed, were but seldom inflamed against each other by religious hatred.

In the Brahma-*g*âla-sutta, i. e. the net of Brahma, in which all philosophical theories are supposed to have been caught like so many fishes, we can discover the faint traces of some of the schools of philosophy which we shall have to examine hereafter. Buddha mentions no less than sixty-two of them, with many subdivisions, and claims to be acquainted with every one of them, though standing himself above them all.

There are some Samanas and Brâhmans, we are told[1], who are eternalists, and who proclaim that both the soul and the world are eternal[2]. They profess to be able to remember an endless succession of former births, including their names, their lineage, and their former dwelling-places. The soul, they declare, is eternal, and the world, giving birth to nothing new, is steadfast as a mountain peak. Living creatures transmigrate, but they are for ever and ever.

There are some Samanas and Brâhmans who are eternalists with regard to some things, but not with regard to others. They hold that the soul and the world are partly eternal, and partly not. According to them this world-system will pass away, and there will then be beings reborn in the World of Light (Âbhassara), made of mind only, feeding on joy, radiating light, traversing the air and continuing in glory for a long time. Here follows a most peculiar account of how people began to believe in one personal Supreme Being, or in the ordinary God. When the world-system began to re-evolve, there appeared (they say) the palace of Brahmâ, but it was empty. Then a certain being fell from the World of Light and came to life in the palace of Brahmâ. After remaining there in perfect joy for a long period, he became dissatisfied and longed for other beings. And just then other beings fell from the World of Light, in all respects like him. But he who had come first began to think that he was Brahmâ, the Supreme, the Ruler, the Lord of all,

---

[1] Brahma-*g*âla-sutta, translated by Rhys Davids, p. 26 seq.

[2] This would be like the *S*âsvata-vâda.

the Maker and Creator, the Ancient of days, the Father of all that are and are to be. The other beings he looked upon as created by himself, because as soon as he had wished for them, they had come. Nay, these beings themselves also thought that he must be the Supreme Brahmâ, because he was there first and they came after him, and it was thought that this Brahmâ must be eternal and remain for ever, while those who came after him were impermanent, mutable, and limited in duration of life.

This Brahmâ reminds one of the Îsvara of the Sâ*m*khya and other philosophies, which as Brahmâ, masc., must be distinguished from Brahma, neuter. Then we are told that there are some gods who spend their lives in sexual pleasures and then fall from their divine state, while others who abstain from such indulgences remain steadfast, immutable, and eternal. Again, that there are certain gods so full of envy that their bodies become feeble and their mind imbecile. These fall from their divine state, while others who are free from such failings remain steadfast, immutable, and eternal.

Lastly, some Samanas and Brâhmans are led to the conclusion that eye, ear, nose, tongue, and body form an impermanent Self, while heart or mind or consciousness form a permanent Self, and therefore will remain for ever steadfast, immutable, and eternal.

Next follows another class of speculators who are called Antânantikas, and who set forth the infinity and finiteness of the world. They maintain either that the world is finite or that it is infinite, or that it is infinite in height and depth, but finite in lateral extension, or lastly, that it is neither finite nor infinite.

The next description of the various theories held by either Samanas or Brâhma*n*as seems to refer to what is known as the Syâdvâda, the theory that everything may be or may not be. Those who hold to this are called wriggling eels. They will not admit any difference between good and bad, and they will not commit themselves to saying that there is another world or that there is not, that there is chance in the world or that there is not, that anything has a result or reward or that it has not, that man continues after death or that he does not.

It would seem, according to some of the Suttas, that Buddha himself was often disinclined to commit himself on some of the great questions of philosophy and religion. He was often in fact an agnostic on points which he considered beyond the grasp of the human mind, and Mahâvîra, the founder of *G*ainism, took the same view, often taking refuge in Agnosticism or the A*g*ñânavâda [1].

Next, there are Samanas and Brâhmans who hold that everything, the soul and the world, are accidental and without a cause, because they can remember that formerly they were not and now they are, or because they prove by means of logic that the soul and the whole world arose without a cause.

Furthermore, there are Samanas and Brâhmans who hold and defend the doctrine of a conscious existence after death, but they differ on several points regarding this conscious existence.

Some maintain that the conscious soul after death has form, others that it has no form, others again

[1] M. M., Natural Religion, p. 105.

that it has and has not, and others that it neither has nor has not form. Some say it is finite, others that it is infinite, that it is both and that it is neither. Some say that it has one mode of consciousness, others that it has various modes of consciousness, others that it has limited, others that it has unlimited consciousness. Lastly, it is held that the soul after death is happy, is miserable, is both or is neither.

There are, however, others who say that the soul after death is unconscious, and while in that state has either form, or no form, has and has not, or neither has nor has not form; that it is finite, infinite, both or neither.

Again, there are some Samanas and Brâhmans who teach the entire annihilation of all living beings. Their arguments are various, and have in their general outlines been traced back to some of the teachers of Buddha, such as Âlâra Kâlâma, Uddâlaka and others[1]. They uphold the doctrine of happiness in this life, and maintain that complete salvation is possible here on earth. Thus when the soul is in perfect enjoyment of the five pleasures of the senses, they call that the highest Nirvâ*n*a. Against this view, however, it is said that sensuous delights are transitory and always involve pain, and that therefore the highest Nirvâ*n*a consists in putting away all sensuous delights and entering into the first *Gh*âna, i. e. Dhyâna, that is, a state of joy born of seclusion and followed by reflection and meditation. Against this view, again, it is asserted that such happiness involves reasoning, and is there-

---

[1] Rhys Davids, l. c., p. 48.

fore gross, while the highest Nirvâ*n*a can only arise when all reasoning has been conquered and the soul has entered the second *Gh*âna, a state of joy, born of serenity without reasoning, a state of elevation and internal calm. But even this does not satisfy the true Buddhist, because any sense of joy must be gross, and true Nirvâ*n*a can only consist in total absence of all longing after joy and thus entering into the third *Gh*âna, serene and thoughtful. Lastly, even this is outbidden. The very dwelling of the mind on care and joy is declared to be gross, and the final Nirvâ*n*a is said to be reached in the fourth *Gh*âna only, a state of self-possession and complete equanimity.

This abstract may give an idea of the variety of philosophical opinions which were held in India at or even before the time of Buddha. The Brahma-*g*âla-sutta professes that all speculations about the past and the future are included in this Sutta of the net of Brahma. By division and subdivision there are said to be sixty-two theories, arranged into two classes so far as they are concerned either with the past or with the future of the soul; the soul, as it seems, being always taken for granted.

The extraordinary part is that in the end all these theories, though well known by Buddha, are condemned by him as arising from the deceptive perceptions of the senses, which produce desire, attachment, and therefore, reproduction, existence, birth, disease, death, sorrow, weeping, pain, grief, and misery, while Buddha alone is able to cut off the root of all error and all misery, and to impart the truth that leads to true Nirvâ*n*a.

It does not seem, indeed, as if the philosophical teaching of Buddha himself was so very different at first from that of other schools which had flourished before and during his lifetime in India; nay, we can often perceive clear traces of a distant relationship between Buddhism and the six orthodox systems of philosophy. Like streams, all springing from the same summit, they run on irrigating the same expanse of country without proving in the least that one channel of thought was derived from another, as has been so often supposed in the case particularly of Buddhism in its relation to the Sâ*m*khya philosophy, as known to us from the Kârikâs and Sûtras.

Though the Brahma-*g*âla-sutta does not enter into full details, which may be gathered from other Suttas, it shows at all events how large a number of philosophical schools was in existence then, and how they differed from each other on some very essential points.

### Mahâbhârata.

If now we compare one of the numerous passages in the Mahâbhârata, containing descriptions of the philosophical sects then flourishing in India, we shall be struck by the great, almost verbal, similarity between their statements and those which we have just read in the Buddhist Brahma-*g*âla-sutta. Thus we read in the Anugîtâ, chap. XXIV: 'We observe the various forms of piety to be as it were contradictory. Some say piety remains after the body is destroyed; some say that it is not so. Some say everything is doubtful; and others that there is no doubt. Some say the permanent principle is impermanent, and others, too, that it exists, and others that it exists and does not exist. Some say it is of one form or twofold, and others that it is mixed. Some Brâhma*n*as, too, who know Brahman and perceive the truth, believe that it is one; others that it is distinct; and others again that it is manifold. Some say both time and space exist, and others that it is not so. Some have matted hair and skins; and some are clean-shaven and without any covering.' This last can only refer to the followers of Buddha, whatever the date of our Mahâbhârata may be. 'Some people are for bathing; some for the omission of bathing. Some are for taking food; others are intent on fasting. Some people extol actions, and others tranquillity. Some extol final emancipation and various kinds of enjoyments; some wish for riches, and others for indigence.'

The commentator Nîlaka*nth*a refers all these remarks to certain sects known to us from other sources. 'Some hold,' he says, 'that the Self exists after the body is lost; others, that is, the Lokâyatas or *K*ârvâkas, hold the contrary. Everything is doubtful, is the view of the Satyavâdins (Syâdvadins?); nothing is doubtful, that of the Tairthikas, the great teachers. Everything is impermanent, thus say the Târkikas; it is permanent, say the Mîmâ*m*sakas; nothing exists, say the *S*ûnyavâdins; something exists, but only momentarily, say the Saugatas or Buddhists. Knowledge is one, but the ego and non-ego are two different principles, thus say the Yogâ*k*âras; they are mixed, say the U*d*ulomas; they are one, such is the view of the worshippers of the Brahman as possessed of qualities; they are distinct, say other Mîmâ*m*sakas, who hold that special acts are the cause (of everything); manifold they are, say the atomists; time and space they are, say the astrologers. Those who say that it is not so, that is to say, that what we see has no real existence at all, are the ancient philosophers; omission to bathe[1] is the rule of the Naish*th*ika Brahma*k*ârins; bathing that of the householders.'

Thus both from Buddhistic and Brâhmanic sources we learn the same fact, the existence of a large number of religious and philosophical sects in the ancient days of India.

### Buddha.

Out of the midst of this whirlpool of philosophical opinions there rises the form of Buddha, calling for a hearing, at first, not as the herald of any brand new philosophy, which he has to teach, but rather as preaching a new gospel to the poor. I cannot help thinking that it was Buddha's marked personality, far more than his doctrine, that gave him the great influence on his contemporaries and on so many generations after his death.

Whether he existed or not, such as he is described to us in the Suttas, there must have been some one, not a mere name, but a real power in the history of India, a man who made a new epoch in the growth of Indian philosophy, and still more of Indian religion and ethics. His teaching must have acted like a weir across a swollen river. And no wonder, if we consider that Buddha was a prince or nobleman who gave up whatever there was of outward splendour pertaining to his rank. He need not have been a powerful prince, as some have imagined,

[1] Does not this refer to the solemn bathing which is the first step towards the stage of a G*ri*hastha or independent householder?

but he belonged to the royal class, and it does not appear that he and his house had any suzerain over them. Like several of the philosophers in the Upanishads, he was a Kshatriya, and the very fact of his making himself a popular teacher and religious reformer attracted attention as a social anomaly in the eyes of the people. We see in fact that one of the principal accusations brought against him, at a later time, was that he had arrogated to himself the privilege of being a teacher, a privilege that had always been recognised as belonging to those only who were Brâhmans by birth. And as these Brâhmans had always been not only the teachers of the people, but likewise the counsellors of princes, we find Buddha also not only patronised, but consulted by the kings of his own time. Curiously enough one of these kings has the name of A*g*âta*s*atru, a name well known to us from the Upanishads. He, the son of Vaidehî, a Videha princess, sends two of his ministers, who were Brâhmans by birth, to Buddha in order to consult him on what he ought to do. It has been supposed by some scholars that this is the same A*g*âta*s*atru, king of Kâ*s*i (or Benares), who, as we saw in the Upanishads, silenced the Brâhman Bâlâki (Kaush. Up. IV, 2, 1). But, according to others, A*g*âta*s*atru, i.e. 'without an enemy,' should be taken, like Devânâm priya, as a general title of royalty, not as a proper name[1]. However that may be, the coincidence is certainly striking, and requires further explanation. At all events, we see that, as in the Upanishads, so in the Tripi*t*aka also, kings appear as friends and

[1] S. B. E., XI, p. 1, note.

patrons of a philosopher, such as Buddha, long before he had become recognised as the founder of a new religion, that they take a prominent part in public assemblies, convened for discussing the great problems of religion and philosophy, or afterwards for settling the canon of their religious texts. The best known are Bimbisâra, king of Magadha, and Prasena*g*it, king of Ko*s*ala.

There is in this respect a clear continuity between the Upanishads and the earliest appearance of Buddhism; and if some of the tenets and technical terms of the Buddhists also are the same as those of the Hindu schools of philosophy, there would be as little difficulty in accounting for this as for the continuity between Sanskrit and Pâli. The Buddhist monk was clearly prefigured in the Parivrâ*g*aka or itinerant mendicant of the Upanishads (B*ri*h. III, 5). The name of Buddha, as the awakened and enlightened, could hardly be understood without the previous employments of the root Budh in the Veda; nor Bhikshu, beggar, without Bhiksh, to beg, in the Upanishads. Nirvâ*n*a, it is true, occurs in later Upanishads only, but if this shows that they are post-Buddhistic, it suggests at the same time that the old Upanishads must have been pre-Buddhistic. Parâ gati, the highest goal, is taken from the dictionary of the Upanishads, and possibly *K*akrapravartana, the turning of the wheel[1], also is taken from the same source.

But though Buddhism and the Upanishads share

[1] Cf. Anugitâ, chap. XVII: 'You are the one person to turn this wheel, the nave of which is the Brahman, the spoke the understanding, and which does not turn back, and which is checked by the quality of goodness as its circumference.'

many things in common which point back to the same distant antiquity, Buddhism in its practical working produced a complete social revolution in India. Though it did not abolish caste, as has sometimes been supposed, it led to a mixture of classes which had formerly been kept more carefully distinct. Anybody, without reference to his birth, could join the Buddhist fraternity, if only he was of good report and free from certain civil disabilities. He could then become an itinerant (Parivrâ*g*aka) friar, without any of that previous discipline which was required from a Brâhman. Once a member of the Sa*m*gha, he was free from all family ties and allowed to support himself by charitable gifts (Bhikshâ). Though kings and noblemen who had embraced the doctrines of Buddha were not obliged to become actual mendicants and join the fraternity, they could become patrons and lay sympathisers (Upâsakas), as we see in the case of the kings already mentioned, and of wealthy persons such as Anâthapi*nd*ika. Whenever the Buddhist friars appeared in villages or towns, they seem to have been received with splendid hospitality, and the arrival of Buddha himself with his six hundred or more disciples was generally made the occasion of great rejoicings, including a public sermon, a public discussion, and other entertainments of a less spiritual character.

In fact, if we may judge from the Tripi*t*aka, the whole of India at the time of Buddha would seem once more to have been absorbed in religion and philosophy; nay, the old saying that the Indians are a nation of philosophers would seem to have never been so true as at the time of the great

Buddhist Councils, held, we are told, at Râ*g*agr*i*ha, at Vai*s*âlî, and later on at the new residence of A*s*oka, Pâ*t*aliputra.

This A*s*oka, like *G*anaka of old, took the warmest interest in the proceedings of that Council. It is perhaps too much to say that he made Buddhism the state-religion of India. There never was such a thing as a state-religion in India. A*s*oka certainly extended his patronage, formerly confined to Brâhmans only, to the new brotherhood founded by Buddha, but there was nothing in India corresponding to a Defender of the Faith.

It might be objected, no doubt, that the authorities on which we have to rely for a description of the intellectual state of India at the time of these Councils, even that of A*s*oka, 242 B.C., are one-sided and exaggerated; but when we consult the Mahâbhârata which, in its earlier elements, at all events, may be assigned to the same Buddhistic period, we get just the same picture. We meet among the Brâhmans as among the Buddhists with an immense variety of philosophical and religious thought, represented by schools and sects striving against each other, not yet by persecution, but by serious argumentation.

### Greek Accounts.

Nor are the scant accounts which the Greeks have left us of what they saw during and after the invasion of India by Alexander the Great at variance with what we learn from these native authorities. Nothing struck the Greeks so much as the philosophical spirit which seemed to pervade that mysterious country. When Megasthenes [1], the ambassador of Seleucus Nicator at the court of *K*andragupta (Sandrocottus), describes what he saw in India in the third century B.C., he speaks of gymnosophists living on mountains or in tho plains, having their abode in groves in front of cities within moderate-sized enclosures. 'They live,' he writes, 'in a simple style, and lie on beds of rushes or skins. They abstain from animal food and sexual pleasures, and spend their time in listening to serious discourse and in imparting their knowledge to such as will listen to them.' The so-called *S*armanas mentioned by Megasthenes, have generally been accepted as representing the *S*ramana*s* or Samanas, the members of the Buddhist brotherhood who then seemed to have lived most amicably with the Brâhmans. Nothing at least is said of any personal enmity between them, however much they may have differed in their philosophical and religious opinions. His Hylobioi or forest-dwellers are probably meant for the Brâhmanic Vânaprasthas, the members of the third Â*s*rama who had to live in the forest, at a certain distance from their villages, and give themselves up to asceticism and meditation, such as we see described in the Upanishads. Even if their name did not tell us, we are distinctly informed that they lived in the forest, subsisting on leaves and wild fruits, and wore garments made of the bark of trees (Vâlkala) [2]. They communicated, we are told, with kings, who, like *G*anaka and A*g*âta*s*atru, Prasena*g*it and Bimbisâra, or in later

[1] Ancient India, by J. W. McCrindle, 1877, p. 97 seq.

[2] Clement Alex., Strom. i. p. 305, adds that they neither live in cities nor even in houses.

times King Harsha, consulted them by messengers regarding the causes of things, and who through them worshipped and supplicated their gods. Clement of Alexandria, after repeating all this, adds at the end that there are also philosophers in India who follow the precepts of Butta, whom they honour as a god on account of his extraordinary holiness. This is the first Greek mention of Buddha, for no one else can have been meant by Clement. The name was never mentioned by Alexander's companions, though there are early coins, which point to Greek influence, with the figure and name of Boddo. We are also told that these philosophers practised fortitude, both by undergoing active toil, and by enduring pain, remaining for whole days motionless in a fixed attitude.

### Buddhist Pilgrims, Hiouen-thsang.

Some centuries later we have another and independent source of information on the intellectual state of India, and this also is in perfect accordance with what we have hitherto learnt about India as the home of philosophers. Beginning with the fourth century of our era, that is, at the time when what I call the Renaissance of Sanskrit literature and national independence began, Chinese Buddhists who made their pilgrimages to India, as to their Holy Land, described to us the state of the country such as they saw it. Those who came early, such as Fa-hian, saw Buddhism flourishing in the fifth century, those who came later in the sixth and seventh centuries, witnessed already the evident signs of its decline. The most important among them was Hiouen-thsang who visited India from 629 to

645, and whose travels have been translated by my late friend, Stanislas Julien. No one can doubt the trustworthiness of this witness, though he may have been deceived in some of his observations. He describes the Buddhist monasteries scattered all over the country, the schools of the most illustrious teachers whose lectures he attended, and their public assemblies, particularly those that took place at the court of *S*îlâditya Harshavardhana 610–650, commonly called *S*rî-Harsha of Kanyâkub*g*a. This king, who is described as having conquered the five Indias, seems to have been in his heart a Buddhist, though he bestowed his patronage and protection on all sects alike, whether followers of the Vedas or of Buddha. No one, we are told, was allowed to eat flesh in his dominions, and whoever had killed a living thing was himself put to death [1]. He built many hospitals and monasteries, and entertained many Buddhist friars at his own expense. Every year he assembled the *S*rama*n*as from different kingdoms, and made them discuss in his presence the most important points of Buddha's doctrine. Each disputant had his chair, and the king himself was present to judge of their learning and their good behaviour. Hiouen-thsang, who by this time had made himself a proficient Sanskrit scholar and Buddhist theologian, having studied the Buddhist writings under some of the most illustrious teachers of the time, was invited by the king to be present at one of these great assemblies, on the southern bank of the Ganges. Twenty kings were gathered there, each bringing with him both *S*rama*n*as and Brâhma*n*as.

---

[1] Mémoires sur les Contrées Occidentales, Julien, i. p. 251 seq.

A large camp was constructed, and every day rich alms were bestowed on the *S*rama*n*as. This, as it would seem, excited the anger of some Brâhmans who were present. They tried to set fire to the camp and the magnificent buildings erected by the king. And when they failed in this, they actually hired an assassin to kill the monarch. The king, however, escaped, and forgave the would-be assassin, but exiled a large number of Brâhmans from his kingdom. This gives us the first idea of what at that time religious persecution meant on the part of Buddhists as well as of Brâhmans. These persecutions may have been exaggerated, but they cannot be altogether denied. Hiouen-thsang himself seems to have taken an active part in this Congress of Religion, and I still believe it was he who is mentioned by his Sanskrit name as 'Mokshadeva' or as the 'Master of the Tripi*t*aka.' After making all reasonable deductions, such as we should make in the case of the descriptions of any enthusiastic witness, enough seems to me to remain to show that from the time of the Upanishads to the time of Hiouen-thsang's sojourn in India, one dominant interest pervaded the whole country, the interest in the great problems of humanity here on earth. While in other countries the people at large cared more for their national heroes, as celebrated in their epic poetry on account of their acts of bravery or cunning, India under the sway of its Vedic poets, most of them of a priestly rather than a warrior origin, remained true to its character. Its kings surrounded themselves with a court of sages rather than of warriors, and the people at large developed and strengthened their old taste for religious and philosophical problems that has endured for centuries, and is not extinct even at the present day. Of course, if we call the people of India a nation of philosophers, this is not meant to deny that the warrior class also had their popular heroes, and that their achievements also excited the interest of the people. India is large enough for many phases of thought. We must not forget that even in the Vedic hymns Indra, the most popular of their gods, was a warrior. The two great epic poems are there to testify that hero-worship is innate in the human heart, and that in early days men and even women will place muscle higher than brain. But many even of these epic heroes have a tinge of philosophical sadness about them, and Ar*g*una, the greatest among them, is at the same time the recipient of the highest wisdom communicated to him by K*r*ish*n*a, as described in the Bhagavad-gîtâ.

K*r*ish*n*a himself, the hero of the Bhagavad-gîtâ, was of Kshatriya origin, and was looked upon as the very incarnation of the Deity. It is curious that the Sanskrit language has no word for epic poetry. Itihâsa refers to the matter rather than to the poetical form of what we should call epic poems, and the Hindus, strange to say, speak of their Mahâbhârata as a Law-book, Dharma*s*âstra [1], and to a certain extent it may have fulfilled that purpose.

### King Harsha.

If the account given by Hiouen-thsang of the spiritual state of India at the time of his visit

---

[1] See Dahlmann, Das Mahâbhârata.

and of his stay at the court of Harsha should seem to be tinged too much by the sentiments of the Buddhist priest, we have only to consult the history of Harsha as written in Sanskrit by Bâ*n*a, to feel convinced of the faithfulness of his account. No doubt Hiouen-thsang looked at India with the eyes of a follower of Buddha, but Bâ*n*a also, though not a Buddhist, represents to us the different schools and teachers, whether followers of Buddha or of the Veda, as living together apparently in perfect peace, and obeying the orders of the same king. They would naturally discuss their differences and exchange opinions on points on which they were agreed or opposed to each other, but of violent persecutions by one side or the other, or of excommunications and massacres, we hear very little or nothing. The king himself, the friend and patron of Hiouen-thsang, tolerated both Buddhism and Brâhmanism in his realm, and we feel doubtful sometimes which of the two he favoured most in his own mind. We see him, for instance, pay his respects to a sage of the name of Divâkara, who had been by birth and education a Brâhman, but had been converted to Buddha's doctrine, without, as it would seem, incurring thereby the displeasure of the king or of his friends. In the Harsha-*k*arita[1] the king is represented to us as entering a large forest, surrounded by his retinue. When approaching the abode of the sage, the king leaves his suite behind and proceeds on foot, attended by only a few of his vassals. While still at a distance from the holy man's abode, the king perceived a large

---

[1] Harsha-*k*arita, translated by Cowell and Thomas, p. 235.

number of 'Buddhists from various provinces, perched on pillows, seated on rocks, dwelling in bowers of creepers, lying in thickets or in the shadow of branches, or squatting on the roots of trees,—devotees dead to all passions, *G*ainas in white robes (*S*vetâmbaras), with mendicants (Bhikshus or Parivrâ*g*akas), followers of K*ri*sh*n*a (Bhâgavatas), religious students (Brahma*k*ârins), ascetics who pulled out their hair, followers of Kapila (Sâ*m*khyas), *G*ainas, Lokâyatikas (atheists), followers of Ka*n*âda (Vai*s*eshikas), followers of the Upanishads (Vedântins), believers in God as a creator (Naiyâyikas), assayers of metals (?), students of legal institutes, students of the Purâ*n*as, adepts in sacrifices requiring seven priests, adepts in grammar, followers of the Pañ*k*arâtras, and others beside, all diligently following their own tenets, pondering, urging objections, raising doubts, resolving them, giving etymologies, and disputing, discussing and explaining moot points of doctrine,' and all this, it would seem, in perfect peace and harmony.

Now I ask once more, is there any other country in the world of which a similar account could be given, always the same from century to century? Such a life as here described may seem very strange to us, nay, even incredible, but that is our fault, because we forget the totally different conditions of intellectual life in India and elsewhere. We cannot dissociate intellectual life from cities, from palaces, schools, universities, museums, and all the rest. However, the real life of India was not lived in towns, but in villages and forests. Even at present it should be remembered that towns are the exception in India, and that the vast majority of people live in the country, in villages, and their adjoining groves. Here the old sages were free to meditate on the problems of life and on all that is nearest to the heart of man. If they were not philosophers, let them be called dreamers, but dreamers of dreams without which life would hardly be worth living.

An insight into this state of things seemed to me necessary as a preliminary to a study of Indian philosophy as being throughout the work of the people rather than that of a few gifted individuals. As far back as we can trace the history of thought in India, from the time of King Harsha and the Buddhist pilgrims back to the descriptions found in the Mahâbhârata, the testimonies of the Greek invaders, the minute accounts of the Buddhists in their Tripi*t*aka, and in the end the Upanishads themselves, and the hymns of the Veda, we are met everywhere by the same picture, a society in which spiritual interests predominate and throw all material interests into the shade, a world of thinkers, a nation of philosophers.

## CHAPTER II.

### The Vedas.

If after these preliminary remarks we look for the real beginnings of philosophy on the soil of India, we shall find them in a stratum where philosophy is hardly differentiated as yet from religion, and long before the fatal divorce between religion and philosophy had been finally accomplished, that is in the Vedas.

There have been curious misunderstandings about this newly-discovered relic of ancient literature, if literature it may be called, having nothing whatever to do in its origin with any *litera scripta*. No one has ever doubted that in the Veda we have the earliest monument of Aryan language and thought, and, in a certain sense, of Aryan literature which, in an almost miraculous way, has been preserved to us, during the long night of centuries, chiefly by means of oral tradition. But seeing that the Veda was certainly more ancient than anything we possess of Aryan literature elsewhere, people jumped at the conclusion that it would bring us near to the very beginning of all things, and that we should find in the hymns of the Rig-veda the 'very songs of the morning stars and the shouts of the sons of God.' When these expectations were disappointed, many of these ancient hymns, turning out to be very simple, nay sometimes very commonplace, and with little of positive beauty, or novel truth, a reaction set in, as it always does after an excessive enthusiasm. The Vedic hymns were looked on askance, and it was even hinted that they might be but forgeries of those very suspicious individuals, the Brâhmans or Pandits of India. In the end, however, the historical school has prevailed, and the historian now sees that in the Vedas we have to deal, not with what European philosophers thought ought to have been, but with what is and has been; not with what is beautiful, but with what is true and historically real. If the Vedic hymns are simple, natural, and often commonplace, they teach us that very useful lesson that the earliest religious aspirations of the Aryan conquerors of India were simple and natural, and often, from our point of view, very commonplace. This too is a lesson worth learning. Whatever the Vedas may be called, they are to us unique and priceless guides in opening before our eyes tombs of thought richer in relics than the royal tombs of Egypt, and more ancient and primitive in thought than the oldest hymns of Babylonian or Accadian poets. If we grant that they belonged to the second millennium before our era, we are probably on safe ground, though we should not forget that this is a constructive date only, and that such a date does not become positive by mere repetition. It may be very brave to postulate 2000 B.C. or even 5000 B.C. as a minimum date for the Vedic hymns, but what is gained by such bravery? Such assertions are safe so far as they cannot be refuted, but neither can they be proved, considering that we have no contemporaneous dates to attach them to. And when I say that the Vedic hymns are more ancient and primitive than the oldest Babylonian and Accadian hymns, all that I mean and could mean is that they contain fewer traces of an advanced civilisation than the hymns deciphered from cuneiform tablets, in which we find mention of such things as temples in stone and idols of gold, of altars, sceptres and crowns, cities and libraries, and public squares. There are thoughts in those ancient Mesopotamian hymns which would have staggered the poets of the Veda, such as their chief god being called the king of blessedness, the light of mankind, &c. We should look in vain in the Veda for such advanced ideas as 'the holy writing of the mouth of the deep,' 'the god of the pure incantation,' 'thy will is made known in heaven and the angels bow their faces,' 'I fill my hand with a mountain of diamonds, of turquoises and of crystal,' 'thou art as strong bronze,' 'of bronze and lead thou art the mingler,' or 'the wide heaven is the habitation of thy liver.' All this may be very old as far as the progression of the equinoxes is concerned, but in the progress of human thought these ideas mark a point, not yet reached by the poets of the Veda. In that sense, whatever their age, these Babylonian hymns are more modern in thought than the very latest hymns of the Rig-veda, though I confess that it is that very fact, the advanced civilisation at that early time which they reflect, that makes the Babylonian hymns so interesting in the eyes of the historian. I do not speak here of philosophical ideas, for we have learnt by this time that they are of no age and of any age.

Whatever may be the date of the Vedic hymns,

whether 1500 or 15000 B.C., they have their own unique place and stand by themselves in the literature of the world. They tell us something of the early growth of the human mind of which we find no trace anywhere else. Whatever aesthetic judgements may be pronounced on them, and there is certainly little of poetical beauty in them, in the eyes of the historian and the psychologist they will always retain their peculiar value, far superior to the oldest chronicles, far superior to the most ancient inscriptions, for every verse, nay every word in them, is an authentic document in the history of the greatest empire, the empire of the human mind, as established in India in the second millennium B.C.

### The Philosophical Basis of the Vedic Gods.

Let us begin with the simplest beginnings. What can be simpler than the simple conviction that the regularly recurring events of nature require certain agents? Animated by this conviction the Vedic poets spoke not only of rain (Indu), but of a rainer (Indra), not only of fire and light as a fact, but of a lighter and burner, an agent of fire and light, a Dyaus (*Ζεύς*) and an Agni (ignis). It seemed impossible to them that sun and moon should rise every day, should grow strong and weak again every month or every year, unless there was an agent behind who controlled them. We may smile at such thoughts, but they were natural thoughts, nor would it be easy even now to prove a negative to this view of the world. One of these agents they called Savitar (**ὑέτηρ, or ὑέτιος*), the enlivener, as distinguished yet inseparable from Sûrya, the heavenly, the sun, Greek Hêlios. Soma, from the same root Su, was likewise at first what enlivens, i.e. the rain, then the moon which was supposed to send dew and rain, and lastly the enlivening draught, used for sacrificial purposes and prepared from a plant called Soma or the enlivener, a plant known to Brâhmans and Zoroastrians before the separation of the two. In this way both the religion and the mythology of the Vedic sages have a philosophical basis, and deserve our attention, if we wish to understand the beginnings not only of Indian mythology and religion, but of Indian philosophy also. 'No one,' as Deussen truly says, 'can or should in future talk about these things who does not know the Rig-veda[1].' The process on which originally all gods depended for their very existence, the personification of, or the activity attributed to the great natural phenomena, while more or less obscured in all other religions, takes place in the Rig-veda as it were in the full light of day. The gods of the Vedic, and indirectly of all the Aryan people, were the agents postulated behind the great phenomena of nature. This was the beginning of philosophy, the first application of the law of causality, and in it we have to recognise the only true solution of Indo-European mythology, and likewise of Aryan philosophy. Whatever may have existed before these gods, we can only guess at, we cannot watch it with our own eyes, while the creation of Dyaus, light and sky, of P*r*ithivî, earth, of Varu*n*a, dark sky, of Agni, fire, and other such Vedic deities, requires neither hypothesis nor induction.

[1] Deussen, Allgemeine Geschichte der Philosophie, p. 83.

There was the sky, Dyaus, apparently active, hence there must be an agent, called Dyaus. To say that this Aryan Theogony was preceded by a period of fetishism or totemism, is simply gratuitous. At all events, it need not be refuted before it has been proved. Possibly the naming of the sky as an agent and as a masculine noun came first, that of the mere objective sky, as a feminine, second.

### Three Classes of Vedic Gods.

We know now by what very simple process the Vedic Âryas satisfied their earliest craving for causes, how they created their gods, and divided the whole drama of nature into three acts and the actors into three classes, those of the sky, those of mid-air, and those of the earth. To the first belong Dyaus, the agent of the sky; Mitra, the agent of the bright sky and day; Varu*n*a, the agent of the dark sky and evening; Sûrya, the agent of the sun; Savit*ri*, the agent of the enlivening or morning sun; A*s*vinau, the twin agents of morning and evening; Ushas, the maiden of the dawn.

To mid-air belong Indra, the agent of the atmosphere in its change between light and darkness, the giver of rain; the Marutas, the agents of the storm-clouds; Vâyu and Vâta, the agents of the air; Par*g*anya, the agent of the rain-cloud; Rudra, the agent of storm and lightning, and several others connected with meteoric phenomena.

To the earth belong P*ri*thivî herself, the earth as active; Agni, the agent of fire; Sarasvatî and other rivers; sometimes the Dawn also, as rising from the earth as well as from the sky. These gods were the first philosophy, the first attempt at explaining the wonders of nature. It is curious to observe the absence of anything like star-worship in India among the Aryan nations in general. A few of the stars only, such as were connected with human affairs, determining certain seasons, and marking the time of rain (Hyades), the return of calmer weather (Pleiades), or the time for mowing (K*r*ittikâs), were noticed and named, but they never rose to the rank of the high gods. They were less interesting to the dwellers in India, because they did not exercise the same influence on their daily life as they do in Europe. There was of course no settled system in this pantheon, the same phenomena being often represented by different agents, and different phenomena by the same agents. The gods, however, had evidently been known before they were distributed into three classes, as gods of the sky, of the earth, and of the clouds [1].

### Other Classifications of Gods.

If we call this creation and likewise classification of the Devas or gods, the first philosophy of the human race, we can clearly see that it was not artificial or the work of one individual only, but was suggested by nature herself. Earth, air, and sky, or again, morning, noon, and night, spring, summer, and winter, are triads clearly visible in nature, and therefore, under different names and forms, mirrored in ancient mythology in every part of the world. These triads are very different from the later number assigned to the gods. Though the Devas are known in the Rig-veda and the

---

[1] M. M., Contributions to the Science of Mythology, p. 475.

Avesta as thirty-three, I doubt whether there is any physical necessity for this number [1]. It seems rather due to a taste very common among uncivilised tribes of playing with numbers and multiplying them to any extent [2]. We see the difficulty experienced by the Brâhmans themselves when they had to fill the number of thirty-three and give their names. Sometimes they are called three times eleven; but when we ask who these three times eleven are, we find no real tradition, but only more or less systematising theories. We are told that they were the gods in the sky, on earth, and in the clouds (I, 139, 11), or again that they were Vasus, Rudras, Âdityas, Visve Devas, and Maruts [3], but the number of each of these classes of gods seems to have been originally seven rather than eleven. Even this number of seven is taken by some scholars in the general sense of many, like devânâm bhûyish*thâh*; but it is at all events recognised in the Rig-veda VIII, 28, 5, though possibly in a late verse. What we look for in vain in the Veda are the names of seven Maruts or seven Rudras. We can perhaps make out seven Vasus, if, as we are told, they are meant for Agni, the Âdityas, the Marutas, Indra, Ushas, the Asvins and Rudra. The seven Âdityas, too, may possibly be counted as Varu*n*a, Mitra, Aryaman, Bhaga, Daksha, A*m*sa, and Tvash*tri*, but all this is very uncertain. We see in fact the three times eleven replaced by the eight Vasus, the eleven Maruts, and the twelve Âdityas, to which two other

[1] Satap. Br. XII, 6, 1, p. 205.

[2] Contributions, p. 475.

[3] Vedânta-Sûtras I, 3, 28; and Rig-veda X, 122, 1.

gods are added as leaders, to bring their number up to the required thirty-three.

In still later times the number of the Âdityas, having been taken for the solar light in each successive month, was raised to twelve. I look upon all these attempts at a classification of the Vedic gods as due once more to the working of a philosophical or systematising spirit. It is not so much the exact number or names of these gods, as the fact that attempts had been made at so early a time to comprehend certain gods under the same name, that interests the philosophical observer.

### The Visve or All-gods.

The first step in this direction seems to be represented by the Visve or the Visve Devas. Visva is different from Sarva, all. It means the gods together, *Gesammtgötter* (cuncti), not simply all the gods (omnes). Sometimes, therefore, the two words can be used together, as Taitt. Br. III, 1, 1, Vísvâ bhuvanâni sarvâ, 'all beings together.' The Maruts are called Vísve Marútah, in the sense of all the Maruts together. These Visve, though they belong to the class-gods (Ganas), are different from other class-gods inasmuch as their number is hardly fixed. It would be endless to give the names of all the gods who are praised in the hymns addressed to the Visve Devas. Indra often stands at their head (Indragyeshthâh), but there is hardly one of the Vedic gods who does not at times appear as one of them. What is really important in these Visve is that they represent the first attempt at comprehending the various gods as forming a class, so that even the other classes (Ganas), such as Âdityas, Vasus, or Rudras may be comprehended under the wider concept of Visve. It is all the more curious that this important class, important not only for mythological but for philosophical and religious purposes also, should have attracted so little attention hitherto. They are passed over, as a class, even in that rich treasure-house of Vedic Mythology, the fifth volume of Muir's Original Sanskrit Texts, but they ought not to be ignored by those who are interested in the progress of the ancient mythological religions from given multiplicity to postulated unity, as an essential character of the godhead.

### Tendencies towards Unity among the Gods.

But while this conception of Visve Devas marks the first important approach from the many incoherent gods scattered through nature to a gradually more and more monotheistic phase of thought in the Veda, other movements also tended in the same direction. Several gods, owing to their position in nature, were seen to perform the same acts, and hence a poet might well take upon himself to say that Agni not only acted with Indra or Savit*ri*, but that in certain of his duties Agni was Indra and was Savit*ri*. Hence arose a number of dual gods, such as Indra-Agnî, Mitrâ-Varu*n*au, Agni-Shomau, also the two Asvins. On other occasions three gods were praised as working together, such as Aryaman, Mitra and Varu*n*a, or Agni, Soma and Gandharva, while from another point of view, Vish*n*u with his three strides represented originally the same heavenly being, as rising in the morning, culminating at noon, and setting in the evening. Another god or goddess, Aditi, was identified with the sky and the air, was called mother, father, and son, was called all the gods and the five races of men, was called the past and the future. Professor Weber has strangely misunderstood me if he imagines that I designated this phase of religious thought as Henotheism.

### Henotheism.

To identify Indra, Agni, and Varu*n*a is one thing, it is syncretism; to address either Indra or Agni or Varu*n*a, as for the time being the only god in existence with an entire forgetfulness of all other gods, is quite another; and it was this phase, so fully developed in the hymns of the Veda, which I wished to mark definitely by a name of its own, calling it Henotheism[1].

### Monotheism and Monism.

All these tendencies worked together in one direction, and made some of the Vedic poets see more or less distinctly that the idea of god, if once clearly conceived, included the ideas of being one and without an equal. They thus arrived at the conviction that above the great multitude of gods there must be one supreme personality, and, after a time, they declared that there was behind all the gods that one (Tad Ekam) of which the gods were but various names.

Rv. I, 164, 46. Ekam sat viprâ*h* bahudhâ vadanti, Agnim, Yamam, Mâtarisvânam âhu*h*.

The sages call that One in many ways, they call it Agni, Yama, Mâtarisvan.

---

[1] This phase of religious thought has been well described in the same fifth volume of Muir's Original Sanskrit Texts, p. 352; see also Deussen, Geschichte der Philosophie, I, p. 104.

Rv. X, 129, 2. Ânît avâtam svadhayâ tat ekam, tasmât ha anyat na para*h* kim *k*ana âsa.

That One breathed breathlessly by itself, other than it there nothing since has been.

*The former thought led by itself to a monotheistic religion, the latter, as we shall see, to a monistic philosophy.*

In trying to trace the onward movement of religious and philosophical thought in the Veda, we should recognise once for all the great difficulties with which we have to contend. Speaking as yet of the hymns only, we have in the Rig-veda a collection of 1,017 hymns, each on an average containing about ten verses. But this collection was made at different times and in different places, systematically in some respects, but in others, more or less at random. We have no right to suppose that we have even a hundredth part of the religious and popular poetry that existed during the Vedic age. We must therefore carefully guard against such conclusions as that, because we possess in our Rig-veda-sa*m*hitâ but one hymn addressed to a certain deity, therefore that god was considered as less important or was less widely worshipped than other gods. This has been a very common mistake, and I confess that there is some excuse for it, just as there was for looking upon Homer as the sole representative of the whole epic poetry of Greece, and upon his mythology as the mythology of the whole of Greece. But we must never forget that the Rig-veda is but a fragment, and represents the whole of Vedic mythology and religion even less than Homer represents the whole of Greek mythology and religion. It is wonderful enough that such a collection should have escaped destruction or forgetfulness, when we keep in mind that the ancient literature of India was purely mnemonic, writing being perfectly unknown, but the art of mnemonics being studied all the more as a discipline essential to intellectual life. What has come down to us of Vedic hymns, by an almost incredible, yet well attested process, is to us a fragment only, and we must be on our guard not to go beyond the limits assigned to us by the facts of the case. Nor can the hymns which have come down to us have been composed by one man or by members of one family or one community only; they reach us in the form of ten collections (Ma*nd*alas) composed, we are told, by different men, and very likely at different periods. Though there is great similarity, nay even monotony running through them, there are differences also that cannot fail to strike the attentive reader. In all such matters, however, we must be careful not to go beyond the evidence before us, and abstain as much as possible from attempting to systematise and generalise what comes to us in an unsystematised, nay often chaotic form.

### Pra*g*âpati.

Distinguishing therefore, as much as possible, between what has been called tentative monotheism, which is religion, and tentative monism, which is philosophy, we can discover traces of the former in the famous hymn X, 121, which, years ago, I called the hymn to the Unknown God. Here the poet asks in every verse to whom, to what Deva, he should offer his sacrifice, and says towards the end whether it should be, yá*h* devéshu ádhi devá*h* éka*h* âsît, 'he who alone was god above gods.' Many of the ordinary gods are constantly represented as supreme, with an entire forgetfulness that one only can be so; but this is very different from the distinct demand here made by the poet for a god that should be above all other gods. It is much more like the Semitic demand for a god above all gods (Exod. xviii. 11), or for a father of gods and men, as in Greece (πατὴρ ἀνδρῶν τε θεῶν τε). Aristotle already remarked that, as men have one king, they imagined that the gods also must be governed by one king[1]. I believe, however, that the ground for this lies deeper, and that the idea of oneness is really involved in the idea of God as a supreme and unlimited being. But Aristotle might no doubt have strengthened his argument by appealing to India where ever so many clans and tribes had each their own king, whether Râ*g*ah or Mahârâ*g*ah, and where it might seem natural to imagine a number of supreme gods, each with their own limited supremacy. Still all this would have satisfied the monistic craving for a time only. Here too, in the demand for and in the supply of a supreme deity, we can watch a slow and natural progress. At first, for instance, when (Rv. VIII, 89) Indra was to be praised for his marvellous deeds, it was he who had made the sun to shine. He was called *S*atakratu, the all-powerful and all-wise, or Abhibhu, the conqueror. At the end the poet sums up by saying: Vi*s*vá-karmâ vi*s*vá-deva*h* mahấn asi, 'thou art the maker of all things, thou art the great Vi*s*vadeva (all-god).' The last word is difficult to translate, but its real purport becomes clear, if we

---

[1] Arist. Politics, 1, 2, 7; Muir, O. S. T., V, p. 5.

remember what we saw before with reference to the origin of the Visve Devas.

### Visvakarman.

In such adjectives as *S*atakratu, and still more in Visvakarman, the maker of all things, we see the clear germs that were to grow into the one supreme deity. As soon as Visvakarman was used as a substantive, the Brâhmans had what they wanted, they had their All-maker, their god above all gods, the god whose friendship the other gods were eager to secure (VIII, 89, 3).

### Tvash*tri*.

The maker or creator of all things is the nearest approach to the one and only god of later times. It should not be forgotten, however, that there was already another maker, called Tvash*tri*, i.e. τέκτων, only that he did not rise to the position of a real creator of all things. He seems to have been too old, too mythological a character for philosophical purposes. He remained the workman, the Hephaestos, of the Vedic gods, well known as the father of Sara*n*yû and Visvarûpa. He had all the requisites for becoming a supreme deity, in fact, he is so here and there, as when he is addressed as having formed heaven and earth (X, 110, 9), nay, as having begotten everything (visvam bhuvana*m* *g*a*g*âna). He is in fact all that a Creator can be required to be, being supposed to have created even some of the gods, such as Agni, Indra, and Brahma*n*aspati (Rv. X, 2, 7; II, 23, 17). If Agni himself is called Tvash*tri* (Rv. II, 1, 5), this is merely in consequence of that syncretism which identified Agni with ever so many gods, but more particularly with Tvash*tri*, the shaper of all things.

When Tvash*tri* is called Savit*ri*, this does not necessarily imply his identity with the god Savit*ri*, but the word should in that case be taken as a predicate, meaning the enlivener, just as in other places he is praised as the nourisher or preserver of all creatures, as the sun (Rv. III, 55, 19). One of the causes why he did not, like Pra*g*âpati or Vi*s*vakarman, become a supreme god and creator was his having belonged to a more ancient pre-Vedic stratum of gods. This might also account for Indra's hostility to Tvash*tri*, considering that he (Indra), as a new god, had himself supplanted the older gods, such as Dyaus. We must be prepared for many such possibilities, though I give them here as guesses only. It is possible also that the name of Asura, given to Tvash*tri* and to his son Vi*s*varûpa, points in the same direction, and that we should take it, not in the sense of an evil spirit, but in the sense of an ancient daimon in which it is applied in other hymns to Varu*n*a, and other ancient Devas. Tvash*tri* is best known as the father of Sara*n*yû and the grandfather therefore of the A*s*vins (day and night), but it is a mistake to suppose that as father of Yama and Yamî he was ever conceived as the progenitor of the whole human race. Those who so confidently identify Yama and Yamî with Adam and Eve seem to have entirely forgotten that Yama never had any children of Yamî. In his mythological character, Tvash*tri* is sometimes identical with Dyaus (Zeus)[1], but he never becomes, as has sometimes been supposed, a purely abstract

---

[1] Contributions, II, p. 560.

deity; and in this we see the real difference between Tvash*tri* and Vi*s*vakarman. Vi*s*vakarman, originally a mere predicate, has no antecedents, no parents, and no offspring, like Tvash*tri* (Rv. X, 81, 4). The work of Vi*s*vakarman is described in the following words, which have a slight mythological colouring: 'What was the stand, the support, what and how was it, from whence the all-seeing Vi*s*vakarman produced by his might the earth and stretched out the sky? The one god who on every side has eyes, mouths, arms and feet, blows (forges) with his two arms and with wings, while producing heaven and earth[1].'

How vague and uncertain the personal character of Vi*s*vakarman was in Vedic times, we can see from the fact that the Taittirîya Brâhma*n*a ascribes the very acts here ascribed to Vi*s*vakarman to Brahman[2]. At a later time, Vi*s*vakarman, the All-maker, became with the Buddhists, as Vi*s*vakamma, a merely subordinate spirit, who is sent to act as hairdresser to Buddha. The gods also have their fates!

### Search for a Supreme Deity.

The same human yearning for one supreme deity which led the Vedic priests to address their hymns to the Vi*s*ve Devas or to Vi*s*vakarman as the maker of all things, induced them likewise to give a more personal character to Pra*g*âpati. This name, meaning

---

[1] This blowing has reference to the forge on which the smith does his work. Wings were used instead of bellows, and we must take care not to ascribe angels' wings to Tvash*tri* or to any god of Vedic times, unless he is conceived as a bird, and not as a man.

[2] Taitt. Br. II, 8, 9, 6; Muir, O.S.T., V, p. 355.

lord of creatures, is used in the Rig-veda as a predicate of several gods, such as Soma, Savit*ri*, and others. His later origin has been inferred from the fact that his name occurs but three times in the Rig-veda [1]. These arithmetical statistics should, however, be used with great caution. First of all my *index verborum* is by no means infallible, and secondly our Sa*m*hitâ of the Rig-veda is but a segment, probably a very small segment, of the mass of religious poetry that once existed. In the case of Pra*g*âpati I had left out in my Index one passage, X, 121, 10, and though, for very good reasons, I considered and still consider this verse as a later addition, this was probably no excuse for omitting it, like all that is omitted in the Pada-text of the Rig-veda. The whole hymn must have been, as I thought, the expression of a yearning after one supreme deity, who had made heaven and earth, the sea and all that in them is. But many scholars take it as intended from the very first verse for the individualised god, Pra*g*âpati. I doubt this still, and I give therefore the translation of the hymn as I gave it in 1860, in my 'History of Ancient Sanskrit Literature' (p. 568). It has been translated many times since, but it will be seen that I have had but little to alter.

**Hymn to the Unknown God.**

1. In the beginning there arose the germ of golden light, Hira*n*yagarbha; he was the one born lord of all that is. He stablished the earth and this sky—Who is the god to whom we should offer our sacrifice?

2. He who gives life, he who gives strength; whose command all the bright gods revere; whose shadow is immortality

---

[1] Muir, O.S.T., V, 390.

and mortality (gods and men)—Who is the god to whom we should offer our sacrifice?

3. He who through his power became the sole king of this breathing and slumbering world—he who governs all, man and beast—Who is the god to whom we should offer our sacrifice?

4. He through whose greatness these snowy mountains are, and the sea, they say, with the Rasâ, the distant river, he whose two arms these regions are—Who is the god to whom we should offer our sacrifice?

5. He through whom the sky is strong, and the earth firm, he through whom the heaven was established, nay the highest heaven, he who measured the light in the air—Who is the god to whom we should offer our sacrifice?

6. He to whom heaven and earth (or, the two armies) standing firm by his help, look up, trembling in their minds, he over whom the rising sun shines forth—Who is the god to whom we should offer our sacrifice?

7. When the great waters went everywhere, holding the germ and generating fire, thence he arose who is the sole life of the bright gods—Who is the god to whom we should offer our sacrifice?

8. He who by his might looked even over the waters, which gave strength and produced the sacrifice, he who alone is god above all gods—Who is the god to whom we should offer our sacrifice?

9. May he not destroy us, he, the creator of the earth, or he, the righteous, who created the heaven, he who also created the bright and mighty waters—Who is the god to whom we should offer our sacrifice?

Then follows the verse which I treated as a later addition, because it seemed to me that, if Pra*g*âpati had been known by the poet as the god who did all this, he would not have asked, at the end of every verse, who the god was to whom sacrifice should be offered. However, poets have their own ways. But the strongest argument against the final verse, which my critics have evidently overlooked, is the fact that this verse has not been divided by the Padakâra. I still hold, therefore, that it was a later addition, that it is lame and weak, and spoils the character of the hymn. It runs as follows:—

10. 'O Pra*g*âpati, no other but thou has held together all these things; whatever we desire in sacrificing to thee, may that be ours, may we be the lords of wealth.'

With this conception of Pra*g*âpati as the lord of all created things and as the supreme deity, the monotheistic yearning was satisfied, even though the existence of other gods was not denied. And what is curious is that we see the same attempt[1] repeated again and again. Like Vi*s*vakarman and Pra*g*âpati we find such names as Purusha, man; Hira*n*yagarbha, golden germ; Prâ*n*a, breath, spirit; Skambha, support (X, 81, 7); Dhât*ri*, maker; Vidhât*ri*, arranger; Nâmadhâ, name-giver of the gods, ὀνοματοθέτης and others, all names for the Eka Deva, the one god, though not, like Pra*g*âpati, developed into fullgrown divine personalities. These names have had different fates in later times. Some meet us again during the Brâhma*n*a period and in the Âtharva*n*a hymns, or rise to the surface in the more modern pantheon of India; others have disappeared altogether after a short existence, or have resumed their purely predicative character. But the deep groove which they made in the Indian mind has remained, and to the present day the religious wants of the great mass of the people in India seem satisfied through the idea of the one supreme god, exalted above all other gods, whatever names may have been given to him. Even the gods of modern times

[1] M. M., Theosophy, pp. 244 seq.

such as *S*iva and Vish*n*u, nay goddesses even, such as Kâlî, Pârvatî, Durgâ, are but new names for what was originally embodied in the lord of created things (Pra*g*âpati) and the maker of all things (Vi*s*vakarman). In spite of their mythological disguises, these modern gods have always retained in the eyes of the more enlightened of their worshippers traces of the character of omnipotence that was assigned even in Vedic times to the one supreme god, the god above all gods.

### Brahman, Âtman, Tad Ekam.

We have now to take another step in advance. By the side of the stream of thought which we have hitherto followed, we see in India another powerful movement which postulated from the first more than a god above, yet among, other gods. In the eyes of more thoughtful men every one of the gods, called by a personal and proper name, was limited *ipso facto*, and therefore not fit to fill the place which was to be filled by an unlimited and absolute power, as the primary cause of all created things. No name that expressed ideas connected with the male or female sex, not even Pra*g*âpati or Vi*s*vakarman, was considered as fit for such a being, and thus we see that as early as the Vedic hymns it was spoken of as Tad Ekam, that One, as neither male nor female, that is, as neuter. We come across it in the hymn of Dîrghatamas (I, 164, 6 [1]), where,

---

[1] This hymn, the author of which is called Dîrghatamas, i.e. Long Darkness, is indeed full of obscure passages. It has been explained by Haug (Vedische Räthselfragen und Räthselsprüche, 1875) and more successfully by Deussen, in his Allgemeine Geschichte der Philosophie, p. 108, but it still contains much that has to be cleared up.

after asking who he was that established these six spaces of the world, the poet asks, 'Was it perhaps the One (neuter), in the shape of the Unborn (masc.)?' This should be read in connection with the famous forty-sixth verse:—

'They call (it) Indra, Mitra and Varu*n*a, Agni: then (comes) the heavenly bird Garutman; *that which is the One*, the poets call in many ways, they call it Agni, Yama, Mâtari*s*van.'

Here we see the clear distinction between the One that is named and the names, that is, the various gods, and again between the One without form or the unborn, that is, the unmanifested, and those who established the whole world. This One, or the Unborn, is mentioned also in X, 82, 6, where we read 'The One is placed in the nave of the unborn where all beings rested.' Again in a hymn to the Vi*s*ve Devas, III, 54, 8, the poet, when speaking of heaven and earth, says:—

'They keep apart all created things, and tremble not, though bearing the great gods; the One rules over all that is unmoving and that moves, that walks or flies, being differently born.'

The same postulated Being is most fully described in hymn X, 129, 1, of which I likewise gave a translation in my 'History of Ancient Sanskrit Literature' (1859), p. 569. It has been frequently translated since, but the meaning has on the whole remained much the same.

**Nâsadîya Hymn.**

1. There was then neither what is nor what is not, there was no sky, nor the heaven which is beyond. What covered? Where was it, and in whose shelter? Was the water the deep abyss (in which it lay)?

2. There was no death, hence was there nothing immortal. There was no light (distinction) between night and day. That One breathed by itself without breath, other than it there has been nothing.

3. Darkness there was, in the beginning all this was a sea without light; the germ that lay covered by the husk, that One was born by the power of heat (Tapas).

4. Love overcame it in the beginning, which was the seed springing from mind; poets having searched in their heart found by wisdom the bond of what is in what is not.

5. Their ray which was stretched across, was it below or was it above? There were seed-bearers, there were powers, self-power below, and will above.

6. Who then knows, who has declared it here, from whence was born this creation? The gods came later than this creation, who then knows whence it arose?

7. He from whom this creation arose, whether he made it or did not make it, the Highest Seer in the highest heaven, he forsooth knows; or does even he not know?

There are several passages in this hymn which, in spite of much labour spent on them by eminent scholars, remain as obscure now as they were to me in 1859. The poet himself is evidently not quite clear in his own mind, and he is constantly oscillating between a personal and impersonal or rather super-personal cause from whence the universe emanated. But the step from a sexual to a sexless god, from a mythological πρῶτος to a metaphysical πρῶτον, had evidently been made at that early time, and with it the decisive step from mythology to philosophy had been taken. It is strange to meet with this bold guess in a collection of hymns the greater part of which consists of what must seem to us childish petitions addressed to the numerous Devas or gods of nature. Even the question which in Europe was asked at a much later date, where the Creator could have found a ποῦ στῶ for creating the world out of matter or out of nothing, had evidently passed through the minds of the Vedic seers when they asked, Rv. X, 81, 2 and 4: 'What was the stand, what was the support, what and how was it, from whence the all-seeing Visvakarman produced by his might the earth and stretched out the sky?' These startling outbursts of philosophic thought seem indeed to require the admission of a long continued effort of meditation and speculation before so complete a rupture with the old conception of physical gods could have become possible. We must not, however, measure every nation with the same measure. It is not necessary that the historical progress of thought, whether religious or philosophical, should have been exactly the same in every country, nor must we forget that there always have been privileged individuals whose mind was untrammelled by the thoughts of the great mass of the people, and who saw and proclaimed, as if inspired by a power not themselves, truths far beyond the reach of their fellow men. It must have required considerable boldness, when surrounded by millions who never got tired of celebrating the mighty deeds achieved by such Devas as Agni, Indra, Soma, Savit*ri*, or Varu*n*a, to declare that these gods were nothing but names of a higher power which was at first without any name at all, called simply Tad Ekam, that One, and afterwards addressed by such dark names as Brahman and Âtman. The poets who utter these higher truths seem fully conscious of their own weakness in grasping them. Thus, in I, 167, 5 and 6, the poet says:—

'As a fool, ignorant in my own mind, I ask for the hidden

places of the gods; the sages, in order to weave, stretched the seven strings over the newborn calf[1].'

'Not having discovered I ask the sages who may have discovered, not knowing, in order to know: he who supported the six skies in the form of the unborn—was he perchance that One?'

And again in ver. 4 of the same hymn:—

'Who has seen the firstborn, when he who had no bones (no form) bears him that has bones (form)? Where is the breath of the earth, the blood, the self? Who went to one who knows, to ask this?'

In all this it is quite clear that the poets themselves who proclaimed the great truth of the One, as the substance of all the gods, did not claim any inspiration *ab extra*, but strove to rise by their own exertions out of the clouds of their foolishness towards the perception of a higher truth. The wise, as they said, had perceived in their heart what was the bond between what is and what is not, between the visible and the invisible, between the phenomenal and the real, and hence also between the individual gods worshipped by the multitude, and that One Being which was free from the character of a mere Deva, entirely free from mythology, from parentage and sex, and, if endowed with personality at all, then so far only as personality was necessary for will. This was very different from the vulgar personality ascribed by the Greeks to their Zeus or Aphrodite, nay even by many Jews and Christians to their Jehovah or God. All this represented an enormous progress, and it is certainly difficult to imagine how

[1] This calf seems meant for the year, and in the seven strings we might see a distant recollection of a year of seven seasons; see Galen, v. 347. Pra*g*âpati is often identified with the year.

it could have been achieved at that early period and, as it were, in the midst of prayers and sacrifices addressed to a crowd of such decidedly personal and mythological Devas as Indra and Agni and all the rest. Still it was achieved; and whatever is the age when the collection of our Rig-veda-sa*m*hitâ was finished, it was before that age that the conviction had been formed that there is but One, One Being, neither male nor female, a Being raised high above all the conditions and limitations of personality and of human nature, and nevertheless the Being that was really meant by all such names as Indra, Agni, Matarisvan, nay even by the name of Pra*g*âpati, lord of creatures. In fact the Vedic poets had arrived at a conception of the Godhead which was reached once more by some of the Christian philosophers of Alexandria, but which even at present is beyond the reach of many who call themselves Christians.

Before that highest point of religious speculation was reached, or, it may be, even at the same time, for chronology is very difficult to apply to the spontaneous intuitions of philosophical truths, many efforts had been made in the same direction. Such names as Brahman and Âtman, which afterwards became so important as the two main supports of Vedânta-philosophy, or Purusha, the name of the transcendent soul as used in the Sâ*m*khya system, do not spring into life without a long previous incubation.

**Brahman, its various Meanings.**

If then we find Bráhman used as another name of what before was called Tad Ekam, That One, if later on we meet with such questions as—

'Was Brahman the first cause? Whence are we born? By what do we live? Whither are we hastening? By whom constrained do we obtain our lot in life whether of happiness or of misery, O ye knowers of Brahman? Is time, is the nature of things, is necessity, is accident, are the elements, or is Purusha to be considered the source?'

We naturally ask, first of all, whence came these names? What did Bráhman mean so as to become fit to signify τὸ ὄντως ὄν? It is curious to observe how lightly this question has been answered [1]. Bráhman, it was said by Dr. Haug, means prayer, and was derived from the root Barh or B*r*ih, to swell or to grow, so that originally it would have meant what swells or grows. He then assigned to Bráhman the more abstract meaning of growth and welfare, and what causes growth and welfare, namely sacred songs. Lastly, he assigned to Bráhman the meaning of force as manifested in nature, and that of universal force as the Supreme Being. I confess I can see no continuity in this string of thought. Other scholars, however, have mostly repeated the same view. Dr. Muir starts from Bráhman in the sense of prayer, while with the ordinary change of accent Brahmán means he who prays.

Here the first question seems to be how Bráhman could have come to mean prayer. Prof. Roth maintained that Bráhman expressed the force of will directed to the gods; and he gave as the first meaning of Bráhman, '*Die als Drang und Fülle des Gemüths auftretende und den Göttern zustrebende Andacht*,' words difficult to render into intelligible

---

[1] M. M., Theosophy, p. 240.

English. The second meaning, according to him, is a sacred or magic formula; then sacred and divine words, opposed to ordinary language; sacred wisdom, holy life; lastly, the absolute or impersonal god. These are mighty strides of thought, but how are they to be derived one from the other?

Prof. Deussen (p. 10) sees in Bráhman 'prayer,' the lifting up of the will above one's own individuality of which we become conscious in religious meditation. I must confess that here too there seem to be several missing links in the chain of meanings. Though the idea of prayer as swelling or exalted thought may be true with us, there is little, if any, trace of such thoughts in the Veda. Most of the prayers there are very matter-of-fact petitions, and all that has been said of the swelling of the heart, the elevation of the mind, the fervid impulse of the will, as expressed by the word Bráhman, seems to me decidedly modern, and without any analogies in the Veda itself. When it is said that the hymns make the gods grow (V*ri*dh), this is little more than what we mean by saying that they magnify the gods (Deussen, l. c., p. 245). Even if a more profound intention were supposed to be necessary for the word Bráhman in the sense of prayer, there would be nothing to prevent its having originally grown out of Bráhman in the sense of word. Of course we cannot expect perfect certainty in a matter like this, when we are trying to discover the almost imperceptible transitions by which a root which expresses the idea of growing forth (V*ri*ddhau), growing strong, bursting forth, increasing, came to supply a name for prayer as well as for deity. This evolution of thought must have taken place long before the Vedic period, long before the Aryan Separation, long before the final constitution of the Aryan language of India. We can but guess therefore, and we should never forget this in trying to interpret the faint traces which the earliest steps of the human mind have left on the half-petrified sands of our language. That Bráhman means prayer is certain, and that the root B*ri*h meant to grow, to break forth, is equally certain, and admitted by all. What is uncertain are the intermediate links connecting the two.

I suppose, and I can say no more, that V*ri*h or B*ri*h, which I take to be a parallel form of V*ri*dh, to grow, meant to grow, to come forth, to spread. Hence B*ri*hat means simply great (like great from growing), broad, strong; Barhish*th*a, strongest. We should note, however, though we cannot attribute much importance to the fact, that B*rim*hati and B*rim*hayati also were quoted by Indian grammarians in the sense of speaking and shining. Here we can see that speaking could originally have had the meaning of uttering, and that 'word' has been conceived as that which breaks forth, or is uttered, an utterance (Ausdruck), as we say.

The next step to consider is the name B*ri*haspati. We must start from the fact that B*ri*haspati is synonymous with Vâ*k*as-pati, lord of speech. Unless B*ri*h had once meant speech, it would have been impossible to form such a name as B*ri*has-pati, as little as Brahma*n*as-pati could have been possible without Bráhman[1].

---

[1] See *Kh*ând. Up. I, 2, 11, vâg ghi b*ri*hatî, tasyâ esha pati*h*; and VII, 2, 2, yo vâ*k*am brahma-ity upâsate. Cf. B*ri*h. I, 3, 20.

From this point once gained I make the next step and suppose that Bráh-man was formed to express what was uttered, what broke forth, or shone forth, that is, the word or speech. If we have arrived at this, we can easily understand how the general concept of word was specialised in the sense both of sacred utterance or formula and of prayer; without any idea of swelling meditation or lifting up of hearts, so alien to Vedic poets, such as they are known to us. But if I am right in seeing in Bráhman the original meaning of what breaks forth, of a force that manifests itself in audible speech, it will become easy to understand how Bráhman could also, from the very beginning though in a different direction, have been used as a name of that universal force which manifests itself in the creation of a visible universe. We need not suppose that it had to ascend a scale first from holy word, holy wisdom to the source of that wisdom, the absolute god.

### B*ri*h and Brahman, Word.

We may suppose therefore—I say no more—that Bráhman meant force or even germ, so far as it bursts forth, whether in speech or in nature[1]. But now comes a much more perplexing question. It can hardly be doubted that V*ri*h or B*ri*h is a parallel form of V*ri*dh; and it is a well-known fact that both the Latin *verbum* and the German *Wort* can be regularly derived from the same root, corresponding to a possible Sanskrit V*ri*h-a or V*ri*dh-a. In that

[1] Divyadâsa Datta quotes a passage from the Yogavasish*th*a: 'Brahmav*rim*haiva hi *gagag*, *gagak* *k*a brahmav*rim*hanam (Vedântism, p. 28).

case Bráhman also may be taken as a direct derivation in the sense of the uttered word, and brahmán as the speaker, the utterer. So far we are still on safe ground, and in the present state of our knowledge I should not venture to go much beyond. But Colebrooke and other Vedic scholars have often pointed out the fact that in the Veda already we find a goddess Vâ*k*, speech, which we met in Vâ*k*ás-páti and B*r*í*h*as-páti[1], the lord of speech. This Vâ*k*, as Colebrooke pointed out as early as 1805, was 'the active power of Brahmâ, proceeding from him[2].' After reading Colebrooke's remarks on it, few Sanskrit scholars could help being reminded of the Logos or the Word that was in the beginning, that was with God, and by whom all things were made. The important question, however, which, even after Colebrooke's remarks, remained still undecided, was whether this idea of the creative Word was borrowed by the Greeks from India, or by the Indians from Greece, or whether it was an idea that sprang up independently in both countries. This is a question the answer of which must lead to the most far-reaching consequences. Professor Weber in his 'Indische Studien,' IX, 473, published an article with the object of showing that 'the Logos-idea had *no* antecedents in Greece to account for it.' This was certainly a startling assertion, but in the face of well-known facts he added: 'Without wishing to give a de-

[1] In the Rig-veda we have only vầ*kah* pate, X, 166, 3, as two words; and again pâti*m* vâ*k*â*h*, IX, 26, 4. Bráhma*n*as pâti*h* occurs frequently in Rig-veda, as II, 23, 1, *g*yesh*th*arầ*g*am bráhma*n*âm brahma*n*as pate, &c.

[2] Miscellaneous Essays, I, p. 28.

cision on this question, the surmise is obvious, considering the close relations at that time existing between Alexandria and India, that the growth of this Neoplatonic idea was influenced by the like views of the philosophical systems of India.' He says again, 'that it may have been simply on account of the invigorating influence which the gods were believed to derive from the hymns, that the goddess of Speech was conceived as furnishing to Pra*g*âpati the strength of creation, though at last, particularly in the shape of Om, she obtained the highest position, being identified with the absolute Bráhman.'

I hope I have thus given a correct account of Professor Weber's somewhat vague yet startling assertion, that the Alexandrian Logos idea had no antecedents in Greek philosophy, but was influenced by the Vedic Vâ*k*. There are, no doubt, similarities, but there are dissimilarities also which ought not to be ignored. To say nothing else, Vâ*k* is a feminine, Logos a masculine, and that involves more than a difference of grammatical gender.

I have tried to show in my 'Lectures on Theosophy,' that the facts of the case lead us to a very different, nay to the very opposite opinion. If I did not enter on a discussion of the arguments which were intended to prove the absence of antecedents of the Alexandrian Logos idea in Greek philosophy, it was because I thought it better to state the facts as they really are, without entering on any useless controversy, leaving classical and Sanskrit scholars to form their own conclusions. While Professor Weber had asserted that the Logos appears in Alexandria without any preparatory steps,

I did my best to point out these very steps leading up to the Logos, which are very well known to every student of the early history of Greek philosophy[1]. If I have succeeded in this, the presumption in favour of any Indian influence having been exercised on the philosophers of Alexandria, would fall to the ground of itself, and the claims of India and Greece would be equal so far as the original idea of the Word, as a *potentia* of the absolute Being, was concerned. 'Real Indian philosophy,' I had said before, 'even in that embryonic form in which we find it in the Upanishads, stands completely by itself. We cannot claim for it any historical relationship with the earliest Greek philosophy. The two are as independent of each other as the Greek Charis, when she has become the wife of Hephaestos, is of the Haritas, the red horses of the Vedic Dawn' (p. 79).

Then the question arose, was there at least a distant relationship, such as exists between Charis and the Haritas, between Zeus and Dyaus, between Vâ*k* and the Logos also? As there were no linguistic indications whatever in support of such a view, I arrived in the end at the conclusion, that striking as are the coincidences between the Vedic Vâ*k* and the Greek Logos, we must here also admit that what was possible in India was possible in Greece likewise, and that we have no evidence to support us in any further conclusions. In all this I thought that facts would speak far better than words. It is quite true that Professor Weber was careful to add

[1] Theosophy, p. 384, The Historical Antecedents of the Logos.

the clause 'that he did not intend to give any opinion on this question,' but after such a confession it is hardly becoming to hint that those who have given an opinion on this question, had derived their information from him. It is easy to state the pros and cons, the Pûrvapaksha and the Uttarapaksha, but both are meant in the end to lead on to the Siddhânta, the conclusion. Even stronger coincidences between Vâ*k* and the Sophia of the Old Testament[1] might have been adduced, for as we read of Vâ*k* as the companion of Pra*g*âpati[2], Wisdom, in Prov. viii. 30, is made to say, 'I was by him, as one brought up with him; and I was daily his delight, rejoicing always before him.'

While in the Kâ*th*aka we read of Vâ*k* being impregnated by Pra*g*âpati, we read in Prov. viii. 22, 'The Eternal possessed me in the beginning of his way, before his works of old.'

But with all this I cannot admit that there is any evidence of borrowing or of any kind of interaction between Indian and Greek philosophy, and I should have thought that after the historical antecedents of the Logos and the Logoi in Greece had been clearly laid open, the idea of the Greeks having borrowed their Logos from Vedic Vâ*k* or from the O. T. Sophia, would not have been revived. The historical consequences of such an admission would carry us very far indeed, and it would require a far stronger lever to lift and to remove the weight of evidence on the other side than the arguments hitherto brought forward. If

---

[1] M. M., Theosophy, p. 381.

[2] Kâ*th*aka 12, 5 (27, 1).

the Greeks had really borrowed their idea of the Logos from India, why should they not have adopted any of the consequences that followed from it?

### East and West.

This requires some fuller consideration. Every indication of a possible intellectual intercourse between Greeks and Hindus in ancient as well as in more modern times, has been carefully noted and strongly urged of late, but I feel bound to say that, particularly for ancient times, nothing beyond mere possibilities of an exchange of religious or philosophical ideas between Greece and India has as yet been established. It seems not to have been perceived that an exchange of philosophical thought is very different from an adoption of useful arts, such as alphabetic writing, astronomical observations, coined money, or articles of trade whether jewels, wood, or clothing materials. It is only a philosopher that can teach or influence a philosopher, and even in the cases of two such men meeting, the difficulties of an interchange of thought, without a perfect knowledge of the languages, are far greater than we imagine. We have an instance of a foreign philosopher becoming a proficient in the philosophical language of India in the case of Hiouen-thsang. Has he left any trace of Chinese thought, whether derived from Confucius or Lao-tze, in India? Modern missionaries, if unsuccessful in conversions, may, no doubt, have left some imprint of Christianity and European philosophy on the native mind, but the position of the Christian missionary in India, accredited by membership in the ruling race, is very different from what the position of a few Buddhist monks could possibly have been in ancient times, even if they had reached Alexandria, and learnt to speak and converse on certain subjects in Greek or Egyptian. A courier may be very conversant with French or Italian, but let him try to discuss metaphysical questions, or even to translate a book of Vico's into English, and it will be perceived what difference there is between an interpreter and a philosopher capable of discussing religious and metaphysical problems.

That there was a time when the ancestors of the Aryan speakers had the same language and held many of their mythological and religious names and ideas in common, is no longer doubted, though, even here, we must be satisfied with names, and could not expect common mythological speculations. Later contact between Indians and Greeks, whether in Persia, Asia Minor or Greece, assumed no importance till we come to the invasion of Asia Minor, Persia, and India by Alexander the Great. But long before that time both Greeks and Hindus had invented many things, such as kings, priests, numbers, and seasons, marriages and funerals, without our having to imagine that there was at that time any exchange of ideas between the two countries on such points. If then we meet in India as well as in Greece with similar philosophic ideas, as, for instance, with a name meaning atom and with the atomic theory, should we suggest at once that Epicurus must have borrowed his atoms from Ka*n*âda, or Ka*n*âda his A*n*us from Epicurus? It is interesting, no doubt, to point out coincidences between Kapila and Zenon, Pythagoras, Plato and Aristotle, but it is even more interesting to point out the shades of difference in cases where they seem most to agree. If the Vedânta could elaborate an ideal Monism, why not the Eleatics as well? And yet where is there a trace of such a philosophical theory as the absolute identity of Âtman (the Self), and Brahman (the absolute being), to be found in Greek philosophy? Who would see more than a very natural coincidence between the Sanskrit triad of Dharma, virtue, Artha, wealth, Kâma, love, and the Platonic *τὰ καλά*, what is good, *τὰ ὠφέλιμα*, what is useful, and *τὰ ἡδέα* what is pleasant? How widely the triad of thought, word, and deed is spread has been shown very clearly by my old friend Professor Cowell and others, but no one would venture to accuse either Greeks or Indians of borrowing or of theft on such evidence.

The real character of most of these coincidences between Greek and Hindu philosophy, is best exhibited by the often attempted identification of the names of Pythagoras and Buddha-guru. At first sight it is certainly startling, but if traced back to its origin, it evaporates completely. First of all, Buddha-guru does not occur, least of all as a name of the teacher Buddha, and whether as a common Aryan name or as borrowed, Pytha could never be the same as Buddha, or Goras as Guru. The belief in transmigration among the Buddhists, besides being borrowed from the Veda, is very different from that of Pythagoras and other philosophers, both civilised and uncivilised, while ascetic practices were certainly not confined to either India or Greece.

It is quite true that after Alexander's conquests, and after the establishment of a Bactrian kingdom, in the North of India, there was a more real intercourse even between philosophers of Greek and Indian origin, and many of the facts bearing on this subject have been very carefully put together by Count Goblet d'Alviella in his *Ce que l'Inde doit à la Grèce*, 1897. But even he brings forward coincidences, which require more convincing proofs. With regard to Indian coinage, it should be observed that the three gods mentioned by Patañ*g*ali as used for commerce, i.e. on coins, are the very gods found on the earliest Mauryan coins, *S*iva, Skanda, and Vi*s*âkha, cf. Pâ*n*. V, 3, 99; provided that Vi*s*âkha can refer to Kâma shooting his arrows?

It cannot be doubted that the art of coining money was introduced into India by the Greeks, and if the images of Indian gods and even of Buddha on ancient coins, may be supposed to have favoured idolatry in India, that too may be admitted. Indian gods, however, were anthropomorphic, had legs and arms, heads, noses and eyes, as early as the Veda, and the absence of workable stone in many parts of India would naturally have been unfavourable to a development of sculptured idols. The Hindus had a god of love in the Veda, but he was very different from the Kâma, imaged on more modern coins as an archer sitting on the back of a parrot.

We are now in possession of specimens of much earlier Greek workmanship in India, than this Kâma on the back of a parrot, nor is there any reason to doubt that the idea of temples or monasteries or monuments, built and carved in stone, came from Greece, while some of the Indian architecture, even when in stone, shows as clear surviving traces of a native wood-architecture as, for instance, the Lycian tombs.

The later influence which Christianity is supposed

to have exercised in originating or in powerfully influencing the sectarian worship of K*r*ish*n*a does not concern us here, for, if it should be admitted at all, it would have to be referred to a much later period than that which gave rise to the six systems of philosophy. Ever since the beginning of Sanskrit studies, nay even before, these startling similarities between K*r*ish*n*a and Christos have been pointed out again and again. But iteration yields no strength to argument, and we are as far as ever from being able to point to any historical channel through which the legends of Christ or K*r*ish*n*a could have travelled. No one can deny the similarities, such as they are, but no one, I believe, can account for them. Some of those who have been most anxious to gather coincidences between the Bhagavad-gîtâ and the New Testament, have been rightly warned by native scholars themselves, that they should learn to translate both Sanskrit and Greek before they venture to compare. It should not be forgotten that as the Bhagavad-gîtâ bears the title of Upanishad, it may belong to the end of the Upanishad-period, and may, as the late Professor Telang maintained, be older even than the New Testament. If Damascius tells us that there were Brâhmans living at Alexandria[1], we must not forget that this refers to the end of the fifth century A. D., and does not help us much even as indicating the way by which the idea of the Creative Word could have reached Clement of Alexandria or Origen. That Clement of Alexandria knew the name of Butta is well known, he even knew that he had

[1] See Goblet d'Alviella, l.c., p. 167.

been taken for a god. Nor should it be forgotten, that Pantaenus who, according to Eusebius, had preached the Gospel in India, was one of the teachers of Clement. But all this is far from proving that Clement or Origen was able to study the Vedânta-Sûtras or the Buddhist Abhidharmas, or that their opinions were influenced by a few Indian travellers staying at Alexandria who cared for none of these things.

Some of the coincidences between Buddhism and Christianity are certainly startling, particularly by their number, but in several cases they exist on the surface only and are not calculated to carry conviction on one side or the other. I have treated of them on several occasions, for the last time in my paper on 'Coincidences,' but the same coincidences, which have been proved to be anything but real coincidences, are repeated again and again. The story of Buddha sitting under an Indian fig-tree (*ficus religiosa*) has nothing whatever in common with Nathaniel sitting under a Palestinian fig-tree, and the parable of the Prodigal Son in the Buddhist scriptures is surely very different in spirit from that in the New Testament. There remain quite sufficient similarities to startle and perplex us, without our dragging in what has no power of proving anything. No critical historian would listen for one moment to such arguments as have been used to establish a real exchange of thought between India and Europe in ancient times. On this point we owe a great deal to students of ethnology, who have pointed out coincidences quite as startling between the religious and philosophical folklore of uncivilised and civilised races, without venturing to suggest any borrowing or any historical community of origin. The *K*invat[1] bridge, for instance, which seems so peculiar to the Persians, had its antecedents as far back as the Veda, and is matched by a similar bridge among the North American Indians[2]. I say, a similar bridge, for it differs also, as I pointed out, very characteristically from the Persian bridge. Again, it is well known that the creation of the world by the Word has been discovered among so low a race as the Klamaths[3], but no one has ventured to say that the two accounts had a common origin or were borrowed one from the other. This should serve as a useful warning to those who are so fond of suggesting channels through which Indian thought might have influenced Palestine or Greece, and *vice versa*.

No doubt, such channels were there; neither mountains nor seas would have formed impassable barriers. Besides, Buddhism, as early as the third century B.C., was certainly a missionary religion quite as much as Christianity was at a later time. Alexandria was known by name, as Alasando, to the author of the Mahâva*m*sa[4]. On the other hand, the name of King Gondaphoros, who is mentioned in the legend of St. Thomas' travels to India, has been authenticated on Indo-Parthian coins as Gondophares, likewise the name of his nephew Abdayases, and possibly, according to M. S. Lévi, that of Vasu Deva as Misdeos. All this is true, and shows that the way between Alexandria and Benares was wide open in the first century A. D. Nor should

---

[1] Contributions to the Science of Mythology.

[2] Theosophy, p. 168.

[3] Theosophy, p. 383.

[4] Le Comte d'Alviella, l.c., p. 177.

it have been forgotten that in the Dialogues between Milinda and Nâgasena we have a well authenticated case of a Greek king (Menandros), and of a Buddhist philosopher, discussing together some of the highest problems of philosophy and religion. All this is true, and yet we are as far as ever from having discovered a Greek or Indian go-between *in flagrante delicto.* We have before us ever so many possibilities, nay even probabilities, but we could not expect any *bonâ fide* historian to accept any one of them as a proof of a real influence having been exercised by Greece on India or by India on Greece, at a time when Greek philosophy and religion might still have been amenable to Eastern guides, or Indian schools of thought might have gratefully received fresh impulses from the West. Though the literature of India has no trustworthy chronology, still, unless the whole structure of the literary development of India is once more to be revolutionised, we can hardly imagine that the occurrence of such names as Bodda and Zarades (Zoroaster) among the followers of Mani, or that of Terebinthos the pupil of Scythianos [1], the very founder of the Manichaean sect in Babylon, would help us to discover the secret springs of the wisdom of Kapila or Buddha *S*âkya Muni. They may point out whence these heresiarchs derived their wisdom, but they leave the question which concerns us here totally untouched. Görres, in spite of all his mysticism, was right when he looked for a similarity

[1] It has been suggested that Scythianos may have been an adaptation of *S*âkya the Scythian, a name of Buddha, and Terebinthos may contain traces of Thera (elder). All this is possible, but no more.

in technical terms in order to establish an Indian influence on Greek or a Greek influence on Indian philosophy. His principle was right, though he applied it wrongly. It is the same as in Comparative Mythology. There may be ever so many similarities between two mythologies, such as changes of men and women into animals or plants, worship of trees and ancestors, belief in spirits and visions in sleep or dreams, but one such equation as Dyaus = Zeus, is more convincing than all of them taken together. If people ask why, they might as well ask why the discovery of one coin with the name of Augustus on it is a more convincing proof of Roman influence in India than the discovery of ever so many pieces of uncoined gold.

To return to the origin of the word Brahman. Tempting[1] as the distant relationship between Bráhman and B*ri*h, in the sense of speech, with *verbum* and Word may be, we could not admit it without admitting at the same time a community of thought, and of deep philosophical thought, at a period

---

[1] There is a curious passage in Bhart*ri*hari's Brahmakâ*nd*a which seems to identify Speech and Brahman. See Sarva-dar*s*ana-sangraha, Bibl. Ind., p. 140:—

> Anâdinidhanam brahma *s*abdatattva*m* yad aksharam,
> Vivartate*r*thabhâvena prakriyâ *g*agato yathâ.

> Brahman without beginning or end, which is the eternal essence of speech,
> Is changed into the form of things, like the evolution of the world.

Equally strong is the statement of Mâdhava himself, Spho*t*âkhyo niravayavo nitya*h* *s*abdo brahmaiveti, 'The eternal word which is called Spho*t*a and does not consist of parts, is indeed Brahman.'

previous to the Aryan Separation; and we certainly have no evidence sufficiently strong to support so bold a hypothesis. What we may carry away from a consideration of the facts hitherto examined is that in India itself Bráhman, as a name of the *πρῶτον κινοῦν*, need not have passed through a stage when Bráhman meant prayer only, and that Bráhman, prayer, could not have assumed the meaning of the object of prayers, that is, the Universal Spirit, who never required any prayers at all.

In order to show what direction the thoughts connected with Vâ*k* took in the Veda, I shall first of all subjoin here a few passages from the hymns, the Brâhma*n*as and Upanishads:—

Vâ*k*, speech, speaking in her own name, is introduced in hymn X, 125, also in Atharva-veda IV, 30, as saying:—

'1. I wander with the Vasus and the Rudras, I wander with the Âdityas and the Visve Devas, I support Mitra and Varu*n*a both, I support Agni and the two Asvins;

2. I support the swelling (?) Soma, I support Tvash*t*ri and Pûshan and Bhaga. I bestow wealth on the zealous offerer, on the sacrificer who presses Soma.

3. I am the queen, the gatherer of riches, the knowing, first of those who merit worship; the gods have thus established me in many places, staying with many, entering into many.

4. By me it is that he who sees, he who breathes, he who hears what is spoken, eats food; without knowing it, they rest on me. Hear, one and all! I tell thee what I believe. (?)

5. I, even I myself, say this, what is good for gods, and also for men; whomsoever I love, him

I make formidable, him I make a Brahmán, him a Rishi, him a sage.

6. I bend the bow for Rudra (the storm-god) that his arrow may strike the hater of Brahman; I make war for the people, I have entered both heaven and earth.

7. I bring forth the (my?) father (Dyaus) on the summit of this world, my origin is in the waters, in the sea; from thence I spread over all beings, and touch yonder heaven with my height.

8. I indeed spread forth like the wind, to lay hold on all things, beyond the sky, beyond the earth; such have I become through my greatness.'

I ask is there any trace in these utterances of the thoughts that led in the end to the conception of the Greek Logos? There is another hymn (X, 71) which is very obscure and has for the first time been rendered more intelligible by Professor Deussen (A. G. P., p. 148), where we meet with some important remarks showing that language formed an object of thought even at that early time. But here also there is nothing, as yet, approaching to the conception of the Word as a creative power. We meet with such observations as that words were made in the beginning in order to reveal what before had been hidden. This is, no doubt, an important thought, showing that those who uttered it had not yet ceased, like ourselves, to wonder at the existence of such a thing as language. The struggle for life that is going on among words is alluded to by saying that the wise made speech by mind (Manas), sifting as by a sieve the coarsely ground flour. The power of speech is greatly extolled, and eloquence is celebrated as a precious gift. All men shout when the eloquent man appears, holding the assembly subdued or spellbound by his words (Sabhâsaha), nay he is supposed to remove all sin and to procure sustenance for his friends. The knowledge of all things or, as Deussen says, the knowledge of the origin of things, is taught by the Bráhman.

We meet with passages of a very similar character, in various parts of the Brâhma*n*as. One of the most startling is found in a verse inserted in the Purusha-hymn, as given in the Taittirîya-âra*n*yaka (III, 12, 17), 'I know that great sun-coloured Purusha, when on the verge of darkness, he, the wise, rests, addressing them, after having thought all forms, and having made their names.' Here we have only to translate forms by εἴδη, and names by λόγοι, and we shall not be very far from the world of thought in which Plato and Aristotle[1] moved.

But although we can discover in this hymn an appreciation of the mysterious nature of speech, we look in vain for the clear and definite idea that language and thought are one, which can be so clearly read in the Greek word Logos, both word and thought, nor do we find more than slight anticipations of the Neo-platonist dogma that the creation of the universe was in reality an utterance of the hidden thoughts and words of the Deity.

### Mind and Speech.

The following passages will give some idea of what was thought in India about mind and language and their mutual relation. They may be

---

[1] See Deussen, l.c., p. 290.

vague and mystical, but they show at all events that a good deal of thought must have been expended by the early thinkers of India on this problem, the nature of speech and the relation between speech and thought.

*S*atap. Brâhma*n*a VI, 1, 1: 'Pra*g*âpati, after having created the Veda (Brahman, neut.), created the waters out of Vâ*k* (speech), for Vâ*k* was his. That was created (sent forth). He then entered the waters with Brahman, i.e. the threefold Veda, and there arose from the water an egg which he touched and commanded to multiply. Then from the egg there arose first Brahman, neut., that is, the threefold Veda.'

Pañ*k*avi*m*sa Brâhma*n*a XX, 14, 2: 'Pra*g*âpati alone was this, and Vâ*k* was his own, Vâ*k* as the second. He thought, Let me create (send forth) this Vâ*k*, for she will go and become all this.'

*S*atap. Brâhm. VII, 5, 2, 21: 'The unborn is Vâ*k*, and from Vâ*k* Visvakarman (the all-maker) begat living beings.'

B*ri*h. Âr. Up. I, 5, 3: 'The Âtman consists of speech, mind, and breath. There are also the three worlds; speech is this world, mind the air, breath the sky. The same are the three Vedas, speech the Rig-veda, mind the Ya*g*ur-veda, breath the Sâma-veda. The same are gods, ancestors, and men, speech the gods, mind the ancestors, breath men, &c.'

B*ri*h. Âr. Up. I, 1, 24: 'He desired, let a second body be born of me, and he (death or hunger) embraced speech with his mind.'

And ibid. I, 4, 17: 'This world in the beginning was Âtman (Self), alone and lonely. He desired,

May I have a wife . . . Manas (mind) is the Self, speech the wife, breath the child.'

The same or very similar and often contradictory ideas occur in later works also. Thus we read in Manu I, 21: 'In the beginning he (Brahmâ) fashioned from the words of the Veda, the several names, works, and conditions of all things.'

And to quote but one passage from the Mahâbhârata, *S*ânti-parva, 8533: 'In the beginning Vidyâ (knowledge, Sophia) without beginning or end, the divine Vâ*k* (speech) of the Vedas, was sent forth by Svayambhû, the self-existent.'

*S*a*m*kara, when treating of Spho*t*a[1] (word), of which we shall have to treat further on, quotes from the B*ri*h. Âr. Up. I, 2, 4: 'He with his mind united himself with speech,' and he adds an important verse from some Sm*ri*ti: 'In the beginning divine Vâ*k*, Speech, eternal, without beginning or end, consisting of Veda, was uttered by Svayambhû, from which all activities proceeded';

And again: 'In the beginning Mahe*s*vara shaped from the words of the Veda the names and forms of all beings and the procedure of all activities.'

The Laws of Manu, or, more correctly, of the Mânavas, the clan of Manu, are no doubt later than the Brâhma*n*as, but they often contain old thoughts.

These utterances, to which many more might be added, are certainly vague, and chaotic, and often contradictory, because they sprang from different minds without any prearranged system; but they seem to me to show at all events that thought and language must have occupied the philosophers of

---

[1] Ved. Sûtras I, 3, 28.

India far more than they did the philosophers of Greece, and even in later times those of modern Europe. And if some of them assigned the first place to thought and others to speech, this also serves to show that at all events these early guessers did not accept language simply as a matter of course, as most of our modern philosophers are so apt to do, but tried hard to discover whence it came and what was its true relation to thought. Thus we read in the *S*atap. Br. I, 4, 5, 8: 'A dispute once took place between Mind and Speech as to which was the better of the two. Both said, "I am excellent." Mind said: "Surely I am better than thou, for thou dost not speak anything that is not understood by me, and since thou art only an imitator of what is done by me and a follower in my wake, I am surely better than thou." Speech said: "Surely I am better than thou, for what thou knowest I make known, I communicate."

'They went to appeal to Pra*g*âpati for his decision, and Pra*g*âpati decided in favour of Mind, &c.'

In the Anugîtâ (p. 262) we read on the contrary: 'Then the lord of speech was produced, that lord of speech looks up to the mind. First, verily, are words produced, and the mind runs after them.'

Some of the Brâhmanic thinkers say in so many words that Speech is Brahman (*S*atap. Br. II, 1, 4, 10, Vâg vai Brahma), and the co-existence of B*ri*haspati and Brahma*n*as-pati could hardly have failed to suggest to them the identity of Brahman and B*ri*h in the sense of speech, just as every thoughtful Greek must have known that there was a reason why Logos meant both word and thought. But that ancient chapter of thought which lies beyond the childhood of all philosophy is for ever lost to us and can be reconstructed by conjectures only, which, though they produce conviction in some minds, cannot be expected to produce the same in all.

Taking into account all these scattered indications, I cannot bring myself to accept the evolution of the various meanings of the word Brahman as elaborated by former scholars. I am particularly reluctant to differ on such a point from Professor Deussen. Professor Deussen holds that Brahman had a ritualistic origin (p. 239), and from prayer came to mean he who is prayed to, the *Urgrund der Welt.* He calls it *der zum Heiligen, Göttlichen emporstrebende Wille des Menschen*, which is much the same idea to which Roth and others have given currency, but which certainly requires a fuller justification. Instead of beginning with the specialised meaning of prayer, whether ritualistic or unpremeditated, and then rising to the object of prayer, I prefer to begin with Bráhman as a synonym of B*ri*h in B*ri*haspáti, meaning word or speech, and to admit by the side of it another Bráhman, meaning that which utters or drives forth (Pra*k*yâvayati) or manifests or creates, that which is the universal support (Skambha) or force (Daksha), in fact the Bráhman, such as we find it afterwards, whether as a neuter, Bráhman, or, for more popular purposes, as a masculine, Bráhmâ [1]. No doubt in those dark passages through which words passed silently before they emerged into the full light of literature, we may often fail to discover the right footsteps of

[1] Taitt. Br. II, 7, 17, 1.

their progress, and we must be prepared for differences of opinion. But the really important point is that on which all scholars agree, by assigning to Bráhman the final meaning of τὸ ὄν, τὸ ὄντως ὄν, τὸ πρῶτον κινοῦν, though, even of those terms, as we shall see, not one corresponds fully and exactly to the character of Bráhman as developed in the history of the Indian mind.

### Âtman.

The next word we have to examine is Âtman. It is next in importance to Brahman only, and the two together may be called the two pillars on which rests nearly the whole of the edifice of Indian philosophy, more particularly of the Vedânta and Sâ*m*khya systems.

As early as the time of the Âpastamba-Sûtras, that is, at the end of the Vedic period, we read, I, 8, 23, 1:—

'The Brâhma*n*a who is wise and recognises all things to be in the Âtman, who does not become bewildered when pondering (on it), and who recognises the Âtman in every (created) thing, he shines indeed in heaven . . .'

And in the same Sûtras, I, 8, 23, 2, we find a definition of Brahman, as the cause of the world, which presupposes, as clearly as possible, the prevalence of Vedântic ideas[1] at the time of the author of this Sûtra:—

'He who is intelligence itself and subtler than the thread of the lotus-fibre, He who pervades the

[1] Yoga and Mîmâ*m*sâ also are mentioned by name in the Âpastamba-Sûtras, but not yet as definite systems of philosophy. Cf. I, 8, 23, 5; II, 4, 8, 13.

universe and who, unchangeable and larger than the earth, contains this universe; He who is different from the knowledge of this world which is obtained by the senses and is identical with its objects, possesses the highest (form of absolute knowledge). From him who divides himself, spring all (objective) bodies. He is the primary cause, eternal and unchangeable.'

The etymology of Âtman is again extremely obscure, probably because it belongs to a pre-Sanskritic, though Aryan stratum of Indian speech. However, there can be little doubt that in the Veda Âtman, in several places, still means breath, as in Rv. X, 16, 3, sûryam *k*ákshu*h* ga*kkh*atu, vấtam âtmấ, words addressed to a dead person, 'May the eye go to the sun, the breath (Âtmâ) to the wind.' It then came to mean vital breath, life, and, like the spirit or breath, was frequently used in the sense of what we call soul. In some passages it is difficult to say whether we should translate it by life or by spirit. From soul there is but a small step to Self, and that step is often grammatical rather than real. If in the Atharva-veda IX, 5, 30 we read:—

Âtmấnam pitáram putrám paútram pitâmahám,
*G*âyấm *g*ánitrîm mâtáram yé priyâs tấn úpa hvaye,

we have to translate in English, 'Myself, father, son, grandson, grandfather, wife, mother, whoever are dear,—I call upon them.' But Self may here be translated by soul or person also, just as we may say, 'My soul doth magnify the Lord,' instead of 'I magnify the Lord.' Again we read, Rv. IX, 113, 1, balám dádhâna*h* âtmáni, 'putting strength into oneself.' In the end Âtman became the regular pronoun self. I need not go through all the evidence which may be seen in any Sanskrit dictionary[1], but we have still to see at what stage in its development Âtman became the definite name of the soul or Self within. This transition of meaning in Âtman offers a curious parallel to that of As, in Asu and Asti, which we examined before. There are passages such as Rv. I, 164, 4, bhûmyâ*h* ásu*h* ásr*i*k âtmâ kvà svit, 'Where was the breath, the blood, the spirit of the world?' Here Âtmâ may be rendered by spirit or life. But in other passages Âtman signifies simply the inmost nature of anything, and more particularly of man, so that in the end it means much the same as what medieval philosophers would have called the quiddity, or Indian philosophers the Idantâ of things. Thus we read at first âtmânam âtmanâ pasya, 'see thy Self by thy Self;' âtmaiva hy âtmana*h* sâkshî, 'Self is the witness of Self.' In this sense Âtman is afterwards used as the name of the highest person, the soul of the world (Paramâtman), and we read (*S*atap. Br. XIV, 5, 5, 15): sa vâ ayam âtmâ sarveshâm bhûtânâm adhipati*h*, sarveshâm bhûtânâ*m* râ*g*â, 'That Âtman is the sovereign of all beings, he is the king of all beings.'

### Pra*g*âpati, Brahman, Âtman.

We have thus seen three words growing up in the hymns and Brâhma*n*as of the Veda, Pra*g*âpati, Brahman, and Âtman, each of which by itself represents *in nuce* a whole philosophy or a view of the world.

---

[1] See Anthropological Religion, pp. 200 seq.; Theosophy, pp. 247 seq., or more recently, Deussen's Geschichte der Philosophie, pp. 324 seq.

In Pra*g*âpati we have the admission of a personal and supreme being, a god above all gods, a creator and ruler of the world. He created the primeval waters and rose from them as Hira*n*yagarbha, in order to send forth, to animate, and to rule all things. Whether this Pra*g*âpati was himself the material cause of the world may seem doubtful. Many times it is said that he was everything and that he desired to become many, and thus created the world, in which case matter also would have come out of him. In other places, however, the primeval waters seem to have been admitted as existing by themselves and apart from Pra*g*âpati (Rv. X, 121, 7). We also read that in the beginning there was water over which Pra*g*âpati breathed as wind and produced the earth, or that the waters themselves produced a golden egg from whence arose Pra*g*âpati, the creator of gods and men. There occur even in the Brâhma*n*as allusions to the legend well known from the Purâ*n*as, that a boar brought forth (Udbabarha or Udvavarha from V*ri*h) the earth, or that a tortoise supported it[1].

A belief in that Pra*g*âpati, as a personal god, was the beginning of monotheistic religion in India, while the recognition of Brahman and Âtman, as one, constituted the foundation of all the monistic philosophy of that country.

---

[1] M. M., India, pp. 134, 287.

# CHAPTER III.

## THE SYSTEMS OF PHILOSOPHY.

### Growth of Philosophical Ideas.

We have thus learnt the important lesson that all these ideas, metaphysical, cosmological, and otherwise, burst forth in India in great profusion and confusion, and without any preconceived system.

We must not suppose that these ideas follow each other in chronological succession. Here once more the *Nebeneinander* gives us the true key, much more than the *Nacheinander*. We must remember that this earliest philosophy existed for a long time without being fixed by writing, that there was neither control, authority, nor public opinion to protect it. Every Â*s*rama or settlement was a world by itself, even the simplest means of communication, such as high-roads or rivers, being often wanting. The wonder is that, in spite of all this, we should find so much unity in the numerous guesses at truth preserved to us among these Vedic ruins. This was due, we are told, to the Paramparâ, i.e. to those who handed down the tradition and at last collected whatever could be saved of it. It would be a mistake to imagine that there was a continuous development in the various meanings assumed by or assigned to such pregnant terms as Pra*g*âpati, Brahman, or even Âtman. It is much more in accordance with what we learn from the Brâhma*n*as and Upanishads of the intellectual life of India, to admit an infinite number of intellectual centres of thought, scattered all over the country, in which either the one or the other view found influential advocates. We should then understand better how Brahman, while meaning what bursts or drives forth, came to signify speech and prayer, as well as creative power and creator, and why Âtman meant not only breath, but life, spirit, soul, essence, or what I have ventured to render by the Self, *das Selbst*, of all things.

But if in the period of the Brâhma*n*as and Upanishads we have to find our way through religious and philosophical thoughts, as through clusters of thickly tangled creepers, the outlook becomes brighter as soon as we approach the next period, which is characterised by persistent attempts at clear and systematic thought. We must not imagine that even then we can always discover in the various systems of philosophy a regular historical growth. The Sûtras or aphorisms which we possess of the six systems of philosophy, each distinct from the other, cannot possibly claim to represent the very first attempts at a systematic treatment; they are rather the last summing up of what had been growing up during many generations of isolated thinkers.

### Prasthâna Bheda.

What the Brâhmans themselves thought of their philosophical literature we may learn even from such modern treatises as the Prasthâna-bheda, from which I gave some extracts by way of introduction to some papers of mine on one of the systems of Indian philosophy, published as long ago as 1852 in the Journal of the German Oriental Society. It is but fair to state that the credit of having discovered that tract of Madhusûdana Sarasvatî, and perceived its importance, belonged really to Colebrooke. I myself came to be acquainted with it through my old friend, Dr. Trithen, who had prepared a critical edition of it, but was prevented by illness and death from publishing it. It was published in the meantime by Professor Weber in his Indische Studien, 1849, and I think it may be useful to give once more some extracts from it [1].

'Nyâya [2],' he writes, 'is logic [3], as promulgated by Gotama [4] in five Adhyâyas (lessons). Its object is knowledge of the nature of the sixteen Padârthas by means of name, definition, and examination.' These Padârthas are the important or essential topics of the Nyâya philosophy; but it has proved very misleading to see Padârtha here translated by categories. No one could understand why such things as doubt, example, wrangling, &c., could possibly be called categories or *praedicabilia*, and it is no wonder that Ritter and others should have spoken of the Nyâya with open

---

[1] A new translation of the Prasthâna-bheda has been published by Prof. Deussen as an Introduction to his Allgemeine Geschichte der Philosophie, vol. i, p. 44, 1894.

[2] Nyâya is derived from ni 'into,' and î 'to go.' The fourth member of a syllogism is called Upanaya, 'leading towards' or 'induction.' Ballantyne translates Nyâya by μέθοδος.

[3] Anvîkshikî as an old name of philosophy, more particularly of logic, occurs also in Gautama's Dharmasâstra II, 3. It is used sometimes as synonymous with Mîmâ*m*sâ, and is more comprehensive than logic.

[4] As the MSS. vary between Gotama and Gautama, I have kept the former for the Nyâya, 'philosopher,' the latter for Buddha.

contempt, as they have done, if such things were represented to them as the categories of Indian logic.

'There is also the Vaiseshika philosophy in ten lessons, promulgated by Kaṇâda. Its object is to establish by their similarities and dissimilarities[1] the six Padârthas, viz.:—

1. Dravya, substance.
2. Guṇa, quality.
3. Karman, activity.
4. Sâmânya, what is general and found in more than one object. The highest Sâmânya is Sattâ or being.
5. Visesha, the differentia or what is special, residing in eternal atoms, &c.
6. Samavâya, inseparable inherence, as between cause and effect, parts and the whole, &c.

To which may be added

7. Abhâva, negation.

This philosophy also is called Nyâya.'

These Padârthas of the Vaiseshikas, at least 1–5, may indeed be called categories, for they represent what can be predicated, in general, of the objects of our experience, or, from an Indian point of view, what is predicated by, or what is the highest sense (Artha) of words (Pada). Thus it has come to pass that Padârtha, literally the meaning of a word, was used in Sanskrit in the sense of things in general, or objects. It is rightly translated by category when applied to the five Padârthas of Kaṇâda, but such a translation, doubtful even in

[1] Barthélemy St. Hilaire, in his work on Indian Logic, p. 356, remarks, 'Mais le philosophe Vaiseshika n'a point cherché à distinguer les catégories entre elles, en énumerant leurs propriétés, comme l'a fait le Stagirite. Il n'a point montré, comme Aristote, leurs rapports et leurs différences.' But this is exactly what he has done, cf. Sûtras I, 8 seq.

the case of the sixth or seventh Padârtha of the Vaiseshikas, would of course be quite misleading when applied to the Padârthas of Gotama. The real categories would, in Gotama's system, find their place mostly under Prameya, meaning not so much what has to be proved or established, as what forms the object of our knowledge.

Madhusûdana continues: 'The Mîmâ*m*sâ also is twofold, viz. the Karma-Mîmâ*m*sâ (work-philosophy) and the *S*ârîraka-Mîmâ*m*sâ (philosophy of the embodied spirit). The Karma-Mîmâ*m*sâ has been brought out by the venerable *G*aimini in twelve chapters.'

The objects of these twelve chapters are then indicated very shortly, and so as to be hardly intelligible without a reference to the original Sûtras. Dharma, the object of this philosophy, is explained as consisting of acts of duty, chiefly sacrificial. The second, third, and fourth chapters treat[1] of the differences and varieties of Dharma, its parts (or appendent members, contrasted with the main act), and the principal purpose of each sacrificial performance. The fifth chapter tries to settle the order of all sacrificial performances, and the sixth the qualifications of its performers. The subject of indirect precepts is opened in the seventh chapter and carried on more fully in the eighth. Inferrible changes, adapting to any variation or copy of certain sacrificial acts what was designed for the types or models of them, are discussed in the ninth, and bars or exceptions in the tenth. Concurrent efficacy is considered in the eleventh chapter, and co-ordinate effect in the twelfth; that is, the co-operation of several acts for a single

[1] I give this more intelligible description from Colebrooke, Miscellaneous Essays, vol. i, p. 330 seq.

result is the subject of the one, and the incidental effect of an act, of which the chief purpose is different, is discussed in the other[1].

'There is also the Sa*m*karsha*n*a-kâ*n*d*a, consisting of four chapters, composed by *G*aimini, and this, which is known by the name of Devatâ-kâ*nd*a, belongs to the Karma-Mîmâ*m*sâ, because it teaches the act called Upâsanâ or worship.

'Next follows the *S*ârîraka-Mîmâ*m*sâ, consisting of four chapters. Its object is to make clear the oneness of Brahman and Âtman (Self), and to exhibit the rules which teach the investigation (of it) by means of Vedic study, &c.' It is in fact much more what we call a system of philosophy than the Pûrva-Mîmâ*m*sâ, and it is quoted by different names, such as Uttara-Mîmâ*m*sâ, Brahma-Mîmâ*m*sâ, Vedânta, &c.[2]

'In the first lecture is shown the agreement with which all Vedânta passages refer, directly or indirectly, to the inward, undivided, second-less Brahman. In the first section are considered Vedic passages which have clear indications of Brahman; in the second, passages which have obscure indications of Brahman, and refer to Brahman so far as he is an object of worship; in the third, passages which have obscure indications of Brahman, and mostly refer to Brahman, so far as he or it is an object of knowledge. Thus the consideration of the Vedânta

---

[1] Professor Deussen has given a somewhat different version of these titles. He gives, for instance, as the subject of the fifth chapter the successive order of recitation, as enjoined by *S*ruti, but to judge from Mîm. Sûtras V, 1, 1, the right meaning seems to be the 'settling of the order of performance, according to *S*ruti, subject-matter, recitation, &c.'

[2] Read Âdya for Âkhya in the Prasthâna bheda.

texts has been finished, and in the fourth section such words as Avyakta, A*g*â, &c., are considered, of which it can be doubtful whether they may not refer to ideas, adapted and formulated by the Sâ*m*khya philosophers, such as Pradhâna, Prak*ri*ti, which is generally, though quite wrongly, translated by nature, as independent of Brahman or Purusha.

'The convergence of all Vedânta texts on the second-less Brahman having thus been established, Vyâsa or Bâdarâya*n*a, fearing an opposition by means of arguments such as have been produced by acknowledged Sm*ri*tis and various other systems, undertakes their refutation, and tries to establish the incontrovertible validity of his own arguments in the second lecture. Here, in the first section, the objections to the convergence of the Vedânta passages on Brahman, as stated by the Sm*ri*tis of the Sâ*m*khya-yoga, the Kâ*n*âdas, and by the arguments employed by the Sâ*m*khyas, are disposed of. In the second section is shown the faultiness of the views of the followers of the Sâ*m*khya, because every examination should consist of two parts, the establishment of our own doctrine and the refutation of the doctrine of our opponents. In the third section the contradictions between the passages of the Veda, referring to the creation of the elements and other subjects, are removed in the first part, and in the second those referring to individual souls. In the fourth section are considered all apparent contradictions between Vedic passages referring to the senses and their objects.

'In the third chapter follows the examination of the means (of salvation). Here in the first section, while considering the going to and returning from another world (transmigration), dispassionateness has to be examined. In the second section the meaning of the word Thou is made clear, and afterwards the meaning of the word That. In the third section there is a collection of words, if not purely tautological, all referring to the unqualified Brahman, as recorded in different *S*âkhâs or branches of the Veda; and at the same time the question is discussed whether certain attributes recorded by other *S*âkhâs in teaching a qualified or unqualified Brahman, may be taken together or not. In the fourth section the means of obtaining a knowledge of the unqualified Brahman, both the external, such as sacrifices and observing the four stations in life, and the internal, such as quietness, control, and meditation, are investigated.

'In the fourth chapter follows an inquiry into the special rewards or fruits of a knowledge of the qualified and unqualified Brahman. In the first section is described salvation of a man even in this life, when free from the influence of good or bad acts, after he has realised the unqualified Brahman by means of repeated study of the Veda, &c. In the second section the mode of departure of a dying man is considered. In the third, the further (northern) road of a man who died with a full knowledge of the unqualified Brahman is explained. In the fourth section the obtainment of disembodied aloneness by a man who knows the unqualified Brahman is first described, and afterwards the abode in the world of Brahman, promised to all who know the qualified (or lower) Brahman.

'This, the Vedânta, is indeed the principal of all doctrines, any other doctrine is but a complement of it, and therefore it alone is to be reverenced by all who wish for liberation, and this according to the interpretation of the venerable *S*a*m*kara—this is the secret!'

Here we see clearly that Madhusûdana considered the Vedânta-philosophy as interpreted by *S*a*m*kara, if not as the only true one, still as the best of all philosophies. He made an important distinction also between the four, the Nyâya, Vai*s*eshika, Pûrva, and Uttara-Mîmâ*m*sâ on one side, and the remaining two, the Sâ*m*khya and Yoga-philosophies on the other. It is curious indeed that this distinction has been hitherto so little remarked. According to Madhusûdana, the philosophies of Gotama and Ka*n*âda are treated simply as Sm*ri*tis or Dharma*s*âstras, like the Laws of Manu, nay like the Mahâbhârata [1] of Vyâsa, and the Râmâya*n*a of Valmîki. Of course these systems of philosophy cannot be called Sm*ri*ti in the ordinary sense of Dharma*s*âstra; but, as they are Sm*ri*ti or tradition, and not *S*ruti or revelation, they may be said to teach Dharma, if not in the legal, at least in the moral sense of that word. Anyhow it is clear that Sâ*m*khya and Yoga were looked upon as belonging to a class different from that to which the two Mîmâ*m*sâs, nay even Nyâya and Vai*s*eshika, and the other recognised branches of knowledge belonged, which together are represented as the eighteen branches of the Trayî (the Veda). Though it may be difficult to understand the exact reason of this distinction, the distinction itself should not be passed over.

---

[1] See Dahlmann, Das Mahâbhârata als Epos und Rechtsbuch, 1896.

'The Sâ*m*khya,' Madhusûdana continues, 'was brought out by the venerable Kapila in six Adhyâyas. In the first Adhyâya the objects for discussion are considered; in the second the effects or products of Pradhâna, or original matter; in the third aloofness from sensuous objects; in the fourth stories about dispassionate persons, such as Piṅgalâ (IV, 11), the fletcher (IV, 18), &c.; in the fifth there is refutation of opposite opinions; in the sixth a *résumé* of the whole. The chief object of the Sâ*m*khya-philosophy is to teach the difference between Prak*ri*ti and the Purushas.

'Then follows the Yoga-philosophy as taught by the venerable Patañ*g*ali, consisting of four parts. Here in the first part meditation, which stops the activity and distraction of the mind, and, as a means towards it, repeated practice and dispassionateness are discussed; in the second the eight accessories which serve to produce deep meditation even in one whose thoughts are distracted, such as (II, 29) restraint, observances, posture, regulation of breath, devotion, contemplation, and meditation; in the third, the supernatural powers; in the fourth aloneness. The chief object of this philosophy is to achieve concentration by means of stopping all wandering thoughts.'

After this follows a short account of the Pâ*s*upata and Pâñ*k*arâtra-systems, and then a recapitulation which is of interest. Here Madhusûdana says, 'that after the various systems have been explained, it should be clear that there are after all but three roads.

1. The Ârambha-vâda, the theory of atomic agglomeration.

2. The Pari*n*âma-vâda, the theory of evolution.

3. The Vivarta-vâda, the theory of illusion.

The first theory holds that the four kinds of atoms (A*n*u), those of earth, water, fire, and air, by becoming successively double atoms, &c., begin the world which culminates in the egg of Brahman.

This first theory, that of the Târkikas (Nyâya and Vai*s*eshika) and the Mîmâ*m*sakas, teaches that an effect which was not (the world), is produced through the activity of causes which are.

The second theory, that of the Sâ*m*khyas, Yoga-pâtañ*g*alas, and Pâ*s*upatas, says that Pradhâna alone, sometimes called Prak*ri*ti or original matter, composed, as it is, of the Gu*n*as of Sattva (good), Ra*g*as (moderate), and Tamas (bad), is evolved through the stages of Mahat (perceiving) and Aha*m*kâra (subjectivity) into the shape of the (subjective and objective) world. From this point of view the effected world existed before as real, though in a subtile (invisible) form, and was rendered manifest through the activity of a cause.

The third theory, that of the Brahmavâdins (Vedânta), says that the self-luminous and perfectly blissful Brahman which has no second, appears by mistake, through its own power of Mâyâ, as the world, while the Vaish*n*avas (Râmânu*g*a, &c.) hold that the world is an actual and true evolution of Brahman.

But in reality all the Munis who have put forward these theories agree in wishing to prove the existence of the one Supreme Lord without a second, ending in the theory of illusion (Vivarta). These Munis cannot be in error, considering that they are omniscient; and these different views have only been propounded by them, in order to keep off all nihilistic theories, and because they were afraid that human beings, with their inclinations towards the objects of the world, could not be expected at once to know the true goal of man. But all comes right when we understand that men, from not understanding their true object, imagined that these Munis would have propounded what is contrary to the Veda, and thus, accepting their opinions, have become followers of various paths.'

Much of what has here been translated from Madhusûdana's Prasthâna-bheda, though it gives a general survey, is obscure, but will become more intelligible hereafter when we come to examine each of the six philosophies by itself; nor is it at all certain that his view of the development of Indian philosophy is historically tenable. But it shows at all events a certain freedom of thought, which we see now and then in other writers also, such as Vi*gñ*âna-bhikshu, who are bent on showing that there is behind the diversity of Vedânta, Sâ*m*khya, and Nyâya one and the same truth, though differently expressed; that philosophies, in fact, may be many, but truth is one.

But however we may admire this insight on the part of Madhusûdana and others, it is our duty, as historians of philosophy, to study the different paths by which different philosophers, whether by the light of revelation or by that of their own unfettered reason, have striven to discover the truth. It is the very multiplicity and variety of these paths that form the chief interest of the history of philosophy, and the fact that to the present day these six different systems of philosophy have held their own in the midst of a great multitude of philosophic theories, propounded by the thinkers of India, shows that we must first of all try to appreciate their characteristic peculiarities, before attempting with Madhusûdana to eliminate their distinctive features.

These philosophers are—

1. Bâdarâyana, called also Vyâsa Dvaipâyana or Krishna Dvaipâyana, the reputed author of the Brahma-Sûtras, called also Uttara-Mîmâmsâ-Sûtras, or Vyâsa-Sûtras.

2. Gaimini, the author of the Pûrva-Mîmâmsâ-Sûtras.

3. Kapila, the author of the Sâmkhya-Sûtras.

4. Patañgali, also called Sesha or Phanin, the author of the Yoga-Sûtras.

5. Kanâda, also called Kanabhug, Kanabhakshaka, or Ulûka, the author of the Vaiseshika-Sûtras.

6. Gotama, also called Akshapâda, the author of the Nyâya-Sûtras.

It is easy to see that the philosophers to whom our Sûtras are ascribed, cannot be considered as the first originators of Indian philosophy. These Sûtras often refer to other philosophers, who therefore must have existed before the time when the Sûtras received their final form. Nor could the fact that some of the Sûtras quote and refute the opinions of other Sûtras, be accounted for without admitting a growing up of different philosophical schools side by side during a period which preceded their last arrangement. Unfortunately such references hardly ever give us the title of a book, or its author, still less the *ipsissima verba*. When they refer to such topics as Purusha and Prakriti we know that they refer to the Sâmkhya, if they speak of Anus or atoms, we know that their remarks are pointed at the Vaiseshikas. But it by no means follows that they refer to the Sâmkhya or Vaiseshika-Sûtras exactly as we now possess them. Some of these, as has been proved, are so modern that they could not possibly be quoted by ancient philosophers. Our Sâmkhya-Sûtras, for instance, have been proved by Dr. F. Hall to be not earlier than about 1380 A. D., and they may be even later. Startling as this discovery was, there is certainly nothing to be said against the arguments of Dr. Hall or against those by which Professor Garbe[1] has supported Dr. Hall's discovery. In this case, therefore, these Sûtras should be looked upon as a mere *rifaccimento*, to take the place of earlier Sûtras, which as early as the sixth cent. A. D. had probably been already superseded by the popular Sâmkhya-kârikâs and then forgotten. This late date of our Sâmkhya-Sûtras may seem incredible, but though I still hold that the Sûtra-style arose in a period when writing for literary purposes was still in its tentative stage, we know that even in our time there are learned Pandits who find no difficulty in imitating this ancient Sûtra-style. The Sûtra-period, reaching down as far as Asoka's reign in the third century, and his Council in 242 B.C., claims not only the famous Sûtras of Pânini, but has also been fixed upon as the period of the greatest philosophical activity in India, an activity called forth, it would seem, by the strong commotion roused by the rise of the Buddhist school of philosophy, and afterwards of religion.

---

[1] Garbe, Die Sâmkhya-Philosophie, p. 71.

### Literary References in the Upanishads.

It is of considerable importance to remember that of the technical names of the six systems of philosophy, two only occur in the classical Upanishads, namely Sâ*m*khya and Yoga or Sâ*m*khya-yoga. Vedânta does not occur, except in the *S*vetâ*s*vatara, Mu*nd*aka and some of the later Upanishads[1]. Mîmâ*m*sâ occurs in the general sense of investigation, Nyâya and Vai*s*eshika are altogether absent, nor do we meet with such words as Hetuvidyâ, or Ânvîkshikî, nor with the names of the reputed founders of the six systems, except those of the two Mîmâ*m*sâs, Bâdarâya*n*a and *G*aimini. The names of Patañ*g*ali, or Ka*n*âda, are absent altogether, while the names of Kapila and Gotama, when they occur, refer, it would seem, to quite different personalities.

### The Six Systems of Philosophy.

No one can suppose that those whose names are mentioned as the authors of these six philosophical systems, were more than the final editors or redactors of the Sûtras as we now possess them. If the third century B.C. should seem too late a date for the introduction of writing for literary purposes in India, we should remember that even inscriptions have not yet been found more ancient than those of A*s*oka, and there is a wide difference between inscriptions and literary compositions. The Southern Buddhists do not claim to have reduced their

---

[1] A curious distinction is made in a commentary on the Gautama-Sûtras XIX, 12. where it is said that 'those parts of the Âra*n*yakas which are not Upanishads are called Vedântas.'

Sacred Canon to writing before the first century B.C., though it is well known that they kept up close relations with their Northern co-religionists who were acquainted with writing[1]. During all that time, therefore, between 477 and 77 B.C., ever so many theories of the world, partaking of a Vedânta, Sâmkhya or Yoga, nay even of a Buddhist character, could have sprung up and have been reduced to a mnemonic form in various Âsramas. We need not wonder that much of that literature, considering that it could be mnemonic only, should have been irretrievably lost, and we must take care also not to look upon what has been left to us in the old Darsanas, as representing the whole outcome of the philosophical activity of the whole of India through so many generations. All we can say is that philosophy began to ferment in India during the period filled by Brâhmanas and Upanishads, nay even in some of the Vedic hymns, that the existence of Upanishads, though not necessarily our own, is recognised in the Buddhist Canon, and lastly that the name of Suttas, as a component part of the Buddhist Canon, must be later than that of the earliest Brâhmanic Sûtras, because in the meantime the meaning of the word had been changed from short mnemonic sentences to fully developed discourses. Possibly Sûtra was originally meant for the text to be elucidated in a sermon, so that the long Buddhistic sermons came to be called Suttas in consequence.

---

[1] The sacred Bo-tree in the city of Anurâdhapura in Ceylon was grown, we are told, from a branch of the tree at Buddha Gayâ.

### B*ri*haspati-Sûtras.

That some of the earlier philosophical Sûtras were lost, is shown in the case of the B*ri*haspati-Sûtras. These are said to have contained the doctrines of the out and out materialists, or sensualists, the Laukâyatikas or *K*ârvâkas, who deny the existence of everything beyond what is given by the senses. They are referred to by Bhâskarâ*k*ârya at Brahma-Sûtras III, 3, 53[1], and as he gives an extract, it is likely that they still existed in his time, though no MS. of them has been found as yet in India. The same applies to such Sûtras as the Vaikhânasa-Sûtras, possibly intended for the Vânaprasthas, and the Bhikshu-Sûtras[2], quoted by Pâ*n*ini, IV, 3, 110, and intended, it would seem, for Brâhmanic, and not yet for Buddhistic mendicants. It is a sad truth which we have to learn more and more, that of the old pre-Buddhistic literature we have but scanty fragments, and that even these may be, in some cases, mere reproductions of lost originals, as in the case of the Sâ*m*khya-Sûtras. We know now that such Sûtras could have been produced at any time, and we should not forget that even at present, in the general decay of Sanskrit scholarship, India still possesses scholars who can imitate Kâlidâsa, to say nothing of such poems as the Mahâbhârata and Râmâya*n*a, and so successfully that few scholars could tell the difference. It is not long ago that I received a Sanskrit treatise written in Sûtras with a commentary, the work of a living

---

[1] Colebrooke, Misc. Essays[2], I, 429.

[2] They were identified by Târânâtha Tarkavâ*k*aspati with the Vedânta-Sûtras; see Siddhânta Kaumudî, vol. i, p. 592.

I

scholar in India, which might have deceived many a European scholar of Sanskrit literature [1]. If that is possible now, if, as in the case of the Kapila-Sûtras, it was possible in the fourteenth century, why should not the same have taken place during the period of the Renaissance in India, nay even at an earlier time? At all events, though grateful for what has been preserved, and preserved in what may seem to us an almost miraculous manner, we should not imagine that we possess all, or that we possess what we possess in its original form.

### Books of Reference.

I shall mention here some of the most important works only, from which students of philosophy, particularly those ignorant of Sanskrit, may gain by themselves a knowledge of the six recognised systems of Indian Philosophy. The titles of the more important of the original Sanskrit texts may be found in Colebrooke's Miscellaneous Essays, vol. ii, p. 239 seq., and in the Catalogues, published since his time, of the various collections of Sanskrit MSS. in Europe and India.

For the Vedânta-philosophy of Bâdarâya*n*a the most useful book is Thibaut's English translation of the text of the Sûtras and *S*a*m*kara's commentary in the S. B. E., vols. xxxiv and xxxviii.

Of books written in German, Deussen's translation of the same work, 1887, preceded as it was by his

---

[1] It is called Kâtantra*kkh*anda*h*prakriyâ by *K*andrakânta Tarkâlaṅkâra, 1896, and gives additional Sûtras to the Kâtantra on Vedic Grammar. He makes no secret that Sûtra*m* v*r*ittis *k*obhayam api mayaiva vyarâ*k*i, 'the Sûtra and the commentary, both were composed by me.'

'System des Vedânta,' 1883, can be thoroughly recommended.

Of the Sâ*m*khya-system we have the Sûtras translated by Ballantyne in 1882–1885, the Aphorisms of the Sâ*m*khya Philosophy of Kapila, with illustrative extracts from the Commentaries, 1852, 1865, 1885.

In German we have the Sâ*m*khya-Prava*k*ana-Bhâshya, Vi*gñ*âna-bhikshu's Commentar zu den Sâ*m*khya-Sûtras, übersetzt von R. Garbe, 1889. Also Aniruddha's Commentary and the original parts of Vedântin Mahâdeva's commentary on the Sâ*m*khya-Sûtras, by Richard Garbe, 1892.

Der Mondschein der Sâ*m*khya Wahrheit, Vâ*k*aspatimi*s*ra's Sâ*m*khya-tattva-kaumudi, übersetzt von R. Garbe, 1892, is also a very useful work.

The Sámkhya Káriká by Íswarakṛishṇa, translated from the Sanscrit by H. T. Colebrooke, also the Bháshya or commentary by Gaurapáda; translated and illustrated by an original comment by H. H. Wilson, Oxford, 1837, may still be consulted with advantage.

Other useful works are :—

John Davies, Hindu Philosophy. The Sānkhya Kārikā of Īswarakṛishṇa, London, 1881.

Die Sâ*m*khya-Philosophie, nach den Quellen, von R. Garbe, 1894.

Of the Pûrva-Mîmâ*m*sâ or simply Mîmâ*m*sâ, which deals chiefly with the nature and authority of the Veda with special reference to sacrificial and other duties, we have the Sûtras with *S*abarasvâmin's commentary published in the original; but there is as yet no book in English in which that system may be studied, except Professor Thibaut's translation of

Laugâkshi Bhâskara's Arthasa*m*graha, a short abstract of that philosophy, published in the Benares Sanskrit Series, No. 4.

The Vai*s*eshika system of philosophy may be studied in an English translation of its Sûtras by A. E. Gough, Benares, 1873; also in a German translation by Roer, Zeitschrift der Deutschen Morgenländischen Gesellschaft, vols. 21 and 22, and in some articles of mine in the same Journal of the German Oriental Society, 1849.

The Nyâya-Sûtras of Gotama have been translated, with the exception of the last book, by Ballantyne, Allahabad, 1850–57.

The Yoga-Sûtras are accessible in an English translation by Rájendralála Mitra, in the Bibliotheca Indica, Nos. 462, 478, 482, 491, and 492.

### Dates of the Philosophical Sûtras.

If we consider the state of philosophical thought in India such as it is represented to us in the Brâhma*n*as and Upanishads, and afterwards in the canonical books of the Buddhists, we cannot wonder that all attempts at fixing the dates of the six recognised systems of philosophy, nay even their mutual relationship, should hitherto have failed. It is true that Buddhism and *G*ainism were likewise but two philosophical systems out of many, and that it has been possible to fix their dates. But if in their case we know something about their dates and their historical development, this is chiefly due to the social and political importance which they acquired during the fifth, the fourth, and the third centuries B.C., and not simply to their philosophical tenets. We know also that there were many teachers, contemporaries of Buddha, but they have left no traces in the literary history of India.

Nor should we forget that, though the date of the Buddhist Canon may be fixed, the date of many of the texts which we now possess and accept as canonical is by no means beyond the reach of doubt.

In the Buddhist annals themselves other teachers such as *G*ñâtiputra, the Nirgrantha, the founder of *G*ainism, Pûra*n*a Kâ*s*yapa, Kakuda Kâtyâyana, A*g*ita Ke*s*akambali, Sa*m*g*a*ya Vaira*tt*i-putra, Go*s*âli-putra, the Maskarin, are mentioned by the side of Gautama, the prince of the clan of the Sâkyas. One of these only became known in history, *G*ñâtiputra, the Nirgrantha or gymnosophist, because the society founded by him, like the brotherhood founded by Buddha, developed into a powerful sect, the *G*ainas. Another, Go*s*âli with the bamboo stick, originally an  Â*g*îvaka, then a follower of Mahâvîra, became likewise the founder of a sect of his own, which, however, has now disappeared[1]. *G*ñâtiputra or Nâtaputta was actually the senior of Buddha.

Though it seems likely that the founders of the six systems of philosophy, though not the authors of the Sûtras which we possess, belonged to the same period of philosophical and religious fermentation which gave rise to the first spreading of Buddha's doctrines in India, it is by no means clear that any of these systems, in their literary form, are pre-supposed by Buddhism. This is owing to the vagueness of the quotations which are hardly ever given *verbatim.* In India, during the mnemonic period of literature, the contents of a book may have become

---

[1] Kern, Buddhismus, I, p. 182.

considerably modified, while the title remained the same. Even at a much later time, when we see Bhart*ri*hari (died 650 A.D.) referring to the Mîmâ*m*saka, Sâ*m*khya, and Vai*s*eshika Dar*s*anas, we have no right to conclude that he knew these Dar*s*anas exactly as we know them, though he may well have known these philosophies after they had assumed their systematic form. Again, when he quotes Naiyâyikas, it by no means follows that he knew our Gotama-Sûtras, nor have we any right to say that our Gotama-Sûtras existed in his time. It is possible, it is probable, but it is not certain. We must therefore be very careful not to rely too much on quotations from, or rather allusions to, other systems of philosophy.

### Sâ*m*khya-Sûtras.

The Sâ*m*khya-Sûtras, as we possess them, are very chary of references. They clearly refer to Vai*s*eshika and Nyâya, when they examine the six categories of the former (V, 85) and the sixteen Padârthas of the latter (V, 86). Whenever they refer to the A*n*us or atoms, we know that they have the Vai*s*eshika-philosophy in their minds; and once the Vai*s*eshikas are actually mentioned by name (I, 25). *S*ruti, which the Sâ*m*khyas were supposed to disregard, is very frequently appealed to, Sm*ri*ti once (V, 123), and Vâmadeva, whose name occurs in both *S*ruti and Sm*ri*ti, is mentioned as one who had obtained spiritual freedom. But of individual philosophers we meet only with Sanandana Â*k*ârya (VI, 69) and Pañ*k*a*s*ikha (V, 32; VI, 68), while the teachers, the Â*k*âryas, when mentioned in general, are explained as comprehending Kapila himself, as well as others.

### Vedânta-Sûtras.

The Vedânta-Sûtras contain more frequent references, but they too do not help us much for chronological purposes.

Bâdarâyana refers more or less clearly to the Buddhists, the *G*ainas, Pâsupatas, and Pâñkarâtras, all of whom he is endeavouring to refute. He never refers, however, to any literary work, and even when he refers to other philosophical systems, he seems to avoid almost intentionally the recognised names of their authors, nay even their technical terms. Still it is clear that the systems of the Pûrva-Mîmâmsâ, the Yoga, Sâmkhya, and Vaiseshika were in his mind when he composed his Sûtras, and among Mîmâmsic authorities he refers by name to *G*aimini, Bâdari, Audulomi, Âsmarathya, Kâsakritsna, Karshnâgini, and Âtreya, nay to a Bâdarâyana also. We cannot be far wrong therefore if we assign the gradual formation of the six systems of philosophy to the period from Buddha (fifth century) to Asoka (third century), though we have to admit, particularly in the cases of Vedânta, Sâmkhya, and Yoga a long previous development reaching back through Upanishads and Brâhmanas to the very hymns of the Rig-veda.

It is equally difficult to fix the relative position[1] of the great systems of philosophy, because, as I explained before, they quote each other mutually. With regard to the relation of Buddhism to the six orthodox systems it seems to me that all we can honestly say is that schools of philosophy handing down doctrines very similar to those of our six classical or orthodox systems, are presupposed by

[1] Bhandarkar, Sâmkhya Philosophy (1871), p. 3.

the Buddhist Suttas. But this is very different from the opinion held by certain scholars that Buddha or his disciples actually borrowed from our Sûtras. We know nothing of Sâ*m*khya-literature before the Sâ*m*khya-kârikâs, which belong to the sixth century after Christ. Even if we admit that the Tattva-samâsa was an earlier work, how could we, without parallel dates, prove any actual borrowing on the part of Buddha or his disciples at that early time?

In the Upanishads and Brâhma*n*as, though there is a common note running through them all, there is as yet great latitude and want of system, and a variety of opinions supported by different teachers and different schools. Even in the hymns we meet with great independence and individuality of thought, which occasionally seems to amount to downright scepticism and atheism.

We must keep all this in mind if we wish to gain a correct idea of the historical origin and growth of what we are accustomed to call the six philosophical systems of India. We have seen already that philosophical discussions were not confined to the Brâhmans, but that the Kshatriyas also took a very active and prominent part in the elaboration of such fundamental philosophical concepts as that of Âtman or Self.

It is out of this floating mass of philosophical and religious opinion, which was common property in India, that the regular systems slowly emerged. Though we do not know in what form this took place, it is quite clear that what we now possess of philosophical manuals, in the form of Sûtras, could not have been written down during the time when writing for any practical purposes except inscriptions on monuments and coins was still unknown in India, or at all events had not yet been employed for literary purposes, so far as we know.

### Mnemonic Literature.

It has now been generally admitted, I believe, that whenever writing has once become popular, it is next to impossible that there should be no allusion to it in the poetical or prose compositions of the people. Even as late as the time of *S*a*m*kara, the written letters are still called unreal (An*ri*ta) in comparison with the audible sounds, as classified in the Prâti*s*âkhyas, which are represented by them (Ved. Sûtras II, 1, 14, p. 451). There is no allusion to writing in the hymns, the Brâhma*n*as and Upanishads; very few, if any, in the Sûtras. The historical value of these allusions to writing which occur in the literature of the Buddhists depends, of course, on the date which we can assign, not to the original authors, but to the writers of our texts. We must never forget that there was in India during many centuries a purely mnemonic literature, which continued down to the Sûtra-period, and which was handed down from generation to generation according to a system which is fully described in the Prâti*s*âkhyas. What would have been the use of that elaborate system, if there had been manuscripts in existence at the same time?

When that mnemonic literature, that Sm*ri*ti, came for the first time to be reduced to writing, this probably took place in something like the form of Sûtras. The very helplessness of the Sûtra-style would thus become intelligible. Letters at that time were as yet monumental only, for in India also monumental writing is anterior to literary writing, and to the adoption of a cursive alphabet. Writing material was scarce in India, and the number of those who could read must have been very small. At the same time there existed the old mnemonic literature, invested with a kind of sacred character, part and parcel of the ancient system of education, which had so far answered all purposes and was not easy to supplant. Much of that mnemonic literature has naturally been lost, unless it was reduced to writing at the proper time. Often the name may have survived, while the body of a work was entirely changed. Hence when we see the Sâ*m*khya mentioned by name in the Buddhist texts, such as the Visuddhi-magga (chap. XVII), it is impossible to tell whether even at that time there existed a work on the Sâ*m*khya-philosophy in the form of Sûtras. It is clear at all events that it could not have been our Sâ*m*khya-Sûtras, nor even the Sâ*m*khya-kârikâs which seem to have superseded the ancient Sûtras early in the sixth century, while our present Sûtras date from the fourteenth.

It might be possible, if not to prove, at all events to render probable the position assigned here to Buddha's teaching as subsequent to the early growth of philosophical ideas in their systematic and more or less technical form, by a reference to the name assigned to his mother, whether it was her real name or a name assigned to her by tradition. She was called Mâyâ or Mâyâdevî. Considering that in Buddha's eyes the world was Mâyâ or illusion, it seems more likely that the name was given to his mother by early tradition, and that it was given not without a purpose. And if so this could only have been after the name of Avidyâ (nescience) in the Vedânta, and of Prakriti in the Sâmkhya-philosophy had been replaced by the technical term of Mâyâ. It is well known that, in the old classical Upanishads, the name of Mâyâ never occurs; and it is equally significant that it does occur in the later and more or less apocryphal Upanishads. In the Svetâsvatara, for instance, I, 10, we read, Mâyâm tu Prakritim vidyât, 'Let him know that Prakriti is Mâyâ or Mâyâ Prakriti.' This refers, it would seem, to the Sâmkhya system in which Prakriti acts the part of Mâyâ and fascinates the Purusha, till he turns away from her and she ceases to exist, at all events as far as he is concerned. But whether in Sâmkhya or Vedânta, Mâyâ in its technical meaning belongs certainly to a secondary period, and it might therefore be argued that Mâyâ, as the name of Buddha's mother, is not likely to have found a place in the Buddhistic legend during the early period of Indian philosophy, as represented in the early Upanishads, and even in the Sûtras of these two prominent schools.

There was, no doubt, a certain amount of philosophical mnemonic composition after the period represented by the old Upanishads, and before the systematic arrangement of the philosophical Sûtras, but whatever may have existed in it, is for ever lost to us. We can see this clearly in the case of the Brihaspati-philosophy.

### The Brihaspati-Philosophy.

Brihaspati is no doubt a very perplexing character. His name is given as that of the author of two Vedic hymns, X, 71, X, 72, a distinction being made between a B*ri*haspati Âṅgirasa and a B*ri*haspati Laukya (Laukâyatika?). His name is well known also as one of the Vedic deities. In Rv. VIII, 96, 15, we read that Indra, with B*ri*haspati as his ally, overcame the godless people (ádevî*h* vísâ*h*). He is afterwards quoted as the author of a law-book, decidedly modern, which we still possess. B*ri*haspati is besides the name of the planet Jupiter, and of the preceptor or Purohita of the gods, so that B*ri*haspati-purohita has become a recognised name of Indra, as having B*ri*haspati for his Purohita or chief priest and helper. It seems strange, therefore, that the same name, that of the preceptor of the gods, should have been chosen as the name of the representative of the most unorthodox, atheistical, and sensualistic system of philosophy in India. We may possibly account for this by referring to the Brâhma*n*as and Upanishads, in which B*ri*haspati is represented as teaching the demons his pernicious doctrines, not for their benefit, but for their own destruction. Thus we read, Maitrâya*n*a Up. 7, 9:—

'B*ri*haspati, having become or having assumed the shape of *S*ukra, brought forth that false knowledge, for the safety of Indra and for the destruction of the Asuras (demons). By it they show that good is evil and that evil is good, and they say that this new law, which upsets the Veda and the other sacred books, should be studied (by the Asuras, the demons). That being so, it is said, Let no man (but the demons only) study that false knowledge, for it is wrong; it is, as it were, barren. Its reward lasts only as long as the pleasure lasts, as with one who has fallen from his station (caste).

Let that false doctrine not be attempted, for thus it is said[1] :—

1. Widely divergent and opposed are these two, the one known as false knowledge, the other as knowledge. I (Yama) believe Na*k*iketas to be possessed of a desire for knowledge; even many pleasures do not tempt him away.

2. He who knows at the same time both the imperfect knowledge (of ritual) and the perfect knowledge (of Self), crosses death by means of the imperfect, and obtains immortality by means of the perfect knowledge[2].

3. Those who are wrapt up in imperfect knowledge fancy themselves alone wise and learned, they wander about floundering and deceived, like the blind led by a man who is himself blind[3].'

And again :—

'The gods and the demons, wishing to know the Self, went once into the presence of Brahman (their father Pra*g*âpati[4]). Having bowed before him, they said: "O blessed one, we wish to know the Self, do thou tell us!" Thus, after considering, he thought, these demons believe in a difference of the Âtman (from themselves), and therefore a very different Self was taught to them. On that Self these deluded demons take their stand, clinging to it, destroying the true boat of salvation, and praising untruth. What is untrue they see as true, like jugglery. But in reality, what is said in the Vedas, that is true. What is said in the Vedas, on that the wise take their stand. There-

---

[1] Ka*th*a Upanishad II, 4.

[2] Vâ*g*. Up. II.

[3] Ka*th*. Up. II, 5.

[4] *Kh*ând. Up. VIII, 8.

fore let no Brâhman study what is not in the Vedas, or this will be the result (as in the case of the demons).'

This passage is curious in several respects. First of all it is a clear reference of one Upanishad to another, namely to the *Kh*ândogya, in which this episode of B*ri*haspati giving false instruction to the demons is more fully detailed. Secondly we see an alteration which was evidently made intentionally. In the *Kh*ândogya Upanishad it is Pra*g*âpati himself who imparts false knowledge of the Âtman to the Asuras, while in the Maitrâya*n*a Upanishad B*ri*haspati takes his place. It is not unlikely that B*ri*haspati was introduced in the later Upanishad in order to take the place of Pra*g*âpati, because it was felt to be wrong that this highest deity should ever have misled anybody, even the demons. In the *Kh*ândogya the demons who believed in the Anyatâ (otherness) of the Âtman, that is to say, in the possibility that the Âtman could be in some place different from themselves, were told to look for it in the person seen in the pupil of the eye, or in the image in a looking-glass, or in the shadow in the water. All this would, however, refer to a visible body only. Then Pra*g*âpati goes on to say that the Âtman is what moves about full of pleasures in a dream, and as this would still be the individual man, he declares at last that Âtman is what remains in deep sleep, without however losing its own identity.

If then in the Upanishads already B*ri*haspati was introduced for the purpose of teaching wrong and unorthodox opinions, we may possibly be able to understand how his name came to cling to sensualistic opinions, and how at last, however unfairly, he was held responsible for them. That such opinions existed even at an earlier time, we can see in some of the hymns in which many years ago I pointed out these curious traces of an incipient scepticism. In later Sanskrit, a Bârhaspatya, or a follower of B*ri*haspati, has come to mean an infidel in general. Among the works mentioned in the Lalita-vistara as studied by Buddha a Bârhaspatyam is mentioned, but whether composed in Sûtras or in metre does not appear. Besides, it is well known that the Lalita-vistara is rather a broken reed to rest upon for chronological purposes. If we may trust, however, to a scholion of Bhâskara on the Brahma-Sûtras, he seems to have known, even at that late time, some Sûtras ascribed to B*ri*haspati[1], in which the doctrines of the *K*ârvâkas i. e. unbelievers, were contained. But although such Sûtras may have existed, we have no means of fixing their date as either anterior or posterior to the other philosophic Sûtras. Pâ*n*ini knew of Sûtras which are lost to us, and some of them may be safely referred to the time of Buddha. He also in quoting Bhikshu-Sûtras and Na*t*a-Sûtras, mentions (IV, 3, 110) the author of the former as Pârâ*s*arya, of the latter as *S*ilâlin. As Pârâ*s*arya is a name of Vyâsa, the son of Parâ*s*ara, it has been supposed that Pâ*n*ini meant by Bhikshu-Sûtras, the Brahma-Sûtras[2], sometimes ascribed to Vyâsa, which we still possess. That would fix their date about the fifth century B.C., and has been readily accepted therefore by all who wish to claim the

[1] Colebrooke, II, 429. [2] See before, p. 113.

greatest possible antiquity for the philosophical literature of India. But Pârâsarya would hardly have been chosen as the titular name of Vyâsa; and though we should not hesitate to assign to the doctrines of the Vedânta a place in the fifth century B.C., nay even earlier, we cannot on such slender authority do the same for the Sûtras themselves.

When we meet elsewhere with the heterodox doctrines of B*ri*haspati, they are expressed in verse, as if taken from a Kârikâ rather than from Sûtras. They possess a peculiar interest to us, because they would show us that India, which is generally considered as the home of all that is most spiritual and idealistic, was by no means devoid of sensualistic philosophers. But though it is difficult to say how old such theories may have been in India it is certain that, as soon as we get any coherent treatises on philosophy, sensualistic opinions crop up among them.

Of course the doctrines of Buddha would be called sceptical and atheistic by the Brâhmans, and *K*ârvâka as well as Nâstika are names freely applied to the Buddhists. But the doctrines of B*ri*haspati, as far as we know them, go far beyond Buddhism, and may be said to be hostile to all religious feelings, while Buddha's teaching was both religious and philosophical, though the lines that separate philosophy and religion in India are very faint.

There are some tenets of the followers of B*ri*haspati which seem to indicate the existence of other schools of philosophy by their side. The Bârhaspatyas speak as if being *inter pares*, they differ from others as others differed from them. Traces of an opposition against the religion of the Vedas (Kautsa) appear in the hymns, the Brâhma*n*as, and the Sûtras, and to ignore them would give us an entirely false idea of the religious and philosophical battles and battle-fields of ancient India. As viewed from a Brâhmanic point of view, and we have no other, the opposition represented by B*ri*haspati and others may seem insignificant, but the very name given to these heretics would seem to imply that their doctrines had met with a world-wide acceptance (Lokâyatikas). Another name, that of Nâstika, is given to them as saying No to everything except the evidence of the senses, particularly to the evidence of the Vedas, which, curiously enough, was called by the Vedântists Pratyaksha, that is, self-evident, like sense-perception.

These Nâstikas, a name not applicable to mere dissenters, but to out and out nihilists only, are interesting to us from a historical point of view, because in arguing against other philosophies, they prove, *ipso facto*, the existence of orthodox philosophical systems before their time. The recognised schools of Indian philosophy could tolerate much; they were tolerant, as we shall see, even towards a qualified atheism, like that of the Sâ*m*khya. But they had nothing but hatred and contempt for the Nâstikas, and it is for that very reason, and on account of the strong feelings of aversion which they excited, that it seemed to me right that their philosophy should not be entirely passed over by the side of the six Vedic or orthodox systems.

Mâdhava, in his Sarvadar*s*ana-sa*m*graha or the Epitome of all philosophical systems, begins with an account of the Nâstika or *K*ârvâka system. He looks upon it as the lowest of all, but nevertheless, as not to be ignored in a catalogue of the philosophical forces of India. *K*ârvâka (not *K*arvâka) is given as the name of a Râkshasa, and he is treated as a historical individual to whom B*ri*haspati or Vâ*k*aspati delivered his doctrines. The name of *K*ârvâka is clearly connected with that of *K*ârva, and this is given as a synonym of Buddha by Bâla*s*âstrin in the Preface to his edition of the Kâ*s*ikâ (p. 2). He is represented as a teacher of the Lokâyata or world-wide system, if that is the meaning originally intended by that word. A short account of this system is given in the Prabodha*k*androdaya 27, 18, in the following words: 'The Lokâyata system in which the senses alone form an authority, in which the elements are earth, water, fire, and wind (not Âkâ*s*a or ether), in which wealth and enjoyment form the ideals of man, in which the elements think, the other world is denied, and death is the end of all things.' This name Lokâyata occurs already in Pâ*n*ini's Ga*n*a Ukthâdi. It should be noted however, that Hema*k*andra distinguishes between Bârhaspatya or Nâstika, and *K*ârvâka or Lokâyatika, though he does not tell us which he considers the exact points on which the two are supposed to have differed. The Buddhists use Lokâyata for philosophy in general. The statement that the Lokâyatas admitted but one Pramâ*n*a, i. e. authority of knowledge, namely sensuous perception, shows clearly that there must have been other philosophical systems already in existence. We shall see that the Vai*s*eshika acknowledged two, perception (Pratyaksha) and inference (Anumâna); the Sâ*m*khya three, adding trustworthy affirmation (Âptavâkya); the Nyâya four, adding comparison (Upamâna); the two Mîmâ*m*sâs six, adding presumption (Arthâpatti) and privation (Abhâva). Of these and others we shall have to speak hereafter. Even what seems to us so natural an idea as that of the four or five elements, required some time to develop, as we see in the history of the Greek στοιχεῖα, and yet such an idea was evidently quite familiar to the *K*ârvâkas. While other systems admitted five, i. e. earth, water, fire, air, and ether, they admitted four only, excluding ether, probably because it was invisible. In the Upanishads we see traces of an even earlier triad of elements. All this shows the philosophical activity of the Hindus from the earliest times, and exhibits to us the *K*ârvâkas as denying rather what had been more or less settled before their time, than as adding any new ideas of their own.

So it is again with regard to the soul. Not only philosophers, but every Ârya in India had a word for soul, and never doubted that there was something in man different from the visible body. The *K*ârvâkas only denied this. They held that what was called soul was not a thing by itself, but was simply the body over again. They held that it was the body that felt, that saw and heard, that remembered and thought, though they saw it every day rotting away and decomposing, as if it never had been. By such opinions they naturally came in conflict with religion even more than with philosophy. We do not know how they accounted for the evolution of consciousness and intellect out of mere flesh, except that they took refuge with a simile, appealing to the intoxicating power that can be developed by mixing certain ingredients, which by themselves are not intoxicating, as an analogy to the production of soul from body.

Thus we read :—

'There are four elements, earth, water, fire, and air,

And from these four elements alone is intelligence produced—

Just like the intoxicating power from Ki*n*wa, &c., mixed together ;—

Since in "I am fat," "I am lean," these attributes abide in the same subject,

And since fatness, &c., resides only in the body, it alone is the soul and no other,

And such phrases as "my body" are only significant metaphorically.'

In this way the soul seems to have been to them the body qualified by the attribute of intelligence, and therefore supposed to perish with the body. Holding this opinion, it is no wonder that they should have considered the highest end of man to consist in sensual enjoyment, and that they should have accepted pain simply as an inevitable concomitant of pleasure.

A verse is quoted :—

'The pleasure which arises to men from contact with sensible objects,

Is to be relinquished as accompanied by pain—such is the warning of fools ;

The berries of paddy, rich with the finest white grains,

What man, seeking his true interest, would fling them away, because covered with husks and dust [1] ?'

---

[1] See for these verses Cowell and Gough's translation of the Sarvadar*s*ana-sa*m*graha, p. 4.

From all this we see that, though fundamental philosophical principles are involved, the chief character of the *K*ârvâka system was practical, rather than metaphysical, teaching utilitarianism and crude hedonism in the most outspoken way. It is a pity that all authoritative books of these materialistic philosophers should be lost, as they would probably have allowed us a deeper insight into the early history of Indian philosophy than the ready-made manuals of the six Dar*s*anas on which we have chiefly to rely. The following verses preserved by Mâdhava in his Epitome are nearly all we possess of the teaching of B*ri*haspati and his followers :—

'Fire is hot, water cold, and the air feels cool;

By whom was this variety made? (we do not know), therefore it must have come from their own nature (Svabhâva).'

B*ri*haspati himself is held responsible for the following invective :—

'There is no paradise, no deliverance, and certainly no Self in another world,

Nor are the acts of the Â*s*ramas (stations in life) or the castes, productive of rewards.

The Agnihotra, the three Vedas, the three staves (carried by ascetics) and smearing oneself with ashes,

They are the mode of life made by their creator[1] for those who are devoid of sense and manliness.

If a victim slain at the *G*yotish*t*oma will go to heaven,

Why is not his own father killed there by the sacrificer?

---

[1] Dhât*ri*, creator, can here be used ironically only, instead of Svabhâva, or nature.

If the *S*râddha-offering gives pleasure to beings that are dead,

Then to give a *viaticum* to people who travel here on earth, would be useless.

If those who are in heaven derive pleasure from offerings,

Then why not give food here to people while they are standing on the roof?

As long as he lives let a man live happily; after borrowing money, let him drink Ghee,

How can there be a return of the body after it has once been reduced to ashes?

If he who has left the body goes to another world,

Why does he not come back again perturbed by love of his relations?

Therefore funeral ceremonies for the dead were ordered by the Brâhmans.

As a means of livelihood, nothing else is known anywhere.

The three makers of the Vedas were buffoons, knaves, and demons.

The speech of the Pandits is (unintelligible), like *G*arpharî Turpharî.

The obscene act there (at the horse sacrifice) to be performed by the queen has been

Proclaimed by knaves, and likewise other things to be taken in hand.

The eating of flesh was likewise ordered by demons.'

This is certainly very strong language, as strong as any that has ever been used by ancient or modern materialists. It is well that we should know how old and how widely spread this materialism was, for without it we should hardly understand the efforts that were made on the other side to counteract it by establishing the true sources or measures of knowledge, the Pramâ*n*as, and other fundamental truths which were considered essential both for religion and for philosophy. The idea of orthodoxy, however, is very different in India from what it has been elsewhere. We shall find philosophers in India who deny the existence of a personal god or Î*s*vara, and who, nevertheless, were tolerated as orthodox as long as they recognised the authority of the Veda, and tried to bring their doctrines into harmony with Vedic texts. It is this denial of the authority of the Veda which, in the eyes of the Brâhmans, stamped Buddha at once as a heretic, and drove him to found a new religion or brotherhood, while those who followed the Sâ*m*khya, and who on many important points did not differ much from him, remained secure within the pale of orthodoxy. Some of the charges brought by the Bârhaspatyas against the Brâhmans who followed the Veda are the same which the followers of Buddha brought against them. Considering therefore, that on the vital question of the authority of the Veda the Sâ*m*khya agrees, however inconsistently, with orthodox Brâhmanism and differs from the Buddhists, it would be far easier to prove that Buddha derived his ideas from B*ri*haspati than from Kapila, the reputed founder of the Sâ*m*khya. If we are right in the description we have given of the unrestrained and abundant growth of philosophical ideas in ancient India, the idea of borrowing, so natural to us, seems altogether out of place in India. A wild mass of guesses at truth was floating in the air, and there was no controlling authority whatever, not even, as far as we know, any binding public opinion to produce anything like order in it. Hence we have as little right to maintain that Buddha borrowed from Kapila as that Kapila borrowed from Buddha. No one would say that the Hindus borrowed the idea of building ships from the Phenicians, or that of building Stûpas from the Egyptians. In India we move in a world different from that which we are accustomed to in Greece, Rome, or Modern Europe, and we need not rush at once to the conclusion that, because similar opinions prevail in Buddhism and in the Sâ*m*khya-philosophy of Kapila, therefore the former must have borrowed from the latter, or, as some hold, the latter from the former.

Though we can well imagine what the spirit of the philosophy of the ancient Indian heretics, whether they are called *K*ârvâkas or Bârhaspatyas, may have been, we know, unfortunately, much less of their doctrines than of any other school of philosophy. They are to us no more than names, such as the names of Yâ*gñ*avalkya, Raikva, or any other ancient leaders of Indian thought mentioned in the Upanishads, and credited there with certain utterances. We know a few of the conclusions at which they arrived, but of the processes by which they arrived at them we know next to nothing. What we may learn from these utterances is that a large mass of philosophical thought must have existed in India long before there was any attempt at dividing it into six well-defined channels of systematic philosophy, or reducing it to writing. Even when the names of certain individuals, such as *G*aimini, Kapila, and others, are given us as the authors of certain systems of philosophy, we must not imagine that they were the original creators of a philosophy in the sense in which Plato and Aristotle seem to have been so.

### Common Philosophical Ideas.

It cannot be urged too strongly that there existed in India a large common fund of philosophical thought which, like language, belonged to no one in particular, but was like the air breathed by every living and thinking man. Thus only can it be explained that we find a number of ideas in all, or nearly all, the systems of Indian philosophy which all philosophers seem to take simply for granted, and which belong to no one school in particular.

### 1. Metempsychosis—Sa*m*sâra.

The best known of these ideas, which belong to India rather than to any individual philosopher, is that which is known under the name of Metempsychosis. This is a Greek word, like Metensomatosis, but without any literary authority in Greek. It corresponds in meaning to the Sanskrit Sa*m*sâra, and is rendered in German by *Seelenwanderung.* To a Hindu the idea that the souls of men migrated after death into new bodies of living beings, of animals, nay, even of plants, is so self-evident that it was hardly ever questioned. We never meet with any attempt at proving or disproving it among the prominent writers of ancient or modern times. As early as the period of the Upanishads we hear of human souls being reborn both in animal and in vegetable bodies. In Greece the same opinion was held by Empedocles; but whether he borrowed this idea from the Egyptians, as is commonly supposed to have been the case, or whether Pythagoras and his teacher Pherecydes learnt it in India, is a question still hotly discussed. To me it seems that such a theory was so natural that it might perfectly well have arisen independently among different races. Among the Aryan races, Italian, Celtic, and Scythic or Hyperborean tribes are mentioned as having entertained a faith in Metempsychosis, nay, traces of it have lately been discovered even among the uncivilised inhabitants of America, Africa, and Eastern Asia. And why not? In India certainly it developed spontaneously; and if this was so in India, why not in other countries, particularly among races belonging to the same linguistic stock? It should be remembered, however, that some systems, particularly the Sâ*m*khya-philosophy, do not admit what we commonly understand by *Seelenwanderung*. If we translate the Sâ*m*khya Purusha by Soul instead of Self, it is not the Purusha that migrates, but the Sûkshma-*s*arîra, the subtile body. The Self remains always intact, a mere looker on, and its highest purpose is this recognition that it is above and apart from anything that has sprung from Prak*ri*ti or nature.

### 2. Immortality of the Soul.

The idea of the immortality of the soul also should be included in what was the common property of all Indian philosophers. This idea was so completely taken for granted that we look in vain for any elaborate arguments in support of it. Mortality with the Hindus is so entirely restricted to the body which decays and decomposes before our very eyes, that such an expression as Âtmano *mritatvam, immortality of the Self, sounds almost tautological in Sanskrit. No doubt, the followers of B*ri*haspati would deny a future life, but all the other schools rather fear than doubt a future life, a long-continued metempsychosis; and as to a final annihilation of the true Self, that would sound to Indian ears as a contradiction in itself. There are scholars so surprised at this unwavering belief in a future and an eternal life among the people of India, that they have actually tried to trace it back to a belief supposed to be universal among savages who thought that man left a ghost behind who might assume the body of an animal or even the shape of a tree. This is a mere fancy, and though it cannot of course be disproved, it does not thereby acquire any right to our consideration. Besides, why should the Âryas have had to learn lessons from savages, as they at one time were no doubt savages themselves, and need not have forgotten the so-called wisdom of savages as little as the *S*ûdras themselves from whom they are supposed to have learnt it?

### 3. Pessimism.

All Indian philosophers have been charged with pessimism, and in some cases such a charge may seem well founded, but not in all. People who derived their name for good from a word which originally meant nothing but being or real, Sat, are not likely to have looked upon what is as what ought not to be. Indian philosophers are by no means dwelling for ever on the miseries of life.

They are not always whining and protesting that life is not worth living. That is not their pessimism. They simply state that they received the first impulse to philosophical reflection from the fact that there is suffering in the world. They evidently thought that in a perfect world suffering had no place, that it is something anomalous, something that ought at all events to be accounted for, and, if possible, overcome. Pain, certainly, seems to be an imperfection, and, as such, may well have caused the question why it existed, and how it could be annihilated. But this is not the disposition which we are accustomed to call pessimism. Indian philosophy contains no outcry against divine injustice, and in no way encourages suicidal expedients. They would, in fact, be of no avail, because, according to Indian views, the same troubles and the same problems would have to be faced again and again in another life. Considering that the aim of all Indian philosophy was the removal of suffering, which was caused by nescience, and the attainment of the highest happiness, which was produced by knowledge, we should have more right to call it eudæmonistic than pessimistic.

It is interesting, however, to observe the unanimity with which the principal systems of philosophy in India, nay some of their religious systems also, start from the conviction that the world is full of suffering, and that this suffering should be accounted for and removed. This seems to have been one of the principal impulses, if not the principal impulse to philosophical thought in India. If we begin with *G*aimini, we cannot expect much real philosophy from his Pûrva-Mîmâ*m*sâ, which is chiefly concerned with ceremonial questions, such as sacrifices, &c. But though these sacrifices are represented as being the means of a certain kind of beatitude, and so far as serving to diminish or extinguish the ordinary afflictions of men, they were never supposed to secure the highest beatitude for which all the other philosophers were striving. The Uttara-Mîmâ*m*sâ and all the other philosophies take much higher ground. Bâdarâya*n*a teaches that the cause of all evil is Avidyâ or nescience, and that it is the object of his philosophy to remove that nescience by means of science (Vidyâ), and thus to bring about that true knowledge of Brahman, which is also the highest bliss (Taitt. Up. II, 1). The Sâ*m*khya-philosophy, at least such as we know it from the Kârikâs and the Sûtras, not however the Tattva-samâsa, begins at once with the recognition of the existence of the three kinds of suffering, and proclaims as its highest object the complete cessation of all pain; while the Yoga philosophers, after pointing out the way to meditative absorption (Samâdhi), declare that this is the best means of escaping from all earthly troubles (II, 2), and, in the end, of reaching Kaivalya or perfect freedom. The Vaiseshika promises to its followers knowledge of truth, and through it final cessation of all pain; and even Gotama's philosophy of logic holds out in its first Sûtra complete blessedness (Apavarga) as its highest reward, which is obtained by the complete destruction of all pain by means of logic. That Buddha's religion had the same origin, a clear perception of human suffering and its causes, and had the same object, the annihilation of Du*h*kha or suffering (Nirvâ*n*a) is too well known to require further elucidation, but it should be remembered that other systems also have one and the same name for the state to which they aspire, whether Nirvâ*n*a or Du*h*khânta, i.e. end of Du*h*kha, pain.

If therefore all Indian philosophy professes its ability to remove pain, it can hardly be called pessimistic in the ordinary sense of the word. Even physical pain, though it cannot be removed from the body, ceases to affect the soul, as soon as the Self has fully realised its aloofness from the body, while all mental pain, being traced back to our worldly attachments, would vanish by freeing ourselves from the desires which cause these attachments. The cause of all suffering having been discovered in ourselves, in our works and thoughts, whether in this or in a previous existence, all clamour against divine injustice is silenced at once. We are what we have made ourselves, we suffer what we have done, we reap what we have sown, and it is the sowing of good seed, though without any hope of a rich harvest, that is represented as the chief purpose of a philosopher's life on earth.

Besides this conviction that all suffering can be removed by an insight into its nature and origin, there are some other ideas which must be traced back to that rich treasury of thought which was open to every thinking man in India. These common ideas assumed, no doubt, different guises in different systems, but this ought not to deceive us, and a little reflection allows us to perceive their common source. Thus, when the cause of suffering is inquired for, they all have but one answer to give, though under different names. The Vedânta gives Avidyâ, nescience, the Sâ*m*khya, Aviveka, non-discrimination, the Nyâya, Mithyâ*g*ñâna, false knowledge, and these various aberrations from knowledge are generally represented as Bandha or bondage, to be broken again by means of that true knowledge which is supplied by the various systems of philosophy.

### 4. Karman.

The next idea that seems ingrained in the Indian mind and therefore finds expression in all the systems of philosophy is a belief in Karman, deed, that is, the continuous working of every thought, word, and deed through all ages. 'All works, good or bad, all must bear and do bear fruit,' is a sentiment never doubted by any Hindu, whether to-day or thousands of years ago[1].

And the same eternity which is claimed for works and their results is claimed for the soul also, only with this difference, that while works will cease to work when real freedom has been obtained, the soul itself continues after the obtainment of freedom or final beatitude. The idea of the soul ever coming to an end is so strange to the Indian mind that there seemed to be no necessity for anything like proofs of immortality, so common in European philosophy. Knowing what is meant by 'to be,' the idea that 'to be' could ever become 'not to be' seems to have been impossible to the mind of the Hindus. If by 'to be' is meant Sa*m*sâra or the world, however long it may last, then Hindu philosophers would never look upon it as real. It never was, it never is, and never will be. Length of time, however enormous, is nothing in the eyes of Hindu

---

[1] Cf. The Mysteries of Karma, revealed by a Brahmin Yogee, Allahabad, 1898.

philosophers. To reckon a thousand years as one day would not satisfy them. They represent length of time by much bolder similes, such as when a man once in every thousand years passes his silken kerchief over the chain of the Himalayan mountains. By the time he has completely wiped them out by this process the world or Sa*m*sâra may indeed come to an end, but even then eternity and reality lie far beyond. In order to get an easier hold of this eternity, the very popular idea of Pralayas, i.e. destructions or absorptions of the whole world, has been invented. According to the Vedânta there occurs at the end of each Kalpa a Pralaya or dissolution of the universe, and Brahman is then reduced to its causal condition (Kâra*n*âvasthâ), containing both soul and matter in an Avyakta (undeveloped) state [1]. At the end of this Pralaya, however, Brahman creates or lets out of himself a new world, matter becomes gross and visible once more, and souls become active and re-embodied, though with a higher enlightenment (Vikâsa), and all this according to their previous merits and demerits. Brahman has then assumed its new Kâryâvasthâ or effective state which lasts for another Kalpa. But all this refers to the world of change and unreality only. It is the world of Karman, the temporary produce of Nescience, of Avidyâ, or Mâyâ, it is not yet real reality. In the Sâ*m*khya-philosophy these Pralayas take place whenever the three Gu*n*as of Prak*ri*ti recover their equipoise [2], while creation results from the upsetting of the equipoise between them. What is truly eternal, is not

---

[1] Thibaut, V. S. I, p. xxviii. [2] Sâ*m*khya-Sûtras VI, 42.

affected by the cosmic illusion, or at least is so for a time only, and may recover at any moment its self-knowledge, that is, its self-being, and its freedom from all conditions and fetters.

According to the Vai*s*eshikas this process of creation and dissolution depends on the atoms. If they are separated, there ensues dissolution (Pralaya), if motion springs up in them and they are united, there follows what we call creation.

The idea of the reabsorption of the world at the end of a Kalpa (æon) and its emergence again in the next Kalpa, does not occur as yet in the old Upanishads, nay even the name of Sa*m*sâra is absent from them; and Professor Garbe is inclined therefore to claim the idea of Pralaya as more recent, as peculiar to the Sâ*m*khya-philosophy, and as adopted from it by the other systems[1]. It may be so, but in the Bhagavad-gîtâ IX, 7, the idea of Pralayas, absorptions, and of Kalpas or ages, of their end and their beginning (Kalpakshaye and Kalpâdau), are already quite familiar to the poets. The exact nature of the Pralayas differs so much, according to different poets and philosophers, that it is far more likely that they may all have borrowed it from a common source, that is, from the popular belief of those among whom they were brought up and from whom they learnt their language and with it the materials of their thoughts, than that they should each have invented the same theory under slightly varying aspects.

[1] Sâ*m*khya-Philosophie, p. 221.

### 5. Infallibility of the Veda.

One more common element presupposed by Indian philosophy might be pointed out in the recognition of the supreme authority and the revealed character ascribed to the Veda. This, in ancient times, is certainly a startling idea, familiar as it may sound to us at present. The Sâ*m*khya-philosophy is supposed to have been originally without a belief in the revealed character of the Vedas, but it certainly speaks of *S*ruti (Sûtras I, 5). As long as we know the Sâ*m*khya, it recognises the authority of the Veda, calling it *S*abda, and appeals to it even in matters of minor importance. It is important to observe that the distinction between *S*ruti and Sm*ri*ti, revelation and tradition, so well known in the later phases of philosophy, is not to be found as yet in the old Upanishads.

### 6. Three Gu*n*as.

The theory of the three Gu*n*as also, which has been claimed as originally peculiar to the Sâ*m*khya-philosophy, seems in its unscientific form to have been quite familiar to most Hindu philosophers. The impulse to everything in nature, the cause of all life and variety, is ascribed to the three Gu*n*as. Gu*n*a means quality, but we are warned expressly not to take it, when it occurs in philosophy, in the ordinary sense of quality, but rather as something substantial by itself, so that the Gu*n*as become in fact the component constituents of nature. In the most general sense they represent no more than thesis, antithesis, and something between the two, such as cold, warm, and neither cold nor warm ; good, bad, and neither good nor bad; bright, dark, and neither bright nor dark, and so on through every part of physical and moral nature. Tension between these qualities produces activity and struggle: equilibrium leads to temporary or final rest. This mutual tension is sometimes represented as Vishamatvam, unevenness, caused by a preponderance of one of the three, as we read, for instance, in the Maitrâya*n*a Upanishad V, 2: 'This world was in the beginning Tamas (darkness) indeed. That Tamas stood in the Highest. Moved by the Highest, it became uneven. In that form it was Ra*g*as (obscurity). That Ra*g*as, when moved, became uneven, and this is the form of Sattva (goodness). That Sattva, when moved, ran forth as essence (Rasa).' Here we have clearly the recognised names of the three Gu*n*as, but the Maitrâya*n*a Upanishad shows several Sâ*m*khya influences, and it might therefore be argued that it does not count for much, in order to establish the general acceptance of the theory of the Gu*n*as, not for more, at all events, than the later Upanishads or the Bhagavad-gîtâ, in which the three Gu*n*as are fully recognised.

## CHAPTER IV.

### Vedânta or Uttara-Mîmâ*m*sâ.

If now we pass on to a consideration of the six orthodox systems of philosophy, and begin with the Vedânta, we have to take as our chief guides the Sûtras of Bâdarâya*n*a, and the commentary of *S*a*m*kara. We know little of Bâdarâya*n*a, the reputed author of our Sûtras. Of course when we possess commentaries on any Sûtras, we know that the Sûtras must have existed before their commentaries, that the Sûtras of Bâdarâya*n*a were older therefore than *S*a*m*kara, their commentator. In India he has been identified with Vyâsa, the collector of the Mahâbhârata, but without sufficient evidence, nor should we gain much by that identification, as Vyâsa of the Mahâbhârata also is hardly more than a name to us. This Vyâsa is said by *S*a*m*kara, III, 3, 32, to have lived at the end of the Dvâpara and the beginning of the Kali age, and to have had intercourse with the gods, l. c., I, 3, 33. But though he calls him the author of the Mahâbhârata, l. c., II, 3, 47, *S*a*m*kara, in the whole of his commentary on the Vedânta-Sûtras, never mentions that the Vyâsa of the epic was the author of the book on which he is commenting, though he mentions Bâdarâya*n*a as such. This convinced Windischmann that *S*a*m*kara himself did not consider these two Vyâsas as one and the same person, and this judgment ought not to have been lightly disturbed. It was excusable in Colebrooke, but not after what had been said by Windischmann, particularly when no new argument could be produced. All we can say is that, whatever the date of the Bhagavad-gîtâ is, and it is a part of the Mahâbhârata, the age of the Vedânta-Sûtras and of Bâdarâyana must have been earlier.

We may also say that Bâdarâyana himself never refers to any work which could be assigned with any amount of certainty to any time after our era. Even when Bâdarâyana quotes the Smriti, it does not follow that *S*amkara is always right when suggesting passages from the Mahâbhârata (Bhagavad-gîtâ), or from Manu, for it is not too much to say that similar passages may have occurred in other and more ancient Smriti works also. Bâdarâyana is certainly most provoking in never quoting his authorities by name. If we could follow *S*amkara, Bâdarâyana would have referred in his Sûtras to Bauddhas, *G*ainas, Pâsupatas and Pâñkarâtras, to Yogins, Vaiseshikas, though not to Naiyâyikas, to Sâmkhyas, and to the doctrines of *G*aimini[1]. By the name of *S*ruti Bâdarâyana, according to *S*amkara, meant the following Upanishads, Brihad-âranyaka, *Kh*ândogya, Kâthaka, Kaushîtaki, Aitareya, Taittirîya, Mundaka, Prasna, *S*vetâsvatara, and *G*âbâla.

This must suffice to indicate the intellectual sphere in which Bâdarâyana moved, or was supposed to have moved, and so far may be said to determine his chronological position as far anterior to that of another Vyâsa, who was the father of *S*uka, the teacher of Gaudapâda, the teacher of Govinda, the

---

[1] Deussen, System des Vedânta, p. 24.

teacher of *S*a*m*kara, and who, if *S*a*m*kara belonged to the eighth century, might have lived in about the sixth century of our era [1].

The literary works to which *S*a*m*kara refers in his commentary are, according to Deussen (System, p. 34), among the Sa*m*hitâs, that of the Rig-veda, of the Vâ*g*asaneyins, Maitrâya*n*îyas and Taittirîyas, and Ka*th*as, (nothing from the Sâma and Atharva-sa*m*hitâs); among the Brâhma*n*as, the Aitareya, Ârsheya, Sha*d*vi*m*sa, *S*atapatha, Taittirîya, Tâ*nd*ya, *Kh*ândogya; among the Âra*n*yakas, Aitareya and Taittirîya; and among the Upanishads, Aitareya, B*ri*had-âra*n*yaka, Î*s*â, Ka*th*a, Kaushîtaki-brâhma*n*a, Kena, *Kh*ândogya, Maitrâya*n*îya, Mu*nd*aka, Pra*s*na, *S*vetâ*s*vatara, Taittirîya. These are sometimes called the old or classical Upanishads, as being quoted by *S*a*m*kara, though Pai*m*gi, Agnirahasya, Nârâya*n*îya and *G*âbâla may have to be added. As belonging to Sm*ri*ti *S*a*m*kara quotes Mahâbhârata (Bhagavad-gîtâ), Râmâya*n*a, Mârka*nd*eya-purâ*n*a, Manu, Yâska, Pâ*n*ini, Paribhâshâs, Sâ*m*khya-kârikâ, and he refers to Sâ*m*khya-Sûtras (though it is important to observe that he gives no *ipsissima verba* from our Sâ*m*khya-Sûtras), to Yoga-Sûtras, Nyâya-Sûtras, Vai*s*eshika-Sûtras, and to Mîmâ*m*sâ-Sûtras. When he alludes to Sugata or Buddha he refers once to a passage which has been traced in the Abhidharma-Ko*sh*a-vyâkhyâ. He also knew the Bhâgavatas and the Svapnâdhyâyavids.

Though the name of Vedânta does not occur in the old Upanishads, we can hardly doubt that it was the

---

[1] Another stemma of Vyâsa, given by native writers, is Nârâya*n*a, Vasish*th*a (Padmabhava), *S*akti, Parâsara, Vyâsa, *S*uka, Gau*d*apâda, Hastâmalaka (*S*ishya), Tro*t*aka, Vârttika-kâra, &c.

Vedântic thoughts, contained in the Upanishads, which gave the first impulse to more systematic philosophical speculations in India. Several scholars have tried to prove that Sâmkhya ideas prevailed in India at an earlier time than the Vedântic ideas. But though there certainly are germs of Sâmkhya theories in the Upanishads, they are but few and far between, while the strictly Vedântic concepts meet us at every step in the hymns, the Brâhmanas, the Âranyakas, and in the Sûtras. Vedânta is clearly the native philosophy of India. It is true that this philosophy is not yet treated systematically in the Upanishads, but neither is the Sâmkhya. To us who care only for the growth of philosophical thought on the ancient soil of India, Vedânta is clearly the first growth ; and the question whether Kapila lived before Bâdarâyana, or whether the systematic treatment of the Sâmkhya took place before that of the Vedânta, can hardly arise.

I only wonder that those who maintain the priority of the Sâmkhya, have not appealed to the Lalita-vistara, twelfth chapter, where, among the subjects known to Buddha, are mentioned not only Nirghantu, *Kh*andas, Yagñakalpa, *G*yotisha, but likewise Sâmkhya, Yoga, Vaiseshika, Vesika (Vaidyaka ?), Arthavidyâ, Bârhaspatya, Âs*k*arya, Âsura, Mrigapakshiruta, and Hetuvidyâ (Nyâya). There are several names which are difficult to identify, but there can be no doubt that the five philosophical systems here mentioned were intended for Sâmkhya, Yoga, Vaiseshika, Nyâya, and Bârhaspatya. The two Mîmâmsâs are absent, but their absence does not prove that they did not exist, but only that they were considered too orthodox to form a proper subject of study for Buddha. This shows the real character of the antagonism between Buddhism and Brâhmanism, now so often denied or minimised[1], and is confirmed by similar references, as when Hema*k*andra in his Abhidhâna mentions indeed such names as Ârhatas or *G*ainas, Saugatas or Buddhists, Naiyâyikas, Yoga, Sâ*m*khya or Kâpila, Vaiseshika, Bârhaspatya or Nâstika, *K*ârvâka or Lokâyatika, but carefully omits the two really dangerous systems, the Mîmâ*m*sâ of Bâdarâya*n*a and that of *G*aimini.

It should also be remembered that considerable doubt has recently been thrown on the age of the Chinese translation of the Lalita-vistara, which seemed to enable us to assign the original to a date at all events anterior to 70 A. D. The case is not quite clear yet, but we must learn to be more cautious with Chinese dates.

It has been the custom to give the name of Vedânta-philosophy to the Uttara-Mîmâ*m*sâ of Bâdarâya*n*a, nor is there any reason why that name should not be retained. If Vedânta is used as synonymous with Upanishad, the Uttara-Mîmâ*m*sâ is certainly the Vedânta-philosophy, or a systematic treatment of the philosophical teaching of the Upanishads. It is true, no doubt, that Vasish*th*a as well as Gautama distinguishes between Upanishads and Vedântas (XXII, 9), and the commentator to Gautama XIX, 7 states distinctly that those parts only of the Âra*n*yakas which are not Upanishads are to be called Vedântas. But there is no real harm in the received name, and we see that the followers of the Vedânta were often called Aupanishadas.

---

[1] See Brahmavâdin, Feb., 1898, p. 454.

### Bâdarâya*n*a.

As to Bâdarâya*n*a, the reputed author of the Vedânta-Sûtras, we had to confess before that we know nothing about him. He is to us a name and an intellectual power, but nothing else. We know the date of his great commentator, *S*a*m*kara, in the eighth century A.D., and we know that another commentator, Bodhâyana, was even earlier. We also know that Bodhâyana's commentary was followed by Râmânu*g*a. It is quite possible that Bodhâyana, like Râmânu*g*a, represented a more ancient and more faithful interpretation of Bâdarâya*n*a's Sûtras, and that *S*a*m*kara's philosophy in its unflinching monism, is his own rather than Bâdarâya*n*a's. But no MS. of Bodhâyana has yet been discovered.

A still more ancient commentator, Upavarsha by name, is mentioned, and *S*a*m*kara (III, 3, 53) calls him Bhagavad or Saint. But it must remain doubtful again whether he can be identified with the Upavarsha, who, according to the Kathâ-sarit-sâgara, was the teacher of Pâ*n*ini.

It must not be forgotten that, according to Indian tradition, Bâdarâya*n*a, as the author of the Vedânta-Sûtras, is called Vyâsa or Vedavyâsa, Dvaipâyana or K*r*ish*n*a Dvaipâyana. Here we are once more in a labyrinth from which it is difficult to find an exit. Vyâsa or K*r*ish*n*a Dvaipâyana is the name given to the author of the Mahâbhârata, and no two styles can well be more different than that of the Vyâsa of the Mahâbhârata and that of Vyâsa, the supposed author of the so-called Vyâsa-Sûtras. I think we should remember that Vyâsa, as a noun, meant no more than compilation or arrangement,

Bhagavad-gîtâ, nor do they give any *ipsissima verba* from it, and as every Smriti presupposes a Sruti, these references may have been meant for passages which the Bhagavad-gîtâ had adapted, and may have shared with other Smritis. Brahma-Sûtra, on the contrary, is a distinct title, all the more significant where it occurs, because neither the word Sûtra nor Brahma-Sûtra occurs again in any other passage of the Gîtâ. However, even admitting that the Brahma-Sûtras quoted from the Bhagavad-gîtâ, as the Gîtâ certainly appeals to the Brahma-Sûtras, this reciprocal quotation might be accounted for by their being contemporaneous, as in the case of other Sûtras which, as there can be no doubt, quote one from the other, and sometimes verbatim.

As to the commentary on Patañgali's Yoga-Sûtras being the work of the same Vyâsa, this seems to me altogether out of the question. There are hundreds of people in India who have the name of Vyâsa. Nor has it ever been positively proved that Patañgali, the reputed author of the Yoga-Sûtras, was the same person as Patañgali, the author of the Mahâbhâshya, the great commentary on Pânini's grammar, and on Kâtyâyana's Vârttikas. Some scholars have rushed at this conclusion, chiefly in order to fix the date of the Yoga-Sûtras, but this also would force us to ascribe the most heterogeneous works to one and the same author[1].

Even the age of Patañgali, the grammarian and author of the Mahâbhâshya, seems to me by no

---

[1] Both Lassen and Garbe, Die Sâmkhya-Philosophie, p. 46, seem inclined to accept the identity of the two Patañgalis.

means positively settled. I gladly admit the plausibility of Goldstücker's arguments that if Patañ*g*ali presupposed the existence of the Maurya-dynasty he might be placed in the third century B.C. I look upon the Ar*k*â*h*, which he mentions in the famous Maurya-passage, as having been devised by the Mauryas for the sake of trade, as the first coins with images of the gods, introduced by the Maurya-dynasty. Such coins, when they contain images of the gods, should not, according to the grammarian, be called simply by the names of the gods, but by a derivative name, not *S*iva, but *S*ivaka, just as we distinguish between an Angel and an Angelot. And I pointed out before, the very gods mentioned here by Patañ*g*ali are the gods the images of which do occur on the oldest Indian coins which we possess, viz. *S*iva, Skanda, and Vi*s*âkha, the last, if taken for Kâma. As a constructive date therefore, that assigned by Goldstücker to Patañ*g*ali might stand, but that is very different from a positive date. Besides, the name of Maurya in the Mahâbhâshya is doubtful and does not occur again in it.

We saw before that Bâdarâya*n*a refers in his Sûtras to *G*aimini, the author of the Pûrva-Mîmâ*m*sâ-Sûtras, and that *G*aimini returns the compliment by referring to Bâdarâya*n*a by name. Bâdarâya*n*a is likewise acquainted with the atheistical doctrines of Kapila and the atomistic theories of Ka*n*âda, and tries to refute them. But in India this is far from proving the later date of Bâdarâya*n*a. We must learn to look on Bâdarâya*n*a, *G*aimini, Kapila, and similar names, as simply eponymous heroes of different philosophies; so that at whatever time these systems were reduced to the form of Sûtras, certain opinions could be called by their names. Colebrooke states, on the authority of a scholiast to Manu and Yâ*gñ*avalkya, that the instructions of a teacher were often reduced to writing by his pupils, and that this would account for the fact that the author of a system is often quoted in the third person in his own book. It would be interesting if this could be established with reference to ancient texts, but I remember nothing of the kind. All this is very discouraging to students accustomed to chronological accuracy, but it has always seemed to me far better to acknowledge our poverty and the utter absence of historical dates in the literary history of India, than to build up systems after systems which collapse at the first breath of criticism or scepticism.

When I speak of a chronology of thought, what I mean is that there is a chronology which enables us to distinguish a period of Vedic thought, subdivided into three periods of Mantras, Brâhma*n*as, and Upanishads. No one would doubt the succession of these three periods of language, but if some scholars wish to extend each period to thousands of years, I can only wish them success. I confess I do not share the idea that we should claim for Indian literature as remote an antiquity as possible. The same attempts were made before, but nothing was gained by them, and much was lost as soon as more sober and critical ideas began to prevail. After the Upanishad-period would follow that of Buddhism, marked, on the Buddhist side, by the Suttas, on the Brâhmanic side, and possibly somewhat earlier, by the large mass of Sûtra literature. To that period seem to me to belong, by similarity of thought, if not of style, the six systems of philosophy. I should have said by style also, because the earliest form in which we possess these systems is that of Sûtras. Unfortunately we know now how easily even that very peculiar style can be, and in case of the Sâ*m*khya and some of the legal Sm*ri*tis, has been imitated. We must not therefore ascribe too much weight to this. The next period would be what I have called that of the Renaissance, beginning at a time when Sanskrit had ceased to be the language spoken by the people, though it continued, as it has to the present day, to be cultivated by the learned.

Such are the difficulties that meet us when we attempt to introduce anything like chronological order into the literature of India, and it seems to me far better to state them honestly than to disguise them. After all, the importance of that literature, and more particularly of its philosophical portion, is quite independent of age. It has something to teach us quite apart from the names and dates of its authors; and grateful as we should feel for any real light that can be thrown on these chronological mazes, we must not forget that the highest interest of the Vedânta and the other philosophies is not their age, but their truth.

### Fundamental Doctrines of the Vedânta.

If we ask for the fundamental doctrines of the Vedânta, the Hindus themselves have helped us and given us in a few words what they themselves consider as the quintessence of that system of thought. I quoted these words at the end of my 'Three Lectures on the Vedânta' (1894):—

'In one half verse I shall tell you what has been taught in thousands of volumes: Brahman is true, the world is false, the soul is Brahman and nothing else[1].'

And again:—

'There is nothing worth gaining, there is nothing worth enjoying, there is nothing worth knowing but Brahman alone, for he who knows Brahman, is Brahman.'

This *résumé* of the Vedânta is very true, and very helpful as a *résumé* of that system of philosophy. After all we must distinguish in every philosophy its fundamental doctrines and its minute details. We can never carry all these details in our memory, but we may always have present before our mind the general structure of a great system of thought and its salient points, whether it be the philosophy of Kant or of Plato or of Bâdarâya*n*a. It would be quite impossible in a historical sketch of the six Indian philosophical systems to give all their details. They are often unimportant, and may easily be gathered from the texts themselves, such as we have them in the original or in translations; but they must not be allowed to crowd and to obscure that general view of the six systems which alone is meant to be given in these pages.

We have another and still shorter abstract of the Vedânta in the famous words addressed by Uddâlaka Âru*n*i to his son *S*vetaketu (*Kh*ând. Up. VI, 8), namely, 'Tat tvam asi,' 'Thou art That.' These words, however, convey little meaning without the context in which they occur, that is to say, unless we know what is meant by the Tat, that, and by the Tvam, thou. The Tat is what we saw shadowed forth in

---

[1] See also Theosophy, p. 317.

the Upanishads as the Brahman, as the cause of the world, the Tvam is the Âtman, the Self in its various meanings, from the ordinary I to the divine Soul or Self, recognised in man; and it is the highest aim of the Vedânta to show that these two are in reality one[1]. This fearless synthesis, embodied in the simple words Tat tvam asi, seems to me the boldest and truest synthesis in the whole history of philosophy. Even Kant, who clearly recognised the Tat or it, that is the *Ding an sich* behind the objective world, never went far enough to recognise the identity of the Tat, the objective *Ding an sich*, and the Tvam, the *Ding an sich* on the subjective side of the world. Among ourselves such a synthesis of the subjective with the objective Self would even now rouse the strongest theological, if not philosophical, protests, whereas the theologians of India discuss it with perfect equanimity, and see in it the truest solution of the riddle of the world. In order fully to understand it, we must try to place ourselves firmly on the standpoint of the Vedânta philosophers, forgetting all our own inherited theological misgivings. Their idea of the Supreme Cause of the universe went far beyond what is meant by God, the creator and ruler of the world (Pra*g*âpati). That being was to them a manifestation only of the Supreme Cause or Brahman, it was Brahman as phenomenal, and it followed that, as Brahman, as they held, was indeed the cause of everything, the All in All, man also could be nothing but a phenomenon of Brahman. The idea therefore that it would be blasphemy to make the creature

[1] Mâ*nd*ûkya Up. II, Ayam Âtmâ Brahma.

equal to the creator so far as their substance was concerned, never presented itself to their minds. Their Tat was something behind or above the purely personal creator, it was the absolute divine essence, the Godhead, manifested in a subjective and personal creator, and present likewise in all its phenomenal manifestations, including gods and men. Even their god beyond all gods (Deveshu adhi eka*h*) did not satisfy them any longer, as it did in the hymns of the Rig-veda; and though they might have shrunk from identifying gods and men with that personal divine being, Pra*g*âpati, the lord of all creatures, they saw nothing but truth in the doctrine that man in his true nature was the same with Brahman, that he shares in the nature of Brahman, or in the spirit of God. They saw, in fact, that God is hardly a name that can be used for that Supreme Brahman, the absolute Cause of the universe, and the absolute Cause of Pra*g*âpati also, when taken as the creative god. I say when taken as such, for we ought never to forget that we have always to be satisfied with what we take God to be (Vidyâmâtra), and that we can never go beyond. Translated into the language of the early Christian philosophers of Alexandria, this lifting up of the Tvam into the Tat might prove the equivalent of the idea of divine sonship, but from the Vedânta point of view it means real identity, real recognition of the original divine nature of man, however much hidden and disfigured for a time by Avidyâ, or ignorance, and all its consequences. With us unfortunately such questions can hardly be discussed in a calm philosophical spirit, because theology steps in and protests against them as irreligious and blasphemous, just as the Jews declared it blasphemy in Christ to teach that He was equal to God, nay that He and the Father were one, Tat tvam asi. If properly understood, these Vedânta teachings may, though under a strange form, bring us very near to the earliest Christian philosophy, and help us to understand it, as it was understood by the great thinkers of Alexandria. To maintain the eternal identity of the human and the divine is very different from arrogating divinity for humanity; and on this point even our philosophy may have something to learn which has often been forgotten in modern Christianity, though it was recognised as vital by the early fathers of the Church, the unity of the Father and the Son, nay, of the Father and all His sons.

The teachers of the Vedânta, while striving to resuscitate in man the consciousness of the identity of the Tat and the Tvam, and, though indirectly, of man and God, seem to be moving in the most serene atmosphere of thought, and in their stiff and algebraic Sûtras they were working out these mighty problems with unfaltering love of truth, and in an unimpassioned and truly philosophic spirit.

It is as difficult to give an idea of the form of the Upanishads as of the spirit that pervades the Upanishads. A few extracts, however, may help to show us the early Vedântists as they were, groping their way in the dark. We do not indeed get there the pure wine of the Vedânta, but we get the grapes from which the juice was extracted and made into wine. The first is taken from the *Kh*ândogya Upanishad which belongs to the Sâma-veda and is generally regarded as one of the earlier Upanishads [1].

---

[1] Translated in S. B. E., I, p. 92

## First Khanda.

1. *S*vetaketu was the son of Aru*n*i, the grandson of Aru*n*a. To him his father (Uddâlaka, the son of Aru*n*a) said: '*S*vetaketu, go to school; for there is none belonging to our race, darling, who, not having studied (the Veda), is, as it were, a Brahmabandhu, i.e. a Brâhma*n*a by birth only.'

2. Having begun his apprenticeship (with a teacher) when he was twelve years of age, *S*vetaketu returned to his father, when he was twenty-four, having then studied all the Vedas,—conceited, considering himself well-read, and stubborn.

3. His father said to him: '*S*vetaketu, as you are so conceited, considering yourself well-read, and so stubborn, my dear son, have you ever asked for that instruction by which we hear what is not heard, by which we perceive what is not perceived, by which we know what is not known?'

4. 'What is that instruction, Sir?' he asked.

The father replied: 'My dear son, as by one clod of clay all that is made of clay is known, the difference being only the name, arising from speech, but the truth being that all is clay;

5. 'And as, my dear son, by one nugget of gold all that is made of gold is known, the difference being only the name, arising from speech, but the truth being that all is gold;

6. 'And as, my dear son, by one pair of nail-scissors all that is made of steel (Kârsh*n*âyasam) is known, the difference being only the name, arising from speech, but the truth being that all is steel,—thus, my dear son, is that instruction.'

7. The son said: 'Surely those venerable men

(my teachers) did not know that. For if they had known it, why should they not have told it me? Do you, Sir, therefore tell me that.' 'Be it so,' said the father.

### SECOND KHA*ND*A.

1. 'In the beginning, my dear son, there was that only which is (τὸ ὄν), one only, without a second. Others say, 'in the beginning there was that only which is not (τὸ μὴ ὄν), one only, without a second; and from that which is not, that which is, was born.

2. 'But how could it be so, my dear son?' the father continued. 'How could that which is, be born of that which is not? No, my dear son, only that which is, was in the beginning, one only, without a second.

3. 'It thought, may I be many, may I grow forth. It sent forth fire.

'That fire thought, may I be many, may I grow forth. It sent forth water.

'And therefore whenever anybody anywhere is hot and perspires, water is produced on him from fire alone.

4. 'Water thought, may I be many, may I grow forth. It sent forth earth (food).

'Therefore whenever it rains anywhere, most food is then produced. From water alone is eatable food produced.

### SEVENTH KHA*ND*A.

1. 'Man (Purusha), my son, consists of sixteen parts. Abstain from food for fifteen days, but drink as much water as you like, for breath comes

from water, and will not be cut off, if you drink water.'

2. *S*vetaketu abstained from food for fifteen days. Then he came to his father and said: 'What shall I say?' The father said: 'Repeat the *Ri*k, Ya*g*us, and Sâman verses.' He replied: 'They do not occur to me, Sir.'

3. The father said to him: 'As of a great lighted fire one coal only of the size of a firefly may be left, which would not burn much more than this (i.e. very little), thus, my dear son, one part only of the sixteen parts (of you) is left, and therefore with that one part you do not remember the Vedas. Go and eat!

4. 'Then wilt thou understand me.' Then *S*vetaketu ate, and afterwards approached his father. And whatever his father asked him, he knew it all by heart. Then his father said to him:

5. 'As of a great lighted fire one coal of the size of a firefly, if left, may be made to blaze up again by putting grass upon it, and will thus burn more than this,

6. 'Thus, my dear son, there was one part of the sixteen parts left to you, and that, lighted up with food, burnt up, and by it you remember now the Vedas.' After that, he understood what his father meant when he said: 'Mind, my son, comes from food, breath from water, speech from fire.' He understood what he said, yea, he understood it.

## NINTH KHA*N*DA.

1. 'As the bees, my son, make honey by collecting the juices of distant trees, and reduce the juice into one form,

2. 'And as these juices have no discrimination,

so that they might say, I am the juice of this tree or that, in the same manner, my son, all these creatures, when they have become merged in the True (either in deep sleep or in death), know not that they are merged in the True.

3. 'Whatever these creatures are here, whether a lion, or a wolf, or a boar, or a worm, or a midge, or a gnat, or a musquito, that they become again and again.

4. 'Now that which is that subtile essence, in it all that exists has its Self. It is the True. It is the Self, and thou, O *S*vetaketu, art it.'

'Please, Sir, inform me still more,' said the son.

'Be it so, my child,' the father replied.

### TENTH KHA*N*DA.

1. 'These rivers, my son, run, the eastern (like the Gangâ) toward the east, the western (like the Sindhu) toward the west. They go from sea to sea (i. e. the clouds lift up the water from the sea to the sky, and send it back as rain to the sea). They become indeed sea. And as those rivers, when they are in the sea, do not know, I am this or that river,

2. 'In the same manner, my son, all these creatures, when they have come back from the True, know not that they have come back from the True. Whatever these creatures are here, whether a lion, or a wolf, or a boar, or a worm, or a midge, or a gnat, or a musquito, that they become again and again.

3. 'That which is that subtile essence, in it all that exists has its Self. It is the True. It is the Self, and thou, O *S*vetaketu, art it.'

'Please, Sir, inform me still more,' said the son.

'Be it so, my child,' the father replied.

### ELEVENTH KHA*N*D*A*.

1. 'If one were to strike at the root of this large tree here, it would bleed, but it would live. If he were to strike at its stem, it would bleed, but it would live. If he were to strike at its top, it would bleed, but it would live. Pervaded by the living Self that tree stands firm, drinking in its nourishment and rejoicing;

2. 'But if the life (the living Self) leaves one of its branches, that branch withers; if it leaves a second, that branch withers; if it leaves a third, that branch withers. If it leaves the whole tree, the whole tree withers. In exactly the same manner, my son, know this.' Thus he spoke:

3. 'This (body) indeed withers and dies when the living (Self) has left it; the living (Self) dies not.

'That which is that subtile essence, in it all that exists has its Self. It is the True. It is the Self, and thou, *S*vetaketu, art it.'

'Please, Sir, inform me still more,' said the son.

'Be it so, my child,' the father replied.

### TWELFTH KHA*N*D*A*.

1. 'Fetch me from thence a fruit of the Nyagrodha tree.'

'Here is one, Sir.'

'Break it.'

'It is broken, Sir.'

'What do you see there?'

'These seeds, almost infinitesimal.'

'Break one of them.'

'It is broken, Sir.'

'What do you see there?'

'Not anything, Sir.'

2. The father said: 'My son, that subtile essence which you do not perceive there, of that very essence this great Nyagrodha tree exists.

3. 'Believe it, my son. That which is the subtile essence, in it all that exists has its Self. It is the True. It is the Self, and thou, O *S*vetaketu, art it.'

'Please, Sir, inform me still more,' said the son.

'Be it so, my child,' the father replied.

### Thirteenth Kha*nd*a.

1. 'Place this salt in water, and then wait on me in the morning.'

The son did as he was commanded.

The father said to him; 'Bring me the salt, which you placed in the water last night.'

The son having looked for it, found it not, for, of course, it was melted.

2. The father said: 'Taste it from the surface of the water. How is it?'

The son replied: 'It is salt.'

'Taste it from the middle. How is it?'

The son replied: 'It is salt.'

'Taste it from the bottom. How is it?'

The son replied: 'It is salt.'

The father said: 'Throw it away and then wait on me.'

He did so; but the salt continued to exist.

Then the father said: 'Here also, in this body, indeed, you do not perceive the True (Sat), my son; but there indeed it is.

3. 'That which is the subtile essence, in it all that exists has its Self. It is the True. It is the Self, and thou, O *S*vetaketu, art it.'

'Please, Sir, inform me still more,' said the son.

'Be it so, my child,' the father replied.

## FOURTEENTH KHA*N*DA.

1. 'As one might lead a person with his eyes covered away from the Gandhâras, and leave him then in a place where there are no human beings; and as that person would turn towards the east, or the north, or the west, and shout, "I have been brought here with my eyes covered, I have been left here with my eyes covered,"

2. 'And as thereupon some one might loose his bandage and say to him, "Go in that direction, it is the Gandhâras, go in that direction;" and as thereupon, having been informed and being able to judge for himself, he would by asking his way from village to village arrive at last at the Gandhâras,—in exactly the same manner does a man, who meets with a teacher to inform him, learn that there is delay so long only as "I am not delivered (from this body); and then I shall be perfect."

3. 'That which is the subtile essence, in it all that exists has its Self. It is the True. It is the Self, and thou, O *S*vetaketu, art it.'

'Please, Sir, inform me still more,' said the son.

'Be it so, my child,' the father replied.

## FIFTEENTH KHA*N*DA.

1. 'If a man is ill, his relatives assemble round him and ask: "Dost thou know me? Dost thou know me?" Then, as long as his speech is not merged in his mind, his mind in breath, breath in heat (fire), heat in the Highest Being (Devatâ), he knows them.

2. 'But when his speech is merged in his mind, his mind in breath, breath in heat (fire), heat in the Highest Being, then he knows them not.

'That which is the subtile essence, in it all that exists has its Self. It is the True. It is the Self, and thou, O *S*vetaketu, art it.'

'Please, Sir, inform me still more,' said the son.

'Be it so, my child,' the father replied.

---

The next extract is from the Ka*th*a Upanishad of the Ya*g*ur-veda, and has by many scholars been classed as of later date.

FIRST VALLÎ.

1. Vâ*g*as*r*avasa, desirous (of heavenly rewards), surrendered (at a sacrifice) all that he possessed. He had a son of the name of Na*k*iketas.

4. He (knowing that his father had promised to give up at a sacrifice all that he possessed, and therefore his son also) said to his father: 'Dear father, to whom wilt thou give me?'

He said it a second and a third time. Then the father replied (angrily):

'I shall give thee unto Death.'

(The father, having once said so, though in haste, had to be true to his word and to sacrifice his son.)

5. The son said: 'I go as the first, at the head of many (who have still to die); I go in the midst of many (who are now dying). What will be the work of Yama (the ruler of the departed) which to-day he has to do unto me?

6. 'Look back how it was with those who came before, look forward how it will be with those who come hereafter. A mortal ripens like corn, like corn he springs up again.'

(Na*k*iketas then enters into the abode of Yama Vaivasvata, and there is no one to receive him. Thereupon one of the attendants of Yama is supposed to say:)

7. 'Fire enters into the houses, when a Brâhma*n*a enters as a guest. That fire is quenched by this peace-offering;—bring water, O Vaivasvata!

8. 'A Brâhma*n*a that dwells in the house of a foolish man without receiving food to eat, destroys his hopes and expectations, his possessions, his righteousness, his sacred and his good deeds, and all his sons and cattle.'

(Yama, returning to his house after an absence of three nights, during which time Na*k*iketas had received no hospitality from him, says:)

9. 'O Brâhma*n*a, as thou, a venerable guest, hast dwelt in my house three nights without eating, therefore choose now three boons. Hail to thee! and welfare to me!'

10. Na*k*iketas said: 'O Death, as the first of the three boons I choose that Gautama, my father, be pacified, kind, and free from anger towards me; and that he may know me and greet me, when I shall have been dismissed by thee.'

11. Yama said: 'With my leave, Auddâlaki Âru*n*i, thy father, will know thee, and be again towards thee as he was before. He shall sleep peacefully through the night, and free from anger, after having seen thee freed from the jaws of death.'

12. Na*k*iketas said: 'In the heaven-world there is no fear; thou art not there, O Death, and no one is afraid on account of old age. Leaving behind both hunger and thirst, and out of the reach of sorrow, all rejoice in the world of heaven.'

13. 'Thou knowest, O Death, the fire-sacrifice which leads us to heaven; tell it to me, for I am full of faith. Those who live in the heaven-world reach immortality,—this I ask as my second boon.'

14. Yama said: 'I will tell it thee, learn it from me, and when thou understandest that fire-sacrifice which leads to heaven, know, O Na*k*iketas, that it is the attainment of the eternal worlds, and their firm support, hidden in darkness.'

15. Yama then told him that fire-sacrifice, in the beginning of the worlds, and what bricks are required for the altar, and how many, and how they are to be placed. And Na*k*iketas repeated all as it had been told to him. Then M*ri*tyu, being pleased with him, said again:

19. 'This, O Na*k*iketas, is thy fire which leads to heaven, and which thou hast chosen as thy second boon. That fire all men will proclaim as thine. Choose now, O Na*k*iketas, thy third boon.'

20. Na*k*iketas said: 'There is that doubt, when a man is dead,—some saying, he is; others, he is not. This I should like to know, taught by thee; this is the third of my boons.'

21. Death said: 'On this point even the gods have been in doubt formerly; it is not easy to understand. That subject is subtle. Choose another boon, O Na*k*iketas, do not press me, and let me off that boon.'

22. Na*k*iketas said: 'On this point even the gods have been in doubt indeed, and thou, Death, hast declared it to be not easy to understand, and another teacher like thee is not to be found:—surely no other boon is like unto this.'

23. Death said: 'Choose sons and grandsons who

shall live a hundred years, herds of cattle, elephants, gold, and horses. Choose the wide abode of the earth, and live thyself as many harvests as thou desirest.'

24. 'If thou canst think of any boon equal to that, choose wealth, and long life. Be (king), Na*k*iketas, on the wide earth. I make thee the enjoyer of all desires.'

25. 'Whatever desires are difficult to attain among mortals, ask for them according to thy wish;—these fair maidens with their chariots and musical instruments,—such are indeed not to be obtained by men,—be waited on by them whom I give to thee, but do not ask me about dying.'

26. Na*k*iketas said: 'Thoughts of to-morrow, O Death, wear out the present vigour of all the senses of man. Even the whole of life is short. Keep thou thy horses, keep dance and song for thyself.'

27. 'No man can be made happy through wealth. Shall we have wealth, when we see thee? Let us live, as long as thou rulest? Only that boon (which I have chosen) is to be chosen by me.'

28. 'What mortal, slowly decaying here below, and knowing, after having approached them, the freedom from decay enjoyed by the immortals, would delight in a long life, after he has pondered on the pleasures which arise from beauty and love?'

29. 'No, that on which there is this doubt, O Death, tell us what there is in that great Hereafter. Na*k*iketas does not choose another boon but that which enters into what is hidden.'

### SECOND VALLÎ.

1. Death said: 'The good is one thing, the pleasant another; these two, having different objects, chain a man. It is well with him who clings to the good; he who chooses the pleasant, misses his end.'

2. 'The good and the pleasant approach man: the wise goes round about them and distinguishes them. Yea, the wise prefers the good to the pleasant, but the fool chooses the pleasant through greed and avarice.'

3. 'Thou, O Na*k*iketas, after pondering all pleasures that are or seem delightful, hast dismissed them all. Thou hast not gone into the road that leadeth to wealth, in which many men perish.'

4. 'Wide apart and leading to different points are these two, ignorance, and what is known as wisdom. I believe Na*k*iketas to be one who desires knowledge, for even many pleasures did not tear thee away.'

5. 'Fools dwelling in darkness, wise in their own conceit, and puffed up with vain knowledge, go round and round, staggering to and fro, like blind men led by the blind.'

6. 'The Hereafter never rises before the eyes of the careless child, deluded by the delusion of wealth. "This is the world," he thinks, "there is no other;"—thus he falls again and again under my sway.'

7. 'He (the Self) of whom many are not even able to hear, whom many, even when they hear of him, do not comprehend; wonderful is a man, when found, who is able to teach this (the Self); wonderful is he who comprehends this, when taught by an able teacher.'

9. 'That doctrine is not to be obtained by argument, but when it is declared by another, then, O dearest, it is easy to understand. Thou hast obtained it now; thou art truly a man of true resolve. May we have always an inquirer like thee!'

10. Na*k*iketas said: 'I know that what is called treasure is transient, for the eternal is not obtained by things which are not eternal. Hence the Nâ*k*iketa fire-sacrifice has been laid by me first; then, by means of transient things, I have obtained what is not transient (the teaching of Yama).'

11. Yama said: 'Though thou hadst seen the fulfilment of all desires, the foundation of the world, the endless rewards of good deeds, the shore where there is no fear, that which is magnified by praise, the wide abode, the rest, yet being wise thou hast with firm resolve dismissed it all.'

12. 'The wise who, by means of meditation on his Self, recognises the Ancient, who is difficult to be seen, who has entered into darkness, who is hidden in the cave, who dwells in the abyss, as God, he indeed leaves joy and sorrow far behind.'

13. 'A mortal who has heard this and embraced it, who has removed from it all qualities, and has thus reached that subtle Being, rejoices, because he has obtained what is a cause for rejoicing. The house (of Brahman) is open, I believe, O Na*k*iketas.'

18. 'The knowing Self is not born, it dies not; it sprang from nothing, nothing sprang from it. The Ancient is unborn, eternal, everlasting; he is not killed, though the body is killed.'

19. 'If the killer thinks that he kills, if the killed thinks that he is killed, they do not understand; for this one does not kill, nor is that one killed.'

20. 'The Self, smaller than small, greater than great, is hidden in the heart of the creature. A man who is free from desires and free from grief, sees the majesty of the Self by the grace of the Creator (or through the serenity of the elements).'

21. 'Though sitting still, he walks far; though lying down, he goes everywhere. Who, save myself, is able to know that God, who rejoices and rejoices not?'

22. 'The wise who knows the Self as bodiless within the bodies, as unchanging among changing things, as great and omnipresent, he never grieves.'

23. 'That Self cannot be gained by the Veda, nor by understanding, nor by much learning. He whom the Self chooses, by him the Self can be gained. The Self chooses him (his body) as his own.'

24. 'But he who has not first turned away from his wickedness, who is not tranquil, and subdued, or whose mind is not at rest, he can never obtain the Self (even) by knowledge.'

## THIRD VALLÎ.

1. 'There are the two, drinking their reward in the world of their own works, entered into the cave (of the heart), dwelling on the highest summit (the ether in the heart). Those who know Brahman call them shade and light; likewise, those householders who perform the Tri*nâk*iketa sacrifice.'

2. 'May we be able to master that Nâ*k*iketa rite which is a bridge for sacrificers; which is the highest, imperishable Brahman for those who wish to cross over to the fearless shore.'

3. 'Know the Self to be sitting in the chariot,

the body to be the chariot, the intellect (buddhi) the charioteer, and the mind the reins.'

4. 'The senses they call the horses, the objects of the senses their roads. When he (the Highest Self) is in union with the body, the senses, and the mind, then wise people call him the Enjoyer.'

5. 'He who has no understanding and whose mind (the reins) is never firmly held, his senses (horses) are unmanageable, like vicious horses of a charioteer.'

6. 'But he who has understanding and whose mind is always firmly held, his senses are under control, like good horses of a charioteer.'

7. 'He who has no understanding, who is unmindful and always impure, never reaches that place, but enters into the round of births.'

8. 'But he who has understanding, who is mindful and always pure, reaches indeed that place, from whence he is not born again.'

9. 'But he who has understanding for his charioteer, and who holds the reins of the mind, he reaches the end of his journey, and that is the highest place (step) of Vish*n*u.'

10. 'Beyond the senses there are the objects, beyond the objects there is the mind, beyond the mind there is the intellect, the Great Self is beyond the intellect.'

11. 'Beyond the Great there is the Undeveloped, beyond the Undeveloped there is the Person (Purusha). Beyond the Person there is nothing—this is the goal, the furthest road.'

12. 'That Self is hidden in all beings and does not shine forth, but it is seen by subtle seers through their sharp and subtle intellect.'

13. 'A wise man should keep down speech and

mind; he should keep them within the Self which is knowledge; he should keep knowledge within the Self which is the Great; and he should keep that (the Great) within the Self which is the Quiet.'

14. 'Rise, awake! having obtained your boons, understand them! The sharp edge of a razor is difficult to pass over; difficult is the path (to the Self); the wise tell it.'

15. 'He who has perceived that which is without sound, without touch, without form, without decay, without taste, eternal, without smell, without beginning, without end, beyond the Great, and unchangeable, is freed from the jaws of death.'

### Translation of the Upanishads.

May I be allowed to say here a few words with regard to my translation. Those who know my translation of the Upanishads, published in 1879 and 1884, will easily see that I have altered it in several places. But I do not wish it to be understood that I consider my translation even now as quite free from doubt. Our best scholars know how far we are still from a perfect understanding of the Upanishads. When therefore, in 1879, I undertook a translation of all the more important Upanishads, all I could hope for was to give a better translation than what we had before. Though I was well aware of the difficulties of such an undertaking, I knew that I could count on the same indulgence which is always granted to a first attempt at translating, nay, often, as in our case, at guessing and deciphering an ancient text. Nor have I been at all convinced that I was wrong in following a text, such as it is presupposed by the commentaries of *Samkara*, instead of introducing conjectural emendations, however obvious they seem to be. Scholars should learn that the more obvious their emendations are, the more difficult it becomes to account for the introduction of such palpable corruptions into an ancient text, such as it was at the time of *Samkara*. My determination also, whenever it was impossible to discover a satisfactory meaning, to be satisfied with *Samkara's* interpretations, who after all lived a thousand years ago, may be criticised, and I never represented it as more than a *pis aller*. Besides that, all the translators of the S. B. E. had to make a sacrifice in giving what they could give at the time, without waiting for the ninth year. Though I have hardly ever referred to the mistakes made by earlier translators of the Upanishads, but have simply corrected them, anybody who will take the trouble to compare them with my own will find a good harvest of them, as those who come after me will no doubt glean many a stray ear even in a field which so many mowers have mowed. But the work of the children that glean some ears is very different from that of the mower who has to mow a whole field alone. Such a work as Colonel Jacob's Concordance of the Principal Upanishads and the Bhagavad-gîtâ, published in 1891, has placed at the disposal of all Vedântic students what may almost be called a mowing machine in place of a sickle; and the careful and brilliant translation of the Sixty Upanishads published by Professor Deussen, in 1897, shows what an immense advance has been made with its help. I have adopted many emendations in the extracts given above, from Professor Deussen's work, and when my translations differ from his, all I can say is that I always differ most reluctantly from one who has devoted so many years to Vedântic studies, and whose mind is so thoroughly imbued with Vedântic ideas. If we could always know at what time each Upanishad was finally settled and reduced to writing, whether before or after the time when the Vedânta and Sâ*m*khya-philosophy assumed each its own independent and systematic form, our task would be much lightened. Whenever we come across such words as Âtman and Brahman we suspect Vedântic influences, whereas Purusha and Prak*ri*ti at once remind us of Sâ*m*khya doctrines. But Âtman is by no means unknown to early Sâ*m*khya philosophers, nor is Purusha entirely outside the Vedântic horizon. To say, therefore, that Purusha must always be taken in the technical Sâ*m*khya sense, and Âtman in that of the Vedânta, is going too far, at least at present. We go still further out of our depth if we maintain, with regard to the Ka*th*a Upanishad, for instance, that there was a time when it consisted of one chapter and three Vallîs only. It may have been so, and who shall prove that it was not so? But on the other hand, what do we know of the compilers of the Upanishads to enable us to speak so positively on such a subject? Everybody can see that there was a division at III, 13, or 16, or 17. The technical repetition of certain words in IV, 17 might indicate that the Upanishad originally ended there, and that V, 18 is later. Anybody can see also that the second Adhyâya differs in spirit from the first. The name of Na*k*iketas, for instance, is never mentioned in the second chapter, except in the last and probably spurious or additional verse, and then it appears as Nâ*k*iketa, as derived from Na*k*iketa, not from the old form Na*k*iketas. We may easily discover a different spirit in the third, as compared with the first and second Vallî. In fact, there is still plenty of work left for those who come after us, for with all that has been achieved we are on the threshold only of a truly historical study of Indian philosophy and literature. Here, also, we are still like children playing on the sea-shore and finding now and then a pebble or a shell, whilst the great ocean of that ancient literature lies before us undiscovered and unexplored.

### Character of the Upanishads.

Such utterances as I have here quoted from the Upanishads will hardly seem worthy of the name of philosophy. It would have been almost impossible to describe them so as to give a clear idea of what the Upanishads really are. With us philosophy always means something systematic, while what we find here are philosophic rhapsodies rather than consecutive treatises. But that is the very reason why the Upanishads are so interesting to the historical student. Nowhere, except in India, can we watch that period of chaotic thought, half poetical, half religious, which preceded, in India at least, the age of philosophy, properly so called. Possibly, if we knew more of the utterances of such men as Heraclitus or Epimenides in Greece, they might show some likeness to the outpourings of the authors of the Upanishads. What is quite clear, however, is that the systematic philosophy of India would be perfectly unintelligible without the previous chapter of the Upanishads. And however unsystematic these relics of the childhood of philosophy may seem, there is really more system in them than appears at first sight. They contain a number even of technical terms which show that the Upanishads did not spring up in one day, and that there must have been a good deal of philosophical controversy during the age that is recorded to us in the Upanishads. If *S*vetaketu is represented as attending the schools of famous teachers till he is twenty-four years of age, and is then only learning from his father the highest wisdom, we see that that highest wisdom had already been fully elaborated in the formula of 'Tat tvam asi,' 'Thou art that,' that is, thou, man, art not different from that divine nature which pervades the whole world, as salt pervades the sea. You cannot see it, you cannot handle it, but you can taste it and know that, though invisible, it is there. That divine essence, that which is alone true and real in this unreal or phenomenal world, is present likewise, though invisible, as the germ of life in the smallest seed, and without it there would be no seed, no fruit, no tree, as without God there would be no world. That this ancient wisdom should be so often mixed up with what seems to us childish and absurd, is as true as it is difficult to explain, but we must remember that a long continued oral tradition must naturally leave a wide door open to additions of every kind.

Whatever we may think of these Upanishads, it cannot be doubted that they represent the soil which contained the seeds of philosophy which sprang up and had their full growth in the great systems of philosophy of a later age.

### Vedânta-Sûtras.

If now we turn to these, and first of all, to the philosophy elaborated by Bâdarâya*n*a, we find no longer rhapsodies, but a carefully reasoned system, contained in 555 short paragraphs, the so-called Vedânta-Sûtras. We read there in the first Sûtra and as a kind of title, 'Now then a desire to know Brahman,' or as Deussen translates *Gig*ñâsâ, 'Now then research of Brahman.' The two words Atha and Ata*h* which, I believe, were originally no more than introductory, and which occur again and again at the beginning of Sanskrit works, always give rise to endless and most fanciful interpretations. If we must assign to them any special meaning, it seems to me best to take Atha in the sense of Now, and Ata*h* in the sense of Then or Therefore, implying thereby that the student has fulfilled certain preliminary conditions, such as Upanayana, reception by a teacher, Vedâdhyayana, learning by heart the text of the Veda, including the Upanishads, and that he is therefore likely to feel a desire to understand the Veda and to know Brahman. It may be true also, as some commentators maintain, that in real life the first step would have been to study the Pûrva-Mîmâ*m*sâ, or what is called Dharma, law, virtue, &c.; and that only after having gained a knowledge of Dharma, particularly of the sacrificial Dharma, would there arise a desire to know Brahman. In that case the Mîmâ*m*sâ might be looked upon as one body, the Pûrva-Mîmâ*m*sâ forming the first, the Uttara-Mîmâ*m*sâ the second part, and we should have to consider the practice of virtue and the performance of sacrificial acts as a necessary preliminary to a study of the Vedânta-philosophy, or, as it is generally expressed, we should have to consider works as essential for producing that purity and serenity of the mind without which a knowledge of Brahman is impossible. I confess I doubt whether all this was present to the mind of Bâdarâya*n*a. He may have used *Gig*ñâsâ, wish to know, instead of Vi*k*âra, research or discussion, on purpose, because in the true sense Brahman cannot be defined or known. But although Brahman cannot be known like all other things, by being defined as So and So, it can be explained negatively as Not so and Not so, and can thus be cleared from many doubts which arise from the various utterances about it in the Upanishads. When we read, however, that food is Brahman[1], that Manas is Brahman[2], that Vigñâna is Brahman[3], that the sun is Brahman[4], nay that Nârâya*n*a is Brahman[5], there is surely room enough for trying to determine what Brahman really is, or at least what he or it was to Bâdarâya*n*a and his predecessors.

The best answer, however, to all these questions is that given in the next Sûtra, 'That *from which the origin &c.* (origin, subsistence, and dissolution) *of this* world proceed[6].' The full sense of this Sûtra, according to the commentator, is: 'That

---

[1] *Kh*ând. Up. VII, 7, 9, 2; B*r*ih. Âr. V, 12, 1.

[2] *Kh*ând. Up. III, 18, 1; VII, 3, 2; B*r*ih. Âr. IV, 1, 6.

[3] *Kh*ând. Up. VII, 7, 2.

[4] *Kh*ând. Up. III, 19, 1; B*r*ih. Up. II, 1, 2.

[5] Mahânâr. Up. XI, 4.

[6] The words which actually occur in the Sûtra are printed in italics, to give an idea of the enigmatical style of the Sûtras, and their utter uselessness without a commentary.

omniscient, omnipotent cause from which proceed the origin, subsistence and dissolution of the world, which world is differentiated by names and forms, contains many agents and enjoyers, and is the abode of fruits or effects, caused by former actions, these fruits having their definite places, times and causes, and the nature of whose arrangement cannot be conceived by the mind—that cause is Brahman.

If it be asked, how this is known, the commentator insists very strongly that such knowledge is not to be gained by sense perception or by inference, but simply by the Veda (Upanishads), passages of which have been collected and properly arranged in the Sûtras. If in some places he admits as a second source of knowledge Sâkshâtkâra, or manifestation, that can only be meant for intuition, but, strictly speaking, such intuition also presupposes a previous working of the organs of sensuous perception, while the object of such Sâkshâtkâra, i. e. Brahman, can at first be supplied by the Veda only. In support therefore of our Sûtra which is intended to give a general idea of Brahman, a passage is quoted from the Taitt. Up. III, 1, where Varu*n*a explains to his son that 'that from which these beings are born, that by which, when born, they live, that into which at their death they re-enter, try to know that, that is Brahman.'

### Appeals to the Veda.

And here we should mark a curious feature of orthodox Indian philosophy. Though the Vedânta appeals to the Veda, it appeals to it, not as having itself grown out of it or as belonging to it, but rather as an independent witness, looking back to it for sanction and confirmation. The same applies, though in a less degree, to other systems also. They all speak as if they had for several generations elaborated their doctrines independently, and, after they had done so, they seem to come back to get the approval of the Veda, or to establish their conformity with the Veda, as the recognised highest authority. This shows that a certain time must have elapsed after the final redaction of the Upanishads and the return, as it were, of their offspring, the Sûtras, to their original home. How this came about, we cannot tell, because we have no historical documents, but that there had been something very important intervening between the old Upanishads and the first attempts at systematising Vedânta and Sâ*m*khya doctrines in the form of Sûtras is very clear by the manner in which the Sûtras appeal to the Veda. This constant appeal to the Veda as the highest authority was justified by the most elaborate arguments, as part of the question, How do we know? a question which forms an essential preliminary to all philosophy in India.

### Pramâ*n*as.

We saw how the *K*ârvâkas admitted but one source of knowledge, the evidence of the senses, excluding all others. How they defended that sensuous knowledge against the uncertainties inherent in it, we do not know, because we do not possess those Sûtras. But it is characteristic of the Vedânta-Sûtras, that they pay much smaller attention to the Pramâ*n*as, the sources and authorities of knowledge, than the other systems. These questions of Pramâ*n*a are often referred to in the commentaries, but not so much in the text. Pramâ*n*a is originally the instrument of measuring, from Mâ, to measure, and Pra, forth. It may be translated by measure, standard, authority, and survives in the modern Persian Fermân, an authoritative order.

### Pramâ*n*as according to the Sâ*m*khya.

The Pramâ*n*a which serves as a means (Sâdhana) of determining, produces Pramiti, accurate knowledge, just as a Sâdhana (means) produces Siddhi, truth or certainty. When we come to the Sâ*m*khya, we shall find there a very full and perhaps the oldest description of the three essential Pramâ*n*as, viz. Pratyaksha, Anumâna, and *S*abda. The first Pramâ*n*a, Pratyaksha, is what we mean by sensuous perception, though it is also used in the sense of what can be perceived by the senses, the D*r*ish*t*a, i.e. what is seen. It is explained (Sâ*m*khya-Sûtra I, 89) as cognition which arises from contact (with objects) and represents their form.

### Pratyaksha.

It is generally explained by Indriyârtha-sa*m*nikarsha, contact of the senses and their respective objects, and is said to involve really three stages, contact of the sense-organ with its object, and at the same time union of the sense with Manas, mind, and union of Manas, mind, with Âtman, Self. There is a distinction made between two kinds of Pratyaksha, called Savikalpa and Nirvikalpa, with doubt and without doubt. The former seems to consist in our seeing an object, and then declaring that it is this or that; the latter in simply accepting a thing such as it is, without any previous idea of it, such as when we awake from sleep, see a tiger, and at once run away. Each sense working by itself, and on its own objects only, is the Asâdhâranakârana, the special or exclusive instrument of the knowledge conveyed by it. Sound, for instance, is heard by the ear only, and is conveyed by Âkâsa or ether. But not every sound is brought into immediate contact with the ear; it is transmitted through the ether, as we are told, by means of waves (Vîkita), so that we may perceive the beating of a distant drum, one wave propelling the other across the vast ocean of ether, till it strikes the shore, i.e. the ear.

### Anumâna.

The next Pramâna is Anumâna or inference, which is explained (l. c., I, 100) as knowledge of the connected on the part of one who knows the connection, or as knowledge of something that is not perceptible, but is known as being invariably connected (Vyâpya) with something else that is perceived, as when we perceive fire (Vyâpaka) from perceiving smoke (Vyâpta). This is a very imperfect description of Anumâna, which will be more fully explained hereafter, but it suffices for our present purpose. As an illustration, we have the common illustration that we know the presence of fire when we see smoke, and that we know the absence of smoke when we see no fire, always supposing that fire has been proved to be the Vyâpaka or the *sine quâ non* of smoke.

### *S*abda.

*S*abda (I, 101) or word, another Pramâ*n*a, is explained to be instruction given by one that can be trusted (Âptopade*s*a); this one that can be trusted being for the Vedântists the Veda, but for the Sâ*m*khya and other systems, any other person also endowed with authority and therefore considered as trustworthy. It might easily be shown that these three Pramâ*n*as all go back to one, the Pratyaksha, because the invariable concomitance between smoke and fire and the like, on which the Anumâna rests, can have been established by sensuous experience only; and the trustworthiness of any knowledge conveyed by word must equally depend on experience, or on acquaintance with the person who is or is not to be trusted.

The question is, whether this *S*abda, word, was originally taken to signify the Veda such as we possess it[1]. I have elsewhere given my reasons for believing that *S*abda had really a far more general and more philosophical meaning, and that it may have been intended at first for Brahman, the Word, or for verbal knowledge as is conveyed by a word. The Hindus knew quite well that words such as greatness, goodness, nay, also such as animal, plant, metal, nay, even dog or cow, convey knowledge that cannot be gained either by perception or by inference alone, but only by the word. The same applies to Âptava*k*ana, another

[1] Sâ*m*khya-Philosophie, p. 154, Anm. 3. That the connection between sound and meaning, and therefore the authority of words by themselves, occupied the Sâ*m*khyas, we see from Sûtra V, 37.

term for *S*abda, word, used in the Sâ*m*khya-philosophy. Âpta, which is explained by Yogya, can hardly be translated by *aptus*. It means what has been obtained or received, and Âptavâkya or Âptava*k*ana need originally have meant no more than our traditional language such as it is, though it was explained afterwards as meaning the word of a person worthy of confidence, or even of a book believed in by the world at large. However, we must be satisfied with what the Sâ*m*khya philosophers tell us; and there can be no doubt that the followers of the orthodox Sâ*m*khya understood *S*abda in the sense of Veda; though, considering that they admitted a divine, not a human origin of the Veda, it is difficult to understand how they could afterwards take it in the general sense of the word of one that can be trusted. The important question for us to consider is what other systems of philosophy have made of these three Pramâ*n*as. The Sûtras of all the other systems of philosophy are well acquainted with them, and they are even referred to by the commentators of the Vedânta also. It seems strange at first sight, considering that the question of the possibility of knowing or of the instruments of knowledge, forms the foundation of every true system of philosophy, that the Brahma-Sûtras, though not the later Vedânta works, should apparently have attached so little importance to what may be called their *Critique of Pure Reason*. This would seem indeed to lower the Vedânta-philosophy to the level of all Pre-Kantian philosophy, but a little reflection will show us that there was in the Vedânta a sufficient excuse for this neglect. What at first sight makes the case still worse is that while Pratyaksha, perception, and Anumâna, inference, are ignored, the only evidence invoked by Bâdarâyana is Sruti or revelation, which, as we saw, was often invoked by the modern orthodox Sâmkhyas under the name of Sabda or word. To most philosophers revelation would seem a very weak instrument of knowledge, and one that could never claim more than a subordinate place, even if treated as a subdivision of Anumâna or inference. But we must remember that it is the highest object of the Vedânta to prove that there is only one true reality, namely Brahman, and that the manifoldness of the visible world is but the result of that nescience which the Vedânta is meant to destroy. It will then become intelligible why an appeal to the evidence of the senses or to inference would have been out of place and almost self-contradictory in the Vedânta. The commentator admits this when he says, 'If we acquiesce in the doctrine of absolute unity (Brahman), the ordinary means of right knowledge, perception, &c., become invalid, because the absence of manifoldness deprives them of their objects.' Hence, a doctrine which undertakes to prove that the manifold world, presented to us by the senses, is unreal, could not well appeal at the same time to the evidence of the senses, nor to inference which is founded on it, in support of truth or right knowledge, though it may and does readily acknowledge their importance for all the ordinary transactions of life. Thus Samkara continues: 'So long as a person has not reached the true knowledge of the unity of the Self, it does not enter his mind that the world of effects, with its instruments and objects of right knowledge and its results of actions, is untrue; and hence, as long as true knowledge does not present itself, there is no reason why the ordinary course of secular and religious activity should not go on undisturbed.'

How well Bâdarâya*n*a must have been acquainted with the ordinary evidences of knowledge, both Pratyaksha and Anumâna, is best shown by the new meaning which he assigns to them, applying (I, 3, 28) Pratyaksha to *S*ruti (revelation) and Anumâna to Sm*ri*ti (tradition), the Veda being to him self-evident, while other works, such as the Law-books of Manu, the Mahâbhârata (Bhagavad-gîtâ), nay even the Sâ*m*khya and Yoga systems (IV, 2, 21), being Sm*ri*ti, are true in so far only as they are not in opposition to the Veda. But everything else, every kind of Tarka or speculation, is excluded when the fundamental truths of the Vedânta are at stake. Thus *S*a*m*kara, II, 1, 11, says: 'In matters to be known from *S*ruti mere reasoning is not to be relied on. As the thoughts of man are altogether unfettered, reasoning, which disregards the holy texts and rests on individual opinion only, has no proper foundation. One sees how arguments which some clever men had excogitated with great pains, are shown by people still more ingenious to be fallacious, and how the arguments of the latter are refuted in their turn by other men; so that on account of the diversity of men's opinions, it is impossible to accept mere reasoning as having a sure foundation. Nor can we get over this difficulty by accepting as well founded the reasoning of some person of recognised eminence, whether Kapila or any one else, since we observe that even men of the most undoubted intellectual eminence, such as Kapila, Ka*n*âda, and other founders of philosophical schools, have contradicted each other.'

This rejection of reason and reasoning, though not unfamiliar to ourselves, seems certainly strange in a philosopher ; and it is not unnatural that *S*am*k*ara should have been taunted by his adversaries with using reason against reasoning. 'You cannot,' they say, 'maintain that no reasoning whatever is well-founded, for you yourself can found your assertion that reasoning has no foundation, on reasoning only. Moreover, if all reasoning were unfounded, the whole course of practical human life would have to come to an end.' But even this does not frighten *S*am*k*ara. As all reasoning is admittedly founded on perception and inference, he replies, 'that although with regard to some things reasoning is known to be well founded, with regard to the matter in hand there will be no escape, i.e. reasoning cannot there escape from the charge of being ill-founded. The true nature of the cause of the world on which final emancipation depends cannot, on account of its excessive abstruseness, even be thought of without the help of the holy texts ; for it cannot become the object of perception because it does not possess qualities such as form and the like, and, as it is devoid of characteristic signs or qualities, it cannot lend itself to inference and other means of right knowledge.'

Here we approach a very difficult question, and have possibly to admit a weak link in the strong chain armour of both Bâdarâya*n*a and *S*am*k*ara. How is the supreme authority of the Veda to be established against those who doubt it ? It may be enough for the orthodox to say that the Veda is its own proof, that it is self-luminous like the sun : but how are objections to be silenced? The Vedânta philosophers have no superstitions on any other points, and are perfectly fearless in the treatment of all other problems; they can enter into the most subtle controversies, and yet they are satisfied with the mere assertion that the Veda wants no proof, that its authority requires no support from elsewhere (prâmâ*n*yam nirapeksham), that it is direct evidence of truth, just as the light of the sun is its own evidence of light, and at the same time the direct means of our knowledge of form and colour (II, 1, 1).

### Authority of the Vedas.

But who says so? Who but a fallible mortal? It is hardly enough if we were to say that the Veda was the oldest document which the Brâhmans possessed, that it may even have been brought into India from another country, that its very language required to be interpreted by competent persons. All this might have helped to invest the Veda with some kind of mysterious character; but my impression has always been that this would be taking too low a view of the Indian intellect. Veda, I hold, was not merely the name of a text or of texts, but was originally conceived in a far deeper sense.

### The Meaning of Veda.

We often read that Veda is Brahman, and Brahman is Veda, and in such passages Brahman is now generally taken in the sense of the Sa*m*hitâs and Brâhma*n*as such as we possess them. But might it not, like Âptava*k*ana, to which we referred before, have meant originally knowledge or wisdom or Sophia; and as such a Sophia was impossible without words, might we not here also have a faint recollection of Brahman as the Word, the first creation of divine thought. After all, Veda means originally knowledge, and not hymns and Brâhma*n*as, and as such would come very near to Wisdom or Sophia. I do not venture to speak positively on such a subject, because there is so little of real evidence left to which we could appeal. I give it simply as an idea that has presented itself to my mind as a way out of many difficulties. To prevent all misunderstandings I say at once that I do not entertain the idea that such thoughts were borrowed from Greece and Alexandria, or had been matured during the as yet undivided Aryan period. All I should venture to suggest is that the idea of the Word or the Logos being the first revelation, manifestation or creation of a Divine Power is by no means so strange, even in a very early period of thought, as it seems to us. People who have thought at all about what a word is, not a mere sign or a means of communication, but an act embodying for the first time a definite idea which came into existence by being uttered, and afterwards thrown forth and realised in our objective world, would naturally, whether in Greece or in India, recognise in every word an act of a Divine Thinker, just as in every species they have to recognise the will of a Divine Creator. *Sam*kara goes so far as to declare that the Veda is the cause of the distinction of all the different classes and conditions (species) of gods, animals, and men (I, 1, 3, and B*r*ih. Âr. Upan. II, 4, 10). Nay he speaks still more distinctly in I, 3, 28: 'We all know from observation,' he says, 'that any one, when setting about something which he wishes to accomplish, first remembers the word denoting the thing, and after that sets to work.' What should he do when there is as yet no word to remember, but the word, that is, the idea, has first to be created? We therefore conclude that, before the creation, the Vedic words became manifest in the mind of Pra*g*âpati the creator, and that after that he created the things corresponding to these words. The *S*ruti also, when it says 'uttering Bhûr He created the earth, &c.,' shows that the worlds, such as the earth, &c., became manifest, i. e. were created, from the word Bhûr, which had become manifest in the mind (of Pra*g*âpati). In that case the recognition by Indian thinkers of Brahman as the Word or the Divine Thought, or as Veda, would by no means be so surprising as it sounds to us at first. It might then be said quite truly that the *S*abda, sound, or Brahman or Vâ*k* or *B*ri*h = word, was eternal, absolute, self-luminous, self-evident, in fact all that the Veda is said to be. Two such words as Brahman and Âtman would by themselves convey that eternal truth for which the Vedânta-philosophy is fighting, and in support of which there is but one appeal, not to sensuous experience nor to inference, but to the Word itself, i. e. to Brahman, or the Veda. I know full well how entirely hypothetical, if not mystical, this may sound to many Sanskrit scholars, but I could not entirely suppress these thoughts, as they seem to me the only way in which we can free our Vedânta philosophers from the charge of childishness, for imagining that they could establish the highest truths which are within the reach of the human mind, on such authorities as the hymns, the Brâhma*n*as and even some of the Upanishads, as we possess them now.

Returning to the Vedânta, however, such as we know it from the Sûtras, we must be satisfied with the expressed view of Bâdarâya*n*a that the evidence for what the Vedânta teaches is neither perception nor inference, but the Word (*S*abda) alone, such as we find it in our manuscripts, or rather in the oral tradition of the Veda.

### Work-part and Knowledge-part of the Veda.

Of course a distinction has to be made, and has been made by Bâdarâya*n*a between the Knowledge-part, the *Gñ*âna-kâ*nd*a, chiefly the Upanishads, and the Karma-kâ*nd*a, the Work-part, the hymns and Brâhma*n*as. Both are called Veda or *S*ruti, revelation, and yet the work-part does not exist for the true philosopher, except in order to be discarded as soon as he has understood the knowledge-part. *S*a*m*kara is bold enough to declare that the whole Veda is useless to a man who has obtained knowledge, or Mukti, or freedom. 'Not all the Vedas together,' he says, 'are more useful to one who has obtained true knowledge than is a small tank of water in a country flooded with water.' A man who has neglected the Vedas and disregarded the rules of the four Â*s*ramas, in fact, a man who has lost caste, may still be allowed to study the Vedânta as the fountain of all true knowledge, and thus become liberated (III, 4, 36). The hymns and Brâhma*n*as refer in fact to the phenomenal world, they presuppose the existence of a manifold creation, of an enjoyer of what is to be enjoyed, of good works and their fruit. But all this, as we shall see, is not real, but phenomenal; it belongs to the realm of Avidyâ, Nescience, and vanishes as soon as true wisdom or Vidyâ has been obtained. It is to be observed in the world, such as it is, as a lower stage, but as essential in leading on to a higher stage.

### Vidyâ and Avidyâ.

If then the highest truth contained in the Veda is the Tat Tvam Asi, that is, Thou, the *G*îvâtman, art it (the Paramâtman or Brahman), and if, as we are told, there is but one Brahman and nothing beside it, the Vedânta philosopher is at once met by the question, How then are we to account for the manifold Thou's, the many individuals, and the immense variety of the objective world? If the Veda is true, our view of the world cannot be true at the same time. It can therefore be due only to what is called Avidyâ, Nescience, and it is the very object of the Vedânta-philosophy to expel and annihilate this Avidyâ, and replace it by Vidyâ.

### Subject and Object.

This Avidyâ is the next point that has to be discussed. *S*a*m*kara, in the introduction to his commentary, has some important remarks on it[1]. 'As it is well known,' he says, 'that object and subject, which fall under the concepts of We and You (or as we should say, of the Ego and Non-Ego), are in their very essence opposed to each other, like darkness and light, and that the one can never therefore take the place of the other, it follows further that

[1] Three Lectures on the Vedânta, p. 62.

their attributes also can never be interchanged.' This means that object and subject mutually exclude each other, so that what is conceived as object can never in the same act of thought be conceived as subject, and *vice versa*. We can, for instance, never say or think: We are you, or You are we, nor ought we ever to substitute subjective for objective qualities. 'Therefore,' he continues, 'we may conclude that to transfer what is objective, that is what is perceived as You or Non-ego with its qualities, to what is subjective, that is what perceives as We, the Ego, which consists of thought, or *vice versa* to transfer what is subjective to what is objective, must be altogether wrong.' A subject can never be anything but a subject, the object always remains the object. 'Nevertheless,' he adds, 'it is a habit in human nature (a necessity of thought, as we might call it), to say, combining what is true and what is false, "I am this," "this is mine," &c. This is a habit, caused by a false apprehension of subject and predicate, and by not distinguishing one from the other, but transferring the essence and the qualities of the one upon the other.'

It is clear that *Samkara* here uses subject and object not only in their simple logical sense, but that by subject he means what is real and true, in fact the Self, while object means with him what is unreal and phenomenal, such as the body with its organs, and the whole visible world. In 'I am,' the verb has a totally different character from what it has in 'thou art' or 'he is.' Such statements therefore as 'I am strong,' or 'I am blind,' arise from a false apprehension which, though it is inseparable from human thought, such as it is, has slowly to be overcome and at last to be destroyed by the Vedânta-philosophy.

This distinction between subject and object in the sense of what is real and what is phenomenal is very important, and stamps the whole of the Vedânta-philosophy with its own peculiar character.

It follows in fact from this fundamental distinction that we should never predicate what is phenomenal or objective of what is real and subjective, or what is real and subjective of what is phenomenal and objective; and it is in causing this mistake that the chief power of Avidyâ or Nescience consists. I should even go so far as to say that this warning might be taken to heart by our own philosophers also, for many of our own fallacies arise from the same Avidyâ, and are due in the end to the attribution of phenomenal and objective qualities to the subjective realities which we should recognise in the Divine only, and as underlying the Human Self and the phenomenal world.

It must not be supposed, however, that the Avidyâ or Nescience which makes the world what we make it and take it to be, is simply our own individual ignorance, our being unacquainted with the truths of the Vedânta. It should rather be looked upon as inborn in human nature, or, from an Indian point of view, as the result of accumulated thoughts and deeds before the mountains were brought forth. It has truly been called a general cosmical Nescience, inevitable for a time, as darkness is with light. So far as in true reality we are Brahman, our Nescience might indeed be called the Nescience of Brahman, if for a time only; and if we remember that it can be annihilated, we can understand why it was said to be nought, for, according to a general principle of the Vedânta, nothing that is real can ever be annihilated, so that nothing that is liable to annihilation has a right to be called real.

### The Phenomenal Reality of the World.

But it is very curious to find that though *Sam*kara looks upon the whole objective world as the result of Nescience, he nevertheless allows it to be real for all practical purposes (Vyavahârârtham). Thus we read (II, 1, 14), 'The entire complex of phenomenal existence is considered as true so long as the knowledge of Brahman and the Self of all has not arisen, just as the phantoms of a dream are considered to be true until the sleeper wakes. . . .' Hence, as long as true knowledge does not present itself, there is no reason why the ordinary course of secular and religious activity should not go on undisturbed, and more particularly, why all the commands of the Veda, even of the work-part, should not be obeyed.

But apart from this concession, the fundamental doctrine of *Sam*kara remains always the same. There is Brahman and nothing else; and to this Brahman as the subject, nothing must be ascribed that is peculiar to the individual living soul (I, 3, 19). The individual soul is, no doubt, Brahman, for the simple reason that there is nothing but Brahman, but Brahman is not the individual soul, which in its present state is personal, that is conditioned, and phenomenal. All we may predicate of that Highest Brahman is that it is one, never changing, never in contact with anything, devoid of all form, eternally pure, intelligent and free. To ascribe anything phenomenal to that Brahman or Âtman would be the same error as to ascribe blue colour to the colourless ether of the sky.

### Creation or Causation.

If with these ideas, taken as granted, we approach the problem of what we call the creation or the making of the world, it is clear that creation in our sense cannot exist for the Vedântist. As long as creation is conceived as a making or fashioning of matter, it does not exist for Bâdarâyana; only so far as it is a calling forth out of nothing does it approach the ideas of the Vedântist. Creation with Bâdarâyana would be nothing but the result of Nescience, and yet Brahman is again and again represented as the cause of the world, and not only as the efficient, but as the material cause as well, so far as such foreign terms can be applied to the reasoning of the Vedânta. Here lies our great difficulty in rendering Hindu-philosophy intelligible. The terms used by them seem to be the same as those which we use ourselves, and yet they are not. It is easy to say that Kârana is cause and Kârya effect, that the created world is the effect, and that Brahman is the cause. But the Vedântists have elaborated their own theory of cause and effect. According to them cause and effect are really the same thing looked at from two points of view, and the effect is always supposed to be latent in the cause. Hence, if Brahman is everything, and nothing exists besides Brahman, the substance of the world can be nothing but Brahman. Divyadâsa, a living Vedântist, seems therefore to draw a quite legitimate inference when he says[1] that the universe with all its sins

---

[1] Lectures on the Vedânta, p. 24.

and miseries must have existed latent in Brahman, just as steam existed latent in water before it was heated, though it does not become evident as vapour till fire is brought near to water.

### Cause and Effect.

This question of cause and effect and their mutual relation has occupied most of the philosophical systems of India; and when we remember what different views of cause and effect have been held by some of the most eminent philosophers of Europe, it is not surprising that the Hindus also should have arrived at very different results. The Vedântists stand up for Kârya-kâra*n*âbheda, the non-difference or substantial identity of cause and effect, and the Sâ*m*khya philosophers agree with them up to a certain point. In the Vedânta, II, 1, 14, we read in so many words, Tadananyatvam, that is, 'they, cause and effect, are not other, are not different from each other.' On this, as a general principle, rests their dogma of the substantial identity of Brahman and the phenomenal world. Nor does *S*a*m*kara support this principle by passages from the Veda only, but he appeals likewise to observation. Thus he continues, II, 1, 15, 'Only when a cause exists is an effect observed to exist, not when it does not exist. The non-difference of the two (cause and effect) is perceived, for instance, in an aggregate of threads, when we do not perceive the thing which we call cloth in addition to the threads, but merely threads running lengthways, and crossways. In the threads again we perceive finer threads, and in these again still finer threads, and so on. On this ground we conclude that the very finest parts which we can perceive are ultimately identical with their causes, viz. red, white, and black, these again with air, the air with ether, and, at last, the ether with Brahman which is without a second and the ultimate cause of the whole world.' Or again, when we look at a tree and ask what it is, when we see through its leaves and fruits, its bark and wood, and ask again what it is, the answer comes that it would be nothing if it were not Brahman, that it lives through Brahman, that it exists through Brahman, that it would not be at all but for Brahman. This is the real Pantheism of the Vedânta: and strange as it may sound to us, it would not be difficult to match it whether from our own philosophers or our poets. Even so recent a poet as Tennyson is reported to have said, 'Perhaps this earth and all that is in it—storms, mountains, cataracts, the sun and the skies, are the Almighty: in fact, such is our petty nature, we cannot see Him, but we see His shadow, as it were, a distorted shadow.' Is not this pure Vedânta? only that the Vedântists hold that a cause, by its very nature, can never become the object of perception, while what Tennyson calls the distorted shadow would come very near to the Avidyâ of *S*a*m*kara. The Veda has declared 'that what is posterior in time, i.e. the effect, has its being, previous to its actual beginning, in the nature of the cause.' And *S*a*m*kara adds that, even in cases where the continued existence of the cause (in the effect) is not perceived, as, for instance, in the case of seeds of the fig-tree from which spring sprouts and new trees, the term birth, as applied to the sprout, means only that the causal substance, viz. the seed, becomes visible by becoming a sprout through the continued accretion of similar particles, while the term death means no more than that through the secession of these particles, the cause passes again beyond the sphere of visibility.

This problem of cause and effect in connection with the problem of Brahman and the world was no doubt beset with difficulties in the eyes of the Vedântists. If they turned to the Veda, particularly to the Upanishads, there were ever so many passages declaring that Brahman is one and unchangeable, while in other passages the same Brahman is called the Creator, and from him, and not, as the Sâ*m*khyas hold, from a second non-intelligent power, called Prak*ri*ti, the creation, sustentation, and reabsorption of the world are said to proceed. If it be asked how two such opinions can be reconciled, *S*a*m*kara answers: 'Belonging to the Self, as it were, of the omniscient Lord, there are names and forms (Nâmarûpa).' These correspond very closely to the Logoi of Greek philosophy, except that, instead of being the ideas of a Divine Mind, they are the figments of Nescience, not to be defined as either real (Brahman), or as different from it. They are the germs of the entire expanse of the phenomenal world, that is, of what in *S*ruti and Sm*ri*ti is called illusion (Mâyâ), power (*S*akti), or nature (Prak*ri*ti). Different, however, from all this is the Omniscient Lord, and in support of this a number of Vedic passages may be quoted, such as 'He who is called Ether is the revealer of all forms and names; that wherein these forms and names are contained, that is Brahman' (*Kh*ând. Up. VIII, 14, 1); 'Let me evolve names and forms' (*Kh*ând. Up. VI, 3, 2); 'He, the wise one, having defined all forms and having made their names, sits speaking,' i.e. creating (Taitt. Âr. III, 12, 7); 'He who makes the one seed manifold' (*S*vet. Up. VI, 12). The Lord as creator, as Lord or Î*s*vara, depends upon the limiting conditions or the Upâdhis of name and form, and these, even in the Lord, are represented as products of Nescience, not like the Logoi, creations of a Divine Wisdom. The true Self, according to the Vedânta, is all the time free from all conditions, free from names and forms, and for the truly informed or enlightened man the whole phenomenal world is really non-existent.

To steer between all these rocks is no easy matter. Brahman, though called the material cause (Upâdâna) of the world, is himself immaterial, nay the world, of which he is the cause, is considered as unreal, while at the same time cause and effect are held to be identical in substance.

While the Vedântist is threatened by all these breakers, the Sâ*m*khya philosopher is far less imperilled. He starts with a Prak*ri*ti, a power different from Brahman, generally, though very imperfectly, translated by Nature, as the material cause of the world. Prak*ri*ti exists, as far as man is concerned, only so far as it is taken notice of by man (Purusha); and he, the Purusha, on taking notice, may therefore be called the efficient cause of the world, Prak*ri*ti itself being its material cause. Otherwise Kapila takes much the same view of the relation between cause and effect as the Vedântist. The Kârya-kâra*n*âbheda, the identity of cause and effect, is valid as much for Sâ*m*khya as for Vedânta. According to both, no real effect would be possible without the continuance of its cause. Though different in appearance or phenomenally, both are the same substantially. An effect is not something newly produced or created, it is a new manifestation only, the cause being never destroyed, but rendered invisible only. This is so characteristic a dogma of the Sâ*m*khya that this philosophy is often spoken of as the Sat-kâryavâda, the doctrine that every effect pre-exists, and is the effect of something real, while the Asat-kâryavâda is peculiar to Nyâya and Vai*s*eshika, and strongly supported by the Buddhists. Whether this doctrine of the identity of cause and effect was first proclaimed by Kapila or by Bâdarâya*n*a is almost impossible to settle. Professor Garbe[1], who claims it for Kapila, may be right in supposing that it would be a more natural theorem for a follower of the Sâ*m*khya than of the Vedânta, but this could never be used as an argument that the Sâ*m*khya-philosophy is older in its entirety than the Vedânta. *S*a*m*kara himself certainly gives us the impression that with him the recognition of the identity of cause and effect came first, and afterwards its religious application, the identity of Brahman and the world. For he says (II, 1, 20), 'Thus the non-difference of the effect from the cause is to be conceived. And *therefore*, as the whole world is an effect of Brahman, and non-different from it, the promise is fulfilled.' It is curious that Kapila seems, almost in so many words, to guard against what is known to us as Hume's view of causality. For in Sûtra I, 4, 1, he says, 'If it were only priority, there would be no law or hold (Niyama) between cause and effect.'

The Sat-kâryavâda, which might be compared with

[1] Sâ*m*khya-Philosophie, p. 232.

Herbart's *Selbsterhaltung des Realen*, is often illustrated by the very popular simile of the rope which is mistaken for a snake, but which, even in its mistaken character, has the very real effect of frightening those who step on it. There is more in this often-quoted simile than at first sight appears. It is meant to show that as the rope is to the snake, so Brahman is to the world. There is no idea of claiming for the rope a real change into a snake, and in the same way no real change can be claimed for Brahman, when perceived as the world. Brahman presents itself as the world, and apart from Brahman the world would be simply nothing. If, therefore, Brahman is called the material cause of the world, this is not meant in the sense in which the clay is the material cause of a jar. Even the apparent and illusory existence of a material world requires a real substratum, which is Brahman, just as the appearance of the snake in the simile requires the real substratum of a rope. If we once see this clearly, we shall also see that Nescience may quite as well be called the material cause of the world as Brahman, the fact being that, strictly speaking, there is with the Vedântists no matter at all, in our sense of the word.

### Dreaming and Waking.

There is, however, in the Vedânta, as well as in many other systems of philosophy, a certain ambiguity as to what is meant by material and real. One would have thought that philosophers, who look upon everything as the result of Avidyâ or Nescience, would have denied all reality in the highest sense to everything except Brahman. And so in a certain sense they do. But besides the concession to which we alluded before, that for practical purposes (Vyavahârârtham) things may be treated as real, whatever we may think of them in our heart of hearts, a concession, by-the-by, which even Berkeley and Kant would readily have allowed, there is another important argument. It is clearly directed against Buddhist philosophers who, carrying the Vedânta principle to its extreme consequences, held that everything is empty and unreal, and that all we have and know are our perceptions only. This is called the *S*ûnyavâda (doctrine of emptiness or vanity) or Vidyâmâtra (knowledge only). Although some Vedântists have been credited with holding the same opinion, and have actually been called Cryptobuddhists in consequence, *S*a*m*kara himself argues most strongly against this extreme idealism. He not only allows the reality of the objective world for practical purposes (Vyavahârârtham), but he enters on a full argument against the nihilism of the Buddhists. These maintain that perception in dreams is of the same kind as all other perception, and that the admission of the existence of external things is therefore unnecessary. No, says *S*a*m*kara, there is a difference between perceiving viands and perceiving the satisfaction arising from eating them. He holds, therefore, that in perceiving anything we not only perceive our perceptions, but perceive something not ourselves, and not our perceptions. He also points out that there is this difference between dreaming and waking, that dreams on awaking are found to be unreal. Dreams at night are contradicted by full daylight, but perceptions in full daylight are not contradicted by dreams. When the

Buddhist replies that, in spite of that, we never can be said to perceive anything but perceptions, the Vedântist answers that, though we perceive perceptions only, these perceptions are always perceived as perceptions of something. And if the Buddhists answer that these perceptions are illusive only, that they are perceptions of things *as if* they were without us, the Vedântist asks What is meant by that 'without us,' to which all things perceived by us are referred? If our perceptions conform to anything without us, the existence of such perceived objects is *ipso facto* admitted. No one would say that perception and what is perceived are identical; they stand to each other in the relation of instrument and effect, just as when we speak of an impression, we admit something that impresses as well as something that is impressed.

This must suffice to show what the Vedântists thought of the difference between the real and the phenomenal, and what was the meaning they attached to Avidyâ by which not only the individual Egos, but the whole phenomenal world exists or seems to exist. Creation is not real in the highest sense in which Brahman is real, but it is real in so far as it is phenomenal, for nothing can be phenomenal except as the phenomenon of something that is real. No wonder that, with all these ambiguities about the phenomenally real and the really real, different schools even in India should have differed in their views about Avidyâ, and that European scholars also should have failed to form a clear idea of that creative Nescience of which we can neither say that it is or that it is not. Avidyâ, like all other words, has had a history. In the Upanishads it is often used in the simple sense of ignorance, and opposed to Vidyâ, knowledge. Both are in that sense simply subjective. Thus we read, *Kh*ând. Up. I, 1, 10: 'Both perform the sacrificial act, he who knows and he who does not know. But there is a difference between Vidyâ (knowledge) and Avidyâ (nescience). For what is performed with Vidyâ, with faith, and with the Upanishad, that is more efficacious.' Or again, B*ri*h. Âr. Up. IV, 3, 20: 'If he feels in a dream as if he were murdered, then, in his ignorance, he takes that to be real whatever he fears, when awake.' Here we see that it is ignorance alone which imparts a false character of reality to the visions of a dream. In the same Upanishad, IV, 4, 3, a man, when dying, is said to shake off his body and his Avidyâ. We are right therefore, I believe, if historically we trace the concept of Avidyâ back to the subjective ignorance of the individual, just as we saw that the higher concept of the Self, though in the end identical with Brahman, arose from that of the individual personal Self, when as yet not free from the limits of the Ego. In some of the later Upanishads this Nescience or Ignorance assumes a more independent character and even a new name, viz. Mâyâ. It is then no longer the Nescience of the individual, but the result of that universal Nescience, which is the cause of what we should call the phenomenal world. Thus we read in the *S*vet. Up. IV, 10: 'Know Prak*ri*ti (nature) as Mâyâ (magic), and the great Lord as the Mâyin (magician).' Though this is not pure Vedânta, it shows us, at all events, the way by which the ignorance of the individual became the cause of what we call objective reality, and led, at the same time, to the admission of an active and creative Lord, the personal Brahmâ or Îsvara; how Avidyâ in fact became a *S*akti or *potentia*, somehow or other related to Brahman itself.

But before there arises this Mâyâ of objective nature, belonging as it were to Brahman himself, there was the Mâyâ of the internal or subjective world. This was originally the only Mâyâ, and, deceived by that Mâyâ or Avidyâ, the Âtman, or pure Self, was covered up (Upâhita) or blinded, or conditioned by the so-called Upâdhis, the conditions or impositions, if we may say so, in both senses. There is here again a certain ambiguity, the Upâdhis being caused by primeval Avidyâ, and, from another point of view, Avidyâ being caused in the individual soul (*G*îvâtman) by the Upâdhis. These Upâdhis are:—

1. The Mukhyaprâ*n*a, the vital spirit (unconscious);

2. the Manas, the central organ of perception, ready to receive what is conveyed to it by the separate senses, and to react on them by will, Manas being that which, as we say, perceives, feels, thinks and wills;

3. the Indriyas, the five senses, both afferent and efferent. The five afferent (Upalabdhi) senses are the senses of hearing, touch, sight, taste, scent. The five efferent or acting senses (Adhyavasâya[1]) are the senses of speaking, grasping, going, evacuating and generating;

4. the material organic body.

[1] Adhyavasâyo buddhi*h*, Sâ*m*khya-Sûtras II, 13.

To these is sometimes added—

5. The objective environment, or the objects or meanings of the senses (Artha).

All these are not the Âtman, and it is only through Avidyâ that the Âtman has become identified with them.

That there is in man something that can be called Âtman or Self requires no proof, but if a proof were wanted it would be found in the fact that no one can say, 'I am not' (I being the disguised Âtman), for he who would say so, would himself be not, or would not be. The question then is What is really I or what is there real behind the I. It cannot be the body as influenced by our objective environment, for that body is perishable; it cannot be the Indriyas or the Manas or the Mukhyaprâ*n*a, for all these have a beginning, a growth, and therefore an end. All these, called the Upâdhis, conditions, are to be treated as Not-self; and if it be asked why they should ever have been treated as Self, the only possible answer is that it was through Nescience or Avidyâ, but through a Nescience that is not only casual or individual, but universal. What in our common language we call the Ego or Aha*m*kâra is but a product of the Manas and quite as unsubstantial in reality as the Manas itself, the senses and the whole body.

We can understand how this startling idealism or monism—for it is not nihilism, though our philosophy has no better name for it—led to two distinct, yet closely united views of the world. All that we should call phenomenal, comprehending the phenomena of our inward as well as of our outward experience, was unreal; but, as the phenomenal was considered impossible without the noumenal, that is, without the real Brahman, it was in that sense real also, that is, it exists, and can only exist, with Brahman behind it. And this led to the admission by the strict Advaitists or Monists of two kinds of knowledge, well known under the names of Aparâ, the lower, and Parâ, the higher knowledge.

### The Higher and the Lower Knowledge.

The higher knowledge consists in the distinction and thereby the freedom of the Self (Âtman) from all its Upâdhis, and this not for this life only, but for all eternity. This is the true Moksha or freedom which implies knowledge of the identity of the Âtman with Brahman, and deliverance from birth and rebirth in the constant evolution (Sa*m*sâra) of the world. The lower knowledge is likewise founded on the Veda, but chiefly on its work-portion (Karmakâ*nd*a), and teaches, not how Brahman is to be known, but how it or he is to be worshipped in its or his phenomenal state, that is, as a personal Lord and Creator, or even under the name of any individual deity. This worship (Upâsanâ) being enjoined in many parts of the Veda, is recognised as obligatory on all who have not yet reached the highest knowledge. These are even allowed the comfort that, in worshipping a personal god, they are really worshipping Brahman, the true Godhead, though in its phenomenal aspect only, and they are promised, as a reward of their worship, happiness on earth and in heaven, nay by way of preparation, a slow advance (Kramamukti) towards complete Moksha or freedom.

In this sense it has been truly said that *S*a*m*kara

did not attack or destroy idolatry, though with him it was always symbolism rather than idolatry. On this point which has given rise to much controversy among the Hindus themselves, some appealing to *Samkara*'s contempt of all ritualism and Karman, others to his defence of a worship of the popular gods, I may quote the words of a living Vedântist, Divyadás Datta, in his Lecture on Vedântism, p. 12. 'It is certain,' he says, 'that *Samkara* was opposed to the abuse of ritualism, and though he did not cut off all connection with idolatry, he tried to introduce the right spirit of idolatry. Idolatry in the sense of religious symbolism—and I believe the most orthodox Hindus would take no other view—cannot be open to objection. Symbolism there must be, whether in words or things. Verbal symbols appeal to the ear, and the symbols of things to the eye, and that is all the difference between them. Verbal symbolism is language. Who would object to the use of language in religion? But if the one is allowed, why should not also the other? To my mind, idolatry, apart from its attendant corruptions, is a religious algebra. And if verbal symbols, without the spirit or in a corrupted spirit, are not objectionable, [but are they not ?] so, and to the same extent, formal symbols, or stocks and stones also are unobjectionable. At one stage of its growth, idolatry is a necessity of our nature. The tender seed of a religious spirit requires to be carefully preserved in a soft coating of symbols, till it has acquired the strength to resist the nipping frost of worldliness and scepticism. . . . When the religious spirit is mature, symbols are either given up, or suffered to remain from their harmlessness. . . .

*S*a*m*kara did bow to idols, sometimes as symbols of the great Infinite, sometimes as symbols of lower orders of beings in whom he believed. . . . These lower orders of divine beings, Brahmâ, Vish*n*u, Indra, Yama, &c., in whom he believed, are phenomenal, and subject to creation and dissolution as much as ourselves.' *S*a*m*kara himself expresses this opinion very clearly when (I, 3, 28) he says: 'The gods (or deities) must be admitted to be corporeal, and though by their divine powers they can, at one and the same time, partake of oblations offered at numerous sacrifices, they are still, like ourselves, subject to birth and death.'

If *S*a*m*kara did not claim full freedom or Moksha for himself, he did so, as he says, for the sake of others. 'If I,' he says, 'had not walked without remission in the path of works, others would not have followed my steps, O Lord!'

### Is Virtue Essential to Moksha?

Another question which has been hotly contested both in India and in Europe is whether Moksha can be the result of knowledge only, or whether it requires a fulfilment of moral duties also[1]. Though, as far as I understand *S*a*m*kara, knowledge alone can in the end lead to Moksha, virtue is certainly presupposed. It is the same question which meets us with regard to the Buddhist Nirvâ*n*a. This also was in the beginning the result and the reward of moral virtue, of the restraint of passions and of perfect tranquillity of soul, such as we find it described, for

[1] See Moksha or the Vedântic Release, by Divyadâs Datta, Journal of the R. A. S., vol. xx, part 4.

instance, in the Dhammapada; but it soon assumed a different character, as representing freedom from all bondage and illusion, amounting to a denial of all reality in the objective, and likewise in the subjective world. There are a few traces left in the Upanishads, showing that virtue was considered an essential preliminary of Moksha. In the Ka*th*a Upanishad II, 1, which is generally quoted for that purpose, we read: 'The good is one thing, the pleasant another; these two having different objects chain a man. It is well with him, if he clings to the good; but he who chooses the pleasant, misses his end. The good and the pleasant approach a man; the wise goes round about them and distinguishes them. Yea, the wise prefers the good to the pleasant, but the fool chooses the pleasant through greed and avarice.' But even in this passage we are not told that virtue or self-denial by itself could secure Moksha or perfect freedom; nay, if we only read a few lines further, we see: 'Wide apart and leading to different points are those two, ignorance (Avidyâ) and what is known as wisdom (Vidyâ).' And Na*k*iketas is praised because he desires knowledge, and is not tempted away from it by pleasure. Still less convincing are passages taken from the Bhagavad-gîtâ, a work which was meant to present different views of Moksha. All of them, no doubt, though they do not explicitly say so, presuppose high morality on the part of the candidate, so that Ar*g*una is made to say for himself:—

> *G*ânâmi dharma*m*, na *k*a me pravr*i*tti*h*,
> *G*ânâmy adharma*m*, na *k*a me nivr*i*tti*h*,

which has been somewhat freely translated: 'For

what I would that I do not, but what I hate that do I.'

That later treatises, such as the Pañkadasî, should lay great stress on the religious and moral side of Moksha is quite compatible with what has been maintained before, that Moksha cannot be achieved by sacrifices or by moral conduct, but in the end by knowledge only. Hence a prayer such as,—

'May such unchanging love as foolish people feel for earthly pleasures never cease in my heart when I call upon Thee!'

—may well be uttered by worshippers of Brahmâ or Îsvara, but not by the true Mumukshu, who is yearning for Brahman and true Moksha.

Even the prayer from the Brihad-âranyaka (I, 3, 28)—

'Lead me from the unreal to the real! Lead me from darkness to light! Lead me from death to immortality!'

—refers to the lower knowledge only, and has for its reward another world, that is, the heaven world, which will also pass away.

It would not be difficult, no doubt, to produce passages which declare that a sinful man cannot obtain Moksha, but that is very different from saying that Moksha can be obtained by mere abstaining from sin. Good works, even merely ceremonial works, if performed from pure motives and without any hope of rewards, form an excellent preparation for reaching that highest knowledge which it is the final aim of the Vedânta to impart. And thus we read: 'Brâhmanas seek to know Him by the study of the Veda, by sacrifices, by charitable gifts' (Brih. Up. IV, 4, 22).

But when the knowledge of the highest Brahman has once been reached or is within reach, all works, whether good or bad, fall away. 'The fetter of the heart is broken, all doubts are solved, extinguished are all his works, when He has been beheld who is both high and low' (Mu*n*d. Up. II, 2, 8).

Hence, to imagine that true Moksha can be obtained by moral conduct alone is a mistake, while there are passages in the Upanishads to show that some Vedântists taught that a man who had reached Brahman and the highest knowledge, was even in this life above the distinction of good and evil, that is, could do nothing that he considered good and nothing that he considered evil. Dangerous as this principle seems to be, that whosoever knows Brahman cannot sin, it is hardly more dangerous, if properly understood, than the saying of St. John (Ep. I, v. 68), that whosoever is born of God, sinneth not.

### The Two Brahmans.

It sometimes seems as if *S*a*m*kara and Bâdarâya*n*a had actually admitted not only two kinds of knowledge, but two Brahmans also, Sagu*n*am and Nirgu*n*am, with or without qualities, but this would again apply to a state of Nescience or Avidyâ only; and it is in this sense alone that Brahman also may be said to be affected by Avidyâ, nay to be produced by Avidyâ, not by the Avidyâ of single individuals, but by an Avidyâ inherent in sentient nature. The true Brahman, however, remains always Nirgu*n*am or unqualified, whatever we may think about him; and as, with regard to Brahman, to be conceived and to be is the same thing, so likewise, so far as we are concerned,

Brahman is conceived by us and becomes to us qualified, active, creative and personal through the deception of the same universal and inevitable Avidyâ. In the same way the creation of the world and of man is not the work of Brahman, but the result of Avidyâ and of man while under her sway. This ambiguity runs through the whole of the Vedânta, at least according to the interpretation of *S*a*m*kara.

It will be seen how small a step it was from this view to another which looked upon Brahman itself as affected by Avidyâ, nay which changed this Avidyâ into a *S*akti or *potentia* of Brahman, thus lowering him, not raising him, to the character of an active creator. In full reality Brahman is as little affected by qualities as our true Self is by Upâdhis (conditions), but the same Nescience which clouds us for a time, clouds *ipso facto* Brahman also, Âtman (*G*îvâtman) and Brahman being substantially one. If the qualified Brahman makes us, we, the qualified Âtman, make Brahman, as our maker. Only we must never forget that all this is illusion, so that in truth we can predicate nothing of Brahman but Na, na, i.e. No, no; he is not this, he is not that. He is, that is all we can say, and is more than everything else. In that sense Brahman may be called both Sat and Asat, being and not being, being in the highest sense, not being, as different from all that the world calls being or true. If in the later Upanishads Brahman is called Sa*k*-*k*id-ânanda, 'being, perceiving, and blessed,' then these three predicates are in reality but one, for he or it could not be without perceiving itself (*esse est percipere*), and he or it could not perceive himself or itself except as independent, perfect, unaffected and untrammelled by anything else (Advitîya). Having no qualities, this highest Brahman cannot of course be known by predicates. It is subjective, and not liable to any objective attributes. If it knows, it can only know itself, like the sun that is not lighted, but lights itself. Our knowledge of Brahman also can only be consciousness of Brahman as our own subjective Âtman or Self.

It seems only a concession to the prejudices, or let us say, the convictions of the people of India, that an ecstatic perception of Brahman was allowed as now and then possible in a state of trance, such as the Yogins practised in ancient, and even in modern times, though, strictly speaking, this perception also could only be a perception of the Âtman as identical with Brahman. The fatal mistake which interpreters of the Vedânta-philosophy both in India and Europe have made is to represent this absorption or recovery (Sa*m*râdhanam, accomplishment) as an *approach* of the individual soul towards God. There can be no such approach where there is identity, there can only be recovery or restitution, a return, a becoming of the soul of what it always has been, a revival of its true nature. Even Yoga, as we shall see, did not mean technically union, nor Yogin a man united with God, but Yoga is effort towards Nirodha or suppression of *K*itta (the activity of thought) (see Yoga-Sûtras I, 2).

We shall thus understand the distinction which the Vedântists and other Indian philosophers also make between the Brahman, τὸ ὄντως ὄν, and the Brahman as Îsvara, the personal God, worshipped under different names, as creator, preserver, and dissolver of the universe. This Î*s*vara exists, just as everything else exists, as phenomenally only, not as absolutely real. Most important acts are ascribed to him, and whatever he may appear to be, he is always Brahman. When personified by the power of Avidyâ or Nescience, he rules the world, though it is a phenomenal world, and determines, though he does not cause, rewards and punishments. These are produced directly by the acts themselves. But it is He through whose grace deeds are followed by rewards, and man at last obtains true knowledge and Mukti, though this Mukti involves by necessity the disappearance of Îsvara as a merely phenomenal god.

It must be clear to any one who has once mastered the framework of the true Vedânta-philosophy, as I have here tried to explain it, that there is really but little room in it for psychology or kosmology, nay even for ethics. The soul and the world both belong to the realm of things which are not real, and have little if anything to do with the true Vedânta in its highest and truest form. This consists in the complete surrender of all we are and know. It rests chiefly on the tremendous synthesis of subject and object, the identification of cause and effect, of the I and the It. This constitutes the unique character of the Vedânta, unique as compared with every other philosophy of the world which has not been influenced by it, directly or indirectly. If we have once grasped that synthesis, we know the Vedânta. All its other teaching flows naturally from this one fundamental doctrine; and though its carefully thought out and worked out details are full of interest, they contain no thoughts, so entirely new at the time when they were uttered, as this identity of subject and object, or this complete absorption of the object by this subject.

### Philosophy and Religion.

It is interesting to see how this very bold philosophy of the Vedânta was always not only tolerated, but encouraged and patronised by religion and by its recognised representatives. Nor did the Vedânta as a philosophy interfere with popular religion; on the contrary, it accepted all that is taught about the gods in the hymns and in the Brâhma*n*as, and recommended a number of sacrificial and ceremonial acts as resting on the authority of these hymns and Brâhma*n*as. They were even considered as a necessary preliminary to higher knowledge. The creation of the world, though not the making of it, was accepted as an emanation from Brahman, to be followed in great periods by a taking back of it into Brahman. The individual souls also were supposed, at the end of each Kalpa, to be drawn back into Brahman, but, unless entirely liberated, to break forth again and again at the beginning of every new Kalpa.

### Karman.

The individual souls, so far as they can claim any reality, date, we are told, from all eternity, and not from the day of their birth on earth. They are clothed in their Upâdhis (conditions) according to the merit or demerit which they have acquired by their former, though long-forgotten, acts. Here we perceive the principal moral element in the ancient Vedânta, so far as it is meant for practical life; and this doctrine of Karman or deed, to which we alluded before, has remained to the present day, and has leavened the whole of India, whether it was under the sway of Brâhmans or of Buddhists. The whole world, such as it is, is the result of acts; the character and fate of each man are the result of his acts in this or in a former life, possibly also of the acts of others. This is with them the solution of what we venture to call the injustice of God. It is their *Théodicée.* "A man who suffers and suffers, as we say, unjustly, seems to them but paying off a debt or laying up capital for another life." A man who enjoys health and wealth is made to feel that he is spending more than he has earned, and that he has therefore to make up his debt by new efforts. It cannot be by a Divine caprice that one man is born deaf or dumb or blind, another strong and healthy. It can be the result of former acts only, whether, in this life, the doer of them is aware of them or not. It is not even necessarily a punishment, it may be a reward in disguise. It might seem sometimes as if Avidyâ too, which is answerable for the whole of this phenomenal world, had to be taken as the result of acts far back before the beginning of all things. But this is never clearly stated. On the contrary, this primeval Avidyâ is left unexplained, it is not to be accounted for as little as Brahman can be accounted for. Like Brahman it has to be accepted as existent; but it differs from Brahman in so far as it can be destroyed by Vidyâ, which is the eternal life-spring of Brahman. The merit which can be acquired by man even in this state of Avidyâ is such that he may rise even to the status of a god, though for a time only, for at the end of a Kalpa even gods like Indra and the rest have to begin their career afresh. In fact it might be said with some truth that Avidyâ is the cause of everything, except of Brahman; but that the cause of that primeval Avidyâ is beyond our powers of conception.

### Brahman is Everything.

These powers of conception are real indeed for all practical purposes, but in the highest sense they too are phenomenal only. They too are but Nâma-rûpa, name and form; and the reality that lies behind them, the Âtman that receives them, is Brahman and nothing else. This might become clearer if we took Brahman for the Kantian *Ding an sich*, remembering only that, according to the Kantian philosophy, the Rûpa, the forms of intuition and the categories of thought, though subjective, are accepted as true, while the Vedânta treats them also as the result of Nescience, though true for all practical purposes in this phenomenal life. In this sense the Vedânta is more sceptical or critical than even Kant's critical philosophy, though the two agree with each other again when we remember that Kant also denies the validity of these forms of perception and thought when applied to transcendent subjects. According to Kant it is man who creates the world, as far as its form (Nâmarûpa) is concerned; according to the Vedânta this kind of creation is due to Avidyâ. And strange as it may sound to apply that name of Avidyâ to Kant's intuitions of sense and his categories of the understanding, there is a common element in them, though hidden under different names. It would be natural to suppose that this Âtman within had been taken as a part of Brahman, or as a modification of Brahman: but no. According to *Samkara* the world is, as

I tried to show [1] on a former occasion, the whole of Brahman in all its integrity, and not a part only; only, owing to Avidyâ, wrongly conceived and individualised. Here we have in fact the Holenmerian theory of Plotinus and of Dr. Henry More, anticipated in India. If the Âtman within seems limited like the Brahman when seen in the objective world, this is once more due to Avidyâ. Brahman ought to be omnipresent, omniscient, and omnipotent; though we know but too well that in ourselves it is very far from all this.

### The Sthûla- and Sûkshma-*s*arîra.

These are the conditions or Upâdhis which consist of Manas, mind, Indriyas, senses, Prâ*n*as, vital spirits, and the *S*arîra, body, as determined by the outward world. This Vedântic arrangement of our organic structure and our mental organisation is curious. but it seems to have been more or less the common property of all Indian philosophers, and supplied by the common language of the people. What is peculiar in it is the admission of a central organ, receiving and arranging what has been conveyed to it by the separate organs of sense. We have no word corresponding to it, though with proper limitations we may continue to translate it by *mens* or mind. It would represent perception as uniting and arranging the great mass of sensations, but it includes besides Upalabdhi, perception, Adhyavasâya, determination, also, so far as it depends on a previous interaction of percepts. Hence a man is said to see by the mind (Manas, νοῦς), but he may

[1] Theosophy, p. 280.

also be said to decide and act by the mind (Manas). All this may seem very crude, leaving particularly the question of the change of mere sensations into percepts (*Vorstellungen*), a subject so carefully elaborated by modern philosophers, and of percepts into concepts, unapproached and unexplained. Here the philosophy of Herbart would supply what is wanted. He too, being opposed to the admission of various mental faculties, is satisfied with one, the Manas, and tries to explain all psychical phenomena whatever as the result of the action and interaction of elementary *Vorstellungen* (ideas or presentations).

By the side of the vital spirit, the Mukhya Prâ*n*a, we find a fivefold division into Prâ*n*a, Upâna, Vyâna, Samâna, and Udâna, meaning originally forth-, off-, through-, with-, and out-breathing, but afterwards defined differently and without much reference to any physiological data. This also is a doctrine common to most systems of Indian philosophy, though it is difficult to see by what physiological observations it could have been suggested.

What is more interesting is the distinction between the Sthûla- and Sûkshma-sarîra, the coarse and the fine body, the former the visible outward body; the latter invisible and consisting of Mukhya Prâ*n*a, vital spirit, Manas, mind, and Indriyas, organs of sense. This body is supposed to remain after death, while the outer body is dissolved into its material elements. The thin or subtle body, though transparent or invisible, is nevertheless accepted as material; and it is this Sûkshma-*s*arîra which is supposed to migrate after death from world to world, but, for the most part, in an unconscious state. It is not like a human body with arms and legs.

### The Four States.

Here again we come across an original idea of Indian philosophy, the doctrine of the four states, the state of being awake, the state of dreaming, the state of deep and dreamless sleep, to which is added as the fourth, the state of death. In the first state the Âtman is supposed to be perceiving and acting by means of the Manas and the Indriyas. In the second the Indriyas cease to act, but the Manas remains active, and the Âtman, joined to the Manas, moves through the veins of the body and sees dreams made out of the remnants of former impressions (Vâsanâs). The third state arises from a complete separation of Âtman from Manas and Indriyas. While these are absorbed in the vital spirit, which remains in full activity, the Âtman in the heart is supposed to have for a time become one with Brahman, but to return unchanged at the time of awakening. In the fourth or disembodied state the Âtman with the Sûkshma-sarîra is supposed to escape from the heart through a vein in the head or through the hundred veins of the body, and then to take, according to merit and knowledge, different paths into the next life.

### Eschatology.

Such fancies seem strange in systems of philosophy like the Vedânta; and, with the full recognition of the limits of human knowledge, we can hardly understand how Vedântists accepted this account of the Sûkshma-sarîra, the circumstances attending the departure of the soul, in fact, a complete Eschatology, simply on the authority of the Veda. It is taken over from the Upanishads, and that may be the excuse for it. Vedântists had once for all bound themselves to accept the Upanishads as revealed truth, and the usual result followed. But we should see clearly that, while much may be taken over from the Veda as due to Avidyâ, we are here really moving in an Avidyâ within that Avidyâ. For practical purposes Avidyâ may often be called common sense, under its well-understood limitations, or the wisdom of the world. But these dreams about the details of a future life are a mere phantasmagoria. They cannot even be treated as Naisargika, or inevitable. They are simply Mithyâ*g*ñâna, fanciful or false knowledge, if not that which is commonly illustrated by the son of a barren woman—that is, a self-contradictory statement—that kind at least which is unsupported by any evidence, such as the horn of a hare. This is really a weakness that runs through the whole of the Vedânta, and cannot be helped. After the supreme and superhuman authority of the Word or of the Veda had once been recognised, a great portion of the sacred traditions of the Vedic age, incorporated as they are in the hymns, the Brâhma*n*as, and the Upanishads, had to be accepted with the rest, though accepted as part of the Aparâ Vidyâ, the lower knowledge only. All the sacrificial rules, nay the very conception of a sacrifice, had no place in the Parâ Vidyâ, or the highest knowledge, because they involved an actor and an enjoyer of the fruits of such acts, and the truly enlightened man cannot be either an actor or an enjoyer[1]. However, as a preparation, as a means of subduing the passions

---

[1] See *Sam*kara's Introduction to the Aitareya Upanishad.

and purifying the mind by drawing it away from the low and vulgar interests of life, all such commandments, together with the promises of rewards vouchsafed to them, might perhaps have been tolerated. But when we come to a full description of the stations on the road by which the subtle body is supposed to travel from the veins of this body to the very steps of the golden throne of the Lower Brahman, we wonder at the long suffering of the true philosopher who has learnt that the true and highest knowledge of the Vedânta removes in the twinkling of an eye (Âpâtata*h*) the veil that in this life seems to separate Âtman from Brahman. As these eschatological dreams have been included in the Vedânta system, they had to be mentioned here, though they are better studied in the pages of the Upanishads.

We are told there that, in the case of persons who have fulfilled their religious or sacrificial duties and have lived a good life, but have not yet reached the highest knowledge, the subtle body in which the Âtman is clothed migrates, carried along by the Udâna through the Mûrdhanya Nâ*d*î, the capital vein, following either the path of the fathers (Pit*ri*yâ*n*a) or the path of the gods (Devayâna). The former is meant for good people, the latter for those who are good and have already reached the lower, if not the highest knowledge. The former leads on to smoke, night, the waning moon, the waning year, the world of the fathers, the ether, and lastly the moon. In the moon the departed souls remain for a time enjoying the rewards of their good deeds, in company with the Pit*ri*s, and then descend again, supported by the remnant of unrewarded merit due to their good works, to the ether, wind, smoke, cloud, rain, and plants. From the plants springs seed which, when matured in the womb, begins a new life on earth in such a station as the rest of his former deeds (Anusaya), *Anlage*, may warrant. As this is, as far as I know, the earliest allusion to metempsychosis or *Seelenwanderung*, it may be of interest to see in what sense *S*am*k*ara in his commentary on Sûtra III, 1, 22 took it [1]:—

'It has been explained,' he says, 'that the souls of those who perform sacrifices, &c., after having reached the moon, dwell there as long as their works last, and then redescend with a remainder of their good works. We now have to inquire into the mode of that descent. On this point the Veda makes the following statement: "They return again the way they came to the ether, from the ether to the air (wind). Then the sacrificer having become air becomes smoke, having become smoke he becomes mist, having become mist he becomes a cloud, having become a cloud he falls down as rain." Here a doubt arises whether the descending souls pass over into a state of identity (Sâbhâvyam) with ether, &c., or into a state of similarity (Sâmyam) only. The Pûrvapakshin (opponent) maintains that the state is one of identity, because this is directly stated by the text. Otherwise there would take place what is called indication only (Laksha*n*â, i.e. secondary application of a word), and whenever the doubt lies between a directly expressed and a merely indicated meaning, the former is to be preferred. Thus the following words also, "Having become air

---

[1] S.B.E., vol. xxxvii, Thibaut's translation.

he becomes smoke," &c., are appropriate only if the soul be understood to identify itself with them. Hence it follows that the souls (of the departed) become really identical with ether. To this we (*Samkara*) reply that they only pass into a state of similarity to ether, &c. When the body, consisting of water which the soul had assumed in the sphere of the moon for the purpose of enjoyment, dissolves at the time when that enjoyment comes to an end, then it becomes subtle like ether, passes thereupon into the power of the air, and then gets mixed with smoke, &c. This is the meaning of the clauses, "They return as they came to the ether, from the ether to the air," &c. How is this known to be the meaning? Because thus only is it possible. For it is not possible that one thing should become another in the literal sense of the word. If, moreover, the souls became identified with ether, they could no longer descend through the air. And as connection with the ether is, on account of its all-pervadingness, eternal, no other connection (of the souls) with it can here be meant, but their entering into a state of similarity to it. In cases where it is impossible to accept the literal meaning of the text, it is quite proper to assume the meaning which is merely indicated. For these reasons the souls' becoming ether, &c., has to be taken in the secondary sense of their passing into a state of similarity to ether, and so on.'

We see from this that *Samkara* believed in a similarity only, an outward and temporary similarity between the departed (in its Sûkshma-*s*arîra) and the ether, air, mist, cloud, and rain; and it is important to observe how, in doing so, he violently twisted the natural meaning of Sâbhâvya, the word used in the Sûtras, rather than altering a word of the Sûtra, and replacing Sâbhâvyam by Sâmyam.

A similar difficulty arises again when it has to be determined whether the departed, in his further descent, actually becomes a plant, such as rice, corn, sesamum, beans, &c., or becomes merely connected with them. *Samkara* decides strongly in favour of the latter view, though here again the actual words of the Sûtra have certainly to be twisted by him; nay, though *Samkara* himself has to admit that other people may really, on account of their bad deeds, sink so low as to become plants. He only denies this with reference to the departed who, on account of their pious works, have already reached the moon, and are after that redescending upon earth.

Lastly, if it is said that the plant, when eaten, becomes a progenitor, this also, according to *Samkara*, can only mean that it is joined with a progenitor. For the progenitor must exist long before he eats the rice or the beans, and is able to beget a child. Anyhow, the child when begotten is the soul that had ascended to and descended from the moon, and is born again according to his former works.

I must confess that, though the Vedântists may be bound by *Samkara*'s interpretation, it seems to me as if the author of the Sûtras himself had taken a different view, and had looked throughout on ether, air, mist, cloud, rain, plants as the habitat, though the temporary habitat only, of the departed in their subtle body[1].

---

[1] See Vish*n*u Dh. *S.* XLIII, 45.

Little is said in the Upanishads of those who, owing to their evil deeds, do not even rise to the moon and descend again. But Bâdarâyana tries to make it clear that the Upanishads know of a third class of beings (III, 1, 12) who reap the fruits of their evil actions in Samyamana (abode of Yama) and then ascend to earth again. Theirs is the third place alluded to in the *Kh*ând. Upanishad V, 10, 8.

But while evil doers are thus punished in different hells, as mentioned in the Purânas, and while pious people are fully rewarded in the moon and then return again to the earth, those who have been pious and have also reached at least the lower knowledge of Brahman follow a different road. After leaving the body, they enter the flame, the day, the waxing moon, the waxing year (northern precession), the year, the world of the Devas, the world of Vâyu, air, the sun, the moon, and then lightning; but all these, we are told, are not abodes for the soul, but guides only who, when the departed has reached the lightning, hand him over to a person who is said to be not-a-man. This person conducts him to the world of Varuna, then to that of Indra, and lastly to that of Pragâpati or the qualified Brahmâ. Here the souls are supposed to remain till they realise true knowledge or the Samyagdarsana, which does not mean universal, but thorough and complete knowledge, that knowledge which, if obtained on earth, at once frees a man from all illusion. Finally the souls, when fully released, share in all the powers of Brahman except those of creating and ruling the universe. They are not supposed ever to return to the world of Samsâra (IV, 4, 17).

All this is hardly to be called philosophy, neither

do the different descriptions of the road on which the souls of the pious are supposed to wander towards Brahmâ, and which naturally vary according to different schools, help us much towards a real insight into the Vedânta. But it would have been unfair to leave out what, though childish, is a characteristic feature of the Vedânta-philosophy, and must be judged from a purely historical point of view.

### Freedom in this Life.

What is of importance to remember in these ancient fancies is that the enlightened man may become free or obtain Mukti even in this life (*Gîvanmukti* [1]). This is indeed the real object of the Vedânta-philosophy, to overcome all Nescience, to become once more what the Âtman always has been, namely Brahman, and then to wait till death removes the last Upâdhis or fetters, which, though they fetter the mind no longer, remain like broken chains hanging heavy on the mortal body. The Âtman, having recovered its Brahmahood, is even in this life so free from the body that it feels no longer any pain, and cannot do anything, whether good or bad. This has been always laid hold of as the most dangerous doctrine of Vedântism, and no doubt it may be both misunderstood and misapplied. But in the beginning it meant no more than that the Âtman, which is above the distinctions of subject and object, of past and present, of cause and effect, is also by necessity above the distinction of good and evil. This never was intended as freedom in the sense of licence, but as freedom that can

[1] Vedânta-Sûtras III, 3, 28.

neither lapse into sinful acts nor claim any merit for good acts, being at rest and blessed in itself and in Brahman.

It is hardly necessary to say or to prove that the Vedânta-philosophy, even in its popular form, holds out no encouragement to vice. Far from it. No one can even approach it who has not previously passed through a course of discipline, whether as a student (Brahma*k*ârin) or as a householder (G*ri*-hastha). In order to make this quite clear, it may be useful to add a few verses from one of the many popular works intended to teach Vedânta to the masses. It is called the Mohamudgara, the Hammer of Folly, and is ascribed to *S*a*m*kara. Though not strictly philosophical, it may serve at least to show the state of mind in which the true Vedântist is meant to maintain himself. It was carefully edited with Bengali, Hindi and English translations by Durga Das Ray, and published at Darjeeling in 1888.

'Fool! give up thy thirst for wealth, banish all desires from thy heart. Let thy mind be satisfied with what is gained by thy Karman.

Who is thy wife and who is thy son? Curious are the ways of this world. "Who art thou? Whence didst thou come? Ponder on this, O Brother."

Do not be proud of wealth, of friends, or youth. Time takes all away in a moment. Leaving all this which is full of illusion, leave quickly and enter into the place of Brahman.

Life is tremulous like a water-drop on a lotus-leaf. The company of the good, though for a moment only, is the only boat for crossing this ocean of the world.

As is birth so is death, and so is the dwelling in the mother's womb. Thus is manifest the misery of the world. How can there be satisfaction here for thee, O Man !

Day and night, morning and evening, winter and spring come and go. Time is playing, life is waning—yet the breath of hope never ceases.

The body is wrinkled, the hair grey, the mouth has become toothless, the stick in the hand shakes, yet man leaves not the anchor of hope.

To live under a tree of the house of the gods, to sleep on the earth, to put on a goat-skin, to abandon all worldly enjoyment ; when does such surrender not make happy ?

Do not trouble about enemy, friend, son, or relation, whether for war or peace. Preserve equanimity always, if you desire soon to reach the place of Vish*n*u (Vish*n*upada).

The eight great mountains, the seven oceans, Brahmâ, Indra, the Sun and the Rudras, thou, I and the whole world are nothing ; why then is there any sorrow ?

In thee, in me, and in others there dwells Vish*n*u alone, it is useless to be angry with me and impatient. See every self in Self, and give up all thought of difference.

The child is given to play, the youth delights in a beautiful damsel, an old man is absorbed in cares —no one clings to the Highest Brahman.

Consider wealth as useless, there is truly no particle of happiness in it. The rich are afraid even of their son, this is the rule established everywhere.

So long as a man can earn money, his family is kind to him. But when his body becomes infirm through old age, no man in the house asks after him.

Having given up lust, anger, avarice, and distraction, meditate on thyself, who thou art. Fools without a knowledge of Self are hidden in hell and boiled.

In these sixteen verses the whole teaching of the disciples has been told. Those in whom this does not produce understanding, who can do more for them?'

### Different Ways of Studying Philosophy.

This may not be exactly moral teaching as we understand it. But there are two ways of studying philosophy. We may study it in a critical or in a historical spirit. The critic would no doubt fasten at once on the supersession of morality in the Vedânta as an unpardonable flaw. One of the corner-stones, without which the grandest pyramid of thought must necessarily collapse, would seem to be missing in it. The historian on the other hand will be satisfied with simply measuring the pyramid or trying to scale it step by step, as far as his thoughts will carry him. He would thus understand the labour it has required in building up, and possibly discover some counteracting forces that render the absence even of a corner-stone intelligible, pardonable, and free from danger. It is surely astounding that such a system as the Vedânta should have been slowly elaborated by the indefatigable and intrepid thinkers of India thousands of years ago, a system that even now makes us feel giddy, as in mounting the last steps of the swaying spire of an ancient Gothic cathedral. None of our philosophers, not excepting Heraclitus, Plato, Kant, or Hegel, has ventured to erect such a spire, never frightened by storms or lightnings. Stone follows on stone in regular succession after once the first step has been made, after once it has been clearly seen that in the beginning there can have been but One, as there will be but One in the end, whether we call it Âtman or Brahman. We may prefer to look upon the expansion of the world in names and forms as the work of Sophia or as the realised Logos, but we cannot but admire the boldness with which the Hindu metaphysician, impressed with the miseries and evanescence of this world, could bring himself to declare even the Logos to be but the result of Avidyâ or Nescience, so that in the destruction of that Avidyâ could be recognised the highest object, and the *summum bonum* (Purushârtha) of man. We need not praise or try to imitate a Colosseum, but if we have any heart for the builders of former days we cannot help feeling that it was a colossal and stupendous effort. And this is the feeling which I cannot resist in examining the ancient Vedânta. Other philosophers have denied the reality of the world as perceived by us, but no one has ventured to deny at the same time the reality of what we call the Ego, the senses and the mind, and their inherent forms. And yet after lifting the Self above body and soul, after uniting heaven and earth, God and man, Brahman and Âtman, these Vedânta philosophers have destroyed nothing in the life of the phenomenal beings who have to act and to fulfil their duties in this phenomenal world. On the contrary, they have shown that there can be nothing phenomenal without something that is real, and that goodness and virtue, faith and works, are necessary as a preparation, nay as a *sine quâ non*, for the attainment of that highest knowledge which brings the soul back to its source and to its home, and restores it to its true nature, to its true Selfhood in Brahman.

And let us think how keenly and deeply Indian thinkers must have felt the eternal riddles of this world before they could propose so desperate a solution as that of the Vedânta; how desperate they must have thought the malady of mankind to be before they could think of so radical a cure. A student of the history of philosophy must brace himself to follow those whom he wants to reach and to understand. He has to climb like a mountaineer, undismayed by avalanches and precipices. He must be able to breathe in the thinnest air, never discouraged even if snow and ice bar his access to the highest point ever reached by the boldest explorers. Even if he has sometimes to descend again, disappointed, he has at all events strengthened his lungs and his muscles for further work. He has done his athletic exercise, and he has seen views such as are never seen in the valleys below. I am myself not a mountaineer, nor am I altogether a Vedântist; but if I can admire the bold climbers scaling Mount Gaurî-Sa*m*kar, I can also admire the bold thinkers toiling up to heights of the Vedânta where they seem lost to us in clouds and sky. Do we imagine that these ascents were undertaken from mere recklessness, from mere love of danger? It is easy for us to call those ancient explorers reckless adventurers, or dispose of them with the help of other names, such as mystic or pantheist, often but half understood by those who employ them. The Vedântists have often been called Atheists, but as the gods which they denied were only Devas, or what we call false gods, they might thus far have been forgiven. They have been called Pantheists, though their *theos*, or their *theoi*, were not the Pân, but the Pân was their *theos*. They have been called Nihilists, but they themselves have drawn a sharp line between the upholders of the *S*ûnya-vâda [1], the emptiness-doctrine, and their own teaching, which, on the contrary, insists throughout on the reality that underlies all phenomenal things, namely Brahman, and inculcates the duties which even this world of seeming imposes on all who are not yet in possession of the highest truth. That this phenomenal world has no exclusive right to the name of real is surely implied by its very name. Besides, whatever perishes can never have been real. If heaven and earth shall pass away; if we see our body, our senses, and all that has been built up on them, decaying and perishing every day before our very eyes; if the very Ego, the Aham, is dissolved into the elements from which it sprang, why should not the Vedântist also have held to his belief that Brahman alone is really real, and everything else a dream; and that even the Nâma-rûpas, the words and things, will vanish with each Kalpa?

To sum up, the Vedânta teaches that in the highest sense Creation is but Self-forgetfulness, and Eternal Life remembrance or Self-consciousness. And while to us such high abstractions may seem useless for the many, it is all the more surprising that, with the Hindus, the fundamental ideas of the

[1] An important distinction between Buddhists and Vedântists is that the former hold the world to have arisen from what is not, the latter from what is, the Sat or Brahman.

Vedânta have pervaded the whole of their literature, have leavened the whole of their language, and form to the present day the common property of the people at large. No doubt these ideas assume in the streets a different garment from what they wear among the learned in the Â*s*ramas or the forests of the country. May even among the learned few stand up for the complete Advaita or Monism as represented by *S*a*m*kara.

The danger with *S*a*m*kara's Vedântism was that what to him was simply phenomenal, should be taken for purely fictitious. There is, however, as great a difference between the two as there is between Avidyâ and Mithyâ*g*ñâna. Mâyâ[1] is the cause of a phenomenal, not of a fictitious, world; and if *S*a*m*kara adopts the Vivarta (turning away) instead of the Pari*n*âma (evolution) doctrine, there is always something on which the Vivarta or illusion is at work, and which cannot be deprived of its reality.

### Râmânu*g*a.

There are schools of Vedântists who try to explain the Sûtras of Bâdarâya*n*a in a far more human spirit. The best known is the school of Râmânu*g*a, who lived in the twelfth century A.D.[2] If we place *S*a*m*kara's literary activity about the eighth century[3], the claim of priority and of prior authority would belong to *S*a*m*kara. But we must never forget that in India more than anywhere else, philosophy was not the

[1] In the only passage where the Sûtras speak of Mâyâ (III, 2, 3), it need not mean more than a dream.

[2] Wilson, Works, I, p. 35.

[3] I-tsing, Introduction, p. xv, 788–820 A.D.; Kumârila, 750 A.D.

property of individuals, but that, as in the period of the Upanishads, so in later times also, everybody was free to contribute his share. As we find a number of teachers mentioned in the Upanishads, and as they give us long lists of names, pupil succeeding teacher through more than fifty spiritual generations, the commentators also quote ever so many authorities in support of the views which they either accept or reject. Hence we cannot accept *S*a*m*kara as the only infallible interpreter of the Vedânta-Sûtras, but have to recognise in his commentary one only of the many traditional interpretations of the Sûtras which prevailed at different times in different parts of India, and in different schools. A most important passage in this respect is that in which *S*a*m*kara has to confess that others (apare tu vâdina*h*) differ from him, and some, as he adds, even of our own (asmadîyâ*s* *k*a ke*k*it)[1]. This allows us a fresh insight into the philosophical life of India which is worth a great deal, particularly as the difference of opinion refers to a fundamental doctrine, namely the absolute identity of the individual soul with Brahman. *S*a*m*kara, as we saw, was uncompromising on that point. With him and, as he thinks, with Bâdarâya*n*a also, no reality is allowed to the soul (Âtman) as an individual (*G*îva), or to the world as presented to and by the senses. With him the soul's reality is Brahman, and Brahman is one *only*. But others, he adds, allow reality to the individual souls also. Now this is the very opinion on which another philosopher, Râmânu*g*a, has based his own interpretation of Bâdarâya*n*a's Sûtras, and has

[1] S.B.E., XXXIV, p. xx, Thibaut.

founded a large and influential sect. But it does not follow that this, whether heretical or orthodox opinion, was really first propounded by Râmânu*g*a, for Râmânu*g*a declares himself dependent on former teachers (Pûrvâ*k*âryâ*h*), and appeals particularly to a somewhat prolix Sûtra-v*ri*tti by Bodhâyana as his authority. Râmânu*g*a[1] himself quotes not only Bodhâyana, but after him *T*añka, Drami*d*a (or Dravi*d*a), Guhadeva, Kapardin, Bharu*k*i. One of them, Dravi*d*a, is expressly said to have been anterior to *S*a*m*kara, and so must Bodhâyana have been, if he is meant by the V*ri*ttikâra whom *S*a*m*kara himself criticises[2].

We ought, therefore, to look on Râmânu*g*a as a perfect equal of *S*a*m*kara, so far as his right of interpreting Bâdarâya*n*a's Sûtras, according to his own opinion, is concerned. It is the same here as everywhere in Hindu philosophy. The individual philosopher is but the mouthpiece of tradition, and that tradition goes back further and further, the more we try to fix it chronologically. While *S*a*m*kara's system is Advaita, i.e. absolute Monism, that of Râmânu*g*a has been called Vi*s*ish*t*a-Advaita, the doctrine of unity with attributes or Monism with a difference. Of course with Râmânu*g*a also Brahman is the highest reality, omnipotent, omniscient, but this Brahman is at the same time full of compassion or love. This is a new and very important feature in Râmânu*g*a's Brahman, as compared with the icy self-sufficiency ascribed to Brahman by *S*a*m*kara. Even more important and more humanising is the

---

[1] S.B.E., XXXIV, p. xxi.

[2] Deussen, The Vedânta-Philosophy, p. 31.

recognition that souls as individuals possess reality, that *K*it and A*k*it, what perceives and what does not perceive, soul and matter, form, as it were, the body of Brahman [1], are in fact modes (Prakâra) of Brahman. Sometimes *K*it is taken for the Supreme Spirit as a conscious cause, A*k*it for the unconscious effect or matter; but there is always Î*s*vara as a third, the Lord; and this, originally Brahmâ, is later on identified without much ado with Vish*n*u, so that Râmânu*g*a's sect is actually called *S*rî-Vaish*n*ava. It assumed no doubt the greatest importance as a religious sect, as teaching people how to live rather than how to think. But to us its chief interest is its philosophical character, and more particularly its relation to the Bâdarâya*n*a-Sûtras and *S*a*m*kara's explanation of them.

Brahman, whether under the name of Î*s*vara, Vish*n*u or Vâsudeva, or Bhagavat, is with Râmânu*g*a as with *S*a*m*kara both the efficient and the material cause of all that exists, and he is likewise the lord and ruler of the world. But here mythology comes in at once. From this Brahman, according to Râmânu*g*a, spring Sa*m*karsha*n*a, the individual soul (*G*îva), from Sa*m*karsha*n*a Pradyumna, mind (Manas), and from Pradyumna Aniruddha or the Ego (Ahaṅkâra). Brahmâ, masc., here called Vâsudeva, is not without qualities, as *S*a*m*kara holds, but possesses *G*ñâna (knowledge), *S*akti (energy), Bala (strength), Ai*s*varya (supreme power), Vîrya (vigour), and Te*g*as (energy), as his Gu*n*as or qualities. Much more of the same kind may be found in Colebrooke [2].

[1] Colebrooke, Misc. Essays, I, 439 n.

[2] Ibid., I, p. 439.

The real philosophical character of Râmânu*g*a's Vedântism has for the first time been placed in its true light by Professor Thibaut, from whom we may soon expect a complete translation of Râmânu*g*a's own commentary on the Vedânta-Sûtras, the *S*rî-bhâshya. As, according to Râmânu*g*a, Brahman is not Nirgu*n*a, without qualities, such qualities as intelligence, power, and mercy are ascribed to him, while with *S*a*m*kara even intelligence was not a quality of Brahman, but Brahman was intelligence, pure thought, and pure being. Besides these qualities, Brahman is supposed to possess, as constituent elements, the material world and the individual souls, and to act as the inward ruler (Antaryâmin) of them. Hence, neither the world nor the individual souls will ever cease to exist. All that Râmânu*g*a admits is that they pass through different stages as Avyakta and Vyakta. As Vyakta, developed, they are what we know them to be on earth; as Avyakta they are enveloped (Sa*m*ko*k*ita). This involution takes place at the end of each Kalpa, when Brahman assumes its causal state (Kâra*n*âvasthâ), and when individual souls and individual things lose for a time their distinct and independent character. Then follows, by the mere will of Brahmâ, the evolution, or the new creation of gross and visible matter, and an assumption by the individual souls of new material bodies, according to the merit or demerit of their former existence. The important point is that the individual souls, according to Râmânu*g*a, retain their individuality even when they have reached the blissful abode of Brahman. The world is not considered by him as merely the result of Avidyâ, but is real, while Brahman is to be looked upon and worshipped as a personal god, the creator and ruler of a real world. Thus Îsvara, the Lord, is not to be taken as a phenomenal god; and the difference between Brahman and Îsvara vanishes, as much as the difference between a qualified and an unqualified Brahman, between a higher and a lower knowledge. Here we perceive the influence exercised on philosophy by the common sense or the common sentiment of the people. In other countries in which philosophy is, as it were, the private property of individual thinkers, that influence is far less perceptible. But extreme views like those propounded by *S*a*m*kara were, as might be expected, too much for the great mass of the people, who might be willing to accept the doctrines of the Upanishads in their vagueness, but who would naturally shrink from the conclusions drawn from them with inexorable consistency by *S*a*m*kara. If it is impossible to say, as *S*a*m*kara says, 'I am not,' it is difficult at least to say, 'I am not I,' but 'I am Brahman.' It may be possible to say that Îsvara or the Lord is Brahman; but to worship Îsvara, and to be told at the same time that Îsvara is but phenomenal, must be trying even to the most ardent of worshippers. If therefore Râmânu*g*a, while professing his faith in the Upanishads and his allegiance to Bâdarâya*n*a, could give back to his followers not only their own souls, but also a personal god, no wonder that his success should have been so great as it was.

In the absence of any definite historical materials it is quite impossible for us to say whether, in the historical development of the Vedânta-philosophy at the time of Bâdarâya*n*a and afterwards, it was the absolute Monism as represented by *S*a*m*kara that took the lead, or whether the more temperate Monism, as we see it in Râmânu*g*a's commentary, exercised an earlier sway. There are certainly some Sûtras which, as Dr. Thibaut has shown, lend themselves far more readily to Râmânu*g*a's than to *S*a*m*kara's interpretation. The question as to the nature of individual souls seems decided by the author of the Sûtras in favour of Râmânu*g*a rather than of *S*a*m*kara. We read in Sûtra II, 3, 43, 'The soul is a *part* of Brahman.' Here the soul is clearly declared to be a part of Brahman, and this is the view of Râmânu*g*a; but *S*a*m*kara explains it by 'a part, as it were,' since Brahman, being not composed of parts, cannot have parts in the literal sense of the word.

This seems a bold proceeding of *S*a*m*kara's; and, though he tries to justify it by very ingenious arguments, Râmânu*g*a naturally takes his stand on the very words of the Sûtra. Similar cases have been pointed out by Dr. Thibaut; and this very diversity of opinion confirms what I remarked before, that the Vedânta philosophers of India, though they look both on Upanishads and the Sûtras as their highest authorities, often present a body of doctrine independent of them; colonies, as it were, of thought that had grown to be independent of the mother-country, but are anxious nevertheless to prove that their own doctrines can be reconciled with the old authorities. This was the position assumed by Bâdarâya*n*a towards the Upanishads, so much so that nearly the whole of the first book of his Sûtras had to be devoted to showing that his own views of Brahman were not in conflict with certain passages in the Upanishads. Some of them may refer to the lower Brahman, some to the individual soul as one with Brahman; and it is on these points that, at a later time, *S*a*m*kara and Râmânu*g*a would naturally have differed. What was important for Bâdarâya*n*a to show was that no passages from the Upanishads could fairly be quoted in support of other philosophies, such as the Sâ*m*khya, of which both *S*a*m*kara and Râmânu*g*a would disapprove. In the same manner both *S*a*m*kara and Râmânu*g*a are anxious to show that they themselves are in perfect agreement with Bâdarâya*n*a. Both, however, approach the Sûtras as if they had some opinions of their own to defend and to bring into harmony with the Sûtras. We can only suppose that schools in different parts of India had been growing up fast in the hermitages of certain teachers and their pupils, and that all were anxious to show that they had not deviated from such paramount and infallible authorities as the Sûtras and the Upanishads. This was done by means of what is called Mîmâ*m*sâ, or a critical discussion of passages which seemed to be ambiguous or had actually been twisted into an unnatural meaning by important teachers.

Dr. Thibaut therefore seems to me quite right when he says that both *S*a*m*kara and Râmânu*g*a pay often less regard to the literal sense of the words and to tradition than to their desire of forcing Bâdarâya*n*a to bear testimony to the truth of their own philosophical theories. This only confirms what I said before about the rich growth of philosophical thought in India, independent of Sûtras and Upanishads, though influenced by both. Even if we

[1] S.B.E., XXXIV, p. xcvi.

admit that Bâdarâyana wished to teach in his Sûtras nothing but what he found in the Upanishads, it must not be forgotten that the Upanishads contain ever so many conflicting guesses at truth, freely uttered by thinkers who had no personal relations with each other, and had no idea of propounding a uniform system of religious philosophy. If these conflicting utterances of the Upanishads had to be reduced to a system, we can hardly blame *S*am*k*ara for his taking refuge in the theory of a higher and a lower Brahman, the former being the Brahman of philosophy, the other that of religion, and both, as he thought, to be found in different parts of the Veda. By doing that he avoided the necessity of arguing away a number of purely anthropomorphic features, incongruous, if applied to the highest Brahman, and dragging down even the Brahman of the lower Vidyâ to a lower stage than philosophers would approve of. Râmânu*g*a's Brahman is always one and the same, and, according to him, the knowledge of Brahman is likewise but one; but his Brahman is in consequence hardly more than an exalted Îsvara. He is able to perform the work of creation without any help from Mâyâ or Avidyâ; and the souls of the departed, if only their life has been pure and holy, are able to approach this Brahmâ, sitting on his throne, and to enjoy their rewards in a heavenly paradise. The higher conception of Brahman excluded of course not only everything mythological, but everything like activity or workmanship, so that creation could only be conceived as caused by Mâyâ [1]

[1] Ved. Sûtras II, 2, 2, sub fine: Avidyâpratyupasthâpitanâmarûpamâyâvesavasena, 'Through being possessed of the Mâyâ of names and forms brought near by Avidyâ.'

or Avidyâ; while the very idea of an approach of the souls of the departed to the throne of Brahman, or of their souls being merged in Brahman, was incompatible with the fundamental tenet that the two were, and always remain, one and the same, never separated except by Nescience. The idea of an approach of the soul to Brahman, nay, even of the individual soul being a separate part of Brahman, to be again joined to Brahman after death, runs counter to the conception of Brahman, as explained by *S*a*m*kara, however prominent it may be in the Upanishads and in the system of Râmânu*g*a. It must be admitted therefore that in India, instead of one Vedânta-philosophy, we have really two, springing from the same root but extending its branches in two very different directions, that of *S*a*m*kara being kept for unflinching reasoners who, supported by an unwavering faith in Monism, do not shrink from any of its consequences; another, that of Râmânu*g*a, trying hard to reconcile their Monism with the demands of the human heart that required, and always will require, a personal god, as the last cause of all that is, and an eternal soul that yearns for an approach to or a reunion with that Being.

I am well aware that the view of the world, of God, and of the soul, as propounded by the Vedântists, whether in the Upanishads or in the Sûtras and their commentaries, has often been declared strange and fanciful, and unworthy of the name of philosophy, at all events utterly unsuited to the West, whatever may have been its value in the East. I have nothing to say against this criticism, nor have I ever tried to make propaganda for Vedântism, least of all in

England. But I maintain that it represents a phase of philosophic thought which no student of philosophy can afford to ignore, and which in no country can be studied to greater advantage than in India. And I go even a step further. I quite admit that, as a popular philosophy, the Vedânta would have its dangers, that it would fail to call out and strengthen the manly qualities required for the practical side of life, and that it might raise the human mind to a height from which the most essential virtues of social and political life might dwindle away into mere phantoms. At the same time I make no secret that all my life I have been very fond of the Vedânta. Nay, I can fully agree with Schopenhauer, and quite understand what he meant when he said,—'In the whole world there is no study, except that of the original (of the Upanishads), so beneficial and so elevating as that of the Oupnekhat (Persian translation of the Upanishads). It has been the solace of my life, it will be the solace of my death.'

Schopenhauer was the last man to write at random, or to allow himself to go into ecstasies over so-called mystic and inarticulate thought. And I am neither afraid nor ashamed to say that I share his enthusiasm for the Vedânta, and feel indebted to it for much that has been helpful to me in my passage through life. After all it is not everybody who is called upon to take an active part in life, whether in defending or ruling a country, in amassing wealth, or in breaking stones; and for fitting men to lead contemplative and quiet lives, I know no better preparation than the Vedânta. A man may be a Platonist, and yet a good citizen and an honest Christian, and I should say the same of a Vedântist.

They may be called useless by the busy and toiling portion of humanity; but if it is true that 'those also serve who only stand and wait,' then may we not hope that even the quiet in the land are not so entirely useless as they appear to be?

And while some of the most important doctrines of the Vedânta, when placed before us in the plain and direct language of the Vedânta-Sûtras, may often seem very startling to us, it is curious to observe how, if clothed in softer language, they do not jar at all on our ears, nay, are in full harmony with our own most intimate convictions. Thus, while the idea that our own self and the Divine Self are identical in nature might seem irreverent, if not blasphemous, one of our own favourite hymns contains the prayer,—

> And that a higher gift than grace
> Should flesh and blood refine,
> God's Presence and His very Self,
> And Essence all-divine!

This is pure Vedânta. We also speak without hesitation of our body as the temple of God, and of the voice of God within us; nay, we repeat with St. Paul that we live, and move, and have our being in God, yet we shrink from adopting the plain and simple language of the Upanishads that the Self of God and man is the same.

Again, the unreality of the material world, though proved point by point by Berkeley, seems to many a pure fancy; and yet one of our most popular poets, the very type of manliness and strength, both mental and physical, speaks like a Vedântist of the shadows among which we move:—

For more than once when I[1]
Sat all alone, revolving in myself
The word that is the symbol of myself,
The mortal limit of the Self was loosed,
And passed into the Nameless, as a cloud
Melts into Heaven. I touched my limbs—the limbs
Were strange, not mine—and yet no shade of doubt,
But utter clearness, and thro' loss of Self
The gain of such large life as matched with ours
Were Sun to spark—unshadowable in words,
Themselves but shadows of a shadow-world.

It would be easy to add similar passages from Wordsworth, Goethe, and others, to show that after all there is some of the Indian leaven left in us, however unwilling we may be to confess it. Indian thought will never quite square with English thoughts, and the English words which we have to adopt in rendering Indian ideas are never quite adequate. All we can do is to strive to approximate as near as possible, and not to allow these inevitable differences to prejudice us against what, though differently expressed, is often meant for the same.

There is one more point that requires a few remarks.

### Metaphors.

It has often been said that the Vedânta-philosophy deals too much in metaphors, and that most of them, though fascinating at first sight, leave us in the end unsatisfied, because they can only illustrate, but cannot prove. This is true, no doubt; but in philosophy illustration also by means of metaphors has its value, and I doubt whether they were ever meant for more than that. Thus, when the Vedânta has to

[1] Tennyson, The Ancient Sage.

explain how the Sat, the Real or Brahman, dwells within us, though we cannot distinguish it, the author of the *Kh*ândogya Up. VI, 13, introduces a father telling his son to throw a lump of salt into water, and after some time to take it out again. Of course he cannot do it, but whenever he tastes the water it is salt. In the same way, the father says, the Sat, the Divine, is within us, though we cannot perceive it by itself.

Another application of the same simile (B*ri*had. Âr. Up. II, 4, 12) seems intended to show that the Sat or Brahman, in permeating the whole elementary world, vanishes, so that there is no distinction left between the individual Self and the Highest Self[1].

Again, when we read[2] that the manifold beings are produced from the Eternal as sparks spring from a burning fire, we should remember that this metaphor illustrates the idea that all created beings share in the substance of the Supreme Being, that for a time they seem to be independent, but that they vanish again without causing any diminution in the Power from whence they sprang.

The idea of a creating as a making of the world is most repugnant to the Vedântist, and he tries in every way to find another simile by which to illustrate the springing of the world from Brahman as seen in this world of Nescience. In order to avoid the necessity of admitting something extraneous, some kind of matter out of which the world was shaped, the Upanishads point to the spider spinning its web out of itself; and, in order to show that things can spring into existence spontaneously, they

[1] See Deussen, Upanishads, p. 416, for a different explanation.
[2] B*ri*h. Âr. Up. II, 1, 20.

use the simile of the hairs springing from a man's head without any special wish of the man himself.

Now it may be quite true that none of these illustrations can be considered, nor were they intended as arguments in support of the Upanishad-philosophy, but they are at all events very useful in reminding us by means of striking similes of certain doctrines arrived at by the Vedânta philosophers in their search after truth.

# CHAPTER V.

## Pûrva-Mîmâ*m*sâ.

It would be interesting to trace at once the same or very similar tendencies as those of the Vedânta in the development of other Indian philosophies, and particularly of the Sâ*m*khya and Yoga, and to see what they have to say on the existence and the true nature of a Supreme Being, and the relation of human beings to that Divine Being, as shadowed forth in certain passages of the Veda, though differently interpreted by different schools of philosophy. But it seems better on the whole to adhere to the order adopted by the students of philosophy in India, and treat of the other Mîmâ*m*sâ, the Pûrva-Mîmâ*m*sâ, that is the Former Mîmâ*m*sâ, as it is called, in connection with the one we have examined. The Hindus admit a Pûrva-Mîmâ*m*sâ and an Uttara-Mîmâ*m*sâ. They look upon the Vedânta as the Uttara- or later Mîmâ*m*sâ, and on that of *G*aimini as the Pûrva-, or prior. These names, however, were not meant to imply, as Colebrooke[1] seems to have supposed, that the Pûrva-Mîmâ*m*sâ was prior in time, though it is true that it is sometimes called Prâ*k*î[2], previous. It really meant no more than that

[1] Colebrooke, Misc. Essays, vol. i, p. 239. Ritter, History of Philosophy, vol. iv, p. 376, in Morrison's translation.

[2] Sarvadarsana-sa*m*graha, p. 122, l. 3.

the Pûrva-Mîmâmsâ, having to do with the Karmakâṇḍa, the first or work-part of the Veda, comes first, and the Uttara-Mîmâmsâ, being concerned with the *Gñânakâṇḍa*, comes second, just as an orthodox Hindu at one time was required to be a Grihastha or householder first, and then only to retire into the forest and lead the contemplative life of a Vânaprastha or a Samnyâsin. We shall see, however, that this prior Mîmâmsâ, if it can be called a philosophy at all, is very inferior in interest to the Vedânta, and could hardly be understood without the previous existence of such a system as that of Bâdarâyana. I should not like, however, to commit myself so far as to claim priority in time for the Vedânta. It has a decided priority in importance, and in its relation to the *Gñâna*-portion of the Veda. We saw why the fact that Bâdarâyana quotes *G*aimini cannot be used for chronological purposes, for *G*aimini returns the compliment and quotes Bâdarâyana. How this is to be accounted for, I tried to explain before. It is clear that while Bâdarâyana endeavoured to introduce order into the Upanishads, and to reduce their various guesses to something like a system, *G*aimini undertook to do the same for the rest of the Veda, the so-called Karmakâṇḍa or work-portion, that is, all that had regard to sacrifice, as described chiefly in the Brâhmanas. Sacrifice was so much the daily life of the Brâhmans that the recognised name for sacrifice was simply Karman, i.e. work. That work grew up in different parts of India, just as we saw philosophy springing up, full of variety, not free even from contradictions. Every day had its sacrifice, and in some respects these regular sacrifices may be called the first calendar of India. They depended on the seasons or regulated the seasons and marked the different divisions of the year. There were some rites that lasted the whole year or even several years. And as philosophy existed, independent of the Upanishads, and through Bâdarâyana attempted to make peace with the Upanishads, we must consider that sacrifices also existed for a long time without the Brâhma*n*as, such as we possess them, that they grew up without being restrained by generally binding authorities of any kind, and that at a later time only, after the Brâhma*n*as had been composed and had acquired some kind of authority, the necessity began to be felt of reconciling variant opinions and customs, as embodied in the Brâhma*n*as and elsewhere, giving general as well as special rules for the performance of every kind of ceremony. We can hardly imagine that there ever was a time in India when the so-called priests, settled in distant localities, did not know how to perform their own sacrificial duties, for who were the authors of them, if not the priests? But when the Brâhma*n*as once existed, a new problem had to be solved: how to bring the Brâhma*n*as into harmony with themselves and with existing family and local customs, and also how to discover in them a meaning that should satisfy every new generation. This was achieved by means of what is called Mîmâ*m*sâ, investigation, examination, consideration. There is little room for real philosophy in all this, but there are questions such as that of Dharma or duty, including sacrificial duties, which offer an opportunity for discussing the origin of duty and the nature of its rewards; while in accounting for seeming contradictions, in arriving at general principles concerning sacrificial acts, problems would naturally turn up which, though often in themselves valueless, are generally treated with considerable ingenuity. In this way the work of *G*aimini secured for itself a place by the side of the works ascribed to Bâdarâya*n*a, Kapila and others, and was actually raised to the rank of one of the six classical philosophies of India. It cannot therefore be passed over in a survey of Indian philosophy.

While Bâdarâya*n*a begins his Sûtras with Athâto Brahma*g*i*g*ñâsa, 'Now therefore the desire of knowing Brahman,' *G*aimini, apparently in imitation of it, begins with Athâto Dharma*g*i*g*ñâsâ, 'Now therefore the desire of knowing Dharma or duty.' The two words 'Now therefore' offer as usual a large scope to a number of interpreters, but they mean no more in the end than that now, after the Veda has been read, and because it has been read, there arises a desire for knowing the full meaning of either Dharma, duty, or of Brahman, the Absolute; the former treated in the Uttara-, the latter in the Pûrva-Mîmâ*m*sâ. In fact, whatever native commentators may say to the contrary, this first Sûtra is not much more than a title, as if we were to say, Now begins the philosophy of duty, or the philosophy of *G*aimini.

Dharma, here translated by duty, refers to acts of prescriptive observance, chiefly sacrifices. It is said to be a neuter, if used in the latter sense, a very natural distinction, though there is little evidence to that effect in the Sûtras or in the literature known to us.

This Dharma or duty is enjoined in the Brâhmanas, and these together with the Mantras are held to constitute the whole of the Veda, so that whatever is not Mantra is Brâhmana, whatever is not Brâhmana is Mantra. The Brâhmanas are said to consist of Vidhis, injunctions, and Arthavâdas, glosses. The injunctions are meant either to make us do a thing that had not been done before, or to make us know a thing that had not been known before[1]. Subsequently the Vidhis[2] are divided into Utpatti-vidhis, original or general injunctions, such as Agnihotram guhoti, he performs the Agnihotra, and Viniyoga-vidhi, showing the manner in which a sacrifice is to be performed. The latter comprises injunctions as to the details, such as Dadhnâ guhoti, he performs the sacrifice with sour milk, &c. Then follow the Prayoga-vidhis which settle the exact order of sacrificial performances, and there is lastly a class of injunctions which determine who is fit to perform a sacrificial act. They are called Adhikâra-vidhis.

The hymns or formulas which are to be used at a sacrifice, though they are held to possess also a transcendental or mysterious effect, the Apûrva, are by Gaimini conceived as mainly intended to remind the sacrificer of the gods who are to receive his sacrificial gifts.

He likewise lays stress on what he calls Nâmadheya or the technical name of each sacrifice, such as Agnihotra, Darsapûrnamâsa, Udbhid, &c. These names are found in the Brâhmanas and they are considered important, as no doubt they are, in defining the nature of a sacrifice. The Nishedhas

---

[1] Rigvedabhâshya, vol. i, p. 5.

[2] Thibaut, Arthasamgraha, p. viii.

or prohibitions require no explanation. They simply state what ought not to be done at a sacrifice.

Lastly, the Arthavâdas are passages in the Brâhmanas which explain certain things; they vary in character, being either glosses, comments, or explanatory statements.

### Contents of the Pûrva-Mîmâmsâ.

Perhaps I cannot do better than give the principal contents of Gaimini's Sûtras, as detailed by Mâdhava in his Nyâya-mâlâ-vistara[1]. The Mîmâmsâ consists of twelve books. In the first book is discussed the authoritativeness of those collections of words which are severally meant by the terms injunction (Vidhi), explanatory passage (Arthavâda), hymn (Mantra), tradition (Smriti), and name (Nâmadheya). In the second we find certain subsidiary discussions, as e.g. on Apûrva, relative to the difference of various rites, refutation of erroneously alleged proofs, and difference of performance, as in obligatory and voluntary offerings. In the third are considered revelation (Sruti), 'sign' or sense of a passage (Liṅga), 'context' (Vâkya), &c., and their respective weight, when in apparent opposition to one another; then the ceremonies called Pratipathi-Karmâni, things mentioned by the way, Anârabhyâdhîta, things accessory to several main objects, as Prayâgas, &c., and the duties of the sacrificer. In the fourth the chief subject is the influence of the principal and subordinate rites on other rites, the fruit produced by the Guhû

[1] See Cowell and Gough in their translation of the Sarvadarsana-samgraha, p. 178.

when made of the *Butea frondosa*, &c., and the dice-playing, &c., which forms part of the Râ*g*asûya-sacrifice. In the fifth the subjects are the relative order of different passages of the *S*ruti, &c., the order of different parts of a sacrifice, as the seventeen animals at the Vâ*g*apeya, the multiplication and non-multiplication of rites, and the respective force of the words of the *S*ruti, the order of mention, &c., as determining the order of performance. In the sixth we read of the persons qualified to offer sacrifices, their obligations, the substitutes for prescribed materials, supplies for lost or injured offerings, expiatory rites, the Sattra-offerings, things proper to be given, and the different sacrificial fines. In the seventh is treated the mode of transference of the ceremonies of one sacrifice to another by direct command in the Vaidic text, others as inferred by 'name' or 'sign.' In the eighth, transference by virtue of the clearly expressed or obscurely expressed 'sign' or by the predominant 'sign,' and cases also where no transference takes place. In the ninth, the discussion begins with the adaptation (Ûha) of hymns, when quoted in a new connection, the adaptation of Sâmans and Mantras, and collateral questions connected therewith. In the tenth the occasions are discussed where the non-performance of the primary rite involves the 'preclusion' and non-performance of the dependent rites, and occasions when rites are precluded, because other rites produce their special results, also Graha-offerings, certain Sâmans, and various other things, as well as different kinds of negation. In the eleventh we find the incidental mention and subsequently the fuller discussion of Tantra, where several acts are combined into one, and Âvâpa, or the performing an act more than once. In the twelfth there is the discussion on Prasaṅga, when the rite is performed with one chief purpose, but with an incidental further reference, on Tantra, cumulation of concurrent rites (Samu*kkh*aya), and option.

It is easy to see from this table of contents that neither Plato nor Kant would have felt much the wiser for them. But we must take philosophies as they are given us; and we should spoil the picture of the philosophical life of India, if we left out of consideration their speculations about sacrifice as contained in the Pûrva-Mîmâ*m*sâ. There are passages, however, which appeal to philosophers, such as, for instance, the chapter on the Pramâ*n*as or the authoritative sources of knowledge, on the relation between word and thought, and similar subjects. It is true that most of these questions are treated in the other philosophies also, but they have a peculiar interest as treated by the ritualistic Pûrva-Mîmâ*m*sâ.

### Pramâ*n*as of *G*aimini.

Thus if we turn our attention first to the Pramâ*n*as, the measures of knowledge, or the authorities to which we can appeal as the legitimate means of knowledge, as explained by the Pûrva-Mîmâ*m*sâ, we saw before that the Vedântists did not pay much attention to them, though they were acquainted with the three fundamental Pramâ*n*as —sense-perception, inference, and revelation. The Pûrva-Mîmâ*m*sâ, on the contrary, devoted considerable attention to this subject, and admitted five, (1) Sense-perception, Pratyaksha, when the organs are actually in contiguity with an object; (2) Inference (Anumâna), i. e. the apprehension of an unseen member of a known association (Vyâpti) by the perception of another seen member; (3) Comparison (Upamâna), knowledge arising from resemblance; (4) Presumption (Arthâpatti), such knowledge as can be derived of a thing not itself perceived, but implied by another; (5) *S*abda, verbal information derived from authoritative sources. One sect of Mîmâ*m*sakas, those who follow Kumârila Bha*tt*a, admitted besides, (6) Abhâva, not-being, which seems but a subdivision of inference, as if we infer dryness of the soil from the not-being or absence of clouds and rain.

All these sources of information are carefully examined, but it is curious that Mîmâ*m*sakas should admit this large array of sources of valid cognition, considering that for their own purposes, for establishing the nature of Dharma or duty, they practically admit but one, namely scripture or *S*abda. Duty, they hold, cannot rest on human authority, because the 'ought' which underlies all duty, can only be supplied by an authority that is more than human or more than fallible, and such an authority is nowhere to be found except in the Veda. This leaves, of course, the task of proving the superhuman origin of the Veda on the shoulders of *G*aimini; and we shall see hereafter how he performs it.

#### Sûtra-style.

Before, however, we enter on a consideration of any of the problems treated in the Pûrva-Mîmâ*m*sâ, a few remarks have to be made on a peculiarity in the structure of the Sûtras. In order to discuss a subject fully, and to arrive in the end at a definite opinion, the authors of the Sûtras are encouraged to begin with stating first every possible objection that can reasonably be urged against what is their own opinion. As long as the objections are not perfectly absurd, they have a right to be stated, and this is called the Pûrvapaksha, the first part. Then follow answers to all these objections, and this is called the Uttarapaksha, the latter part; and then only are we led on to the final conclusion, the Siddhânta. This system is exhaustive and has many advantages, but it has also the disadvantage, as far as the reader is concerned, that, without a commentary, he often feels doubtful where the cons end and the pros begin. The commentators themselves differ sometimes on that point. Sometimes again, instead of three, a case or Adhikara*n*a is stated in five members, namely:—

1. The subject to be explained (Vishaya).
2. The doubt (Sa*m*saya).
3. The first side or prima facie view (Pûrvapaksha).
4. The demonstrated conclusion (Siddhânta); and
5. The connection (Sa*m*gati).

This is illustrated in the commentary on the first and second Sûtras of the Mîmâ*m*sâ [1], which declare that a desire to know duty is to be entertained, and then define duty (Dharma) as that which is to be recognised by an instigatory passage, that is by a passage from the Veda. Here the question to be discussed (Vishaya) is, whether the study of Duty in

---

[1] Sarvadarsana-sa*m*graha, p. 122; translation by Cowell and Gough, p. 180; Siddhânta Dîpikâ, 1898, p. 194.

*G*aimini's Mîmâ*m*sâ is really necessary to be undertaken. The Pûrvapaksha says of course, No, for when it is said that the Veda should be learnt (Vedo *dhyetavya*h*), that clearly means either that it should be understood, like any other book which we read, or that it should be learnt by heart without any attempt, as yet, on the part of the pupil to understand it, simply as a work good in itself, which has its reward in heaven. This is a very common view among the ancient Brâhmans; for, as they had no written books, they had a very perfect system for imprinting texts on the memory of young persons, by making them learn every day a certain number of verses or lines by heart, without any attempt, at first, of making them understand what they learnt; and afterwards only supplying the key to the meaning. This acquisition of the mere sound of the Veda was considered highly meritorious; nay, some held that the Veda was more efficacious, if not understood than if understood. This was in fact their printing or rather their writing, and without it their mnemonic literature would have been simply impossible. As we warn our compositors against trying to understand what they are printing, Indian pupils were cautioned against the same danger; and they succeeded in learning the longest texts by heart, without even attempting at first to fathom their meaning. To us such a system seems almost incredible, but no other system was possible in ancient times, and there is no excuse for being incredulous, for it may still be witnessed in India to the present day.

Only after the text had thus been imprinted on the memory, there came the necessity of interpretation or understanding. And here the more enlightened of the Indian theologians argue that the Vedic command 'Vedo-dhyetavya*h*,' 'the Veda is to be gone over, that is, is to be acquired, to be learnt by heart,' implies that it is also to be understood, and that this intelligible purpose is preferable to the purely mechanical one, though miraculous rewards may be held out for that.

But if so, it is asked, what can be the use of the Mîmâ*m*sâ? The pupil learns the Veda by heart, and learns to understand it in the house of his teacher. After that he bathes, marries and sets up his own house, so that it is argued there would actually be no time for any intervening study of the Mîmâ*m*sâ. Therefore the imaginary opponent, the Pûrvapakshin, objects that the study of the Mîmâ*m*sâ is not necessary at all, considering that it rests on no definite sacred command. But here the Siddhântin steps forward and says that the Sm*ri*ti passage enjoining a pupil's bathing (graduating) on returning to his house is not violated by an intervening study of the Mîmâ*m*sâ, because it is not said that, after having finished his apprenticeship, he should immediately bathe; and because, though his learning of the text of the Veda is useful in every respect, a more minute study of the sacrificial precepts of the Veda, such as is given in the Mîmâ*m*sâ, cannot be considered superfluous, as a means towards the highest object of the study of the Veda, viz. the proper performance of its commands.

These considerations in support of the Siddhânta or final conclusion would probably fall under the name of Sa*m*gati, connection, though I must confess that its meaning is not quite clear to me. There are besides several points in the course of this discussion, such as, for instance, the so-called four Kriyâphalas, on which more information is much to be desired.

### Has the Veda a Superhuman Origin?

This discussion leads on to another and more important one, whether the Veda has supreme authority, whether it is the work of man, or of some inspired person, or whether it is what we should call revealed. If it were the work of a person, then, like any other work, it could not establish a duty, nor could it promise any rewards as a motive for the performance of any duty; least of all, a reward in heaven, such as the Veda promises again and again to those who perform Vedic sacrifices. It follows therefore either that the Veda has no binding authority at all, or that it cannot be the work of a personal or human author. This is a dilemma arising from convictions firmly planted in the minds of the ancient theologians of India, and it is interesting to see how they try to escape from all the difficulties arising out of their postulate that the Veda must be the work of a superhuman or divine author. The subject is interesting even though the arguments may not be convincing to us. It is clear that even to start such a claim as being revealed for any book requires a considerable advance in religious and philosophical thought, and I doubt whether such a problem could have arisen in the ancient literature of any country besides India. The Jews, no doubt, had their sacred books, but these books, though sacred, were not represented as having been the work of Jehovah. They were acknowledged to have been composed, if not written down, by historical persons, even if, as in the case of Moses, they actually related the death of their reputed author. The Mîmâ*m*sâ philosopher would probably have argued that as no writer could relate his own death, therefore Deuteronomy must be considered the work of a superhuman writer; and some of our modern theologians have not been very far from taking the same view. To the Brâhmans, any part of the Veda, even if it bore a human or historical name, was superhuman, eternal and infallible, much as the Gospels are in the eyes of certain Christian theologians, even though they maintain at the same time that they are historical documents written down by illiterate people, or by apostles such as St. Mark or St. John. Let us see therefore how the Mîmâ*m*sâ deals with this problem of the Apaurusheyatva, i. e. the non-human origin of the Vedas. Inspiration in the ordinary sense of the word would not have satisfied these Indian orthodox philosophers, for, as they truly remark, this would not exclude the possibility of error, because, however true the message might be, when given, the human recipient would always be a possible source of error, as being liable to misapprehend and misinterpret such a message. Even the senses, as they point out, can deceive us, so that we mistake mother-of-pearl for silver; how much more easily then may we misapprehend the meaning of revealed words!

However, the first thing is to see how the Brâhmans, and particularly the Mîmâ*m*sakas, tried to maintain a superhuman authorship in favour of the Veda.

I quote from Mâdhava's introduction to his commentary on the Rig-veda [1]. He is a great authority in matters connected with the Pûrva-Mîmâ*m*sâ, having written the Nyâya-mâlâ-vistara, a very comprehensive treatise on the subject. In his introduction he establishes first the authority of the Mantras and of the Brâhma*n*as, both Vidhis (rules) and Arthavâdas (glosses), by showing that they were perfectly intelligible, which had been denied. He then proceeds to establish the Apaurusheyatva, the non-human authorship of the Veda, in accordance, as he says, with *G*aimini's Sûtras.

'Some people,' he says, and he means of course the Pûrvapakshins, the recognised objectors, 'uphold approximation towards the Vedas,' that is to say, they hold that as the Raghuva*m*sa of Kâlidâsa and other poems are recent, so also are the Vedas. The Vedas, they continue, are not without a beginning or eternal, and hence we find men quoted in them as the authors of the Vedas. As in the case of Vyâsa's Mahâbhârata and Valmîki's Râmâya*n*a, Vyâsa, Valmîki, &c., are known to be their human authors, thus in the case of the Kâ*th*aka, Kauthuma, Taittirîya, and other sections of the Veda, Ka*th*a, &c., are given us as the names of the authors of these branches of the Veda; and hence it follows that the Vedas were the works of human authors.

And if it were suggested that such names as Ka*th*a, &c., were meant for men who did no more than hand down the oral tradition, like teachers, the Pûrvapakshin is ready with a new objection, namely, that the Vedas must be of human origin,

[1] See my Second Edition, vol. i, p. 10.

because we see in the Vedas themselves the mention of temporal matters. Thus we read of a Babara Prâvâha*n*i, of a Kusuruvinda Auddâlaki, &c. The Vedas, therefore, could not have existed in times anterior to these persons mentioned in them, and hence cannot be prehistoric, pre-temporal, or eternal. It is seen from this that what is claimed for the Veda is not only revelation, communicated to historical persons, but existence from all eternity, and before the beginning of all time. We can understand therefore why in the next Sûtra, which is the Siddhânta or final conclusion, *G*aimini should appeal to a former Sûtra in which he established that even the relation of words to their meanings is eternal. This subject had been discussed before, in answer to the inevitable Objector-general, the Pûrvapakshin, who had maintained that the relation between words and their meanings was conventional (θέσει), established by men, and therefore liable to error quite as much as the evidence of our senses. For as we may mistake mother-of-pearl for silver, we may surely mistake the meaning of words, and hence the meaning of words of the Veda also. *G*aimini, therefore, in this place, wishes us first of all to keep in mind that the words of the Vedas themselves are superhuman or supernatural, nay, that sound itself is eternal, and thus fortified he next proceeds to answer the objections derived from such names as Kâ*th*aka, or Babara Prâvâha*n*i. This is done by showing that Ka*th*a did not compose, but only handed down a certain portion of the Veda, and that Babara Prâvâha*n*i was meant, not as the name of a man, but as a name of the wind, Babara imitating the sound, and Pravahana meaning 'carrying along,' as it were *pro-vehens*.

Then follows a new objection taken from the fact that impossible or even absurd things occur in the Veda; for instance, we read that trees or serpents performed a sacrifice, or that an old ox sang foolish[1] songs fit for the Madras. Hence it is argued once more that the Veda must have been made by human beings. But the orthodox *G*aimini answers, No; for if it had been made by man, there could be no injunction for the performance of sacrifices like the *G*yotish*t*oma, as a means of attaining Svarga or paradise, because no man could possibly know either the means, or their effect; and yet there is this injunction in the case of the *G*yotish*t*oma, and other sacrifices are not different from it. Such injunctions as 'Let a man who desires paradise, sacrifice with the *G*yotish*t*oma' are not like a speech of a madman; on the contrary, they are most rational in pointing out the object (paradise), in suggesting the means (Soma, &c.), and in mentioning all the necessary subsidiary acts (Dîksha*n*îya, &c.). We see, therefore, that the commands of the Veda are not unintelligible or absurd. And if we meet with such passages as that the trees and serpents performed certain sacrifices, we must recognise in them Arthavâdas or glosses, conveying in our case indirect laudations of certain sacrifices, as if to say, 'if even trees and serpents perform them, how much more should intelligent beings do the same!'

As, therefore, no flaws that might arise from human workmanship can be detected in the Veda, *G*aimini concludes triumphantly that its superhuman origin and its authority cannot be doubted.

---

[1] On Mâdraka, see Muir, Sansk. Texts, II, p. 482.

This must suffice to give a general idea of the character of the Pûrva-Mîmâmsâ. We may wonder why it should ever have been raised to the rank of a philosophical system by the side of the Uttara-Mîmâmsâ or the Vedânta, but it is its method rather than the matter to which it is applied, that seems to have invested it with a certain importance. This Mîmâmsâ method of discussing questions has been adopted in other branches of learning also, for instance, by the highest legal authorities in trying to settle contested questions of law. We meet with it in other systems of philosophy also as the recognised method of discussing various opinions before arriving at a final conclusion.

There are some curious subjects discussed by *G*aimini, such as what authority can be claimed for tradition, as different from revelation, how far the recognised customs of certain countries should be followed or rejected, what words are to be considered as correct or incorrect; or again, how a good or bad act, after it has been performed can, in spite of the lapse of time, produce good or bad results for the performer. All this is certainly of interest to the student of Indian literature, but hardly to the student of philosophy, as such.

### Supposed Atheism of Pûrva-Mîmâmsâ.

One more point seems to require our attention, namely, the charge of atheism that has been brought against *G*aimini's Mîmâmsâ. This sounds a very strange charge after what we have seen of the character of this philosophy, of its regard for the Veda, and the defence of its revealed character, nay, its insistence on the conscientious observance of all ceremonial injunctions. Still, it has been brought both in ancient and in modern times. So early a philosopher as Kumârila Bha*tt*a tells us that the Mîmâ*m*sâ had been treated in the world as a Lokâyata [1], i. e. an atheistic system, but that he was anxious to re-establish it as orthodox. Professor Banerjea [2] tells us that Prabhâkara also, the other commentator of the Mîmâ*m*sâ, had openly treated this system as atheistic, and we shall meet with a passage from the Padma-Purâ*n*a supporting the same view. However, there seems to be a misunderstanding here. Atheistic has always meant a great many things, so much so that even the most pantheistic system that could be imagined, the Vedânta, has, like that of Spinoza, been accused of atheism. The reason is this. The author of the Vedânta-Sûtras, Bâdarâya*n*a, after having established the omnipresence of Brahman (III, 2, 36–37) by quoting a number of passages from the Veda, such as 'Brahman is all this' (Mu*n*d. Up. II, 2, 11), 'the Self is all this' (*Kh*ând. Up. VII, 25, 2), proceeds to show (III, 2, 38) that the rewards also of all works proceed directly or indirectly from Brahman. There were, however. two opinions on this point, one, that the works themselves produce their fruit without any divine interference, and in cases where the fruit does not appear at once, that there is a supersensuous principle, called Apûrva, which is the direct result of a deed, and produces fruit at a later time; the other, that all actions are directly or

[1] Lokâyata is explained by Childers, s.v., as controversy on fabulous or absurd points, but in the Amba*tth*a-Sutta, I. 3, it is mentioned as forming part of the studies proper for a Brâhman.

[2] Muir, III, 95.

indirectly requited by the Lord. The latter opinion, which is adopted by Bâdarâya*n*a, is supported by a quotation from B*ri*h. Up. IV, 4, 24, 'This is indeed the great, unborn Self, the giver of food, the giver of wealth.' *G*aimini, however, as we are informed by Bâdarâya*n*a in the next Sûtra, accepted the former opinion. The command that 'he who is desirous of the heavenly world should sacrifice,' implies, as he holds, a reward of the sacrificer by means of the sacrifice itself, and not by any other agent. But how a sacrifice, when it had been performed and was ended, could produce any reward, is difficult to understand. In order to explain this, *G*aimini assumes that there was a result, viz. an invisible something, a kind of after-state of a deed or an invisible antecedent state of the result, something Apûrva or miraculous, which represented the reward inherent in good works. And he adds, that if we supposed that the Lord himself caused rewards and punishments for the acts of men, we should often have to accuse him of cruelty and partiality; and that it is better therefore to allow that all works, good or bad, produce their own results, or, in other words, that for the moral government of the world no Lord is wanted.

Here, then, we see the real state of the case as between *G*aimini and Bâdarâya*n*a. *G*aimini would not make the Lord responsible for the injustice that seems to prevail in the world, and hence reduced everything to cause and effect, and saw in the inequalities of the world the natural result of the continued action of good or evil acts. This surely was not atheism, rather was it an attempt to clear the Lord from those charges of cruelty or undue partiality which have so often been brought against him. It was but another attempt at justifying the wisdom of God, an ancient Theodicée, that, whatever we may think of it, certainly did not deserve the name of atheism.

Bâdarâya*n*a, however, thought otherwise, and quoting himself, he says, 'Bâdarâya*n*a thinks the Lord to be the cause of the fruits of action,' and he adds that he is even the cause of these actions themselves, as we may learn from a well-known Vedic passage (Kaush. Up. III, 8): 'He makes whomsoever he wishes to lead up from these worlds, do good deeds; and makes him whom he wishes to lead down from these worlds, do bad deeds.'

Atheism is a charge very freely brought against those who deny certain characteristics predicated of the Deity, but do not mean thereby to deny its existence. If the Mîmâ*m*sakas were called atheists, it meant no more than that they tried to justify the ways of God in their own way. But, once having been called atheists, they were accused of ever so many things. In a passage quoted by Professor Banerjea from a modern work, the Vidvan-modatarańgi*n*î, we read: 'They say there is no God, or maker of the world; nor has the world any sustainer or destroyer; for every man obtains a recompense in conformity with his own works. Neither is there any maker of the Veda, for its words are eternal, and their arrangement is eternal. Its authoritativeness is self-demonstrated, for since it has been established from all eternity how can it be dependent upon anything but itself?' This shows how the Mîmâ*m*sakas have been misunderstood by the Vedântists, and how much *S*a*m*kara is at cross-purposes with

*G*aimini. What has happened in this case in India is what always happens when people resort to names of abuse rather than to an exchange of ideas. Surely a Deity, though it does not cause us to act, and does not itself reward or punish us, is not thereby a non-existent Deity. Modern Vedântists also are so enamoured of their own conception of Deity, that is, of Brahman or Âtman, that they do not hesitate, like Vivekânanda, for instance, in his recent address on Practical Vedânta, 1896, to charge those who differ from himself with atheism. 'He is the atheist,' he writes, 'who does not believe in himself. Not believing in the glory of your own soul is what the Vedânta calls atheism.'

#### Is the Pûrva-Mîmâ*m*sâ a system of Philosophy?

Let me say once more that, in allowing a place to the Pûrva-Mîmâ*m*sâ among the six systems of Indian Philosophy, I was chiefly influenced by the fact that from an Indian point of view it always held such a place, and that by omitting it a gap would have been left in the general outline of the philosophic thought of India. Some native philosophers go so far as not only to call both systems, that of *G*aimini and Bâdarâya*n*a, by the same name of Mîmâ*m*sâ, but to look upon them as forming one whole. They actually take the words in the first Sûtra of the Vedânta-philosophy, 'Now then a desire to know Brahman,' as pointing back to *G*aimini's Sûtras and as thereby implying that the Pûrva-Mîmâ*m*sâ should be studied first, and should be followed by a study of the Uttara-Mîmâ*m*sâ afterwards. Besides, the authors of the other five systems frequently refer to *G*aimini as an independent thinker, and though his treatment of the sacrificial system of the Veda would hardly seem to us to deserve the name of a system of philosophy, he has nevertheless touched on many a problem which falls clearly within that sphere of thought. Our idea of a system of philosophy is different from the Indian conception of a Dar*s*ana. In its original meaning philosophy, as a love of wisdom, comes nearest to the Sanskrit *Gigñâsâ*, a desire to know, if not a desire to be wise. If we take philosophy in the sense of an examination of our means of knowledge (Epistemology), or with Kant as an inquiry into the limits of human knowledge, there would be nothing corresponding to it in India. Even the Vedânta, so far as it is based, not on independent reasoning, but on the authority of the *S*ruti, would lose with us its claim to the title of philosophy. But we have only to waive the claim of infallibility put forward by Bâdarâya*n*a in favour of the utterances of the sages of the Upanishads, and treat them as simple human witnesses to the truth, and we should then find in the systematic arrangement of these utterances by Bâdarâya*n*a, a real philosophy, a complete view of the Kosmos in which we live, like those that have been put forward by the great thinkers of the philosophical countries of the world, Greece, Italy, Germany, France, and England.

# CHAPTER VI.

### Sâmkhya-Philosophy.

HAVING explored two of the recognised systems of Indian philosophy, so far as it seemed necessary in a general survey of the work done by the ancient thinkers of India, we must now return and enter once more into the densely entangled and almost impervious growth of thought from which all the high roads leading towards real and definite systems of philosophy have emerged, branching off in different directions. One of these and, as it seems to me, by far the most important for the whole intellectual development of India, the Vedânta, has been mapped out by us at least in its broad outlines.

It seemed to me undesirable to enter here on an examination of what has been called the later Vedânta which can be studied in such works as the Pañkadasi or the Vedânta-Sâra, and in many popular treatises both in prose and in verse.

### Later Vedânta mixed with Sâmkhya.

It would be unfair and unhistorical, however, to look upon this later development of the Vedânta as simply a deterioration of the old philosophy. Though it is certainly rather confused, if compared with the system as laid down in the old Vedânta-Sûtras, it represents to us what in the course of time became of the Vedânta, when taught and discussed in the different schools of philosophy in medieval and modern India. What strikes us most in it is the mixture of Vedânta ideas with ideas borrowed chiefly, as it would seem, from Sâmkhya, but also from Yoga, and Nyâya sources. But here again it is difficult to decide whether such ideas were actually borrowed from these systems in their finished state, or whether they were originally common property which in later times only had become restricted to one or the other of the six systems of philosophy. In the Pañkadasî, for instance, we meet with the idea of Prakriti, nature, which we are accustomed to consider as the peculiar property of the Sâmkhya-system. This Prakriti is said there to be the reflection, or, as we should say, the shadow of Brahman, and to be possessed of the three Gunas or elements of goodness, passion, and darkness, or, as they are sometimes explained, of good, indifferent, and bad. This theory of the three Gunas, however, is altogether absent from the original Vedânta; at least, it is not to be met with in the purely Vedântic Upanishads, occurring for the first time in the Svetâsvatara Upanishad. Again in the later Vedânta works Avidyâ and Mâyâ are used synonymously, or, if distinguished from one another, they are supposed to arise respectively from the more or less pure character of their substance[1]. The omniscient, but personal Îsvara is there explained as a reflection of Mâyâ, but as having subdued her, while the

---

[1] I translate Sattva here by substance, for the context hardly allows that we should take it for the Guna of goodness.

individual soul, Prâ*g*ña or *G*îva, is represented as having been subdued by Avidyâ, and to be multiform, owing to the variety of Avidyâ. The individual soul, being endowed with a causal or subtle body, believes that body to be its own, and hence error and suffering in all their variety. As to the development of the world, we are told that it was by the command of Îsvara that Prak*ri*ti, when dominated by darkness, produced the elements of ether, air, fire, water and earth, all meant to be enjoyed, that is, to be experienced by the individual souls.

In all this we can hardly be mistaken if we recognise the influence of Sâ*m*khya ideas, obscuring and vitiating the monism of the Vedânta, pure and simple. In that philosophy there is no room for a Second, or for a Prak*ri*ti, nor for the three Gu*n*as, nor for anything real by the side of Brahman.

How that influence was exercised we cannot discover, and it is possible that in ancient times already there existed this influence of one philosophical system upon the other, for we see even in some of the Upanishads a certain mixture of what we should afterwards have to call the distinctive teaching of Vedânta, Sâ*m*khya, or Yoga-philosophy. We must remember that in India the idea of private property in any philosophic truth did hardly exist. The individual, as we saw before, was of little consequence, and could never exercise the same influence which such thinkers as Socrates or Plato exercised in Greece. If the descriptions of Indian life emanating from the Indians themselves, and from other nations they came in contact with, whether Greek conquerors or Chinese pilgrims, can be trusted, we may well understand that truth, or what was taken to be truth, was treated not as private, but as common property. If there was an exchange of ideas among the Indian seekers after truth, it was far more in the nature of co-operation towards a common end, than in the assertion of any claims of originality or priority by individual teachers. That one man should write and publish his philosophical views in a book; and that another should read and criticise that book or carry on the work where it had been left, was never thought of in India in ancient times. If A. referred to B. often, as they say, from mere civility, Pû*g*ârtham, B. would refer to A., but no one would ever say, as so often happens with us, that he had anticipated the discovery of another, or that some one else had stolen his ideas. Truth was not an article that, according to Hindu ideas, could ever be stolen. All that could happen and did happen was that certain opinions which had been discussed, sifted, and generally received in one Â*s*rama, hermitage, Ârâma, garden, or Parishad, religious settlement, would in time be collected by its members and reduced to a more or less systematic form. What that form was in early times we may see from the Brâhma*n*as, and more particularly from the Upanishads, i. e. *Séances*, gatherings of pupils round their teachers, or later on from the Sûtras. It cannot be doubted that these Sûtras presuppose, by their systematic form, a long continued intellectual labour, nay it seems to me difficult to account for their peculiar literary form except on the ground that they were meant to be learnt by heart and to be accompanied from the very beginning by a running commentary, without which they would have been perfectly unintelligible. I suggested once before that this very peculiar style of the Sûtras would receive the best historical explanation, if it could be proved that they represent the first attempts at writing for literary purposes in India. Whatever the exact date may be of the introduction of a *sinistrorsum* and *dextrorsum* alphabet for epigraphic purposes in India (and in spite of all efforts not a single inscription has as yet been discovered that can be referred with certainty to the period before Asoka, third century B.C.), every classical scholar knows that there always is a long interval between an epigraphic and a literary employment of the alphabet. People forget that a period marked by written literary compositions requires a public, and a large public, which is able to read, for where there is no demand there is no supply. Nor must we forget that the old system of a mnemonic literature, the Paramparâ, was invested with a kind of sacred character, and would not have been easily surrendered. The old mnemonic system was upheld by a strict discipline which formed the principal part of the established system of education in India, as has been fully described in the Prâtisâkhyas. They explain to us by what process, whatever existed at that time of literature, chiefly sacred, was firmly imprinted on the memory of the young. These young pupils were in fact the books, the scribes were the Gurus, the tablet was the brain. We can hardly imagine such a state of literature, and the transition from it to a written literature must have marked a new start in the intellectual life of the people at large, or at least of the educated classes. Anybody who has come in contact with the Pandits of India has been able to observe the wonderful feats that can be achieved by that mnemonic discipline even at present, though it is dying out before our eyes at the approach of printed books, nay of printed editions of their own sacred texts. I need hardly say that even if Bühler's idea of the introduction of a Semitic alphabet into India by means of commercial travellers about 800 or 1000 B.C. were more than a hypothesis, it would not prove the existence of a written literature at that time. The adaptation of a Semitic alphabet to the phonetic system as elaborated in the Prâti*s*âkhyas may date from the third, possibly from the fourth century B.C., but the use of that alphabet for inscriptions begins in the middle of the third century only; and though we cannot deny the possibility of its having been used for literary purposes at the same time, such possibilities would form very dangerous landmarks in the chronology of Indian literature.

But whatever the origin of the peculiar Sûtra-literature may have been—and I give my hypothesis as a hypothesis only—all scholars will probably agree that these Sûtras could not be the work of one individual philosopher, but that we have in them the last outcome of previous centuries of thought, and the final result of the labours of numerous thinkers whose names are forgotten and will never be recovered.

### Relative Age of Philosophies and Sûtras.

If we keep this in mind, we shall see that the question whether any of the texts of the six philosophies which we now possess should be considered as older than any other, is really a question impossible to answer. The tests for settling the relative ages of literary works, applicable to European literature, are not applicable to Indian literature. Thus, if one Greek author quotes another, we feel justified in taking the one who is quoted as the predecessor or contemporary of the one who quotes. But because *G*aimini quotes Bâdarâya*n*a and Bâdarâya*n*a *G*aimini, and because their systems show an acquaintance with the other five systems of philosophy, we have no right to arrange them in chronological succession. Ka*n*âda, who is acquainted with Kapila, is clearly criticised by Kapila, at least in our Kapila-Sûtras. Kapila, to whom the Sâ*m*khya-Sûtras are ascribed, actually adopts one of Bâdarâya*n*a's Sûtras, IV, 1, 1, and inserts it *totidem verbis* in his own work, IV, 3. He does the same for the Yoga-Sûtras I, 5 and II, 46, which occur in II, 33, III, 34, and VI, 24 in the Sâ*m*khya-Sûtras which we possess. Ka*n*âda was clearly acquainted with Gotama, while Gotama attacks in turn certain doctrines of Kapila and Bâdarâya*n*a. It has been supposed, because Patañ*g*ali ignores all other systems, that therefore he was anterior to all of them[1]. But all such conclusions, which would be perfectly legitimate in Greek and Latin literature, have no weight whatever in the literary history of India, because during its mnemonic period anything could be added and anything left out, before each system reached the form in which we possess it.

---

[1] Rajendralal Mitra, l.c., p. xviii.

### Age of Kapila-Sûtras.

The Sûtras of Kapila, which have come down to us, are so little the work of the founder of that system, that it would be far safer to treat them as the last arrangement of doctrines accumulated in one philosophical school during centuries of Paramparâ or tradition. It is easy to see that the Yoga-philosophy presupposes a Sâ*m*khya-philosophy, but while Patañ*g*ali, the reputed author of Yoga-Sûtras has been referred to the second century B.C., it is now generally admitted that our Sâ*m*khya-Sûtras cannot be earlier than the fourteenth century A.D. It is necessary to distinguish carefully between the six philosophies as so many channels of thought, and the Sûtras which embody their teachings and have been handed down to us as the earliest documents within our reach. Yoga, as a technical term, occurs earlier than the name of any other system of philosophy. It occurs in the Taittirîya and Ka*th*a Upanishads, and is mentioned in as early an authority as the Âsvalâyana-G*ri*hya-Sûtras. In the Maitrây. Up. VI, 10 we meet even with Yogins. But it by no means follows that the Yoga, known in those early times, was the same as what we possess in Patañ*g*ali's Sûtras of the Yoga-philosophy. We look in vain in the so-called classical Upanishads for the names of either Sâ*m*khya or Vedânta, but Sâ*m*khya occurs in the compound Sâ*m*khya-Yoga in the *S*vetâ*s*vatara Up. VI, 13 and in several of the minor Upanishads. It should be observed that Vedânta also occurs for the first time in the same *S*vetâ*s*vatara VI, 22, and afterwards in the smaller Upanishads. All such indications may become valuable hereafter for chronological purposes. In the Bhagavad-gîtâ II, 39 we meet with the Sâ*m*khya as the name of a system of philosophy and likewise as a name of its adherents, V, 5.

As to our Sâ*m*khya-Sûtras their antiquity was first shaken by Dr. FitzEdward Hall. Vâ*k*aspati Mi*s*ra, the author of the Sâ*m*khya-tattva-Kaumudî, who, according to Professor Garbe, can be safely referred to about 1150 A.D., quotes not a single Sûtra from our Sâ*m*khya-Sûtras, but appeals to older authorities only, such as Pa*ñk*a*s*ikha, Vârshaga*n*ya, and the Râ*g*avârtika. Even Mâdhava about 1350 A.D., who evidently knew the Sûtras of the other systems, never quotes from our Sâ*m*khya-Sûtras; and why not, if they had been in existence in his time?

But we must not go too far. It by no means follows that every one of the Sûtras which we possess in the body of the Sâ*m*khya-Sûtras, and the composition of which is assigned by Bâla*s*astrin to so late a period as the sixteenth century, is of that modern date. He declares that they were all composed by the well-known Vi*g*ñâna-Bhikshu who, as was then the fashion, wrote also a commentary on them. It is quite possible that our Sâ*m*khya-Sûtras may only be what we should call the latest recension of the old Sûtras. We know that in India the oral tradition of certain texts, as, for instance, the Sûtras of Pâ*n*ini, was interrupted for a time and then restored again, whether from scattered MSS., or from the recollection of less forgetful or forgotten individuals. If that was the case, as we know, with so voluminous a work as the Mahâbhâshya; why should not certain portions of the Sâ*m*khya-Sûtras have been preserved here and there, and have been added to or remodelled from time to time, till they meet us at last in their final form, at so late a date as the fourteenth or even the sixteenth century? It was no doubt a great shock to those who stood up for the great antiquity of Indian philosophy, to have to confess that a work for which a most remote date had always been claimed, may not be older than the time of Des Cartes, at least in that final literary form in which it has reached us. But if we consider the circumstances of the case, it is more than possible that our Sûtras of the Sâ*m*khya-philosophy contain some of the most ancient as well as the most modern Sûtras, the utterances of Kapila, Âsuri, Pa*ñk*a*s*ikha and Vârshaga*n*ya, as well as those of Î*s*vara-K*r*ish*n*a and even of Vi*g*ñâna-Bhikshu.

### Sâ*m*khya-kârikâs.

But if we must accept so very modern a date for our Kapila-Sûtras, we are fortunate in being able to assign a much earlier and much more settled date to another work which for centuries seems to have formed the recognised authority for the followers of the Sâ*m*khya in India, the so-called Sâ*m*khya-kârikâs or the sixty-nine or seventy *Versus memoriales* of Î*s*vara-K*r*ish*n*a (with three supplementary ones, equally ascribed to that author). That these Kârikâs are older than our Sûtras could easily be proved by passages occurring among the Sûtras which are almost literally taken from the Kârikâs [1].

Alberuni, who wrote his account of India in the

---

[1] See Hall, Sâ*m*khya-Sâra, p. 12; Deussen, Vedânta, p. 361.

first half of the eleventh century, was well acquainted not only with Îsvara-Krishna's work, but likewise, as has been shown, with Gaudapâda's commentary on it[1]. Nay, we can even make another step backward. For the Sâmkhya-kârikâs exist in a Chinese translation also, made by *K*an-ti (lit. true truth), possibly Paramârtha, a Tripitaka law-teacher of the *Kh*an dynasty, A.D. 557 to 589 (not 583). Paramârtha came to China in about 547 A.D. in the reign of the Emperor Wu-ti of the Lian dynasty which ruled in Southern China from 502 to 557 A.D.[2], and was followed by the *Kh*an dynasty. He lived till 582 A.D.; and there are no less than twenty-eight of his translations now in existence, that of the Suvarna-Saptati-sâstra being the twenty-seventh (No. 1,300 in B. Nanjio's Catalogue). The name given to it in Chinese, 'the Golden Seventy Discourse,' is supposed to refer to the number of verses in the Kârikâ. *K*an-ti was not considered a good Chinese scholar, and his translation of the Abhidharma-Kosha-sâstra, for instance, had in consequence to be replaced by a new translation by Hiouen-thsang.

But though we are thus enabled to assign the Sâmkhya-kârikâ to the sixth century A.D., it by no means follows that this work itself did not exist before that time. Native tradition, we are told, assigns his work to the first century B.C.

---

[1] Garbe, Sâmkhya und Yoga, p. 7.

[2] See Mayer's Chinese Reader's Manual, which gives the exact dates.

### Date of Gau*d*apâda.

But even here new difficulties arise with regard to the age of Gau*d*apâda, the author of the commentary on the Kârikâs. This commentary also, so we were informed by Beal, had been translated into Chinese before 582 A.D.; but how is that possible without upsetting the little we know of Gau*d*apâda's date? *S*a*m*kara is represented as the pupil of Govinda who was the pupil of Gau*d*apâda. But *S*a*m*kara's literary career began, as is generally supposed, about 788 A.D. How then could he have been the literary grandson of Gau*d*apâda, and son or pupil of Govinda? As Mr. Beal could no longer be consulted I asked one of my Chinese pupils, the late Mr. Kasawara, to translate portions of the Chinese commentary for me; but the specimens he sent me did not suffice to settle the question whether it was really a translation of Gau*d*apâda's commentary. It is but right to state here that Telang in the Indian Antiquary, XIII, 95, places *S*a*m*kara much earlier, in 590 A.D., and that Fleet, in the Indian Antiquary, Jan., 1887, assigns 630 to 655 as the latest date to King V*ri*shadeva of Nepal who is said to have received *S*a*m*kara at his court, and actually to have given the name of *S*a*m*karadeva to his son in honour of the philosopher. In order to escape from all these uncertainties I wrote once more to Japan to another pupil of mine, Dr. Takakusu, and he, after carefully collating the Chinese translation with the Sanskrit commentary of Gau*d*apâda, informed me that the Chinese translation of the commentary was not, and could not in any sense be called, a translation of Gau*d*apâda's commentary. So much trouble may be caused by one unguarded expression! Anyhow this difficulty is now removed, and *S*a*m*kara's date need not be disturbed. The author of the Kârikâs informs us at the end of his work that this philosophy, proclaimed by the greatest sage, i. e. Kapila, had been communicated by him to Âsuri, by Âsuri to Pañ*k*a*s*ikha, and, as the Tattva-samâsa adds, from Pañ*k*a*s*ikha to Patañ*g*ali [1], and had been widely taught until, by an uninterrupted series of teachers, it reached even Î*s*vara-K*ri*sh*n*a [2]. He calls it the Shash*t*i-tantra, the Sixty-doctrine. A similar account is given by Paramârtha in his comment on the first verse, 'Kipila (Kapila),' he says, 'was a *Ri*shi descended from the sky and was endowed with the four virtues, dutifulness (Dharma), wisdom (Pra*g*ñâ), separation from desires (Vairâgya), and freedom (Moksha). He saw a Brâhman of the name of Ö-shu-li (Âsuri) who had been worshipping heaven or the Devas for a thousand years, and said to him: 'O Âsuri, art thou satisfied with the state of a G*ri*hastha or householder? After a thousand years he came again, and Âsuri admitted that he was satisfied with the state of a G*ri*hastha. He then came a third time to Âsuri, whereupon Âsuri quitted the state of a householder and became a pupil of Kapila.' These may be mere additions made by Paramârtha, but they show, at all events, that to him also Kapila and Âsuri were persons of a distant past.

---

[1] This would seem to place the Tattva-samâsa later than Patañ*g*ali.

[2] See Kârikâ, vv. 70, 71.

### Tattva-samâsa.

But however far the Kârikâs of Îsvara-K*ri*sh*n*a may go back, they are what they are, a metrical work in the style of a later age, an age that gave rise to other Kârikâs like Bhart*ri*hari's (about 650 A.D.) Kârikâs on grammar. Everybody has wondered, therefore, what could have become of the real Sâ*m*khya-Sûtras, if they ever existed; or, if they did not, why there should never have been such Sûtras for so important a system of philosophy as the Sâ*m*khya. There is clearly a great gap between the end of the Upanishad period and the literary period that was able to give rise to the metrical work of Îsvara-K*ri*sh*n*a. In what form could the Sâ*m*khya-philosophy have existed in that interval?

To judge from analogy we should certainly say, in the form of Sûtras, such as were handed down for other branches of learning by oral tradition. The Kârikâs themselves presuppose such a tradition quite as much as the much later Sûtras which we possess. They are both meant to recapitulate what existed, never to originate what we should call new and original thoughts. When we see the Kârikâs declare that they leave out on purpose the Âkhâyikâs, the illustrative stories contained in the fourth book of our Sûtras, this cannot prove their posteriority to the Sûtras as we have them; but it shows that at Îsvara-K*ri*sh*n*a's time there existed a body of Sâ*m*khya-philosophy which contained such stories as we find in our modern Sûtras, but neither in the Kârikâs nor in the Tattva-samâsa. Besides these stories other things also were omitted by Îsvara-K*ri*sh*n*a, comprehended under the name of Para-vâda, probably controversies, such as those on the necessity of an Îsvara.

Under these circumstances I venture to say that such a work in Sûtras not only existed, but that we are in actual possession of it, namely in the text of the much neglected Tattva-samâsa. Because it contains a number of new technical terms, it has been put down at once as modern, as if what is new to us must be new chronologically also. We know far too little of the history of the Sâ*m*khya to justify so confident a conclusion. Colebrooke[1] told us long ago that, if the scholiast of Kapila[2] may be trusted, and why should he not? the Tattva-samâsa was the proper text-book of the Sâ*m*khya-philosophy. It was a mere accident that he, Colebrooke, could not find a copy of it. 'Whether that Tattva-samâsa of Kapila be extant,' he wrote, 'or whether the Sûtras of Pañ*k*a*s*ikha be so, is not certain.' And again he wrote: 'It appears from the Preface of the Kapila-bhâshya that a more compendious tract in the form of Sûtras or aphorisms, bears the title of Tattva-samâsa, and is ascribed to the same author, i. e. to Kapila.

I admit that the introductory portion of this tract sounds modern, and probably is so, but I find no other marks of a modern date in the body of the work. On the contrary there are several indications in it of its being an earlier form of the Sâ*m*khya-philosophy than what we possess in the Kârikâs or in the Sûtras. When it agrees with the Kârikâs, sometimes almost verbatim, it is the metrical text

---

[1] Essays, I, p. 244.

[2] Sâ*m*khya-pravα*k*ana-bhâshya, pp. 7, 110.

that seems to me to presuppose the prose, not the prose the metrical version. In the Sûtras themselves we find no allusion as yet to the atheistic or non-theistic doctrines which distinguish the later texts of the Sâ*m*khya, and which are still absent from the Sâ*m*khya-kârikâs also. The so-called Ais*v*aryas or superhuman powers, which are recognised in the Tattva-samâsa, might seem to presuppose the recognition of an Îs*v*ara, though this is very doubtful; but the direct identification of Purusha with Brahman in the Tattva-samâsa points certainly to an earlier and less pronounced Nirîs*v*ara or Lord-less character of the ancient Sâ*m*khya. It should also be mentioned that Vi*g*ñâna-Bhikshu, no mean authority on such matters, and even supposed by some to have been himself the author of our modern Sâ*m*khya-Sûtras, takes it for granted that the Tattva-samâsa was certainly prior to the Kapila-Sûtras which we possess. For why should he defend Kapila, and not the author of the Tattva-samâsa, against the charge of Punarukti or giving us a mere useless repetition, and why should he have found no excuse for the existence of the Kapila-Sûtras except that they are short and complete, while the Tattva-samâsa is short and compact[1]?

Not being able to find a MS. of the Tattva-samâsa Colebrooke decided to translate instead the Sâ*m*khya-kârikâs, and thus it came to pass that most scholars have been under the impression that in India also this metrical version was considered as the most authoritative and most popular manual of the Sâ*m*khya-philosophy. This is the way in which certain

---

[1] Sâ*m*khya-prava*k*ana-bhâshya, Introduction.

prepossessions arise. We have learnt since from Ballantyne [1] that at Benares, where he resided, these Kârikâs were hardly known at all except to those who had seen Professor Wilson's English edition of them, while the Tattva-samâsa was well known to all the native assistants whom he employed. Nor can we doubt that in the part of India best known to Ballantyne it was really an important and popular work, if we consider the number of commentaries written on it [2], and the frequency of allusions to it which occur in other commentaries. The commentary published by Ballantyne is, if I understand him rightly, anonymous. It gives first what it calls the Sâ*m*khya-Sûtrâ*n*i, and then the Samâsâkhya-sûtra-v*ri*tti*h*. Hall, l. c., p. 13, quotes one commentary by Kshemânanda, called Sâ*m*khya-krama-dîpikâ, but it is not quite clear to me whether this is the same as the one published by Ballantyne, nor have I had access to any other MSS.

We must not forget that in modern times the Sâ*m*khya-philosophy has ceased to be popular in several parts of India. Even in the sixteenth century Vi*gñ*âna-Bhikshu, in his commentary on the Sâ*m*khya-Sûtras (v. 5), complains that it has been swallowed up by the sun of the time, and that but a small part of the moon of knowledge remained; while in the Bhâgavata Purâ*n*a I, 3, 10, the Sâ*m*khya is spoken of as Kâla-vipluta, destroyed by time. Professor Wilson told me that, during the whole of his intercourse with learned natives, he met with one Brâhman only who professed to be acquainted with the

---

[1] Drift of the Sâ*m*khya, p. 1.

[2] Five are mentioned by Hall in his Preface, p. 33.

writings of this philosophical school, and Professor Bhandarkar (l. c., p. 3) states that the very name of Sâ*m*khya-prava*k*ana was unknown on his side of India. Hence we may well understand that Sâ*m*khya MSS. are scarce in India, and entirely absent in certain localities. It is possible also that the very smallness of the Tattva-samâsa may have lowered it in the eyes of native scholars, and that in time it may have been eclipsed by its more voluminous commentaries. But if we accept it as what it professes to be, and what, up to the time of Vi*g*ñâna-Bhikshu at least, it was considered to be in India, it seems to me just the book that was wanted to fill the gap to which I referred before. By itself it would fill a few pages only. In fact it is a mere enumeration of topics, and, as such, it would agree very well with the somewhat puzzling name of Sâ*m*khya, which means no more than enumeration. All other derivations of this title seem far-fetched [1] as compared with this. According to Vi*g*ñâna-Bhikshu in his commentary on the Sûtras (pp. 6, 110), ed. Hall, both the Sâ*m*khya-Sûtras and the Yoga-Sûtras are really mere developments of the Tattva-samâsa-Sûtras. Both are called therefore Sâ*m*khya-prava*k*ana, exposition of the Sâ*m*khya, the latter adding the peculiar arguments in support of the existence of an Î*s*vara or Supreme Lord, and therefore called Se*s*vara, in opposition to the Sâ*m*khya, which is called An-î*s*vara, or Lord-less.

And here it is important to remark also that the name of Shash*t*i-tantra, the Doctrine of the Sixty,

---

[1] They are mentioned in the Preface to Hall's edition of the Sâ*m*khya-prava*k*ana-bhâshya, 1856. Some of them are mere definitions without any attempt at etymology.

which is given by Îsvara-K*r*ish*n*a, or at all events by the author of the 72nd of his Kârikâs, should occur and be accounted for in the Tattva-samâsa, as containing the 17 (enumerated in 64 and 65), and the 33, previously exhibited in 62 and 63, together with the 10 Mûlikârthas or fundamental facts which together would make up the sixty topics of the Shash*t*i-tantra. At the end of the 25 great topics of the Tattva-samâsa we find the straightforward declaration: 'Iti tattva-samâsâkhya-sâ*m*khya-sûtrâ*n*i,' Here end the Sâ*m*khya-Sûtras called Tattva-samâsa.

At first sight, no doubt, Samâsa seems to mean a mere abstract; but Samâsa may be used also in opposition to B*r*ihat, and there is no other work in existence of which it could be called an abstract, certainly not either of the Kârikâs or of the modern Sûtras, such as we possess them. The whole arrangement is different from the other and more recent treatments of Sâ*m*khya-philosophy. The three kinds of pain, for instance, which generally form the starting-point of the whole system, are relegated to the very end as a separate topic. We meet with technical subjects and technical terms which are not to be found at all in other and, as it would seem, more modern Sâ*m*khya works. The smallness of the Tattva-samâsa can hardly be used as an argument against its ever having been an important work, for we find similar short, yet old Sûtra-works, for instance, the Sarvânukrama and other Anukrama*n*is described in my History of Ancient Sanskrit Literature[1]. However, in matters

---

[1] These Anukramas have been very carefully published in the Anecdota Oxoniensia by Professor Macdonell, to whom I had handed over my materials.

of this kind we must avoid being too positive either in denying or asserting the age and authenticity of Sanskrit texts. All I can say is that there is no mark of modern age in their language, though the commentary is, no doubt, of a later date. What weighs with me is the fact that Indian Pandits evidently considered the Tattva-samâsa-Sûtras as the original outlines of the Sâ*m*khya-philosophy, while the idea that they are a later spurious production rests, as far as I can see at present, on no real argument whatever.

### Anteriority of Vedânta or Sâ*m*khya.

It must be clear from all this how useless it would be, with the limited means at our disposal, to attempt to prove the anteriority either of the Vedânta or of the Sâ*m*khya, as systems of philosophy, and as distinguished from the Sûtras in which we possess them. External or historical evidence we have none, and internal evidence, though it may support a suggestion, can but seldom amount to positive proof. We can understand how, out of the seeds scattered about in the Upanishads, there could arise in time the systematic arrangement and final representation of systems such as have been handed down to us in the Sûtras of the Vedânta, the Sâ*m*khya, and the other schools. It cannot be denied that in the Upanishad period Vedântic ideas are certainly more prevalent than those of the Sâ*m*khya. I go even a step further and admit that the Sâ*m*khya-philosophy may have been a kind of toning down of the extreme Monism of the Advaita Vedânta. I think we can enter into the misgivings and fears of those who felt startled by the unflinching Monism of the Vedânta, at least as interpreted by the school which was represented rather than founded by *S*am*k*ara. Now, the two points which are most likely to have caused difficulty or given offence to ordinary consciences, would seem to have been the total denial of what is meant by the reality of the objective world, and the required surrender of all individuality on the part of the subject, that is, of ourselves. These are the points which seem most startling even to ourselves, and it is quite possible that they may have given rise to another system free from these startling doctrines, such as we find in the Sâ*m*khya. They certainly formed the chief stumbling-block to Râmânu*g*a and those who had come before him, such as Bodhâyana and other Pûrvâ*k*âryas, and led them to propound their own more human interpretation of the Vedânta, though sacrificing the Îsvara in order to save the reality of each Purusha.

These conflicting views of the world, of the soul, and of God, emerge already in the Upanishads; and in a few of them, the *S*vetâ*s*vatara, Maitrây, and Ka*th*a Upanishads, for instance, there are utterances that come very near to what we know as Sâ*m*khya rather than Vedânta doctrines. Vedânta ideas preponderate, however, so decidedly in the Upanishad literature, that we can well understand that in the oral tradition of the schools the Sâ*m*khya doctrines should have exercised a limited influence only, whatever favour they may have found with those who were repelled by the extreme views of the monistic Vedânta. The followers of Kapila had an advantage over the Vedântists in admitting a Prak*ri*ti, or a something objective, independent of Brahman or Purusha, though called into life and activity by the look of Purusha only, and disappearing when that look ceased. They were also less opposed to the common consciousness of mankind in admitting the reality of individual souls. Dualism is always more popular than rigorous Monism, and the Sâ*m*khya was clearly dualistic when it postulated nature, not only as the result of Avidyâ or Mâyâ, but as something real in the ordinary sense of that word, and when it allowed to the individual souls or *G*îvas also an independent character. It should be remembered that the denial of an Î*s*vara or personal Lord did not probably form part of the original Sâ*m*khya, as presented to us in the Tattva-samâsa. It would seem therefore that on these very important points the Sâ*m*khya was more conciliatory and less defiant to the common sense of mankind than the Vedânta, and though this is far from proving that it was therefore posterior to the Vedânta in its severest form, it might well be accepted as an indication that these two streams of thought followed parallel courses, starting from a common fund of ancient Vedic thoughts, but diverging afterwards, the Vedânta unflinchingly following its straight course, the other, the Sâ*m*khya, avoiding certain whirlpools of thought which seemed dangerous to the ordinary swimmer. To the people at large it would naturally seem as if the Vedânta taught the oneness of all individual souls or subjects in Brahman, and the illusory character of all that is objective, while the Sâ*m*khya allowed at all events the temporary reality of the objective world and the multiplicity of individual souls. Of course, we must leave it an open question for the present whether the extreme monistic view of the Veda was due to *S*a*m*kara, or whether, like Râmânu*g*a, he also could claim the authority of Pûrvâ*k*âryas in his interpretation of Bâdarâya*n*a's Sûtras. If that were so, the difference between the two systems would certainly seem to be irreconcilable, while minor differences between them would in India at least admit of a friendly adjustment.

### Atheism and Orthodoxy.

Even on what seems to us so vital a point in every philosophy as theism or atheism, Indian philosophers seem to have been able to come to an understanding and a compromise. We must remember that in the eyes of the Brâhmans the Sâ*m*khya is atheistic and yet orthodox. This seems to us impossible; but the fact is that orthodoxy has a very different meaning in India from what it has with us. What we mean by orthodoxy was with them not much more than a recognition of the supreme authority of the Veda. The Sâ*m*khya, whatever we may think of its Vedic character, never denies the authority of the Veda in so many words, though it may express a less decided submission to it. Whether in its origin the Sâ*m*khya was quite independent of the Veda, is difficult to say. Some scholars think that the recognition of the supreme authority of the *S*ruti was an afterthought with Kapila, a mere stroke of theological diplomacy. But if so, we should be forced to admit that the Sâ*m*khya philosophers wished, by means of this diplomacy, to be raised to the same position which others, such as the Vedântists, had occupied before them; and so far it might seem to indicate the posteriority of the Sâ*m*khya, as a system of philosophy.

It is important here to remember that the Sâ*m*khya not only declared for the authority of the Veda, but had never openly rejected it, like B*ri*haspati or Buddha. It is quite another question whether it really carried out the spirit of the Veda, particularly of the Upanishads. That *S*a*m*kara, the great defender of Vedântism, should deny the correctness of the interpretation of the Veda, adopted by Kapila, proves after all no more than that a difference of opinion existed between the two, but it would show at the same time that Kapila, as well as *S*a*m*kara, had tried to represent his philosophy as supported by passages from the Veda. To judge from a passage in the beginning of the Sâ*m*khya-kârikâs it might seem indeed that Kapila placed his own philosophy above the Veda. But he really says no more there than that certain remedies for the removal of pain, enjoined by the Veda, are good, and that other remedies enjoined by philosophy are likewise good; but that of the two the latter are better, that is, more efficacious (Tattva Kaumudî, v. 2). This does not affect the authority of the Veda as a whole, as compared with philosophy or human knowledge. We must not forget that after all it is *S*ruti or revelation itself which declares that all remedies are palliative only, and that real freedom (Moksha) from all suffering can be derived from philosophical knowledge only, and that this is incomparably higher than sacrifices or other meritorious acts (Sâ*m*khya-prava*k*ana I, 5).

### Authority of the Veda.

What authority Kapila assigns to the Veda may be gathered from what he says about the three possible sources of knowledge, perception, inference, and Âptavakana, that is the received, correct, or true word, or, it may be, the word of a trustworthy person. He explains Âptavakana in v. 5 by Âpta-sruti, which clearly means received revelation or revelation from a trustworthy source. However the commentators may differ, Sruti can here mean the Veda only, though, no doubt, the Veda as interpreted by Kapila. And that the Veda is not only considered as equal to sensuous perception and inference, but is placed by him on an even higher pedestal, is shown by the fact that Kapila (Sûtras V, 51) declares it to be self-evident, Svatah-pramânam, while perception and inference are not, but are admitted to be liable to error and to require confirmation.

Though it is true, therefore, that with the true Sâmkhya philosopher the Veda does not possess that superhuman authority which is ascribed to it by Bâdarâyana, I cannot bring myself to believe that this concession on the part of Kapila was a mere artifice to escape the fate which, for instance, befell Buddha. There are many passages where Kapila appeals quite naturally to Sruti or revelation. In I, 36 he appeals to both Sruti and Nyâya, reasoning, but in many places he appeals to Sruti alone. That revelation is to be looked upon as superior to experience or sensuous perception is stated by him in so many words in I, 147, where we read 'There is no denial of what is established by *S*ruti.' Again, when the Nyâya philosophy tries to establish by reasoning that the organs of sense are formed of the elements, Kapila squashes the whole argument by a simple appeal to *S*ruti. 'They cannot be so formed,' he says, 'because *S*ruti says that they are formed of Aha*m*kâra, self-consciousness (II, 20)[1].'

Other passages where the authority of *S*ruti is invoked as paramount by Kapila, or supposed to be so by the commentator, may be found in Sâ*m*khya-Sûtras I, 36; 77; 83; 147; 154; II, 20; 22; III, 15; 80; IV, 22; &c.

### Sâ*m*khya hostile to Priesthood.

There is one passage only in which a decidedly hostile feeling towards the Brâhmanic priesthood may be discovered in Kapila's Sûtras, and it seems full of meaning. Among the different kinds of bondage to which men are liable, but ought not to be, is one called Dakshi*n*â-bandha, bondage arising from having to offer gifts to priests, which seems to be condemned as superstitious and mischievous[2].

As springing from the great mass of philosophic thought accumulated in the Upanishads, the Sâ*m*khya, like the Vedânta-philosophy, was probably at first considered as neither orthodox nor unorthodox. It was simply one out of many attempts to solve the riddle of the world, and even the fact that it did not appeal to a personal Lord or creator, was evidently at first not considered sufficient to anathematise it as unorthodox or un-Vedic. It was probably

---

[1] But are not the elements mere Vikâras of Aha*m*kâra?

[2] See Tattva-samâsa 22; Sâ*m*khya-kârikâs 44.

at a much later time when the Vedânta and other systems had already entrenched themselves behind revelation, or the Veda, as the highest authority even on philosophical questions, that other systems, having been proved un-Vedic, came to be considered as objectionable or unorthodox, while the Vedânta, as its very name implied, was safe under the shadow of the Veda. I know that other scholars maintain that with the Sâmkhya any appeal to the Veda was an afterthought only, and not an essential part of the original system, nay, not even quite honest. We may admit that the Sâmkhya has no need of the Veda, but why should it appeal to it even on indifferent questions, if the Veda had not been considered by it as of supreme authority. It is possible that there may have been originally a difference between Sruti, revelation as not human, and Âpta-vakana, authoritative tradition as human, and that with Kapila the Veda was treated at first as coming under Âpta-vakana. But however this may be, unless our conception of the development of Indian philosophy, as we catch glimpses of it now and then in the course of centuries, is entirely wrong, it must be clear that, in the present state of our knowledge, to call one channel of philosophic thought, whether Sâmkhya or Vedânta, in the form in which it has reached us, more ancient than the other, would be mere playing with words.

### Parallel development of Philosophical Systems.

The result of this desire to fix dates, where dates are impossible, has often proved most mischievous. Scholars of recognised authority have arrived at and given expression to convictions, not only widely different, but diametrically opposed to each other. The chief cause of this confusion has been that, by a very natural tendency, we always wish to arrange things *Nacheinander* or in causal connection, instead of being satisfied with taking things as *Nebeneinander*, parallel and formed under similar conditions, springing from a common source and flowing on side by side in the same direction.

A reference to the history of language may make my meaning clearer. No one would say that Greek was older than Latin. Greek has some forms more primitive than Latin, but Latin also has some forms more primitive than Greek. It is true that we know literary productions in Greek at a much earlier time than literary productions in Latin, nor would any Sanskrit scholar deny that the Sûtras of Bâdarâya*n*a are older than the Sâ*m*khya-Sûtras, as we now possess the two. But for all that, Greek, as a language, cannot be a day older than Latin. Both branched off, slowly it may be and almost imperceptibly at first, from the time when the Aryan separation took place. In their embryonic form they both go back to some indefinite date, far beyond the limits of any chronology. In India we may learn how, like language, religion, and mythology, philosophy also formed at first a kind of common property. We meet with philosophical ideas of a Vedântic character, though as yet in a very undecided form, as far back as the hymns of the Rig-veda; they meet us again in the Brâhma*n*as and in some of the Upanishads, while the Sâ*m*khya ideas stand out less prominently, owing, it would seem, to the ascendency gained at that early period already by the Vedânta. Instead of supposing, however, that passages in support of Sâmkhya ideas occurring in certain of the older Upanishads were foisted in at a later time, it seems far more probable to me that they were survivals of an earlier period of as yet undifferentiated philosophical thought.

### Buddhism subsequent to Upanishads.

What remains of the chronological framework of Indian philosophy is in the end not much more than that both Vedânta and Sâmkhya ideas existed before the rise of historical Buddhism. The very name of Upanishad, for instance, is so peculiar that its occurrence in ancient Buddhist texts proves once for all the existence of some of these works before the rise of Buddhism.

The recognition of mendicant friars also, as a social institution, seems to me simply taken over from the Brâhmans. The very name of Bhikkhu, applied to the members of the Buddhist fraternity, comes from the same source. It is true, no doubt, that the name of Bhikshu does not occur in the classical Upanishads, but the right of begging, whether in the first or the third of the Âsramas (Brahmakârin or Vânaprastha), is fully recognised, only that the third and fourth Âsramas are not so clearly distinguished in early times as they are in Manu and afterwards. In the Kaush. Up. II, 2 we read of a man who has begged through a village and got nothing (Bhikshitvâ); in the *Kh*ând. Up. IV, 3, 5, a Brahmakârin is mentioned who has begged. The technical term for this begging is Bhikshâkâryâ in the Brih. Âr. Up. III (V), 5, 1, and exactly the same compound, Bhikkhâ-

*k*ârya, occurs in the Dhammapada 392; Bhaikshâ-*k*ârya occurs also in the Mu*nd*aka I, 2, 11, so that the fact that the substantive Bhikshu does not occur in the classical Upanishads can hardly be used as an argument to prove that the status of the mendicant friar was not known before the spreading of Buddhism. It is true that in its social meaning Â*s*rama, the name of the three or four stages, does not occur in the classical Upanishads; but, as we find Â*s*ramin in the Maitrây. Up. IV, 3, we can hardly doubt that the three or four stages (Brahma*k*ârî, Gaha*tth*o, Vânapa*tth*o, Bhikkhu) were known before the rise of Buddhism, and taken over by the Buddhists from the Vedic Brâhmans. Socially, the only Â*s*ramas that remained among the Buddhists were two, that of the G*ri*hins and that of the Bhikkhus.

That many of the technical terms of the Buddhists (Uposhadha, &c.) could have come from the same source only, has long been known, so much so that it has been rightly said, Without Brâhmanism no Buddhism.

The institution of the Vasso[1], for instance, the retreat during the rainy season, is clearly taken over from the Varshâs, the rainy season, as kept by the Brâhmans, and so is the quinquennial celebration of the Pañ*k*avarsha-parishad, and many other customs adopted by the Buddhists.

### Lalita-vistara.

I have explained before why at present I attribute less importance than I did formerly to the occurrence

[1] S. B. E. VIII, p. 213.

of a number of titles, including Sâ*m*khya, Yoga, Vai*s*eshika, and possibly Nyâya, in the Lalita-vistara. If the date assigned by Stanislas Julien and others to certain Chinese translations of this work could be re-established, the passage so often quoted from the twelfth chapter would be of considerable value to us in forming an idea of Indian literature as it existed at the time when the Lalita-vistara was originally composed. We find here the names not only of the Vedic glossary (Nigha*nt*u ?) the Nigamas (part of Nirukta), Purâ*n*as, Itihâsas, Vedas, grammar, Nirukta, *S*ikshâ, *Kh*andas, ritual (Kalpa), astronomy (*G*yotisha), but, what would be most important for us, the names of three systems of philosophy also, Sâ*m*khya, Yoga, and Vai*s*eshika, while Hetuvidyâ can hardly be meant for anything but Nyâya. But until the dates of the various Chinese translations of the Life of Buddha have been re-examined, we must abstain from using them for assigning any dates to their Sanskrit originals.

### A*s*vaghosha's Buddha-*k*arita.

We may perhaps place more reliance on A*s*vaghosha's Buddha-*k*arita, which, with great probability, has been ascribed to the first century A.D. He mentions Vyâsa, the son of Sarasvatî, as the compiler of the Veda, though not of the Vedânta-Sûtras; he knows Valmîki, the author of the Râmâya*n*a, Âtreya as a teacher of medicine, and *G*anaka, the well-known king, as a teacher of Yoga. By far the most important passage in it for our present purpose is the conversation between Ârâ*d*a and the future Buddha, here already called Bodhisattva in the twelfth book. This Ârâ*d*a is clearly a teacher of Sâ*m*khya-philosophy, it may be of Sâ*m*khya in an earlier state; and, though the name of Sâ*m*khya does not occur, the name of Kapila does (XII, 21), and even a disciple of his is mentioned. Here then we have in a poem, ascribed to the first century A. D., a clear reference to that philosophical system which is known to us under the name of Sâ*m*khya, and we have actually the name of Kapila, the reputed author of that system. The name of Kapila-vâstu[1] also occurs, as the birthplace of Buddha and as the dwelling of the famous sage Kapila. No reference to the Vedânta has been met with in A*s*vaghosha's Buddha-*k*arita, though the substitution of the Vedântic name of Brahman for the Sâ*m*khya name of Purusha deserves attention.

### Buddhist Suttas.

If we consult the Buddhist Suttas, which, whatever the date of their original composition may have been, were at all events reduced to writing in the first century B. C., and may be safely used therefore as historical evidence for that time, we find there also views ascribed to the Brâhmans of Buddha's time which clearly breathe the spirit of the Sâ*m*khya-philosophy. But it would be very unsafe to say more, and to maintain that such passages prove in any way the existence of fully developed systems of philosophy, or of anything very different from what we find already in certain Upanishads. All we can

---

[1] I write Vâstu, because that alone means dwelling-place, while Văstu means thing. Vâstu became Vătthu in Pâli, and was then probably retranslated into Sanskrit as Văstu.

say is that there are a number of terms in the Suttas which are the very terms used in the Vedânta, Sâmkhya and Yoga-philosophies, such as Âtman, Sâsvata, Nitya (? Anitya), Akshobhya, Brahman, Îsvara, Dharma, Parinâma, and many more; but, so far as I know, there is not one of which we could say that it could have been taken from the Sûtras only, and from nowhere else.

We should remember that in the Buddhist Canon we find constant mention of Titthiyas or Tîrthakas and their heretical systems of philosophy. Six contemporaries of Buddha are mentioned, one of them, Nigantho Nâtaputta, being the well-known founder of Gainism, Pûrana Kassapa, Makkhali, Agita, Pakudha and Sañgaya[1]. Nor are the names of the reputed authors of the six systems of Brâhmanic-philosophy absent from the Tripitaka. But we hear nothing of any literary compositions ascribed to Bâdarâyana, Gaimini, Kapila, Patañgali, Gotama or Kanâda. Some of these names occur in the Buddhist Sanskrit texts also, such as the Lankâvatâra where the names of Kanâda, Kapila, Akshapâda, Brihaspati are met with, but again not a single specimen or extract from their compositions.

### Âsvalâyana's Grihya-Sûtras.

Another help for determining the existence of ancient Sûtras and Bhâshyas may be found in the Grihya-Sûtras of Âsvalâyana and Sâmkhâyana, works belonging to the age of Vedic literature, though it may be to the very end of what I call the Sûtra-period. Here, as I pointed out in 1859 in my History

---

[1] Sâmañña-Phala-Sutta 3.

of Ancient Sanskrit Literature, we find not only the Rig-veda with all its subdivisions, but such names as Sumantu, *G*aimini, Vai*s*ampâyana, Paila, Sûtras, Bhâshyas, Bhârata[1], Mahâbhârata, teachers of the law, *G*ânanti, Bâhavi, Gârgya, Gautama, *S*âkalya, Bâbhravya, Mâ*nd*avya, Mâ*nd*ûkeya, Gârgî Vâ*k*aknavî, Vadavâ Prâtîtheyî, Sulâbhâ Maitreyî, Kahola Kaushîtaka, Mahâkaushîtaka, Pai*m*gya, Mahâpai*m*gya, Suya*gñ*a *S*â*m*khâyana, Aitareya, Mahaitareya, the Sâkala (text), the Bâshkala (text), Su*g*âtavaktra, Audavâhi, Mahaudavâhi, Sau*g*âmi, *S*aunaka, Â*s*valâyana. The *S*â*m*khâyana G*ri*hya-Sûtras IV, 10, give the same list, though leaving out a few names and adding others. The most valuable part in both sets of G*ri*hya-Sûtras is their testifying at that early and probably pre-Buddhistic time, not only to the existence of Sûtras, but of Bhâshyas or commentaries also, without which, as I said before, neither the philosophical, nor the grammatical, nor any other Sûtras would ever have been intelligible, or even possible.

### Did Buddha borrow from Kapila?

I may seem very sceptical in all this, but I cannot even now bring myself to believe that the author of Buddhism borrowed from the Sâ*m*khya or any other definite system of philosophy, as known to us in its final Sûtra form, in the sense which we ourselves assign to borrowing. Buddha, it seems to me, had as much

---

[1] How careful we must be, we may learn from the fact that instead of Bhârata and Mahâbhârata, other MSS. read Bhâratadharmâ*k*âryas; while in the *S*â*m*khâyana G*ri*hya-Sûtras IV, 10, 4, Bhârata, Mahâbhârata and Dharmâ*k*âryas are left out altogether.

right to many of the so-called Sâ*m*khya or Vedânta ideas as Kapila or anybody else. Who would say, for instance, that his belief in Sa*m*sâra or migration of souls was borrowed from Bâdarâya*n*a or Kapila? It belonged to everybody in India as much as a belief in Karman or the continuous working of deeds. In the great dearth of historical dates it may no doubt be excusable, if we lay hold of anything to save us from drowning while exploring the chronology of Indian literature. Our difficulties are very great, for even when the names of the principal systems of philosophy and the names of their reputed authors are mentioned, how do we know that they refer to anything written that we possess? Unless we meet with *verbatim* quotations, we can never know whether a certain book of a certain author is intended, or simply the general Paramparâ, that is, the tradition, as handed down in various Â*s*ramas, two things which should be carefully distinguished.

It is strange to see how often our hopes have been roused and disappointed. We were told that in Professor Hardy's most valuable translation of the Aṅguttara a number of philosophical sects were mentioned which existed at the time of Buddha's appearance, such as (1) Â*g*îvakos, (2) Niga*nth*os, (3) Mu*nd*asâvakos, (4) *G*atilakos, (5) Paribbâ*g*akos, (6) Mâgandikos, (7) Teda*nd*ikos, (8) Aviruddhakos, (9) Gotamakos, and (10) Devadhammikos. But not one of these names helps us to a real chronological date. Â*g*îvakos and Niga*nth*os are the names of *G*aina ascetics, the latter belonging to the Digambara sects, which could hardly have been established long before Buddha's appearance, while Mu*nd*asâvakos, i.e. pupils of the shaveling, the Buddha, and Gotamakos would seem to be schools which owed their existence to Buddha himself. The other names *G*atilakos, ascetics, Paribbâ*g*akos, religious mendicants, Teda*nd*ikos, i.e. Sa*m*nyâsins carrying the three staves, would be applicable both to Brâhmanic and Buddhist sects. Mâgandikos, if meant for Mâgadhikos, people of Magadha, would be Buddhists again. Aviruddhakos, a name not clear to me, may have been intended for ascetics no longer impeded by any desires, while Devadhammikos are clearly worshippers of the ancient national Devas, and therefore Brâhmanic, and possibly Vedic. We get no historical dates from the names of any of these schools, if schools they were. All they teach is that at the time Brâhmanic and Buddhist sects were existing side by side in large numbers, but by no means, as is commonly supposed, in constant conflict with each other[1]. Of the six recognised systems of philosophy, of their eponymous heroes or their written works, we do not hear a single word.

#### Bâna's Harsha*k*arita.

Not even in later works, which have been referred to the sixth, seventh, and eighth centuries A.D., do we meet with actual quotations from our Sûtras of the six Dar*s*anas. Bâna, in his Life of King Harsha, knows indeed of Aupanishadas, Kâpilas, Kâ*n*âdas; and if the Kâpilas are the followers of the Sâ*m*khya, Kâ*n*âdas the followers of the Vai*s*eshika school, the Aupanishadas can hardly be meant for anybody but the Vedântins. Varâha-Mihira also, in the sixth

---

[1] Cf. Rhys Davids, J. R. A. S., Jan., 1898, p. 197.

century A. D., mentions Kapila and Ka*n*abhu*g* (Vai*s*eshika), but even this does not help us to the dates of any Sûtras composed by them.

The Chinese translator of the Kârikâs, likewise in the sixth century, informs us that these Kârikâs contain the words of Kapila or of Pañ*k*a*s*ikha, the pupil of Âsuri, who was the pupil of Kapila. We are told even that there were originally 60,000 Gâthâs, and all that Î*s*vara-K*ri*sh*n*a did was to select seventy of them for his seventy or seventy-two Kârikâs.

That Mâdhava (1350 A. D.), while mentioning the Sûtras of the other systems, should not have mentioned those of the Sâ*m*khya, is no doubt, as I pointed out before, a strong argument in support of their non-existence in his time. But it is no proof, as little as we may conclude from the fact that Hiouen-thsang translated the Vai*s*eshika-nikâya-da*s*apadârtha-*s*âstra by *G*ñâna*k*andra, and not the Vai*s*eshika-Sûtras by Ka*n*âda, that therefore these Sûtras did not exist in his time. We cannot be too careful in such matters, for the unreserved acceptance of a purely conjectural date is very apt to interfere with the discovery of a real date. Hiouen-thsang likewise mentions a number of Nyâya works, but not Gotama's Nyâya-Sûtras. Does that prove that Gotama's Sûtras were unknown in the seventh century? It may or may not. He relates that Gu*n*amati defeated a famous Sâ*m*khya philosopher of the name of Mâdhava, but again he tells us no more. His own special study, as is well known, was the Yoga-philosophy. And here again, though he speaks of a number of Yoga works, he says not a word of the most important of them all, the

Sûtras of Patañgali[1]. Yet I doubt whether we may conclude from this that these Sûtras did not exist at his time.

### The Tattva-samâsa.

If then I venture to call the Tattva-samâsa the oldest record that has reached us of the Sâmkhya-philosophy, and if I prefer to follow them in the account I give of that philosophy, I am quite aware that many scholars will object, and will prefer the description of the Sâmkhya as given in the Kârikâs and in the Sûtras. Both of them, particularly the Kârikâs, give us certainly better arranged accounts of that philosophy, as may be seen in the excellent editions and translations which we owe to Professor Garbe, and I may now add to Satish Chandra Banerji, 1898. If, as I believe, the Tattva-samâsa-Sûtras are older than our Sâmkhya-Sûtras, their account of the Sâmkhya-philosophy would always possess its peculiar interest from a historical point of view; while even if their priority with regard to the Kârikâs and Sûtras be doubted, they would always retain their value as showing us in how great a variety the systems of philosophy really existed in so large a country as India.

These Samâsa-Sûtras, it is true, are hardly more than a table of contents, a mere Sâmkhyam or Parisamkhyâ, but that would only show once more that they presuppose the existence of a commentary from the very first. What we possess in the shape of commentaries may not be very old, for commentaries may come and go in different schools, while the

[1] M. M., India, p. 362.

Sûtras which they intend to explain, would remain unchanged, engraved on the memory of teachers and pupils. How tenacious that philosophical Paramparâ was we can see from the pregnant fact that the Âkhyâyikâs or stories, though left out in the Kârikâs, must surely have existed both before and after the time of Îsvara-K*r*ish*n*a, for though absent in the Tattva-samâsa and in the Kârikâs, they reappear in our Sâ*m*khya-Sûtras. Where were they during the interval if not in Sûtras or Kârikâs, now lost to us?

The commentary on the Tattva-samâsa, the publication of which we owe to Ballantyne, begins with an introduction which sounds, no doubt, like a late tradition, but reminds us in some respects of the dialogue at the beginning of the Chinese translation of the commentary on the Sâ*m*khya-kârikâs. But though it may sound like a late tradition, it would be very difficult to prove that it was so. Chronology is not a matter of taste that can be settled by mere impressions.

A certain Brâhman, we are told, overcome by the three kinds of pain, took refuge with the great *R*ishi Kapila, the teacher (not necessarily the originator) of the Sâ*m*khya[1], and having declared his family, his name, and his clan in order to become his pupil, he said: 'Reverend Sir, What is here on earth the highest (the *summum bonum*)? What is truth? What must I do to be saved?'

Kapila said, 'I shall tell thee.' Then follow the topics which are twenty-five in number:—

---

[1] In the Bhâgavata-purâ*n*a I, 3, 11, Kapila is said to have *revived* the Sâ*m*khya (Sâ*m*khya-Sâra, ed. Hall, p. 7, note).

**List of Twenty-five Tattvas.**

I. The eight Prak*r*itis (primary and productive elements),

1. The Prak*r*iti as Avyakta (the non-differentiated or undeveloped principle);
2. The Buddhi (intellect), of eight kinds;
3. The Aha*m*kâra (the subject), of three kinds (Vaikârika, Tai*g*asa, Bhûtâdi);

4–8. The five Tanmâtras (essences) of sound, touch, colour, savour, and odour.

II. The sixteen Vikâras (modifications),

9–13. The five Buddhîndriyas (perceptive organs);

14–18. The five Karmendriyas (active organs);

19. Manas (central organ or mind);

20–24. The Mahâbhûtas (material elements);

III. 25. The Purusha (Spirit or Self).

(The twenty-five Tattvas.)

---

IV. The Traigu*n*ya (triad of forces).

V. The Sa*ñk*ara (evolution).

VI. The Pratisa*ñk*ara (dissolution).

VII. The Adhyâtma
VIII. The Adhîbhûta
IX. The Adhidaivata
} referring to the thirteen instruments, i.e. to Buddhi, Aha*m*kâra, Manas, and the ten Indriyas.

X. The five Abhibuddhis (apprehensions), five acts of Buddhi or the Indriyas.

XI. The five Karmayonis (sources of activity).

XII. The five Vâyus, winds or vital spirits.

XIII. The five Karmâtmans, kinds of Aha*m*kâra.

XIV. Avidyâ (Nescience), fivefold, with sixty-two subdivisions.

XV. A*s*akti (weakness), twenty-eightfold (nine Atush*t*is and eight Asiddhis).

XVI. Tush*t*i (contentment), ninefold.

XVII. Siddhi (perfection), eightfold.

XVIII. Mûlikârthas (cardinal facts), eight.

XIX. Anugrahasarga (benevolent creation).

XX. Bhûtasarga (creation of material elements), fourteen.

XXI. Bandha (bondage), threefold.

XXII. Moksha (freedom), threefold.

XXIII. Pramâ*n*a (authorities), threefold.

XXIV. Du*h*kha (pain), threefold.

I have given these titles or headings in Sanskrit, and shall often have to use these Sanskrit terms, because their English equivalents, even when they can be found, are too often unintelligible or misleading without a commentary. This commentary which follows immediately on the Sûtra, is meant to elucidate their meaning, and it does so on the whole satisfactorily, but the English word seems never to square the Sanskrit terms quite accurately.

The commentator begins by asking, 'Now what are the eight Prak*ri*tis?' and he answers, again in technical terms which will have to be explained: I. '1. The Avyakta (chaos), 2. Buddhi (light or perception), 3. Aha*m*kâra (subjectivity), and 4–8, the five Tanmâtras (transcendental elements).'

### The Avyakta.

He then continues: 1. 'Here then the Avyakta, neuter (the undeveloped), is explained. As in the world various objects such as water-jars, cloth, vases, beds, &c., are manifest, not so is the Avyakta manifest. It is not apprehended by the senses, such as the ear, &c. And why? Because it has neither beginning, middle, nor end, nor has it any parts. It is inaudible, intangible, invisible, indestructible, eternal, without savour and odour. The learned declare it to be without beginning and middle, to be beyond what is great[1], unchanging, pre-eminent. And again, this Avyakta is subtle, without attributes, without beginning or end, producing (Prasûta), but alone of all the eight Prak*ri*tis unproduced (Aprasûta), without parts, one only, but common to all." And these are its synonyms, that is to say, words applicable to the Avyakta, under certain circumstances: Pradhâna (principal), Brahman[2], Pura (abode), Dhruva (unchanging), Pradhânaka (chief), Akshara (indestructible), Kshetra (field, object), Tamas (darkness), Prasûta (productive).'

### Buddhi.

2. 'And what is called Buddhi (intellect)? Buddhi is Adhyavasâya (ascertainment). It is that through which there is in regard to a cow, &c., the conviction (Pratipatti), "This is so and so, not otherwise, this is a cow, not a horse; this is a post, not a man."

---

[1] Mahat in the sense of mind, and Pradhâna in the sense of nature, seem hardly to be appropriate here.

[2] Brahman seems out of place here, and to be synonymous with Purusha or Âtman rather than with the Avyakta. It is given as a synonym of Purusha further on, but strictly speaking Prak*ri*ti also would, from a Vedântic point of view, fall to Brahman as being what is called the substantial cause of the world, but of an immaterial world, as it would seem.

Such is Buddhi, the most wonderful phase of Prakriti.'

Buddhi is generally taken here in its subjective or psychological sense, but whatever native and European authorities may have to say, it is impossible that this should have been its original meaning in the mind of Kapila. If Buddhi meant only determination (Adhyavasâya), even in its widest sense, it would clearly presuppose the later phases, not only Ahamkâra, Manas, Indriyas, as subjective, but likewise something that is knowable and determinable, such as Mahâbhûtas, or at least Tanmâtras. Though this psychological acceptation is the common acceptation of Buddhi among native writers on Sâmkhya, yet sense is more important than commentaries. The Buddhi or the Mahat must here be a phase in the cosmic growth of the universe, like Prakriti in the beginning, and the senses and the other organs of the soul; and however violent our proceeding may seem, we can hardly help taking this Great Principle, the Mahat, in a cosmic sense. Now the first step after Avyakta, the undeveloped, dull, and as yet senseless Prakriti, can only be Prakriti as lighted up, as rendered capable of perception, and no longer as dull matter. If taken in a psychological sense, it supplies, no doubt, in a later stage, the possibility of individual perception also, or of the determination of this and that. But originally it must have been meant as Prakriti illuminated and intellectualised, and rendered capable of becoming at a later time the germ of Ahamkâra (distinction of subject and object), Manas, mind, and Indriyas, apprehensive senses. Only after Prakriti has become lighted up or perceptive, only after mere material contact has become consciousness, can we imagine the distinction, whether general or individual, between subject and object (Aha*m*kâra), and their new relation as perceiver and perceived, as 'I' on one side and 'this' and 'that' on the other.

This may seem a very bold interpretation, and a complete forsaking of native guidance, but unless a more reasonable and intelligible account can be given of Buddhi, there seems no escape from it.

What native interpreters have made of Buddhi may be seen in all their commentaries, for instance, Vâ*k*aspati-Mi*s*ra's commentary on Kârikâ 23: 'Every man uses first his external senses, then he considers (with the Manas), then he refers the various objects to his Ego (Aha*m*kâra), and lastly he decides with his Buddhi what to do.' This may be quite right in a later phase of the development of Prak*ri*ti, it cannot possibly be right as representing the first evolution of Prak*ri*ti from its chaotic state towards light and the possibility of perception. It could not be the antecedent of Aha*m*kâra, Manas, and even the Tanmâtras, if it were no more than the act of fixing this or that in thought. I am glad to find that Mr. S. C. Banerji on p. 146 of his work arrives at much the same conclusion.

There are eight manifestations of this Buddhi (intellect), (1) Dharma, virtue, (2) *G*ñâna, knowledge, (3) Vairâgya, dispassionateness, (4) Ai*s*varya, superhuman power.

As each of these requires explanation, he explains them by a very favourite process, namely, by contrasting them with their opposites, and saying that (1) Dharma, virtue, is the opposite of Adharma, vice, and is enjoined by *S*ruti and Sm*ri*ti, revelation and tradition. It is not opposed to, nay, it is in harmony with, the practice of the best people, and has happiness for its outward mark.

(2) *Gñâna* or knowledge, the opposite of A*g*ñâna or ignorance, is explained as the understanding of the twenty-five subjects (Tattvas), the states of thought (Bhâva), and the elements (Bhûta).

(3) Vairâgya, dispassionateness, is the opposite of passion, and consists in not being dependent on or influenced by external objects, such as sound, &c.

(4) Ai*s*varya, superhuman power, is the opposite of powerlessness, and consists of the eight qualities such as A*n*iman, extreme minuteness, i. e. being able to assume the smallest form and weight, &c.[1]

These four kinds of intellect (Buddhi) are classed as Sâttvika.

Their opposites are classed as Tâmasa, dark or bad.

Through virtue, as a means, there takes place going upward, through knowledge there arises liberation, through dispassionateness men are absorbed in Prak*ri*ti (Prak*ri*tilaya?), through superhuman power there comes unfettered movement.

Thus has Buddhi in its eight forms been described.

Synonyms of Buddhi are, Manas, mind, Mati, thought, Mahat, the great, Brahmâ[2], masc., Khyâti, discrimination, Pra*g*ñâ, wisdom, *S*ruti, inspiration,

---

[1] These Ai*s*varyas are believed in by Sâ*m*khya and Yoga, and are acquired by Yogins by means of long and painful practices.

[2] This also seems out of place here, unless the Sâ*m*khyas give their own meaning both to Brahman and Brahmâ. In later times Buddhi, taken collectively, becomes the Upâdhi or mental limitation of Brahmâ or Hira*n*yagarbha.

Dh*ri*ti, firmness, Pra*gñ*ânasantati, continuity of thought, Sm*ri*ti, memory, and Dhî, meditation.

It is quite clear that in all these explanations Buddhi is taken as intellect, and as personal intellect, and that the idea of a cosmic stage of intellectuality has been entirely forgotten. Thus only can we account for the statement that this Buddhi, if dominated by Sattva (Gu*n*a of purity), is said to assume the form (Rûpa) of virtue, knowledge, dispassionateness, and superhuman powers, while, if dominated by Tamas (Gu*n*a of darkness), it takes the four opposite forms of vice, &c. How could this be possible before the distinction between subject and object has been realised by Aha*m*kâra, and before Buddhi has assumed the character of sense-perception (Buddhîndriyâ*n*i)? We have, in fact, to read the Sâ*m*khya-philosophy in two texts, one, as it were, in the old uncial writing that shows forth here and there, giving the cosmic process, the other in the minuscule letters of a much later age, interpreted in a psychological or epistemological sense.

### Aha*m*kâra.

3. Now, he asks, What is called Aha*m*kâra? And he answers, 'It is Abhimâna, assumption or misconception, and this consists in the belief that I am in the sound, i. e. I hear, I feel, I see, I taste, and I smell, I am lord and rich, I am Î*s*vara, I enjoy, I am devoted to virtue, by me a man was slain, I shall be slain by powerful enemies, &c.'

*S*a*m*kara in his commentary on the Vedânta-Sûtras gives, though from a different point of view, some more instances, as when a man, because his wife and children are unhappy, imagines that he is unhappy, or that he is stout, thin, or fair, that he stands, walks, or jumps, that he is dumb, impotent, deaf, blind, that he has desires, doubts, or fears, whereas all these things do not pertain to him at all, but to Prak*ri*ti only.

'Synonyms of Aha*m*kâra, or rather modifications of it, are Vaikârika, modifying, Tai*g*asa, luminous, Bhûtâdi, the first of elements, Sânumâna, dependent on inference, Niranumâna, not dependent on inference.'

Here we must distinguish again between Aha*m*kâra, as a cosmic power, and Aha*m*kâra as a condition presupposed in any mental act of an individual thinker. Aha*m*kâra was so familiar in the sense of Egoism that, like Buddhi, it was taken in its ordinary rather than in its technical Sâ*m*khya sense. I quite admit that this is a somewhat bold proceeding, but how to get without it at a proper understanding of the ancient Sâ*m*khya, the rival of the Vedânta, I cannot see. We must remember that Aha*m*kâra, whatever it may mean in later times, is in the Sâ*m*khya something developed out of primordial matter, after that matter has passed through Buddhi. Buddhi cannot really act without a distinction of the universe into subject and object, without the introduction of the Ego or I, which again is impossible without a Non-Ego, or something objective. After that only do we watch the development of what is objective in general into what is objectively this or that (the Tanmâtras). But while the creation of what is subjective and objective is the only possible meaning of the cosmic Aha*m*kâra, its psychological interpretation is far more easy. Thus we are told that there are three or four modifications of the Aha*m*kâra, (1) the Vaikârika, dominated by the Sattva-gu*n*a, helps to do good works; (2) the Tai*g*asa, dominated by the Ra*g*as-gu*n*a, helps to do evil works; (3) the Bhûtâdi, dominated by the Tamas-gu*n*a, helps to do hidden works; (4) the Sânumâna Aha*m*kâra is responsible for unintentional good; (5) the Niranumâna, for unintentional evil works. This division, though rather confused, shows at all events that the Aha*m*kâra is here treated as simply a moral agent, dominated by the Gu*n*as, but no longer as a cosmic *potentia*. These five modes of Aha*m*-kâra are spoken of as Karmâtmans also, i.e. the very essence of our acts, while in another place the Tattva-samâsa itself explains that Aha*m*kâra should be taken as an act of Buddhi directed towards the perception of the nature of what is Self (subjective) or Not-Self (objective). Though Aha*m*kâra means only the production of Ego, yet the production of Ego involves that of the Non-Ego, and thus divides the whole world into what is subjective and objective.

### Five Tanmâtras.

4–8. If it is asked, What are the five Tanmâtras (substances)? he answers, The five substances or essences as emanating from Aha*m*kâra, the essence of sound, contact colour, savour, and odour.

The essences of sound are perceived in sounds only. Differences of sound, such as acute, grave, circumflexed, and the notes of the gamut, such as Shad*g*a, C, *Ri*shabha, D, Gândhâra, E, Madhyama, F, Pañ*k*ama, G, Dhaivata, A, Nishada, B, are perceived; but there is no difference in the essence of sound.

The essences of touch are perceived in touch only. Differences of touch, such as soft, hard, rough, slippery, cold, and hot, are perceived, but there is no difference in the essence of touch.

The essences of colour are perceived in colour only. Differences of colour, such as white, red, black, green, yellow, purple, are perceived, but there is no difference in the essence of colour.

The essences of savour are perceived in savour only. Differences of savour, such as pungent, bitter, astringent, corrosive, sweet, acid, salt, are perceived, but there is no difference in the essence of savour.

The essences of odour are perceived in odour only. Differences of odour, such as sweet and offensive, are perceived, but there is no difference in the essence of odour.

Thus have the essences been indicated; and their synonyms, though sometimes very inaccurate ones, are said to be: Avi*s*esha, not differentiated, and therefore not perceptible, Mahâbhûtas (?), the great elements; Prak*ri*tis, natures, Abhogya, not to be experienced, A*n*u, atomic, A*s*ânta, not-pleasurable, Aghora, not-terrible, Amû*dh*a, not-stupid; the last three being negations of the qualities of the Mahâbhûtas, according to the three Gu*n*as preponderating in each. And if it is asked why these eight Prak*ri*tis only, from Avyakta to the Tanmâtras, are called Prak*ri*tis, the answer is because they alone Prakurvanti, they alone bring forth, or evolve.

### Sixteen Vikâras.

11. If it be asked 'Which are the sixteen Vikâras or evolutions?' the answer is, 'the eleven sense organs (including Manas), and the five elements.'

### Five Buddhîndriyas.

9–13. 'Now the organs are set forth; the ear, the skin, the eyes, the tongue, and the nose, constitute the five Buddhîndriyas, or perceptive organs. The ear perceives as its object sound, the skin touch, the eye colour, the tongue savour, the nose odour.'

Being produced from the Tanmâtras, the senses, as perceiving, are represented as being of the same nature as the objects perceived, a view of considerable antiquity.

### Five Karmendriyas.

14–18. 'The five Karmendriyas or organs of action, voice, hands, feet, the organ of excretion, and the organ of generation, perform each its own work. The voice utters words, the hands work, the feet perform movement, the organ of excretion evacuation, the organ of generation pleasure.'

### Manas.

19. 'Manas, mind, both perceptive and active, performs its acts of doubting and ascertaining.'

Central organ of the senses or κοινὸν αἰσθητήριον might be the nearest approach to the meaning of Manas; but mind may do, if we only remember its Sâ*m*khya definition, as perceptive, like the other organs, and at the same time active like the Karmendriyas.

'Thus have the eleven organs been explained. Their synonyms are, Kara*n*a, instruments, Vaikârika, changing, Niyata, special, Padâni, appliances[1], Avadhritâni, kept under (?), Anu, atomic, Aksha[2], organ.'

### Five Mahâbhûtas.

20–24. 'The Mahâbhûtas, or gross elements, are earth, water, light, air, and ether.'

Here the earth, we are told, helps the other four, by being their support. Water helps the other four by moistening. Light helps the other four by ripening. Air helps the other four by drying. Ether helps the other four by giving space.

'Earth is possessed of five qualities, sound, touch, colour, savour, and odour. Water is possessed of four qualities, sound, touch, colour, and savour. Light is possessed of three qualities, sound, touch, and colour. Air is possessed of two qualities, sound and touch. Ether has one quality, sound. Thus are the five Mahâbhûtas explained.

Their synonyms are: Bhûtas, elements, Bhûtaviseshas, special elements, Vikâras, modifications, Âkritis, species, Tanu, skin (or body?), Vigraha, shapes, Sânta, pleasurable, Ghora, fearful, Mûdha, stupid. Thus have the sixteen Vikâras been described.'

### Purusha.

III. 25. Now it is asked, 'What is the Purusha?' and the answer is, 'Purusha is without beginning, it is subtle, omnipresent, perceptive, without qualities, eternal, seer, experiencer, not an agent, knower of objects, spotless, not producing.' Why is it called Purusha? Because of its being old (Purânât), because it rests in the body (Puri sayate), and because it serves

---

[1] Garbe, Sâmkhya-Philosophie, p. 257.

[2] Or Akshara, imperishable?

as Purohita (Director).' These are, of course, fanciful etymologies; and we can hardly doubt that we have, in the name of Purusha, a recollection of the Vedic Purusha, one of the many names of the supreme deity, by the side of Visvakarman, Hira*n*yagarbha, Pra*g*âpati, &c. Like Brahman when conceived as Âtman, Purusha also was probably used both for the divine and for the human side of the same power. It is the multiplicity only of the Purusha which is peculiar to the Sâ*m*khya-philosophy.

'And why is the Purusha without beginning? Because there is no beginning, no middle, and no end of it.' This is not a very satisfactory answer, but it is probably meant for no more than that we never perceive a beginning, middle, or end of it. Why is it subtle? Because it is without parts and supersensuous. Why omnipresent? Because, like the sky, it reaches everything, and its extent is endless. Why perceptive? Because it perceives (that is, for a time) pleasure, pain, and trouble. Why without qualities? Because the qualities of good, indifferent, and bad are not found in it. Why eternal? Because it was not made, and cannot be made. Why seer? Because it perceives the modifications of Prak*r*iti. Why enjoyer? Because being perceptive it perceives (for awhile) pleasure and pain. Why not an agent? Because it is indifferent and without the qualities (Gu*n*as). Why the knower of body or of objects? Because it knows the qualities of objective bodies. Why spotless? Because neither good nor evil acts belong to the Purusha. Why not-producing? Because it has no seed, that is, it can produce nothing. Thus has the Purusha of the Sâ*m*khya been described.

The synonyms of Purusha are, Âtman, Self, Pumân, male, Pu*m*gu*n*a*g*antugîva*h*, a male living creature, Kshetra*g*ña, knower of objects or of the body, Nara, man, Kavi, poet, Brahman, Akshara, indestructible, Prâ*n*a, spirit, Ya*h*ka*h* [1], anybody, Sa*t*, He.

Thus have the twenty-five substances been described, viz. the eight Prak*ri*tis, the sixteen Vikâras, and the Purusha. He who knows these twenty-five substances, whatever stage of life he may be in, and whether he wear matted hair, a topknot, or be shaven, he is liberated, there is no doubt. This verse is often quoted by Sâ*m*khya philosophers. Here, it seems, the first part of the Tattva-samâsa is ended, containing a list of the twenty-five Tattvas, in the three divisions of Prak*ri*tis, Vikâras, and Purusha.

Purusha (subject).
|
1. Prak*ri*ti (object).
Avyakta (chaos).
|
2. Mahat or Buddhi (light and intelligence as Samash*t*i, not yet individualised).
|
3. Aha*m*kâra (subjectivation).

5 Tanmâtras (Sâttvika) (subtle elements).

10 Indriyas, organs (Râ*g*asa) + 1 Manas (mind) (5 Buddhîndriyas, 5 Karmendriyas, and Manas).

| Tanmâtras. | Buddhîndriyas. | Karmendriyas. |
|---|---|---|
| 1. Sound, Sabda. | 1. Srotra, hearing in ear. | 1. Speaking in tongue. |
| 2. Touch, Sparsa. | 2. Tva*k*, touch in skin. | 2. Grasping in hands. |
| 3. Colour, Rûpa. | 3. *K*akshus, seeing in eye. | 3. Moving in feet. |
| 4. Savour, Rasa. | 4. *G*ihvâ, tasting in tongue. | 4. Evacuating in Pâyu. |
| 5. Odour, Gandha. | 5. Ghrâ*n*a, smelling in nose. | 5. Generating in Upastha. |

5 Mahâbhûtas (Tâmasa).

1. Âkâsa, ether (sabda).
2. Vâyu, air (sabda + sparsa).
3. Te*g*as, fire (sabda + sparsa + rûpa).
4. Ap, water (sabda + sparsa + rûpa + rasa).
5. P*ri*thivî, earth (sabda + sparsa + rûpa + rasa + gandha).

---

[1] As ya*h*, the relative pronoun could hardly be used as a name, I supposed it might be meant for the indefinite pronoun ya*h*ka*h*, but this is doubtful.

**Is Purusha an Agent?**

Now follow a number of special questions, which seemed to require fuller treatment. The first is, Is the Purusha an agent, or is he not? If Purusha were an agent, he would do good actions only, and there would not be the three different kinds of action. The three kinds of action are (1) Good conduct, called virtue (Dharma), which consists in kindness, control and restraint (of the organs), freedom from hatred, reflection, displaying of supernatural powers.

(2) But passion, anger, greed, fault-finding, violence, discontent, rudeness, shown by change of countenance, these are called indifferent conduct.

(3) Madness, intoxication, lassitude, nihilism, devotion to women, drowsiness, sloth, worthlessness, impurity, these are called bad conduct.

We see here once more that the three Gu*n*as must have had originally a much wider meaning than is here described. They are here taken as purely moral qualities, whereas originally they must have had a much larger cosmic sense. They are not qualities or mere attributes at all; they are on the contrary ingredients of Prak*r*iti in its differentiation of good, indifferent, bad; bright, dim and dark; light, mobile, heavy. We see here the same narrowing of cosmical ideas which we had to point out before in the case of Buddhi and Aha*m*kâra, and which, it seems to me, would render the original conception of the Sâ*m*khya-philosophy quite unmeaning. We must never forget that, even when the Sâ*m*khya speaks of moral qualities, these qualities belong to nature as seen by the Purusha, never to Purusha apart from Prak*r*iti.

### Three Gu*n*as.

Whenever this triad is perceived in the world it is clear that agency belongs to the Gu*n*as, and it follows that Purusha is not the agent.

Deceived by passion and darkness, and taking a wrong view of these Gu*n*as which belong to Prak*ri*ti, not to himself, a fool imagines that he himself is the agent, though in reality he is unable by himself to bend even a straw. Nay, he becomes an agent, as it were, foolish and intoxicated by vain imagination and saying, 'All this was made by me and belongs to me.'

And then it is said (in the Bhagavad-gîtâ III, 27): 'Acts are effected by the qualities (Gu*n*as) of Prak*ri*ti in every way, but the Self (Âtman), deluded by the conceit of the I (Aha*m*kâra), imagines that the I is the agent.'

Ibid. XIII, 31:—

'This imperishable supreme Self, from being without beginning and devoid of qualities, neither acts nor suffers, even while staying in the body.'

And XIII, 29:—

'He sees (aright) who looks upon actions as in all respects performed by Prak*ri*ti alone, and upon the Self as never an agent.'

### Is Purusha one or many?

Now comes the important question, Is that Purusha one or many? The answer to this question divides the Sâ*m*khya from the Vedânta-philosophy. The Sâ*m*khya answer is that the Purusha is clearly many, because of the variety in the acts of pleasure, pain, trouble, confusion and purifying (of race), health, birth and death; also on account of the stages in life (Â*s*rama) and the difference of caste (Var*n*a). If there were but one Purusha, as the Vedântins hold, then if one were happy, all would be happy; if one were unhappy, all would be unhappy, and so on in the case of people affected by trouble, confusion of race, purity of race, health, birth and death. Hence there is not one Purusha, but many, on account of the manifoldness indicated by form, birth, abode, fortune, society or loneliness. Thus Kapila, Âsuri, Pa*ñk*a*s*ikha and Pata*ñg*ali, and all other Sâ*m*khya teachers describe Purusha as many.

### Vedânta Sayings.

But teachers who follow the Vedânta, such as Harihara, Hira*n*yagarbha, Vyâsa and others, describe Purusha as one. And why so? Because (as the Vedânta says),

1. 'Purusha is all this, what has been and what is to be, he is lord of that immortality which springs up by (sacrificial) food, that is, he is beyond the immortality of the ordinary immortal gods[1].

2. That is Agni, that is Vâyu, that is Sûrya, that is *K*andramas, that is pure, that is Brahman, that is water and Pra*g*âpati[2].

3. That is true, that is immortal, it is liberation,

---

[1] These verses are meant to represent the views of the Vedânta, and they are mostly taken from the Upanishads. The first from *S*vet. Up. III, 15, occurs also Taitt. Âr. III, 12, 1, and in the Rig-veda X, 90, 2, where we should read, Yát ánnenâdhiróhati, see Deussen, Geschichte, I, p. 152.

[2] Mahânâr. Up. I, 7; cf. Vâ*g*. Sa*m*h. 32, 1.

it is the highest point, it is indestructible, it is the glory of the sun;

4. Higher than which there is nothing else, nothing smaller, and nothing greater, the One stands like a tree planted in the sky; by him and by the Purusha, all this is filled[1].

5. Having hands and feet everywhere, having mouth, head and eyes everywhere, hearing everywhere in this world, it stands covering everything;

6. Shining[2] through the qualities (Guna) of all the senses, and yet free from all the senses, the master of all, the Lord, the great refuge of all;

7. He is all substances everywhere, the Self of all, the source of all; that in which everything is absorbed, that the sages know as Brahman.

8. For[3] there is but one Self of beings, settled in everybody, it is seen as one and as many, like the moon in the water.

9. For he alone, the great Self, dwells in all beings, whether moving or motionless, he by whom all this was spread out.

10. This Self of the world is one—by whom was it made manifold? Some speak of the Self as several, because of the existence of knowledge, &c. (because knowledge is different in different people).

11. Wise[4] people see the same (Âtman) in the Brahman, in worms and insects, in the outcast, in the dog and the elephant, in beasts, cows, gadflies, and gnats.

12, 13. As one and the same string passes

---

[1] *S*vet. Up. III, 9; Mahânâr. Up. X, 20.

[2] *S*vet. Up. III, 17; cf. Bhag. Gîtâ XIII, 14.

[3] Brahmabindu Up. 12.

[4] Cf. Bhag. Gîtâ V, 18.

through gold, and pearls, jewels, corals, porcelain, and silver, thus is one and the same Self to be known as dwelling everywhere in cows, men, and in elephants, deer,' &c.

We see in these extracts a mixture of Vedânta and Sâ*m*khya terms and ideas; and in verse 10 the two views of Brahman being one, and the Purusha being many, are given in the same breath.

### Early Relation between Vedânta and Sâ*m*khya.

The relation between Sâ*m*khya and Vedânta during the Upanishad-period is by no means clear. Most scholars seem to regard it as a kind of syncretism, but it may also represent to us a period of philosophic thought when these two views of the world were not yet finally differentiated, and were not felt to be altogether incompatible. Though there is in the Upanishads which we possess a decided preponderance of a Vedântic interpretation of the world, the Sâ*m*khya philosophers are not altogether wrong when they maintain that their view also can be supported by Vedic authority. All these views were at first no more than guesses at truth, gropings in the dark; but the idea that if the one was right the other must be wrong, belongs decidedly to a later period, to that of systematised and controversial philosophy. There are certain technical terms, such as Purusha, Buddhi, Gu*n*as, &c., which are looked upon as the peculiar property of the Sâ*m*khya, and others, such as Âtman, Brahman, Avidyâ, Mâyâ, &c., which remind us at once of the Vedânta-philosophy; but even these terms are used far more freely in the Brâhma*n*as and Upanishads than in the Darsanas, nor are they always used in the same sense or in the same order by earlier and later authorities.

Thus we read in the Kâthaka Up. III, 10, 11:—

'Beyond the senses are the objects (Artha), beyond the objects is the mind (Manas), beyond the mind is intellect (Buddhi), the Great Self (Mahân Âtmâ) is beyond the intellect. Beyond the Great there is the Undeveloped (Avyakta), beyond the undeveloped there is the Purusha. Beyond the Purusha there is nothing, that is the goal, the highest point.'

In the same Upanishad, VI, 7, 8, we read:—

'Beyond the senses is the mind, beyond the mind the highest being (Sattvam Uttamam), higher than that being is the great Self (Mahân Âtmâ), beyond this great (Self) is the highest, the Undeveloped.

Beyond the Undeveloped is the Purusha, the all-pervading and imperceptible. Every creature that knows him is liberated, and obtains immortality.'

The successive development, as here described, is not in strict accordance with the systematic Sâmkhya, but still less does it represent to us Vedântic ideas. Even the two accounts, as given in the same Upanishad, vary slightly, showing to us how little of technical accuracy there was as yet during the Upanishad-period. We get—

| | III, 10, 11. | VI, 7, 8. |
|---|---|---|
| 1. | Indriyas. | Indriyas. |
| 2. | Arthas. | ——— |
| 3. | Manas. | Manas. |
| 4. | Buddhi. | Sattvam Uttamam. |
| 5. | Mahân Âtmâ. | Mahân Âtmâ. |
| 6. | Avyakta. | Avyakta. |
| 7. | Purusha. | Purusha. |

The omission of the Arthas as objects would not signify, because, as Indriyârthas, they are implied by the Indriyas or senses. But why should Buddhi, generally the first emanation of Prakriti in its undeveloped (Avyakta) state, be replaced by Sattvam Uttamam, the Highest Being? The word may be meant for Buddhi, for Buddhi is often called Mahat, the Great, but why it should be called Great is difficult to say. It is certainly not an equivalent of the Phenician Mot, as Professor Wilson conjectured many years ago[1]. Mahân Âtmâ looks like a Vedântic term, but even then it would only occupy the place of *G*îvâtmâ, the individualised Self, and how could this be said to emanate from the Avyakta?

Another passage which reminds us of Sâ*m*khya rather than of Vedânta-philosophy occurs in the Maitrây. Up. II, 5, where we read: 'He who has the name of Purusha, and is very small, intangible, invisible, dwells of his own will[2] here in part[3], as a man who is fast asleep awakes of his own will. And this part, which is entirely intelligent, present in every single man, knowing the body, attested by conceiving (Manas), willing (Buddhi), and belief in subject and object (Aha*m*kâra) is Pra*g*âpati, called

---

[1] See Sâ*m*khya-Sûtras I, 61, 71; the Ekâda*s*akam is Sâttvikam, cf. II, 18, that is the five Buddhîndriyas, the five Karmendriyas, and the Manas; see Garbe, Sâ*m*khya-prava*k*anabhâshya, p. 188.

[2] The Anubhûti-prakâ*s*a reads Buddhipûrvam, Deussen translates Abuddhipûrvam.

[3] As to the idea of parts (A*m*sa), see Vedânta-Sûtras II, 3, 43, and Thibaut's remarks in his Introduction, p. xcvii.

Visva. By him, the intelligent, is the body made intelligent, and he is the driver thereof.'

This passage does not contain much of Sâmkhya thought, yet the words Purusha and possibly Buddhipûrvam seem to allude to Kapila's ideas rather than to those of Bâdarâyana. Other words also, such as Samkalpa, Adhyavasâya and Abhimâna, in the sense of Ahamkâra, point to the same source. The whole passage, however, is obscure, nor does the commentator help us much, unless he is right in recognising here the germs of the later Vedântic ideas of a Pragâpati, called Visva or Vaisvânara (Vedânta-sâra, § 138), Taigasa and Prâgña.

One more passage of the Maitrây. Upanishad, III, 2, may here be mentioned, as reminding us of Sâmkhya doctrines. There we read: 'There is indeed that other different one, called the elemental Self (Bhûtâtmâ) who, overcome by the bright and dark fruits of action, enters on a good or evil birth, so that his course is upward or downward, and that overpowered by the pairs (the opposites) he roams about. And this is the explanation. The five Tanmâtras (of sound, touch, light, taste, and smell) are called Bhûta (elements), and the five Mahâbhûtas (gross elements) also are called Bhûta. Then the aggregate of all these is called Sarîra, body, and he who dwells in that body is called Bhûtâtman (the elementary Âtman). True, his immortal Âtman (Self) remains untainted, like a drop of water on a lotus-leaf; but he, the Bhûtâtman, is in the power of the Gunas of Prakriti. Then, thus overpowered, he becomes bewildered, and because thus bewildered, he sees not the creator, i. e. the holy Lord, abiding within him. Carried along by the Gunas, darkened, unstable, fickle, crippled, full of devices, vacillating, he enters into Abhimâna (conceit of subject and object), believing "I am he, this is mine," &c. He binds himself by himself, as a bird is bound by a net, and, overcome afterwards by the fruits of what he has done, he enters on a good or evil birth, downward or upward in his course, and, overcome by the pairs, he roams about.'

Here we see again a mixture of Sâ*m*khya and Vedânta ideas, the Sâ*m*khya claiming such terms as Prak*ri*ti and Gu*n*as, the Vedânta such terms as Âtman and possibly Bhûtâtman. This Bhûtâtman, however, is by no means so clear as has sometimes been imagined. It is a term peculiar to the Maitrây. Upanishad, and seems to have been borrowed from it when it occurs in some of the later Upanishads. If, like many other things in the Maitrây. Upanishad, it is to be looked upon as belonging to the Sâ*m*khya-system, we must remember that Âtman, though quoted sometimes as a synonym of Purusha, cannot be supposed to stand here for Purusha. A compound such as Bhûta-Purusha would be impossible. The Maitrây. Up. III, 1 itself says that the Âtman of Bhûtâtman is another, though likewise called Âtman, and that he dwells in the body, *S*arîra, which is a compound of Tanmâtras, Bhûtas, and Mahâbhûtas. It would therefore correspond to the Vedântic *G*îvâtman. But if this Bhûtâtman is said to spring from Prak*ri*ti, it could not possibly stand for the Purusha of the Sâ*m*khyas, because their Purusha does not spring from Prak*ri*ti, as little as Prak*ri*ti springs from him. Nor could any Âtman be said to be purely objective. In fact, strictly speaking, this Bhûtâtman fits neither into the Vedânta, nor into the Sâmkhya-philosophy, and would rather seem to belong to a philosophy in which these two views of the world were not yet finally separated.

Another difficult and rather obscure expression in the Maitrây. Upanishad is Nirâtman (*selbstlos*), an expression which would be impossible in the Vedânta-philosophy, and is certainly perplexing even in the Sâmkhya.

A similar mixture of philosophical terms meets us in the Svetâsvatara Upanishad. In verse I, 10, for instance, we have Pradhâna, which is Sâmkhya, and Mâyâ, which is Vedânta, at least the later Vedânta, while in IV, 10 Mâyâ is directly identified with Prakriti. Purusha occurs in III, 12, where it evidently stands for Brahman, IV, 1. But though in this Upanishad Sâmkhya ideas would seem to prevail, Vedânta ideas are not excluded. The very name of Sâmkhya[1] and Yoga occurs (VI, 13), but the name of Vedânta also is not absent, VI, 22. In all this we may possibly get a glimpse of a state of Indian philosophy which was, as yet, neither pure Sâmkhya nor pure Vedânta, unless we look on these Upanishads as of a far more modern date, and on their philosophy as the result of a later syncretism.

### Traigunya.

IV. If now we return to the Tattva-samâsa, we meet first of all with some more remarks about the three Gunas, Sattva, explained as

[1] Sâmkhya should be here taken as the title of the two systems, Sâmkhya and Yoga, or better still as one word, Sâmkhyayoga. It cannot well mean *Prüfung*.

virtue, purity, goodness; Ra*g*as, explained as dust, mist, passion, movement, and Tamas, darkness, as ignorance. Colebrooke had already warned us against taking the Gu*n*as of the Sâ*m*khya in the sense of qualities. 'These three qualities,' he says, 'are not mere accidents of nature, but are of its essence, and enter into its composition like different rivers forming one stream, though for a time retaining their different colours.' Constituent 'parts' might be a better rendering, but for the present it is best to retain Gu*n*a, there being neither thought nor word in English corresponding to Gu*n*a, as defined in the Sâ*m*khya. We ourselves have inherited our ideas of substance and quality from Greek and medieval philosophers, but even with us a definition of inherent qualities is by no means easy, considering that our substances never exist without qualities, nor our qualities without substances. Our commentary continues :—

He now asks, What is the triad of Gu*n*as? and the answer is, the triad consists of Goodness, Passion, and Darkness. The triad of Gu*n*as means the three Gu*n*as.

Goodness (Sattva) is of endless variety, such as calmness, lightness, complacency, attainment of what is wished for, contentment, patience, joy, &c. In short it consists of happiness.

Passion is of endless variety, such as grief, distress, separation, excitement, attainment of what is evil, &c. In short it consists of pain.

Darkness is of endless variety, such as covering, ignorance, disgust, misery, heaviness, sloth, drowsiness, intoxication, &c. In short it consists of trouble or madness.

Thus far has the triad of the Gu*n*as been explained. Let it be known that goodness is all that is bright, passion all that excites, and darkness all that is not bright. This is what is named Traigu*n*ya.

These Gu*n*as have been again and again explained as Dravyâ*n*i, matter; quality and what is qualified being considered in the Sâ*m*khya as inseparable. The four sides of a cube, for instance, would be called its Gu*n*as as much as the blue of the sky. These Gu*n*as act a very prominent part in Indian philosophy, and have quite entered into the sphere of popular thought. We can best explain them by the general idea of two opposites and the middle term between them, or as Hegel's thesis, antithesis and synthesis, these being manifested in nature by light, darkness, and mist; in morals by good, bad, and indifferent, with many applications and modifications. If the Sâ*m*khyas look on certain objects as happy instead of happifying, &c., we should remember that we also call sugar sweet, meaning that it calls forth the sensation of sweetness in us. The Hindus look upon the state of equilibrium of the three Gu*n*as as perfect, and they see in the preponderance of any one of them the first cause of movement and activity in Prak*r*iti or nature, in fact the beginning of creation.

### Sañ*k*ara and Pratisañ*k*ara.

V, VI. Then comes the question, What is Sañ*k*ara and what is Pratisañ*k*ara? The answer is, Sañ*k*ara is evolution, Pratisañ*k*ara dissolution or re-involution. Evolution is as follows: From the Avyakta (undeveloped Prak*r*iti) before explained, when superintended by the high and omnipresent Purusha (Spirit), Buddhi (intellect) arises, and this of eight kinds. From this Buddhi, the substance of intellect, arises Aha*m*kâra (conceit of I, or subjectivity). Aha*m*kâra is of three kinds, Vaikârika, modified, that is, modified of Sattva[1]; Tai*g*asa, luminous, as under the influence of Ra*g*as producing the Buddhîndriyas; and Bhûtâdi (first of elements). From the modified or Vaikârika Aha*m*kâra, which under the influence of Tamas produces the gross material elements, spring the gods and the senses; from the first of elements, Bhûtâdi, the Tanmâtras (essences); from the luminous, Tai*g*asa, both. From the Tanmâtras, essences, are produced the material elements. This is the development or Sa*ñk*ara. Pratisa*ñk*ara or dissolution is as follows: The material elements are dissolved into the essences, Tanmâtras, the essences and senses into Aha*m*kâra, Aha*m*kâra into Buddhi (intellect), Buddhi into Avyakta (the undeveloped), all being different forms of Prak*ri*ti. The Undeveloped is nowhere dissolved, because it was never evolved out of anything. Know both Prak*ri*ti and Purusha as having no beginning. Thus has dissolution been explained.

**Adhyâtma, Adhíbhûta, and Adhidaivata.**

VII–IX. Now it is asked, What is meant by Adhyâtma (subjective), Adhibhûta (objective), and Adhidaivata (pertaining to deity)? To this it is answered, Intellect is subjective, what is to be perceived is objective, Brahmâ is deity. Aha*m*kâra is subjective, what is to be received and perceived by

[1] Garbe, Sâ*m*khya-Philosophie, p. 236.

it is objective, Rudra is the deity. Manas, mind, is subjective, what is to be conceived is objective, *K*andra, moon, is the deity. The ear is subjective, what is to be heard is objective, Âkâ*s*a, ether, is the deity. The skin is subjective, what is to be touched is objective, Vâyu, wind, is the deity. The eye is subjective, what is to be seen is objective, Âditya, the sun, is the deity. The tongue is subjective, what is to be tasted is objective, Varu*n*a[1] is the deity. The nose is subjective, what is to be smelled is objective, Earth is the deity. The voice is subjective, what is to be uttered is objective, Agni, fire, is the deity. The two hands are subjective, what is to be grasped is objective, Indra is the deity. The feet are subjective, what has to be gone over is objective, Vish*n*u is the deity. The organ of excretion is subjective, what is to be excreted is objective, Mitra is the deity. The organ of generation is subjective, what is to be enjoyed is objective, Pra*g*âpati, lord of creatures, is the deity. Thus in the case of each of the thirteen instruments is there what is subjective, what is objective, and the deity.

Whoever has properly learnt the substances, the forms of the qualities (Gu*n*asvarûpâ*n*i), and the deity (Adhidaivatam) is freed from evil and released from all his sins; he experiences the qualities (Gu*n*as), but is not united to them. Here ends the discussion of the Tattvas (substances)[2].

---

[1] Evidently taken already as god of the waters.

[2] I ought to say that in this and the subsequent paragraphs I had often to be satisfied with giving the words such as they stand, without being myself able to connect any definite ideas with them. I did not like to leave them out altogether, but while they may be safely passed over by philosophical readers,

### Abhibuddhis (5).

X. Now what are the five Abhibuddhis (apprehensions)? The answer is, They are Vyavasâya, ascertainment, Abhimâna, conceit, Î*kkh*â, desire, Kartavyatâ, determination to act or will, Kriyâ, action.

The apprehension that this has to be done by me is ascertainment; an act of the intellect. Abhimâna, conceit, is directed towards the perception of the nature of Self and not-Self, it is Aha*m*kâra, an act of the intellect. Î*kkh*â, desire, is wish, an idea of the mind, an act of the intellect. Kartavyatâ, the will of doing such acts as hearing, &c., performed by the senses that have sound, &c., for their objects, is an act of the intellect pertaining to the Buddhîndriyas. Kriyâ, the act of the intellect, such as speaking, &c., pertaining to the Karmendriyas, is action[1]. Thus have five Abhibuddhis (apprehensions) been explained.

### Karmayonis (5).

XI. What are the five Karmayonis? The answer is that they are Dh*r*iti, energy, *S*raddhâ, faith or faithfulness, Sukhâ, bliss, Avividishâ, carelessness, Vividishâ, desire of knowledge.

The character of Dh*r*iti or energy is when a man resolves and carries out his resolution. *S*raddhâ, faith or faithfulness, is said to consist in study of the Veda

---

they may, I hope, elicit from Sanskrit scholars some better elucidation than I am able to give. At present most of them seem to me to consist of useless distinctions and hair-splitting definitions of words.

[1] The text is somewhat doubtful.

religious studentship, sacrificing and causing sacrifices to be performed, penance, giving and receiving proper gifts, and making Homa-oblations.

But Sukhâ or bliss arises when a man, in order to obtain blessedness, devotes himself to knowledge, sacrifices and penance, being always engaged in penitential acts.

Avividishâ or carelessness consists in the heart's being absorbed in the sweetness of sensual pleasures.

Vividishâ or desire of knowledge is the source of knowledge of thoughtful people. What has to be known is the oneness (belonging to Prak*ri*ti), the separateness (of Purusha and Prak*ri*ti), &c., (Prak*ri*ti) being eternal, and not-percipient, subtle, with real products, and not to be disturbed; and this is Vividishâ. . . . It is a state belonging to Prak*ri*ti destroying cause and effect. Thus have the five Karmayonis been explained (?).

Some portions of these verses are obscure, and the text is probably corrupt. I have taken *Gñ*eyâ for *Gñ*eyam, referring to each of the subjects with which Vividishâ, the desire of knowledge, is concerned. The construction is very imperfect, but may be excused in what is after all no more than an index. I separate Sûkshmam and take it in the sense of Sûkshmatvam. Satkâryam refers to the Satkâryavâda. The third line is quite unintelligible to me, and Ballantyne has very properly left it altogether untranslated. It may mean that Vividishâ is a state belonging to Prak*ri*ti which helps to destroy cause and effect by showing that they are one and the same, but this is a mere guess.

### Vâyus (5).

XII. What are the Vâyus (winds)? They are Prâ*n*a, Apâna, Samâna, Udâna, and Vyâna, i.e. the winds in the bodies of those who have bodies. The wind called Prâ*n*a is superintended by mouth and nose, and is called Prâ*n*a because it leads out or moves out. The wind called Apâna is superintended by the navel, and is called Apâna because it leads away and moves downward. The wind called Samâna is superintended by the heart, and is called Samâna because it leads equally and moves equally. The wind called Udâna is superintended by the throat. It is called Udâna because it goes upward and moves out. Vyâna is the all-pervader. Thus have the five winds been explained.

The real meaning of these winds has never been discovered. If they are rendered by vital spirits, nothing is gained except explaining *obscurum per obscurius*. They may have been intended to account for the vital processes which make the action of the senses (Indriyas) and of other organs of the body also, possible, but their original intention escapes us altogether. They form a kind of physical organism or Anta*h*kara*n*a, but their special functions are often stated differently by different authors.

### Karmâtmans (5).

XIII. What are the five Karmâtmans, the (Ego as active)? They are Vaikârika, Tai*g*asa, Bhûtâdi, Sânumâna, and Niranumâna. The Vaikârika, modifying, is the doer of good works. The Tai*g*asa, luminous, is the doer of bad works. The Bhûtâdi[1], first of

[1] Bhûtâdi is used in the sense of Manas, because the Bhûtas, though springing from the Tanmâtras, are due to it.

elements, is the doer of hidden works. If associated with inference (Sânumâna), the Aha*m*kâra is the doer of what is good and reasonable; if not associated with inference (Niranumâna) it is the doer of what is not good and not reasonable. Thus have the five Karmâtmans been explained.

### Avidyâ, Nescience (5).

XIV. What is the fivefold Avidyâ (Nescience)? It is Tamas, darkness, Moha, illusion, Mahâmoha, great illusion, Tâmisra, gloom, Andhatâmisra, utter gloom. Here darkness and illusion are again each eightfold, great illusion is tenfold, gloom and utter gloom are eighteenfold. Tamas, darkness, is the misconception that Self is identical with things which are not Self, namely with Prak*ri*ti, Avyakta, Buddhi, Aha*m*kâra, and the five Tanmâtras. Moha, illusion, is the misconception arising from the obtainment of supernatural powers, such as minuteness and the rest. Mahâmoha, great illusion, is when one supposes oneself to be liberated in the ten states with regard to the objects of sound, colour, &c., whether heard or seen, &c. Gloom is unrestrained hatred, directed against the eightfold superhuman powers, such as minuteness, &c., and against the tenfold world of sense causing threefold pain. Utter gloom is that distress which arises at the time of death after the eightfold human power has been acquired, and the tenfold world of sense has been conquered. Thus has ignorance with sixty-two subdivisions been explained.

### A*s*akti, Weakness (28).

XV. What is called the twenty-eightfold weakness? The faults of the eleven organs of sense and the seventeen faults of the intellect. First, with regard to the organs of sense, there is deafness in the ear, dullness in the tongue, leprosy in the skin, blindness in the eye, loss of smell in the nose, dumbness in the voice, crippledness in the hands, lameness in the feet, constipation in the organ of excretion, impotence in the organ of generation, madness in the mind; these are defects of the eleven organs. The seventeen defects of the intellect are the opposites of the Tush*t*is, contentments, and of the Siddhis, perfections.

### Atush*t*i and Tush*t*i.

XVI. First then the opposites of the Tush*t*is or the contentments. They are Anantâ, the conviction that there is no Pradhâna (Prak*r*iti); Tâmasalîna, consisting in recognising the Âtman in the Mahat (Buddhi, intellect); Avidyâ, the non-recognition of the Ego (Aha*m*kâra); Av*r*ish*t*i, the denial that the Tanmâtras, essences, are the causes of the elements; Asutâra, occupation in acquiring the objects of the senses; Asupâra, occupation in their preservation; Asunetra, occupation for wealth, without seeing that it is liable to be lost; Asumarî*k*ikâ, addiction to enjoyment; Anuttamâmbhâsikâ, engaging in enjoyment without seeing the evil of injury (to living beings). Thus have the nine opposites of Tush*t*i, contentment, been explained.

### Asiddhis and Siddhis.

XVII. Next follow the opposites of Siddhi, perfection, which are also called Asiddhis, non-perfections: Atâra, when diversity is mistaken for phenomenal unity; Sutâra, when, after hearing words only, the opposite is understood, as, for instance, when after hearing that a man who knows the various principles (tattvas) is liberated, a man understands the opposite, that such a man is not liberated; Atâratâra, ignorance, when a man, though devoted to hearing and studying, does not succeed in knowing the twenty-five principles, owing either to his obtuseness or to his intellect being impaired by false doctrines. If a man, though overcome by mental suffering, is not anxious to know, being careless as to transmigration, so that knowledge is no pleasure to him, this is Apramodâ. Thus the next pair also of Apramuditâ (mutually not delighted) and Apramodamâna (mutually not delighting) should be considered. Ignorance of a man of undecided mind even with regard to what has been taught him by a friend is Arasya. But failure of an unfortunate man in obtaining knowledge, either because of bad instruction or disregard on the part of the teacher, is Asatpramuditam. Thus have the eight Asiddhis, the opposite of the Siddhis or perfections, been explained, and the twenty-eightfold Asakti (weakness) is finished.

### Tushtis and Siddhis.

Next follow the Tushtis and Siddhis themselves, but as their opposites have already been examined we may dispense with their enumeration here. Some of these technical terms vary in different texts, but they are of very small importance [1]. I am afraid that even what I have given of these long lists,

[1] The names of the nine Tushtis or contentments are: Ambhas, water, Salilâ, Oghâ, Vrishti, Sutârâ, Supârâ, Sunetrâ, Sumarîkikâ, Uttamâ Sâttviki. The names of the eight Siddhis are: Târâ, Sutârâ, Târayanti, Pramodâ, Pramuditâ, Pramodamânâ, Ramyakâ, Satpramuditâ.

which are so characteristic of the Sâ*m*khya-philosophy, may have proved very tedious, and not very closely connected with the great problems of philosophy. I confess that in several cases many of these subdivisions seemed to me entirely meaningless, but I thought that they were of some importance historically, and for a right appreciation of the methods of Indian philosophy. The long lists of the instruments and the acts of intellect, of the sources of activity, of Nescience with its sixty-two subdivisions, &c., though certainly meaningless to my mind, may possibly serve to show how long and how minutely these philosophical questions must have been discussed in order to leave such spoils behind. This large number of technical terms is certainly surprising. Some of them, as, for instance, Su*k*î, Pada, Avadhârita, &c., are not mentioned either in the Kârikâs or in the Sûtras, and this, which has been taken for a sign of their more recent date, seems to me, on the contrary, to speak in favour of an early and independent origin of the Tattva-samâsa and its commentary. If these technical terms were modern inventions, they would occur more frequently in modern works on the Sâ*m*khya-philosophy, but as far as I know, they do not.

### Mûlikârthas.

XVIII. We have still to examine, though as briefly as possible, the Mûlikârthas or eight cardinal facts, that is, the most important subjects established by the Sâ*m*khya[1]. They are with regard to Prak*ri*ti or Pradhâna, its reality (Astitva), its oneness (Ekatva), its having an object or an

[1] See Sâ*m*khya-tattva-kaumudî, p. 59.

intention (Arthavattva), and its being intended for some one else (Parârthya). They are with regard to Purusha his being different from Prakriti (Anyatva), his not being an agent (Akartritva), and his being many (Bahutva). They are with regard to both Prakriti and Purusha, their temporary union and separation, while Sthiti, durability, is said to refer to the Sûkshma- and Sthûla-sarîra, the gross and the subtle bodies. Astitva, reality, might seem to belong to both Prakriti and Purusha, but it is meant as the reality of Prakriti only, which the Sâmkhya is chiefly concerned with establishing as against the Vedântins who deny it with regard to all that is objective, keeping it for the subject only, whether he is called Purusha or Âtman. The commentator, however, and Prof. Garbe also, connect Astitva with Purusha as well as with Prakriti. The matter is of little consequence, unless Astitva is taken in the sense of phenomenal or perceptible reality. The highest reality of the Purusha or the Âtman has of course never been doubted by Sâmkhya or Vedânta philosophers, but that is more than mere Astitva.

### Shashti-tantra.

It should be added that the commentator in this place accounts once more for the name of Shashti-tantra, the Sixty-doctrine, but this time by adding the 17 Tushtis and Siddhis, the 33 (Avidyâ 5 + Asakti 28) and 10, not 8, Mûlikârthas, and thus arriving at 60 topics. The Chinese name presupposes a Saptati-sâstra, or Seventy-treatise, probably with reference to the original number of verses in the Kârikâ.

### Anugraha-sarga.

XIX. But even here the Tattva-samâsa is not yet finished, for it goes on to explain the Anugraha-sarga, lit. the creation of benevolence, which is explained as the production of external objects from the five Tanmâtras or subtle essences *for the sake* of the Purusha. Brahmâ, after seeing these (the organs of sense?) produced, but as yet without a sphere in which their measuring or perceiving power could find scope, created for them the so-called benevolent creation, shaped from the Tanmâtras[1].

### Bhûta-sarga.

XX. After this follows the Bhûta-sarga in fourteen divisions. The divine creation has eight divisions, consisting of good and evil spirits and gods, such as Pi*s*â*k*as, Rakshas, Yakshas, Gandharvas, Indra, Pra*g*âpati, and Brahmâ. The animated creation consists of domestic animals, birds, wild animals, reptiles, and immovable things or plants. The human creation consists of one, of man only, from Brâhmans down to *K*â*nd*âlas. Domestic animals are from cows down to mice; birds from Garu*d*a down to gnats; wild animals from lions down to jackals; reptiles from *S*esha (world-serpent) down to worms; immovable things from the Pâri*g*âta-tree (in paradise) down to grass. This is the threefold creation, consisting of gods, men, and animals, the animals, i. e. living beings, forming again five classes.

---

[1] This passage is very doubtful, unless we connect Mâna with Tanmâtra, and take measuring in the sense of perceiving, so that the creation would be represented as made for man.

### Bandha, Bondage.

XXI. If it be asked what the threefold bondage (Bandha) consists in, it is replied, In the eight Prakritis, in the sixteen Vikâras, and in Dakshinâ (gifts to priests). There are eight Prakritis, as often described before (pp. 321, 329); and as long as a man considers these as the highest, he is absorbed in Prakriti and bound by Prakriti. The bondage of the sixteen Vikâras applies both to ascetics and to men of the world, if they are subdued by the senses, which are Vikâras, if they are devoted to objects of sense, if their organs of sense are not in subjection, if they are ignorant and deluded by passions.

### Dakshinâ-bondage, Gifts to Priests.

The priestly bondage applies to those, whether householders, students, mendicants or anchorets, whose minds are overcome by passions and delusions, and who from misconception bestow sacrificial gifts on priests. A verse is quoted here in support: 'Bondage is spoken of by the name of Prakriti-bondage, Vikâra-bondage, and thirdly bondage through priestly gifts.' This last bondage seems to me very important, and it is strange that it should never have been pointed out as marking the unecclesiastical and unorthodox character of the Sâmkhya-philosophy [1]. What would have become of the Brâhmans without their Dakshinâs or fees, the very name of a Brâhman being Dakshinîya, one to be fee'd? In the Aitareya-Brâhmana already we read of Yatis who condemned sacrifices, but they are said to have been thrown to the jackals. That this

[1] See, however, Kârikâ 44.

feeing of a priest should have been considered one of the three bondages shows at all events that the followers of Kapila were above superstition, and looked upon sacrifice and priestcraft as hindrances rather than as helps to true freedom and Moksha of the spirit.

**Moksha.**

XXII. This Moksha, the highest aim of Kapila's philosophy, is again of three kinds, according as it arises from increase of knowledge, from the quieting of the passions of the senses, or lastly from the destruction of the whole. From increase of knowledge and quieting of the passions of the senses there arises the destruction of all that is commonly considered as merit and demerit; and from the destruction of merit and demerit there arises final beatitude consisting in complete detachment from the world, and in concentration of the Purusha in himself.

**Pramâ*n*as.**

XXIII. The three Pramâ*n*as which follow next require little explanation here, as they have been fully examined before. Still each system of philosophy takes its own view of them, and the character of each is more or less determined by the view taken of the real nature of knowledge. What is most creditable is that each system should have recognised the importance of this question, as a preliminary to every philosophy. This distinguishes Indian philosophy very favourably from other philosophies. All systems of philosophy in India admit Pratyaksha or perception of the senses as the first of Pramâ*n*as. The Vedânta, however, looks upon the Veda as the only source of true knowledge, and actually applies to it the name of Pratyaksha. The ordinary three or six Pramâ*n*as of the Mîmâ*m*sâ would apply to the world of Avidyâ or nescience only, never to the true world of Brahman. See Vedânta-Sûtras II, 1, 14. The names vary sometimes, but the meaning is the same. Sensuous perception, if it is meant for what is perceived, is sometimes called D*ri*sh*t*am, what is seen; and instead of Veda we meet with *S*abda, word, and Âpta-va*k*ana (Sâ*m*khya), right affirmation. Anumâna, inference, is illustrated by the usual examples, such as, inference of rain from the rising of clouds, inference of water from the appearance of cranes, inference of fire from the rising of smoke. Whatever cannot be proved by either sense or inference has to be accepted as Âpta-va*k*ana, as, for instance, the existence of Indra, the king of the gods, the Northern Kurus, Meru, the golden mountain, the Apsaras, or nymphs of Svarga, &c. For all these things, Munis such as Va*s*ish*th*a must be accepted as authorities. Âpta is explained as a name for a man who is assiduous in his work, free from hatred and passion, learned, and endowed with all virtues, and who can therefore be relied upon. These three Pramâ*n*as, or measures, are so called because in the same way as in common life grains are measured by measures such as a Prastha, and sandalwood, &c., weighed by a balance, the Tattvas also, the principles, the Bhâvas (their modifications), and the Bhûtas, elemental substances, are measured or proved by the Pramâ*n*as.

**Du*h*kha.**

XXIV. The last paragraph in the Tattva-samâsa points back to the first. We saw in the beginning how a Brâhman was introduced who, overcome by threefold pain, took refuge with the great *Ri*shi Kapila. If we ask what was meant by that threefold pain, the answer is that it is Âdhyâtmika, Âdhibhautika, and Âdhidaivika. Âdhyâtmika is pain arising from the body, whether produced by wind, bile, or phlegm, &c., and from the mind (Manas), such as is due to desire, anger, greed, folly, envy, separation from what is liked, union with what is disliked, &c. Âdhibhautika is pain that arises from other living beings, such as thieves, cattle, wild beasts, &c. Âdhidaivika is pain that is caused by divine agents, as pain arising from cold, heat, wind, rain, thunderbolts, &c., all under the direction of the Vedic Devas. If a Brâhman is affected by this threefold pain, a desire to know (the reason) arises in him, as a desire for water arises in a thirsty man. Freedom from pain, or final beatitude, is to be gained, as we are told, from a study of the Tattva-samâsa. Whoever knows the philosophy which is contained in the Tattva-samâsa, is not born again. This is the doctrine of the great sage Kapila, and thus is finished the commentary on the Sûtras of the Tattva-samâsa.

### The True Meaning of the Sâ*m*khya.

In giving an account of the Sâ*m*khya, I have followed entirely the Tattva-samâsa, without mixing it up with the Kârikâs or Sûtras. I was quite aware that the Kârikâs or the Sûtras might have supplied us with a clearer and better-arranged account of that philosophy. But if I am right, that the Tattva-samâsa is older than either, it seemed to me more important that we should know what the Sâ*m*khya really was in its original form. By comparing the Tattva-samâsa with the Kârikâs and Sûtras, we can easily see how this dry system was developed in later times. But though the Kârikâs and Sûtras give us a more systematic account of the Sâ*m*khya, all that is essential can be found in the Samâsa, if only we try to arrange the dry facts for ourselves. It must be confessed, no doubt, that neither in the Sûtras, the Kârikâs, nor in the Tattva-samâsa, do we find what we most value in every philosophy, an insight into the mind and heart of the founder of that philosophical system. If we were asked why such a system should ever have been imagined and elaborated, or what kind of comfort, whether intellectual or moral, it could have afforded to any human being, we should indeed have little to answer. All we can learn is that a man crushed by the burden of what is called the threefold misery, and seeing no hope of relief either by means of good actions or of sacrifices, which can promise no more than a temporary happiness on earth or in Heaven, should seek advice from a philosopher, such as Kapila, believing that he could procure for him entire freedom from all his troubles.

### Nature of Pain.

Here we come across something like a really human sentiment. We can well understand why pain, not only as actual suffering, but as an apparent anomaly or imperfection in the universe, should have opened man's eyes to the fact that there was something wrong or limited in his nature, and in the world in which he found himself; and it is quite intelligible that this consciousness of his limitation should have acted as the first impulse to an inquiry for the cause of it. This would naturally lead on either to a religious or to a philosophical solution, and it certainly did so in India. A religion must have existed already before this question of the origin of suffering could well have been mooted: but religion seems rather to have increased the difficulty of the questioner than solved it. The gods or god, even in their imperfect conception, were generally supposed to be good and just. How then could they be the authors of human suffering, particularly of that suffering, bodily or mental, for which the individual was clearly not responsible, such as being 'born blind, or deaf, or dumb, or mad.' This seems to have been keenly felt by the ancient Indian philosophers, who shrink from charging any divine power with injustice or cruelty towards men, however low an opinion they may otherwise have formed of Indra and Agni, nay even of Pra*g*âpati, Vi*s*vakarman or Brahmâ.

Here then it was that philosophy was called in, nay was first brought to life, and the answer which it gave as to the origin of suffering or, in a wider sense, the origin of evil, was that all that seemed wrong in the world must have been the effect of causes, of deeds done, if not in this, then in a former life. No deed (Karman) good or bad, small or great, could ever be without its effect, its reward or punishment. This was the fundamental principle of their ethics, and an excellent principle it was. It was but another version of what we mean by eternal punishment, without which the world would fall to pieces; for it has rightly been observed that eternal punishment is in reality but another name for eternal love. This idea of eternal love, however, cannot hang in the air, it presupposes an eternal lover, a personal God, a creator and ruler of the world: but even this idea Indian philosophers would not have taken for granted. In some cases, though allowing deeds to have their effects, they went so far as to admit at least the superintending care of a Divine Being, just as the giver of rain enables seeds to grow, though the seeds themselves were the deeds performed by men, as independent actors, and therefore liable to take all their consequences upon themselves, whether good or evil.

But though this ought to have sufficed to convince men that the world was exactly as it ought to be, and could not have been otherwise, because man himself had made it what it was, whether as an individual or as a member of a class, there arose a new question which could not well be suppressed, namely, Whether it was beyond the power of man ever to put an end to the unbroken and irresistible sequence of the effects of the deeds of himself and of his fellow creatures; whether, in fact, the cycle of life and death, or what was called Sa*m*sâra, would go on for ever. And here the bold answer was, Yes, the Sa*m*sâra can be stopped, man's former acts can be shaken off and annihilated, but by one means only, by means of knowledge or philosophy. In order to achieve this deliverance from all suffering, from all limitation, from all the bondage of the world, man must learn what he really is. He must learn that he is not the body, for the body decays and dies, and with it all bodily sufferings might seem to end. But this is again denied, because through an invisible agency (Ad*r*ish*t*a or Apûrva) a new Ego would spring up, liable to suffer for its former acts, just as it was in this life. A man must learn therefore that he is not even what is meant by the Ego, for the Ego also has been formed by surroundings or circumstances, and will vanish again like everything else. Then what remains? There remains behind the body, and behind the Ego, or the individual person, what is called the Purusha or the Âtman, the Self, and that Self is to be recognised either as identical with what was in earlier times conceived and called the Divine, the Eternal, the Unconditioned, namely, Brahman, or as Purusha, perfect, independent, and absolute in itself, blissful in its independence and in the complete aloofness from everything else. The former was, as we saw, the view of the Vedânta, the latter is the view of the Sâ*m*khya-philosophy. Both may have had the same roots, but they differ in their later growth. The view which the Vedânta took of man has sometimes been mistaken for human apotheosis. But people forget that for these philosophers there were no *theoi* left whose company man could have joined, and whose eminence they could have reached. The Divine which they meant was the Divine in man, and what they wanted was reconciliation between the Divine within and the Divine without. Their Moksha or Nirvâ*n*a was not meant for *Vergötterung*, not even for the *Vergottung* of Eckhart; it was meant for complete freedom, freedom from all conditions and limitations, selfdom, in fact, whether as recovery of the Divine as Brahman, or as Âtman, or as something beyond all names that had ever been given to the Divine, as the eternal Subject, undetermined by any qualities, satisfied and blissful in his own being and in his own thinking.

Whatever we may think of these two solutions of the world's great riddle, we cannot but admire their originality and their daring, particularly if we compare them with the solutions proposed by other philosophers, whether of ancient or modern times. None of them seems to me to have so completely realised what may be called the idea of the soul as the Phoenix, consumed by the fire of thought and rising from his own ashes, soaring towards regions which are more real than anything that can be called real in this life. Such views cannot be criticised as we criticise ordinary systems of religion or morality. They are visions, if you like, but they are visions which, to have seen is like having been admitted to the vision of another world; of a world that must exist, however different in its eternal silence from what we and from what the ancient seers of India imagined it to be.

The most curious thing is that such views could be held by the philosophers of India without bringing them into conflict with the representatives of the ancient religion of the country. It is true that the Sâ*m*khya-philosophy was accused of atheism, but that atheism was very different from what we mean by it. It was the negation of the necessity of admitting an active or limited personal god, and hence was carefully distinguished in India from the atheism of the Nâstikas or nihilists, who denied the existence of anything transcendent, of anything beyond our bodily senses, of anything divine. To call the Sâ*m*khya atheistic, and the Vedânta not, would be philosophically most unfair, and it does the Indian priesthood great credit that they treated both systems as orthodox, or at all events as not prohibited, provided always that the students had, by a previous severe discipline, acquired the strength and fitness necessary for so arduous a task.

How different the world of thought in India was from our own, we may see by an extraordinary defence set up for the so-called atheism of the Sâ*m*khya-philosophy. It seems to us perfectly absurd, but it was by no means so, if we consider the popular superstitions of the Hindus at the time. It was a common belief in India that man could, by severe penance, raise himself to the status of a god, or Deva. There are ever so many legends to that effect. This might no doubt be called apotheosis; and it was expressly stated that it was in order to put an end to such vain desires of becoming personal gods that Kapila ignored or left out of question the existence of such theomorphic or anthropomorphic beings as could ever excite the rivalry of men. We are hardly prepared for such explanations, and yet in India they seem quite *bonâ fide*.

### Vedânta and Sâ*m*khya.

We have thus finished our account of the Vedânta and of the Sâ*m*khya-philosophy. At first sight no two philosophies would seem to be so different from each other, nay, to start from such opposite points of view as the Vedânta and the Sâ*m*khya. The Vedântist of the school of *S*a*m*kara looks upon the whole world, including animate and inanimate nature, including the small gods and the still smaller men, as a phenomenal manifestation of an unknown power which he calls Brahman. There is nothing beside it, nothing that can be called real except this one invisible Brahman. Then came the question, But whence this phenomenal world? or rather, as he starts with the idea of there being but one real being from eternity to eternity, How could that eternal Brahman ever give rise to the world, not only as its efficient, but also as its material cause, if indeed there is anything material in the objects known to the Vedântist? Under the circumstances thus given, but one answer is possible, That Brahman is the world, and that the world, so far as it is Brahman, but so far only, is real. The phenomenal world, such as we see it and live in it, is changeful, ever passing away, and consequently never, in the Vedântic sense of that word, real. We never see it or know it, as it really is, until we have become Vedântists. It is impossible to think that this eternal Being, whatever name be given to it, could ever change or be changed. This view of the universe as a development of Brahman was possibly the original view taken by Bâdarâya*n*a, and it was clearly that of Râmânu*g*a and his followers, who explain the world as an evolution (Pari*n*âma). But this was not *S*a*m*kara's theory. He accepts the two facts that the world is changing and unreal, and yet that the real cause of it, that is, Brahman, is incapable of change.

### Vedânta, Avidyâ, and Aviveka.

Hence nothing remains but to ascribe the changeful phenomenal character of the world to something else, and, according to the Vedânta, to ignorance, not. however, to our individual ignorance, but to some primeval ignorance directed towards Brahman as manifested and seen. This ignorance or Avidyâ, again, is not to be called real, it is nothing by the side of Brahman, nothing therefore that could ever have dominion over Brahman. All such views are excluded by the postulate that Brahman is free, is one and all; though here again, other Vedântists differ from *Sam*kara, and represent Avidyâ as an actual power (*S*akti) of Brahman, or as Mâyâ, i. e. illusive power, which in fact performs, or is answerable for what we call creation. We should of course ask at once, Whence comes that Avidyâ or that Mâyâ, and what is it? How can it be anything, if not again Brahman, the only thing that exists? The answer given by *Sam*kara, which satisfied his mind, if not the minds of other Vedântists, was that we know as a fact that Avidyâ or Nescience is there, but we also know that it is not there, as soon as we see through it, in fact, as soon as we are able to annihilate it by Vidyâ or knowledge, such as is given to us by the Vedânta-philosophy. The Vedântist holds that nothing that can be annihilated can claim true reality for itself. Therefore Avidyâ, though it is, must not be called something real. The great difficulty how Brahman could ever be affected by Avidyâ, which is a weakness or a defect, is avoided by looking upon Brahman, while affected by Avidyâ or seen through Avidyâ, as for the time under a cloud or forgetful of itself, but never really unreal. We ourselves also, that is the individual souls, can be in full reality nothing but Brahman, though for a while we are divided from it, because forgetful of Brahman through Avidyâ. While that state of Avidyâ lasts the true Brahman, neuter, may become to us Brahmâ, masculine, may become the creator and ruler of the world, and, as such, receive worship from his creatures. But as soon as the cloud of Avidyâ is lifted, this creator also recedes and is restored at once to his true state and dignity. He, the so-called Îsvara, or Lord, or Creator, becomes what he is and always has been, the whole Brahman; and we ourselves also remember and thereby recover our true Brahmahood, or Self-hood, not as if we had ever been divided from it, but only as having been blinded for a while by Avidyâ so as to forget ourselves, our true Self, that is Brahman.

### Sâmkhya, Aviveka.

The Sâmkhya takes what seems a very different attitude towards the problem of the world. These attitudes towards the world form indeed the kernel of every philosophy. If we call the Vedânta monistic, the Sâmkhya is decidedly dualistic. It accepts the whole objective universe as real, and calls it Prakriti, a word often translated by Nature, but in reality untranslatable, because the idea which it represents has never arisen in our philosophy. Prakriti may be called the undeveloped matter or *Urstoff*, containing in itself the possibilities of all things. By itself it has no consciousness, it simply grows or develops into consciousness when seen by Purusha. And it develops not only into an objective or material world, but at the same time, into what we should call the subjective or intellectual world, supplying the instruments of perception and thought, both what perceives and what is perceived. The question whence it came is never asked, as little as we could ask that question with regard to Brahman. It is, it has been, and it has had no beginning. But in order to account for the world of experience, it is supposed that this undeveloped Prakriti is always operative, so long as it is noticed or perceived by a Purusha (Self), and always passing through a process of evolution. This is an important condition. Prakriti is at work so long only as it is perceived by a Purusha or a true Self. This would come very near to the recognition of the subjectivity of all our knowledge, and to the recognition that the world exists for us in the form of knowledge only. If we call Prakriti matter, the Sâmkhya philosopher saw clearly enough that dead, dull, inert matter alone would not account for the world. Therefore he makes Prakriti, under the eye of a Purusha, develop into Buddhi, commonly translated by perception, but really a kind of perception that involves something like what we should call intellect (νοῦς). What, as far as I can see, is really meant by Buddhi in this place, is the lighting up of Prakriti or dull matter by intelligence, so as to render it perceptive, and also perceptible. It is the Indian 'Let there be light.' In this stage Prakriti is called Mahat, the great, possibly in order to indicate its importance in the great development of the universe. It cannot be taken here in an exclusively psychological sense, though it supplies, no doubt, the possibility of the intelligence of the individual also. In the cosmical sense the development of the world is often spoken of as Samashti, in the psychological sense, and as applied to each individual it goes by the name of Vyashti. Thus Vigñâna-Bhikshu (Sâmkhya-Sûtras I, 63) remarks: As, according to passages of Sruti and Smriti, such as (*Kh*ând. Up. VI, 2, 3) 'Let me multiply myself, let me procreate,' the creation of the elements, &c., is preceded by Abhimâna (i. e. Ahamkâra or subjectivity), it follows that this Abhimâna is really the cause of the creation of the world, as preceded by an activity of Buddhi, i.e. the cosmical Buddhi, and not simply the personal organ of deciding, as Buddhi is generally explained when part of the individual or psychological development. For shortness sake, it is sometimes said that Abhimâna or Ahamkâra is the cause of creation, for in the end all the Vikâras or evolutes serve one and the same purpose. Buddhi exists in human nature as the power of perception, and it is then, though not quite correctly, identified with Manas or Antahkarana, the mental activity going on within us, which combines and regulates the impressions of the senses, as we shall see hereafter. But as a cosmic force, Buddhi is that which gives light as the essential condition of all knowledge, and is afterwards developed into the senses, the powers of light and thought, two ideas often comprehended by the root Budh, to awaken or to perceive. Budh means literally to awake. And as a sleeping person is dull and inert to the world, but begins to perceive as soon as he is awake, Prakriti also is inert till it is awakened (Pra-buddha), and thus becomes Buddhi, perceiving or perception.

This Buddhi, however, which, as we must always remember, is here conceived as a development of Prakriti, and as, as yet, neither subjective nor objective, requires a new development before it can serve for conscious intellectual work. Perception, according to the Sâmkhya, cannot work without Ahamkâra, literally I-making or Egoism, but philosophically used with a much larger meaning, namely, if I am right, as that which produces the sense of subject, and in consequence of object also. Nature, in spite of being lighted up or rendered capable of perceiving and being perceived, requires, even after it has reached the stage of Buddhi, the division of the whole world, that is, of itself, into subject and object, before any real perception can take place. Subjectivation, therefore, would seem to be the nearest approach, though naturally there can be no subjectivation without simultaneous objectivation.

After this development of Prak*ri*ti into Buddhi, and its differentiation as subjective and objective, the next step is that it produces the Tanmâtras, the elements of the senses as well as of the sense-objects, such as sight and light, hearing and sound, smelling and odour, tasting and savour, feeling and touch. All these, the faculties as well as the corresponding qualities of sense-perception, are modifications of the same Prak*ri*ti, and therefore in one sense the same thing, only viewed from different points of view, as we should say, as subjective and objective, and as changed at last into the material reality of the sentient powers on one side, and the objective world on the other. Lastly, all this development remains without real consciousness, till it attracts the attention of some Purusha, Spirit or Self, who by becoming conscious of Prak*ri*ti and all its works, produces what is the only reality of which we have any conception, the phenomenal reality of a self-conscious soul. I hope I have understood this train of thought rightly, but there is much that requires fuller light. Does Kapila really look upon perception and thought as an instrument, ready made by Prak*ri*ti for the use of the Purusha, but remaining inert, like a telescope, till it is looked through by the Purusha, or is it the first glance of Purusha at Prakriti in its state of Avyakta or chaos, that gives the first impulse to the activity of Prakriti, which impulse is generally ascribed to the working of the Gunas? Much may be said for either view. I do not feel competent to pronounce so decided an opinion as others have done on this subject.

If the Vedântist explains what we call Creation as the result of Avidyâ or Nescience, the Sâmkhya explains it by the temporary union between Purusha and Prakriti. This union is said to arise from a want of discrimination (Aviveka), and it is not in the highest sense a real union, because it vanishes again by discriminating knowledge (Viveka), nay, it is actually said to have the one object only of evoking at last in the Purusha a revulsion, and in the end a clear recognition of his complete independence, and his freedom from Prakriti (Kârikâ 66). Thus the creation of the phenomenal world and our position in the phenomenal world are due to nescience (Avidyâ) with the Vedântist, but to a want of discrimination (Aviveka) with the Sâmkhya philosopher (S. S. I, 55), and this want of discrimination is actually called by the Vedântic term of Avidyâ in the Yoga-Sûtras II, 24. Where then, we may well ask, is the difference between the two views of the universe? There is a difference in the mode of representation, no doubt, but in the end both Vedânta and Sâmkhya look upon what we call reality as the result of a temporary error, call it nescience, illusion, want of discrimination, or anything else. If, therefore, philosophers like Vignâna-Bhikshu recognised this original similarity in the tendencies both of the Vedânta and the Sâmkhya, it is hardly fair to blame them as having mixed and confounded the two. No doubt these two philosophies diverged in their later development, but they started with the same object in view, and they advanced for a time in the same direction. If the Vedântists desired to arrive at what is called Âtmâ-anâtma-viveka, discrimination between Âtman and Anâtman, the Sâ*m*khyas looked forward to Prak*ri*ti-purusha-viveka, discrimination between Purusha and Prak*ri*ti. Where then is the difference ? If their later defenders forgot their common interest and laid greater stress on the points of difference than on the points of similarity between them, it was but right that those who could see deeper, should bring to light whatever features there were left of the original family likeness between the two philosophies.

### Âtman and Purusha.

Greater, however, than the difference between Nescience, Avidyâ, and want of discrimination, Aviveka, as the causes of the world, according to Vedânta and Sâ*m*khya, is that between the Brahman of the Vedânta, and the many Purushas of the Sâ*m*khya. According to *S*a*m*kara the individual souls are not, according to Kapila they are. According to the former there is in reality but one Âtman or Self, as it were, one sun reflected in the countless waves of the world-ocean ; according to the latter there are many Purushas, as many as there are divine, human, animal, and vegetal souls, and their plurality is conceived as eternal, not as phenomenal only. On this point, therefore, there is a radical difference ; and this is due, as it seems to me, to a want of accurate reasoning on the part of the Sâ*m*khyas. Such a peculiarity must not be slurred over in an account of the Sâmkhya-philosophy, but it is fair to point out what the reason of this aberration may have been. From a higher point of view the Purusha of Kapila is really the same as the Brahman or the Âtman of the Vedânta, the absolute subject. It differs only in that the Purusha was never conceived as the material cause of the universe, while Brahman was, though, of course, with the important proviso that everything material was due to Nescience. Apart from that, if the Purusha was meant as absolute, as eternal, immortal, and unconditioned, it ought to have been clear to Kapila that the plurality of such a Purusha would involve its being limited, determined or conditioned, and would render the character of it self-contradictory. Kapila has certainly brought forward every possible argument in support of the plurality of individual Purushas, but he has forgotten that every plurality presupposes an original unity, and that as trees in the last resort presuppose the tree, as men are descended from man, call him Adam or Manu or any other name, many Purushas, from a metaphysical point of view, necessitate the admission of one Purusha, just as the many gods had to be recognised as in reality the One God without a second, and at last as mere mistakes of Brahman. In this way Vigñâna-Bhikshu was right that Kapila did not differ so much from Bâdarâyana as it would seem, because, if the Purushas were supposed to be many, they would not be Purushas, and being Purusha they would by necessity cease to be many. It may be said that this is going beyond Kapila, but surely we have a right to do so.

It is necessary, at all events, that we should see all this clearly, just as Vigñâna-Bhikshu and other philosophers saw it clearly, in order to perceive the unity that underlies the apparent diversity in the philosophy of India. Nor should we ever forget that our philosophical Sûtras, whatever their age, whether of the fourteenth century A. D. or the fifth century B. C., are but the last outcome of the philosophical activity of a whole country, and that we are entirely ignorant of their historical antecedents. We should remember that the grammatical Sûtras of Pâ*n*ini are contradicted again and again by grammatical forms which have fortunately been preserved to us in the earlier Brâhma*n*as and Mantras of the Vedic period. We have no such remnants of an earlier period of philosophy anterior to the Sûtras, with the exception of the as yet unsystematised Upanishads, and possibly of some of the more ancient parts of the Mahâbhârata; but in other respects we are left without any earlier facts, though not without a firm conviction that such perfect systems as we find in the Sûtras cannot have sprung up in a day, still less from one brain, but that they must have passed through many changes for better or for worse, before they could assume that final and permanent form in which they are now presented to us in literature. The Sûtras are, in fact, the final outcome of ages of inquiry and discussion.

It would seem then to follow from Vi*gñ*âna-Bhikshu's remarks that in India a philosopher might at one and the same time have been a follower of the Vedânta as well as of the Sâ*m*khya, if he could only see that, where the two follow different roads, they started nevertheless from the same point and were proceeding towards the same goal. If this is seen and accepted in a historical spirit, it can do no harm, though no doubt there is danger of the distinctive features of each system becoming blurred, if we dwell too much on what they share in common or on what they may have shared in common at an earlier period of their growth. In one respect Vi*g*ñâna-Bhikshu, to mention him only, has certainly seen more rightly by not resorting at once to the idea that actual borrowing must have taken place, whenever Vedânta and Sâ*m*khya shared the same ideas. We should always remember that there must have been a period of unrestricted growth of philosophical thought in ancient India, and that during that period philosophical ideas, whether true or false, were common property and could be freely adopted by different schools of philosophy. It was in the Sûtras that these schools became sterilised and petrified.

On one point Vi*g*ñâna-Bhikshu may have gone too far, yielding to a temptation which does not exist for us. To him not only Vedânta and Sâ*m*khya, but all the six Dar*s*anas or systems of philosophy were orthodox, they were all Sm*r*iti, though not *S*ruti. Hence his natural desire to show that they did not on any essential points contradict each other. After he had reconciled to his own satisfaction the conflicting tenets of Vedânta and Sâ*m*khya, and had certainly, at least to my mind, succeeded in discovering the common background of both of them, he attempted to do the same for the Nyâya and Vai*s*eshika. These two, as he says, as they represent the Self as endowed with qualities, might seem to be contradicted by the Vedânta and Sâ*m*khya which show that the Self, or the Purusha, cannot be endowed with qualities; but this is not so. Nyâya and Vai*s*eshika are intended, as he thinks, as a first step only towards the truth; and though they admit the Self to be qualified by pain and joy, they teach that the Self is at all events different from the body. This is what marks the first advance toward a right understanding of the Self, not only as different from the body, but as unaffected by pain and joy, as neither suffering nor enjoying, as neither thinking nor acting in any way. To the followers of the Nyâya-philosophy also, Brahman, the Absolute, is Anirva*k*anîya, undefinable or inexpressible. The full light, however, of the Sâ*m*khya-doctrine might dazzle the beginner, and hence, according to Vi*g*ñâna-Bhikshu, the usefulness of the Nyâya and Vai*s*eshika, as slowly preparing him for the acceptance of the highest truth. There does not, however, seem to be any ancient evidence to support this view of Vi*g*ñâna-Bhikshu's, that the Nyâya and Vai*s*eshika were intended as a preparation only, still less that they existed as systems before the doctrines of the Sâ*m*khya began to influence the thinkers of India. The Sâ*m*khya is indeed mentioned in the Mahâbhârata (XII, 111, 98) as the highest truth, but the other systems are never represented as merely preparations for it. They present themselves as independent philosophies, quite as much as the other Dar*s*anas: nor do I remember any passage where Gotama and Ka*n*âda themselves represent their teaching as a mere step leading to the higher knowledge of Vedânta or Sâ*m*khya, nor any utterance of Bâdarâya*n*a or Kapila to the effect that such preparation was required.

### Origin of Avidyâ.

The question which the Sâ*m*khya may seem to have left unanswered, but which is really unanswer-

able, is, How this Aviveka, this failure of Purusha to recognise himself as distinct from Prak*ri*ti, could ever have arisen, and how and by what stages the development of Prak*ri*ti may be supposed to have taken place which led in the end to the delusion of Purusha and made him look on the senses, on the Manas (central sense), on the Aham or ego, nay on Buddhi or intellect, on everything, in fact, within his experience, as belonging to him, as his own? What Kapila wishes to teach is that nothing is in reality his own or belongs to him except his Self, or, as he calls it, the Purusha. Here we can observe a real difference between Sâ*m*khya and Vedânta. And while in all these discussions Bâdarâya*n*a had only to appeal to the Veda in support of any one of his statements, Kapila, with all his regard for Âptava*k*ana, had evidently meant to reason out his system by himself, though without any declared antagonism to the Vedas. Hence the Sûtras of Kapila received the name of Manana-*s*âstra, institute of reasoned truth.

### The *S*âstra.

If then it is asked how Kapila came to know anything about Prak*ri*ti or *Urstoff* which, as superintended by Purusha, is said to stand for the whole of creation, and how we ourselves can know anything about its various developments, beginning with Buddhi or intellect, and going on from Buddhi to Aha*m*kâra, the making of the I or Ego, or subjectivity as inseparable from objectivity, and from Aha*m*kâra to the Tanmâtras or subtle substances, &c., we have to confess with the author of the Sâ*m*khya-sâra (p. 16) that there was nothing but the *S*âstra itself to depend on in support of what may

be felt to be very crude and startling assertions [1]. *S*âstra sometimes stands for Veda, but it cannot well be taken in that sense here. It seems rather to point to the existence of a treatise, such as the Sâ*m*khya-kârikâ or the original text of the Sâ*m*khya-Sûtras, or the whole body of Sâ*m*khya-philosophy, as handed down from time immemorial in various schools in India. At first sight, no doubt, it seems strange to us to derive Buddhi or Intellect from Prak*ri*ti, nature, or from Avyakta, the undeveloped. But we must remember that all these English renderings are very imperfect. Prak*ri*ti is very different from nature or φύσις, though there is hardly a more convenient term to render it by. In the Sâ*m*khya-philosophy Prak*ri*ti is a postulated something that exists, and that produces everything without being itself produced. When it is called Avyakta, that means that it is, at first, chaotic, undeveloped, and invisible.

### Development of Prak*ri*ti, Cosmic.

In place of this one Prak*ri*ti we often read of eight Prak*ri*tis, those beginning with Buddhi or the Mahat being distinguished as produced as well as producing, while the first, the Avyakta, is producing only, but not produced. This need not mean more than that the seven modifications (Vikâras) and

[1] For the actual succession in the evolution of Aha*m*kâra from the Mahat, and of the Mahat from Prak*ri*ti, &c., the *S*âstra alone, we are told, can be our authority, and not inference, because inference can only lead us to the conclusion that all effects must have a cause, while there is no inference to prove either the succession beginning with the elements, or that beginning with the mind in the way in which the Sâ*m*khya-philosophy teaches. Then what is meant by *S*âstra here?

*forms* of Prak*ri*ti are all effects, and serve again as causes, while the Avyakta itself, the undeveloped Prak*ri*ti, has no antecedent cause, but serves as cause only for all the other forms of Prak*ri*ti.

### Retrospect.

After going through the long list of topics which form the elements of the Sâ*m*khya-philosophy, it may be well to try to give a more general view of Kapila's system. Whether we begin with the beginning, the postulated Prak*ri*ti, or with the end, the phenomenal world as reflected by the Indriyas and the Manas, it is but natural that Kapila should have asked himself the question how what was postulated as the beginning, the undeveloped Prak*ri*ti, could account for all that was to follow, or how all that did follow could be traced back to this postulated Prak*ri*ti. Given the undeveloped Prak*ri*ti, he imagined that it was due to the disturbance of the equilibrium of its three constituents (Gu*n*as) that it was first awakened to life and light or thought, to physical and intellectual activity. Some such impulse is required by all metaphysicians, a πρῶτον κινοῦν. This first step in the development of Prak*ri*ti, this first awakening of the inert substance, is conceived by Kapila as Buddhi, the lighting up, and hence, so long as it is confined to Prak*ri*ti, described as Prakâ*s*a, or light, the chief condition of all perception. After Prak*ri*ti has thus been lighted up and become Buddhi, or potential perception, another distinction was necessary in this luminous and perceiving mass, in this so-called Mahat or Buddhi, namely, the differentiation between perceiver and what is perceived, between subject and object. This was the work assigned, I believe, to Aha*m*kâra, which I should prefer to translate by subjectivation (*Subjectivirung*, Garbe) rather than by Ego or Egoism.

This step from Buddhi to Aha*m*kâra has been compared to Des Cartes' *Cogito ergo sum*[1], but is it not rather *Sum, ergo cogito*, as showing that being itself would be impossible unless it were first lighted up, and differentiated into subject and object, that *esse*, in fact, is *percipi*, or even *percipere*?

When the evolution of the Avyakta has gone so far, the question arises, how this process of perception could take place, how perception is possible subjectively, how it is possible objectively. If we begin with the objective side, the answer of Kapila is that there must be Tanmâtras (This-only), potential *perceptibilia*, which are not the potentialities of everything in general, but of this and this only (Tan-mâtra). These five potentialities are Sound, Touch, Odour, Light, and Taste. They are not yet what is actually heard, seen, &c., nor what actually hears and sees, but they contain the possibilities of both. As there is no hearing without sound, the Sâ*m*khyas seem to have argued, neither is there any sound without hearing. But there is in the Tanmâtras the potentiality of both. Hence, according to the division produced by Aha*m*kâra into subject and object, the five Tanmâtras are realised as the five subjective powers of perception, the powers of hearing, touching, smelling, seeing, and tasting, and corresponding to them as the five objects of sense, the objects of sound, touch, odour, sight, and taste. In their final form the five potential Tanmâtras stand before us in their

[1] Davies, Hindu Philosophy, p. 18.

material shape, subjectively as ear, skin, nose, eyes, and tongue, objectively as ether, air, light, water, and earth (the five Mahâbhûtas). These five supply all possible and real forms under which perception can and does take place.

It should be remembered, however, that in order to account for perception such as it really is, another, a sixth sense, is necessary, in addition to the five, which is called Manas, generally translated by mind, but really a kind of central organ of perception, acting as a door-keeper, meant to prevent the crowding in of perceptions, to arrange them into percepts, and, as we should say, into concepts also, being in fact the *conditio sine quâ non* of all well-ordered and rational thought. One might feel inclined to translate Manas by brain, if brain had not become so unscientific a term in our days. It might also be called the point of attention and apperception, but even this would hardly help us to a clear view of what Kapila really meant by Manas. Only we must guard against taking this Manas, or mind, for the true Self. Manas is as much a mere instrument of knowledge and a product of Prak*ri*ti as the five senses. They all are necessary for the work of perception, conception, and all the rest, as a kind of clockwork, quite different from the highest Self, whether it is called Âtman or Purusha. The Purusha watches the clockwork, and is for a time misled into believing in his identity with the workings of Prak*ri*ti.

This is but a poor attempt to make the Sâ*m*khya view of being and knowing intelligible, and I am far from maintaining that we have gained, as yet, a full insight into the problems which troubled Kapila, or into the solutions which he proposed.

What I feel is, that it is not enough simply to repeat the watchwords of any ancient philosophy, which are easily accessible in the Sûtras, but that we must at least make an attempt to bring those ancient problems near to us, to make them our own, and try to follow the ancient thinkers along the few footsteps which they left behind.

There is an illustration in the Sâ*m*khya-tattva-Kaumudî 36, which suggests a very different view of the process of knowing, and deserves to be taken into consideration: 'As the seniors of a village,' they say, 'collect taxes from the householders and hand them over to the governor of the district, who again remits them to the treasurer, and the treasurer to the king, thus do the outer senses, when they have perceived anything, hand it on to the inner sense, the Manas, the organ which determines what there is and then hands it over to Aha*m*kâra, and the Aha*m*kâra, after appropriating it, to the Buddhi, the supreme Lord.' Here Buddhi, though supreme, is decidedly different from the cosmic Buddhi that springs from the Avyakta and leads to Aha*m*kâra; nor is it easy to see how these two Buddhis, or rather that one Buddhi in its two functions, could have been admitted by one and the same philosopher.

### Is Sâ*m*khya Idealism?

There is another point on which it is difficult to come to a clear understanding. We are asked whether the Hindus fully realised the fact that we are conscious of our sensations only, and that all we call bodies, or the outside or objective world, is no more than the result of an irresistible inference of our mind, which may be called Avidyâ. We are conscious, no doubt, that we are not ourselves the cause of our sensations, that we do not make the sky, but that it is given us. But beyond that, our world is only an inductive world, it is, so to say, our creation; we make the sky concave or blue, and all that remains, after deducting both the primary and secondary qualities, is Prakriti as looked at by Purusha, or, as we should say, *das Ding an sich*, which we can never know directly. It is within us, or under our sway, that this Prakriti has grown to all that it is, not excluding our own bodies, our senses, our Manas, our Tanmâtras, our Ahamkâra, our Buddhi. Was this the view taken by the Sâmkhyas? Did they see that the Sañkara, the development of the world, takes place within us, is our growth, though not our work, that the light which, as Buddhi emerges from Prakriti, is the light within us that has the power of perceiving by its light; that both the Aham, the Ego, and the Tvam, the Non-Ego, determine not only ourselves, but the whole world, and that what we call the real, the sensuously perceiving and perceived world, is no more than the development of thoughtless nature as reflected through the senses on our enchanted Self? The riddle of the world which the Sâmkhya-philosophy has to solve would then be no more than to account for the mistaken interest which the Self takes in that reflex, the consciousness which he assumes of it, the fundamental error by which, for a time at least, he actually identifies himself with those images. This identifying process would, from this point of view, really take the place of what we call creation. The closing of the mental eyelids would be the dropping of the curtain and the close of the drama of the world; and this final recognition of our cosmic misconception would lead the Self back from the stage of the world to himself, would undo all creation, and put an end to that suffering which is the result of bondage or finiteness.

It sometimes seems to me as if such views had been at the bottom of all Hindu philosophy, though forgotten again or obscured by a belief in that reality which determines our practical life (Vyavahâra). By admitting this blending of cosmic and psychological views, much in the Sâ*m*khya-philosophy would cease to be obscure, the Buddhi of the world and the Buddhi of ourselves would indeed become one, and the belief in the reality of things, both objective and subjective, might truly be explained as due to Aviveka, the absence of discrimination between the Self and the imagery of nature. It would become intelligible why Prak*ri*ti should be supposed to play her part so long only as it was noticed by Purusha; it would explain why Prak*ri*ti, by itself, was taken as A*k*etana, objective, thoughtless, and the Purusha only as subjective, conscious and thinking; why in its solitude Purusha was conceived as not active, but Prak*ri*ti as always active; why Purusha should sometimes mean the eternal Self, and sometimes man such as he is or imagines himself to be, while interested in the world, believing in the world, and yet with a constant longing after a higher and truer state, freedom from the world, freedom from pain, freedom from all cosmic being, freedom as alone with himself.

### Purusha and Prak*ri*ti.

But if we may credit the founders of the Sâ*m*khya, whether Kapila or Âsuri or Pañ*k*as*i*kha, with such advanced views, if they really had made it quite clear to themselves that human beings cannot have anything but their own knowledge, we can understand why they should have represented the whole process of perception and combination, all joy and pain, and, in consequence, all willing also, as belonging, not to the Purusha or the Self, but to a stranger, to the Manas, and indirectly to Prak*ri*ti, while the Purusha, when he seems to see, to combine, to rejoice, to suffer, and to will, does so by misapprehension only, like a spectator who is carried away by his sympathies for Hecuba, but who in the end dries his tears and stops his sighs, leaves the theatre of the world, and breathes the fresh air of a bright night. The Sâ*m*khya uses this very simile. The whole development of Prak*ri*ti, it is said, takes place only when Purusha is looking on the dancer, that is, on Prak*ri*ti, in all her disguises. If he does not look, she does not dance for him, and as soon as he turns his eyes entirely away from her, she altogether ceases to try to please him. She may please others who are still looking at her, and so far it may be said that she is never annihilated, because there will always be new Purushas to be enchanted and enchained for awhile, but at last to be set free by her.

### State of Purusha, when Free.

Often has the question been asked, What then becomes of the Purusha, after the spell of Prak*ri*ti has been broken, and he has ceased to take any interest in the phantasmagoria of the world, thrown on him by the Manas and all the products of Prak*ri*ti that support the Manas. But this is a question which no philosophy can be expected to answer. All that can be said is that Purusha, freed from all Prak*ri*tic bonds, whether ignorance or knowledge, joy or sorrow, would remain himself, would be what he alone can be, unrestricted, not interfered with, free and independent, and hence, in the highest sense of the word, perfect and happy in himself. This ineffable state of bliss has naturally shared the fate of similar conceptions, such as the oneness with Brahman, the Ni*h*sreyasa or *Non plus ultra*, and the Nirvâ*n*a of the Buddhists. In the eyes of less advanced thinkers, this unfathomable bliss assumed naturally the character of paradisiacal happiness painted in the most brilliant and even sensuous colours, while to the truly enlightened it represented tranquillity (*S*ânti), perfect rest, and self-satisfaction. While I agree with Dr. Dahlmann [1] that the Buddhist idea of Nirvâ*n*a was the same, originally, as that of the higher bliss of the Vedânta and Sâ*m*khya-philosophy, I cannot believe that it was borrowed by the Buddhists from either of those systems. Nirvâ*n*a was one of the ideas that were in the air in India, and it was worked out by Buddha as well as by Kapila and Bâdarâya*n*a, but by each in his own fashion. The name itself, like many technical terms of Buddha's teaching, was no doubt Brâhmanic. It occurs in the Vedânta, though it is absent in the Sâ*m*khya-Sûtras. We see in the Buddhist Suttas how it was used by the Buddhists, at first, in the simple sense of freedom from passion, but was developed higher and higher, till in the

---

[1] Nirvâ*n*a, eine Studie zur Vorgeschichte des Buddhismus von Joseph Dahlmann, S.J. Berlin, 1896.

end it became altogether negative. If it had been simply taken over by Buddha from some individual teacher of an established philosophy, it would betray its origin, while we see it spring up as naturally in Buddha's philosophy as in that of Bâdarâyana and Kapila. They all took their materials from the same stratum of thought, and elaborated them into systems, probably about the same time. But in spite of Dr. Dahlmann's very learned and very able pleading, I must say once more that I cannot yet see any evidence for supposing that either Buddha borrowed direct from Kapila or that Kapila borrowed from Buddha.

Kapila does not enter into a minute analysis of his Nirvâna, or, as he calls it, Kaivalya, aloneness. His object was to show how pain arose and how pain can be absolutely removed. If freedom from limitation and pain is happiness, that happiness can be secured by the Sâmkhya just as much as by the Vedânta and the Buddhist-philosophy; but though the Vedântist admits happiness (Ânanda) by the side of existence and perception (Sak-kit), as peculiar to the highest Brahman, he does not attempt to explain what kind of happiness he means; and some Vedânta philosophers have actually objected to Ânanda or happiness as a positive predicate of the highest Brahman. Negatively, however, this happiness may surely be defined as freedom from pain, freedom from all limits or fetters, and therefore perfect bliss.

### Meaning of Pain.

It would seem extraordinary, and wholly unworthy of a great philosopher, if Kapila had had eyes for the ordinary sufferings only which are entailed on all the sons of men. He must have known that there is happiness also for them, and something between suffering and happiness, the even tenour of a man's life. Kapila meant something else by pain. He seems to have felt what Schelling felt, that sadness cleaves to all finite life, but that is very different from always being intent on getting rid of the sufferings inherent in life on earth. Kapila evidently meant by Du*h*kha or pain something more than physical or even mental suffering, namely the consciousness of being conditioned, limited, or fettered, which is inseparable from this life. But whatever suffering he may have meant, the method suggested by him for its removal is certainly bold and decided. All this suffering, he tells us, is not, as we imagine, our suffering. Like the whole evolution of Prak*ri*ti, this suffering also belongs to Prak*ri*ti and not to ourselves, not to the Purushas.

### Purusha.

In order to explain the world, we have to admit not only Prak*ri*ti, rising in the form of Buddhi, Aha*m*kâra, and Manas to the height or the depth of individual existence, perception, and action, but likewise another quite independent being, the Purusha, the real or the better and truer Self, and therefore very much the same as the Âtman of the Vedânta. Both Purusha and Âtman, it should be remembered, are absent in Buddha's teaching, and by their removal the idea of Nirvâ*n*a has become almost meaningless. But on this point also we must wait for further light.

With Kapila the Purusha or Self always remains, after as well as before his release. It is true he is only the looker on of all that takes place through Prakriti, looking as it were into a glass in which all the doings of Prakriti are mirrored. For a time by some strange want of discernment, this Purusha, always one of many Purushas, forgets his true nature and identifies himself with this image of Prakriti. He imagines therefore that he himself sees and hears, that he himself suffers and rejoices, that he himself is an I, really possessing all that the world offers to him, and unwilling to give it up again, whether in life or in death. His very body, however, his organs of sense, nay his mind and his individuality, are neither he, nor his; and if he can only learn the wisdom of Kapila, he is for ever above the body, above all sensation, above all suffering. Nay Prakriti even, which has no soul, but acts only as impelled by her nature when looked at by Purusha, ceases her jugglery as soon as Purusha turns away.

### Prakriti an Automaton?

It might possibly help us to understand the relation between Purusha and Prakriti better, if we saw in Prakriti an automaton, such as Des Cartes described, performing all the functions which we consider our own and which are common to man and animals, as in fact a mere mechanism, and if we took the rational soul, the Purusha, as the *chose pensante*, superadded to the automaton. It was Professor Huxley who showed that, as a consequence of this assumption, all our mental conditions might be regarded as simply the symbols (Pratibimba) in consciousness of the changes which take place automatically in the organism. In the same way all the changes of Prakriti, from mere sensation to conceptual thought, might be taken as including pain and joy and consequent action, the working of Prak*ri*ti, independent of the looker on, although that looker on in his enchanted state imagines that he is himself doing what in reality Prak*ri*ti is doing for him. This is beautifully illustrated by the simile of the dancing-girl to which we referred before, but who is here represented not only as intent on pleasing and beguiling Purusha, but as trying herself to open his eyes and make him free from her charms and fetters. We thus get a new application of the simile mentioned before.

### Prak*ri*ti's Unselfishness.

We read in the Kârikâs 59–62: 'As a dancer having exhibited herself on the stage ceases to dance, so does Nature (Prak*ri*ti) cease, when she has made herself manifest to Purusha.

60. In many ways Prak*ri*ti serves Purusha, who yet does nothing for her in return; she is noble minded and cares only for the welfare of him who is so ungrateful to her.

61. There is nothing more modest, I think, than Prak*ri*ti, who does not expose herself again to the gaze of Purusha, after she knows that she has been gazed at.

62. No Purusha is therefore really chained, nor does he become free, or wander; Prak*ri*ti alone, dependent as she is on different Purushas, wanders from birth to birth, is bound, and is freed.'

In fact it would seem that Prak*ri*ti, in enchanting or binding Purusha, has no object in view except that Purusha should in the end perceive his fetters, and by discrimination become free from them (Kârikâ 59).

Here is indeed the Gordian knot of the whole Sâ*m*khya-philosophy. We believe for a time in our own physical nature and in the nature by which we are surrounded, and so long as we do this, we suffer. We are exposed to all kinds of pain, till our eyes are opened and we learn that it is Prak*ri*ti that sees and acts, that kills and is killed, that suffers, while we imagine that we ourselves do and suffer all this. As soon as this insight has been gained, as soon as Purusha has distinguished between himself and what is not himself, liberation is achieved at once, and the dance of life is ended for ever, at least so far as the liberated Self is concerned. Until that final liberation has been accomplished and everything like body has been completely removed, transmigration continues, and the Purusha is supposed to be clothed in what is called the Liṅga-*s*arîra, or subtle body. Whatever we may think of the truth of such a system we cannot help admiring its consistency throughout, and its boldness and heroism in cutting the Gordian knot.

### Gross and Subtle Body.

The idea of a subtle body by the side of our gross body is very natural; and we know that among the Greeks also Pythagoras claimed a subtle ethereal clothing for the soul apart from its grosser clothing when united with the body. But the exact nature of that subtle body and its relation to the grosser body is by no means as clear as we could wish it to be.

Both Sâ*m*khyas and Vedântists agreed in admitting the necessity of a subtle body in order to make the process of migration after death intelligible. In the Vedânta the name of that body, or vehicle,

or Âsraya for the journey of the soul from existence to existence is Sûkshma-sarîra, the subtle body. The Vedântists look upon this thin and transparent vehicle of the soul as a seminal or potential (Vî*g*a or *S*akti) body, which at death leaves the coarse material body, without being injured itself. This subtle body arises, according to the Vedânta, from the so-called Upâdhis (conditions), and consists of the senses of the body (Dehendriyas), both perceptive (Buddhîndriyas) and active (Karmendriyas), and of Manas (mind), of Buddhi (intellect), Vedanâ (sensation), implying beyond itself the Vishayas, objects required for sensation and presupposed already by Manas. Its physical life is dependent on the Mukhya Prâ*n*a, the vital spirit, and on the five Prâ*n*as, the specialised spirits. Its Indriyas or senses are not to be taken as the external organs of sense, such as ears, eyes, &c., but as their functions only (V*ri*tti). This subtle and invisible body or Sûkshma-sarîra remains, according to the Vedânta, till true knowledge arises, and the individual soul recovers its true being in Brahman. The Vedântists are, however, by no means consistent in their views on these two bodies, the subtle and the coarse body (Sûkshma*m* and Sthûla*m* *S*arîra*m*), or on the process by which the one affects or controls the other. At the final dissolution of the coarse body we are told that the Indriyas are absorbed in the Manas, the Manas in the Mukhya Prâ*n*a, this in the *G*îva, the individual, and this in the subtle body; but neither the Upanishads nor the Vedânta-Sûtras are always quite consistent and clear in their views on the subject, and it seems to me useless to attempt to reduce their various guesses to one uniform theory.

In the Sâmkhya-philosophy this Sûkshma-sarîra appears as Linga-sarîra, or the sign-body. The Sthûla-sarîra or coarse material body consists, according to some Sâmkhya teachers, of the five or four coarse elements (Bhûtas), according to others of the element of the earth only, and is made up of six coverings, hair, blood, flesh, sinews, bones and marrow. The subtle or inner body, sometimes called the vehicle, or the Âtivâhika-sarîra, is formed of eighteen elements[1], of (1) Buddhi, (2) Ahamkara, (3) Manas, (4–8) the five Tanmâtras or Sûkshmabhûtas, and (9–18) the ten senses. This body is of course invisible, but without it the coarse body would be useless. It forms what we should call our personality, and causes the difference in the characters of individuals, being itself what it has been made to be by former works. All fitness for reward and punishment attaches to it, not to the Purushas who are all alike and unchanging, and it likewise determines by means of its acquired dispositions the gross bodies into which it has to enter from life to life, till final freedom is obtained by the Purusha; and not only the gross body, but the subtle body also is reabsorbed in Prakriti.

### The Atheism of Kapila.

We have still to say a few words about the charge of atheism brought against the Sâmkhyas. It seems certainly strange that at this early time

[1] Kârikâ 40, and Sâmkhya-Sûtras III, 9. Why the Linga-sarîra should be said to consist of seventeen and one (Saptadasaikam) elements, is difficult to say, unless Eka is taken for the Purusha who, for the time being, identifies himself with the subtle body.

and surrounded as he no doubt was by sacrifices and hymns addressed to the innumerable Vedic Devas, nothing should have been said by Kapila either for or against these beings. Most likely at his time and before his time, the different Devas of the popular religion had already been eclipsed in the minds of thoughtful people by one Deity, whether Pra*g*âpati, Visvakarman, or Brahman. Both Pra*g*âpati and Brahmâ are mentioned in the Tattva-samâsa-bhâshya. But even such a supreme Deva or Adhideva is never asserted or denied by Kapila. There is a place in his system for any number of subordinate Devas, but there is none for God, whether as the creator or as the ruler of all things. There is no direct denial of such a being, no out-spoken atheism in that sense, but there is simply no place left for him in the system of the world, as elaborated by the old philosopher. He had, in fact, put nearly everything that belonged to God into Prak*ri*ti, only that this Prak*ri*ti is taken as purely objective, and as working without a conscious purpose, unless when looked at by Purusha, and then working, as we are told, for his benefit only.

This has sometimes been illustrated by what must have been a very old fable, viz. that of a cripple who could not walk, meeting another cripple who could not see. As they could not live by themselves, they lived together, the lame one mounting on the shoulders of the blind one. Prak*ri*ti, we are told, was the blind, Purusha the lame traveller.

We must remember, however, that Prak*ri*ti, though blind, is always conceived as real, because the Sâ*m*khya-philosophy looks upon everything that is, as proceeding out of something that is real (Sat-kâryavâda). And here we see again, the fundamental difference between the Sâmkhya and the other philosophies, as Vâkaspati-Misra has pointed out in his commentary on the Sâmkhya-kârikâ 9. The Buddhist takes the real world as the result of nothing, the Vedântist takes the unreal world as proceeding from something real, Naiyâyika and Vaiseshika derive what does not yet exist from what does exist, while the Sâmkhyas derive what is from what is[1].

If it be asked how the unconscious Prakriti began to work and attract the attention of Purusha, Kapila has an answer ready. The Gunas, he says, are first in a state of equipoise, but as soon as one of the three preponderates, there is tension, and Prakriti enters on the course of her unceasing labours, beginning with the emanation of Buddhi, and ending with the last of the twenty-four Tattvas.

There is this difference also between the atheism of Kapila and that of other atheistic systems of philosophy, that Kapila nowhere puts himself into a hostile attitude towards the Divine idea. He nowhere denies distinctly the existence even of the purely mythological gods, such as Indra, which is strange indeed; nor does he enter on any arguments to disprove the existence of one only God. He simply says—and in that respect he does not differ much from Kant—that there are no logical proofs to establish that existence, but neither does he offer any such proofs for denying it. We know that Kant, honest thinker as he was, rejected all the logical proofs of the existence of Deity as insufficient, and based the arguments for his belief in God on purely

---

[1] Garbe, Sâmkhya-Philosophie, p. 202.

ethical grounds. Though we have no right to assume anything of the kind with regard to Kapila, when brought face to face with this great religious and moral problem, the existence of a supreme God, we ought to mark his impartiality and the entire absence, in the whole of his philosophy, of anything like animus against a belief in God. The Devas he could hardly have seriously believed in, we should say, and yet he spares them and allows them to exist, possibly with the reservation that people, in worshipping them, were unconsciously approaching the true Purusha. We should not forget that with many people atheism meant, and means, a denial of Devas rather than the denial of the one, only God, the First Cause of the world. This whole question, however, will be better discussed when we reach the Yoga-philosophy and have to examine the arguments produced by Patañ*g*ali against Kapila, and in support of the admission of a Supreme Being, generally called Îsvara, the Lord.

### Immorality of the Sâ*m*khya.

It has also been said that Kapila's system is not only without a God, but likewise without any morality. But though it is quite true that, according to Kapila, Purusha in his perfect state is non-moral, neither merit nor demerit, virtue nor vice, existing any longer for him, he is certainly not allowed to be immoral. The Sâ*m*khya, like the Vedânta and other systems of Indian philosophy, implies strong moral sentiment in the belief in Karman (deed) and transmigration. Kapila also holds that deeds, when once done, can never cease, except at the time of Moksha, but produce effect after effect, both in this life and in the lives to come. This is one of the unalterable convictions in the Hindu mind. There is, besides the admission of virtue and vice, the dispraise of passion and the praise of dispassion. These are represented as forms of Buddhi, as Rûpas or Bhâvas, forms or states, inhering in Buddhi, and therefore following the Liṅga-*s*arîra from birth to birth. Nay, it is distinctly added that going upward is due to virtue, going downward to vice, so that virtue, as a preliminary, is really indispensable to final liberation. It may be true that in this way morality is reduced to mere calculation of consequences, but even such a calculation, which is only another name for reasoning, would serve as a strong incentive to morality. Anyhow there is no ground for saying that Kapila's system ignores ordinary morality, still less that it encourages vice.

### Sâ*m*khya Parables.

There is one more feature of the Sâ*m*khya that deserves to be mentioned, because it is not found in the other Indian philosophies, but may be supposed to have suggested to the Buddhists their method of teaching by parables. A whole chapter of the Sûtras, the fourth, is assigned to a collection of stories, each of which is meant to illustrate some doctrine of Kapila's. Some are very much to the point, and they can be appealed to by one word, so as to recall the whole lesson which they were meant to teach. The first is meant to illustrate the complete change that comes over a man when he has been taught his true nature by means of the Sâ*m*khya. 'As in the case of the son of a king.' The story which follows is that a young prince who was born under an unlucky star, was taken out of his capital and brought up by a *S*abara, a kind of wild man of the woods. When he grew up he naturally thought that he himself was a *S*abara, and lived accordingly. But a minister, who had found out that the prince was alive, went to him secretly and told him that he was the son of the king, and not a *S*abara. At once the prince gave up the idea that he was a savage, believed that he was a prince, and assumed a truly royal bearing. In the same manner a man who has been told his true character by his teacher, surrenders the idea that he is a material and mortal being, and recovers his true nature, saying 'As a son of Brahman I am nothing but Brahman, and not a being different from him in this phenomenal world.'

The commentator adds an extract from the Garu*d*a-Purâ*n*a which must have been borrowed from a Sâ*m*khya source:—

'As everything that is made of gold is known as gold, if even from one small piece of gold one has learnt to know what gold is, in the same way from knowing God the whole world becomes known.

As a Brâhman possessed by an evil spirit, imagines that he is a *S*ûdra, but, when the possession is over, knows that he is a Brâhman, thus the soul, possessed by Mâyâ, imagines that it is the body, but after Mâyâ has come to an end, it knows its own true being again, and says, I am a Brâhman.'

The seventh illustration is 'like a cut-off hand,' and is meant to teach that, as no one takes his hand again after it has once been cut off, no one should identify himself with anything objective, after once having surrendered the illusion of the objective. The sixteenth, to which I called attention many years ago as connected with old Aryan folklore, is meant to teach that even an accidental negligence may be fatal to our reaching the highest goal, as in the case of the 'frog-wife.'

The story is that of a king who, while hunting, had seen a beautiful girl in a forest. She became his wife on condition that he should never let her see water. He gave the promise, but once when the queen, tired after playing, asked him for some water, he forgot his promise, and brought her some, whereupon the daughter of the frog-king became a frog (Bhekî), and disappeared in the lake. Neither nets nor anything else was of any avail for bringing her back, the king had lost her for ever. Thus true knowledge also will disappear by one act of negligence, and will never return.

This system of teaching by parables was very popular with the Buddhists, and it is just possible that the first impulse may have come from the followers of Kapila, who are so often called Kryptobuddhists or Pra*kkh*anna-Bauddhas.

I have called attention already to the fact that these illustrative parables, though they do not occur in the Kârikâs and in the Tattva-samâsa, must have existed all the time in the Paramparâ of the Brâhmans, because they appear in the modern Sûtras, that is in the sixteenth century. Like the Sûtras referring to these stories, other Sûtras also may occur in our modern collection of Sâ*m*khya-Sûtras, which existed for centuries, as handed down by tradition, but were omitted in the Kârikâs and even in the Tattva-samâsa.

## CHAPTER VII.

### Yoga and Sâ*m*khya.

THE relation of the Yoga to the Sâ*m*khya-philosophy is not easy to determine, but the Bhagavad-gîtâ V, 4, goes so far as to say that children only, not learned people, distinguish between Sâ*m*khya and Yoga at all, as it were between faith (knowledge) and works. We find the Sâ*m*khya and Yoga represented, each in its own Sûtras, which are ascribed to different authors, Kapila and Patañ*g*ali[1], and they are spoken of in the dual as the two old systems (Mahâbh. XII, 104, 67); but we also find a philosophy called Sâ*m*khya-yoga (Svetâ*s*v. Up. II, 13), and this not as a Dvandva, as it were, Sâ*m*khya and Yoga, but as one philosophy, as a neuter sing., representing Yoga and Sâ*m*khya together as one, or possibly as Yoga belonging to the Sâ*m*khya. Thus we read again in the Bhagavad-gîtâ V, 5, that he who understands Sâ*m*khya and Yoga to be one, understands aright. Yoga, in the sense of ascetic practices and meditations, may no doubt have existed in India in very

[1] The identification of these two names with the name of one person Kâpya Pâtañ*k*ala, who is mentioned in the *S*atapatha-brâhma*n*a, once proposed by Professor Weber, has probably long been given up by him. See also Garbe, Sâ*m*khya-Philosophie, p. 26.

ancient times. It is called Purâtana (old), (B. G. IV, 3), and this is probably what the author of the Bhagavad-gîtâ (IV, 1) meant, when he made the Bhagavat say to Ar*g*una:—

'I declared this imperishable Yoga to Vivasvat. Vivasvat told it to Manu, Manu to Ikshvâku. Thus royal sages came to know it, having received it through tradition; but this Yoga was lost here by long lapse of time.'

A similar oral tradition descending from Pra*g*âpati to Manu, and from Manu to the people (to Ikshvâku, according to *S*a*m*kara) is mentioned already in the *Kh*ândogya Upanishad (III, 11; VIII, 15).

It is much the same with the other philosophies, and we are left in doubt as to whether the three couples, Sâ*m*khya and Yoga, Nyâya and Vai*s*eshika, nay even Pûrva- and Uttara-Mîmâ*m*sâ, were amalgamations of systems which had originally an independent existence, or whether they were differentiations of former systems. Sâ*m*khya and Yoga might easily have formed one comprehensive system, because their divergence with regard to the existence of an Î*s*vara, or Lord, was not so essential a point to them as it seems to us. Those who wanted an Î*s*vara might have him as a first and super-eminent Purusha; while those who had gone beyond this want, need not have quarrelled with those who still felt it. The Nyâya and Vai*s*eshika show clear traces of a common origin; while the two Mîmâ*m*sâs, which in character are more remote from one another than the other systems, seem to sanction, by their names at least, the suspicion of their former unity. But the deplorable scarcity of any historical documents does not enable us to go beyond mere conjectures; and though the names of Kapila, Vyâsa, and Gotama may seem to have an older air than those of Patañgali, *G*aimini, and Ka*n*âda, we must not in such matters allow ourselves to be guided by mere impressions. The often-cited passage from the Vedânta-Sûtras II, 1, 3, Etena Yoga*h* pratyukta*h*, 'By this the Yoga is refuted,' proves of course no more than the existence of a Yoga-philosophy at the time of Bâdarâya*n*a; it cannot be used to prove the existence of the Yoga-Sûtras, such as we possess them, as previous to the composition of the Vedânta-Sûtras.

### Meanings of the word Yoga.

In the Bhagavad-gîtâ Yoga is defined as Samatva, equability (II, 48). It has been repeated again and again that Yoga, from Yu*g*, to join, meant originally joining the deity, or union with it. Even native authors occasionally favour that view. A moment's consideration, however, would have shown that such an idea could never have entered the mind of a Sâ*m*khya, for the simple reason that there was nothing for him that he could have wished to join. Even the Vedântist does not really join Brahman, though this is a very common misconception; nay, a movement of the soul towards Brahman is distinctly guarded against as impossible. The soul is always Brahman, even though it does not know it, and it only requires the removal of ignorance for the soul to recover its Brahmahood, or to become what it always has been. Yu*g*, from meaning to join, came, by means of a very old metaphor, to mean to join oneself to something, to harness oneself for some work. Thus Yu*g* assumed the sense of preparing for hard work, whether preparing others or getting ready oneself. And as people with us use the expression to go into harness, i. e. to prepare for work, or to buckle-to, i. e. to get ready for hard work, Yu*g*, particularly in the Âtmanepada, came to mean to exert oneself. Possibly the German *Angespannt* and *Anspannung* may have been suggested by the same metaphor, though the usual explanation is that it was so by a metaphor taken from the stretching of the bow. In Sanskrit this Yu*g* is often used with such words as Manas, *K*ittam, Âtman, &c., in the sense of concentrating or exerting one's mind; and it is in this sense only that our word Yoga could have sprung from it, meaning, as the Yoga-Sûtras tell us at the very beginning, I, 2, the effort of restraining the activities or distractions of our thoughts (*K*itta-*v*r*i*tti-nirodha), or the effort of concentrating our thoughts on a definite object.

### Yoga, not Union, but Disunion.

A false interpretation of the term Yoga as union has led to a total misrepresentation of Patañ*g*ali's philosophy. Rajendralal Mitra, p. 208, was therefore quite right when he wrote: 'Professor Weber, in his History of Indian Literature (pp. 238–9), has entirely misrepresented the case. He says, "One very peculiar side of the Yoga doctrine—and one which was more and more developed as time went on—is the Yoga practice, that is, the outward means, such as penances, mortifications, and the like, whereby this absorption into the supreme Godhead is sought to be attained." "The idea of absorption," he continues rightly, "into the supreme Godhead forms no part of the Yoga theory." "Patañ*g*ali, like Kapila," he adds, "rests satisfied with the isolation of the soul, and does not pry into the how and where the soul abides after separation."' But when he charges the professor with not having read the Yoga he goes a little too far, and he ought to have known, from his own experience, that it is small blame to a man who writes a complete history of Indian literature, if he has not read every book on which he has to pronounce an opinion. Even the best historian of German literature can hardly have read every German author of any eminence, much less can the first historian of Sanskrit literature.

Rajendralal Mitra, however, is quite right so far that Yoga, in the philosophy of Patañ*g*ali and Kapila, did not mean union with God, or anything but effort (Udyoga, not Sa*m*yoga), pulling oneself together, exertion, concentration. Yoga might mean union, but the proper term would have been Sa*m*yoga. Thus we read in the Bhagavad-gîtâ II, 50 :—

Buddhiyukto *g*ahâtîha ubhe suk*ri*tadushk*ri*te,
Tasmâd yogâya yu*g*yasva, yoga*h* karmasu kau*s*alam.

'He who is devoted to knowledge leaves behind both good and evil deeds; therefore devote yourself to Yoga, Yoga is success in (all) actions.'

That native scholars were well aware of the double meaning of Yoga, we may see from a verse in the beginning of Bho*g*adeva's commentary on the Yoga-Sûtras, where he states that, with a true Yogin, Yoga, joining, means really Viyoga, separation, or Viveka, discrimination between Purusha and Prak*ri*ti, subject and object, self and nature, such as it is taught in the Sâ*m*khya: Pumprak*ri*tyor viyogo*pi yoga ityudito yayâ, 'By which (teaching of Patañ*g*ali) Yoga (union) is said to be Viyoga (separation) of Purusha and Prak*ri*ti.'

### Yoga as Viveka.

We saw that this Viyoga or Viveka was indeed the highest point to which the whole of the Sâmkhya-philosophy leads up. But granted that this discrimination, this subduing and drawing away of the Self from all that is not Self, is the highest object of philosophy, how is it to be reached, and even when reached, how is it to be maintained? By knowledge chiefly, would be the answer of Kapila (by *G*ñânayoga); by ascetic exercises delivering the Self from the fetters of the body and the bodily senses, (by Karmayoga) adds Patañ*g*ali. Patañ*g*ali by no means ignores the *G*ñânayoga of Kapila. On the contrary, he presupposes it; he only adds, as a useful support, a number of exercises, bodily as well as mental, by which the senses should be kept in subjection so as not to interfere again with the concentration of all thoughts on the Self or the Purusha[1]. In that sense he tells us in the second Sûtra that Yoga is the effort of restraining the activity or distractions of our thoughts. Before we begin to scoff at the Yoga and its minute treatment of postures, breathings, and other means of mental concentration, we ought first of all to try to understand their original intention. Everything can become absurd by exaggeration, and this has been, no doubt, the case with the self-imposed discipline and tortures of the Yogins. But originally their

[1] I prefer, even in the Sâmkhya-philosophy, to render Purusha by Self rather than by man, because in English *man* cannot be used in the sense of simply subject or soul. Besides, Âtman, Self, is often used by Patañ*g*ali himself for Purusha, cf. Yoga-Sûtras III, 21; II, 41.

object seems to have been no other than to counteract the distractions of the senses. We all consider the closing of the eyelids and the stopping of the ears against disturbing noises useful for serious meditation. This was the simple beginning of Yoga, and in that sense it was meant to be a useful addition to the Sâ*m*khya, because even a convinced Sâ*m*khya philosopher who had obtained *G*ñânayoga or knowledge-yoga would inevitably suffer from the disturbances caused by external circumstances and the continual inroads of the outer world upon him, i.e. upon his Manas, unless strengthened to resist by Karmayoga or work-yoga the ever present enemy of his peace of mind. More minute directions as to how this desired concentration and abstraction could be achieved and maintained, might at first have been quite harmless, but if carried too far they would inevitably produce those torturing exercises which seemed to Buddha, as they do to most people, so utterly foolish and useless. But if we ourselves must admit that our senses and all that they imply are real obstacles to quiet meditation, the attempts to reduce these sensuous affections to some kind of quietude or equability (Samatva) need not surprise us, nor need we be altogether incredulous as to the marvellous results obtained by means of ascetic exercises by Yogins in India, as little as we should treat the visions of St. Francis or St. Teresa as downright impositions. The real relation of the soul to the body and of the senses to the soul is still as great a mystery to us as it was to the ancient Yogins of India, and their experiences, if only honestly related, deserve certainly the same careful attention as the stigmata of Roman Catholic saints. They may be or they may not be true, but there is no reason why they should be treated as *a priori* untrue. From this point of view it seems to me that the Yoga-philosophy deserves some attention on the part of philosophers, more particularly of the physical school of psychologists, and I did not feel justified therefore in passing over this system altogether, though it may be quite true that, after we have once understood the position of the Sâ*m*khya-philosophy towards the great problem of the world, we shall not glean many new metaphysical or psychological ideas from a study of the Yoga. We must never forget that, although our Sâ*m*khya-Sûtras are very modern, the Sâ*m*khya as such, is not, and is always presupposed by the Yoga. It has its roots in a soil carefully prepared by centuries of philosophical cultivation, and has but little in common with the orgiastic ecstasies which we see among savage tribes of the present day. The Hindus also, before they became civilised and philosophers, may or may not have passed through such a phase. But how little of true similarity there really exists between the Yoga and Tapas of the Hindus, and the sweating processes of the American Indians in their steam-booths, may easily be seen from the excellent Reports of the Bureau of Ethnology, by J. W. Powell, 1892–3, p. 117 seq.; p. 823 seq., to mention no other and more painful reports.

Before we enter upon an examination of the peculiar teaching of the Yoga-philosophy, a few words with reference to the sources on which we have to depend for our information may be useful.

### Patañ*g*ali, Vyâsa.

The Sûtras of the Yoga-philosophy are ascribed to Patañ*g*ali, who is also called Pha*n*in or *S*esha, the divine serpent. He may have been the author or the representative of the Yoga-philosophy without being necessarily the author of the Sûtras. His date is of course uncertain, though some scholars have, with great assurance, assigned him to the second century B.C. It may be so, but we should say no more. Even the commonly received identification of the philosopher Patañ*g*ali with Patañ*g*ali, the grammarian and author of the Mahâbhâshya, should be treated as yet as a hypothesis only. We know too little about the history of Sanskrit proper names to be able to say whether the same name implies the same person. That is not the case in any other country, and can hardly be true in India considering how freely the names of the gods or of great Rishis were taken, and are still taken, as proper names. It has actually been asserted that Vyâsa, the author of a late commentary on Patañ*g*ali's Yoga-Sûtras, is the same person as Vyâsa, the collector of the Vedas, the reputed author of the Mahâbhârata and of the Vedânta-Sûtras. But there are ever so many Vyâsas living even now, and no solid argument could possibly be derived from the mere recurrence of such a name. There are works ascribed to Hira*n*yagarbha, Harihara, Vish*n*u, &c.; then why not to Patañ*g*ali? It is of course as impossible to prove that Patañ*g*ali the philosopher and Patañ*g*ali the grammarian were not the same person, as to prove that they were; but if style of language and style of thought are any safe guides in such matters, we ought certainly to hesitate, and should do so in any other literature, before taking the grammarian and the philosopher Patañgali as one and the same person. It would no doubt be a great help if we could transfer the date of the grammarian, the second century B.C., to the author of our Yoga-Sûtras, but on that point also it seems to me better to wait till we get some more tangible proof. In the present state of knowledge, or rather ignorance, of all dates to be assigned to the philosophical Sûtras, it is the duty of every scholar to abstain from premature assertions which only encumber and obstruct the way to further discoveries.

### Second Century B.C.

The second century would certainly be most welcome as a date for any of our extant philosophical Sûtras, but that is no excuse for saying that the Yoga-philosophy was reduced to the form of Sûtras in that century, because the grammarian Patañgali has been referred to it. Besides, even the date assigned to the grammarian Patañgali is a constructive date only, and should not for the present be considered as more than a working hypothesis. The fact that these Yoga-Sûtras do not enter on any controversy might certainly seem to speak in favour of their being anterior to the other Sûtras; but we saw already why we could no more build any chronological conclusions on this than we should think of proving the anteriority of our Sâmkhya-Sûtras by the attacks on its atheistical doctrines which occur in the Sûtras of the other philosophical systems. I think we must be satisfied with the broad fact that Buddha was later than the classical Upanishads, and that our philosophical Sûtras are later than Buddha, because they evidently refer to his doctrines, though not to his name. As to popular tradition, it is no doubt of little value, particularly in India; still I doubt whether tradition could have gone so completely wrong as to prophesy in the Saṅkshepa-*S*am*kara-Vi*g*aya[1] and elsewhere that *G*aimini, Vyâsa, Patañ*g*ali, and *S*amkara would appear on earth to uproot all heresies, if they had lived before the great heresy of Buddha. Patañ*g*ali is said to have been a portion of Saṅkarsha*n*a or Ananta, the hooded serpent *S*esha, encircling the world, and it may be for the same reason that he is sometimes called Pha*n*in (Pha*n*ibhart*ri*). This is the kind of useless information which tradition gives us.

### Chronology of Thought.

In India we must learn to be satisfied with the little we know, not of the chronology of years, but of the chronology of thought; and taking the Yoga, in its systematic form, i. e. in the Patañ*g*ali-Sûtras, as post-Buddhistic, we can best understand the prominence which it gives both to the exercises which are to help toward overcoming the distracting influences of the outer world, and to the arguments in support of the existence of an Î*s*vara or Divine Lord. This marked opposition became intelligible and necessary as directed against Kapila as well as against Buddha; and in reading the Yoga-Sûtras it is often difficult to say whether the author had his eye on the one or the other. If we took away these

---

[1] Yoga Aphorisms, p. lxvi.

two characteristic features of the Yoga, the wish to establish the existence of an Îsvara against all comers, and to teach the means of restraining the affections and passions of the soul, as a preparation for true knowledge, such as taught by the Sâmkhya-philosophy, little would seem to remain that is peculiar to Patañgali.

But though the Sûtras are post-Buddhistic, there can be no doubt that not only the general outlines of the Sâmkhya, but likewise all that belongs to the Karmayoga or work-yoga was known before the rise of Buddhism. Thus, if we turn to the Mahâbhârata, we find that the twenty-four *principia*, with Purusha as the twenty-fifth, are often mentioned, though arranged and described in different ways. Then we read again (Anugîtâ XXV): 'That which sages by their understanding meditate upon, which is void of smell, of taste, of colour, touch or sound, that is called Pradhâna (Prakriti). That Pradhâna is unperceived; a development of this unperceived power is the Mahat; and a development of the Pradhâna (when it has) become Mahat, is Ahamkâra (egoism). From Ahamkâra is produced the development, namely, the great elements, and from the elements respectively, the objects of sense are stated to be a development.'

As to the Yoga-practices or tortures we know that, after practising the most severe Tapas for a time, Buddha himself declared against it, and rather moderated than encouraged the extravagant exercises of Brâhmanic ascetics. His own experience at the beginning of his career had convinced him of their uselessness, nay, of their danger. But a moderately ascetic life, a kind of *via media*, remained throughout the ideal of Buddhism, and we can well understand that the Brâhmans, in trying to hold their own against the Buddhists, should have tried to place before the people an even more perfect system of asceticism. And, lest it should be supposed that the Sâ*m*khya-philosophy, which was considered as orthodox or Vedic, had given its sanction to Buddha's denial of an Âtman and Brahman, which was far more serious than the denial of an Î*s*vara, Lord, it would have seemed all the more necessary to protest decidedly against such denial, and thus to satisfy the ingrained theistic tendencies of the people at large, by showing that the Sâ*m*khya, by admitting Purusha, admitted a belief in something transcendent, and did by no means, according to Pata*ñg*ali at least, condemn a belief even in an Î*s*vara, or Lord. In that sense it might truly be said that the Yoga-philosophy would have been timely and opportune, if it came more boldly forward, after the rise of Buddhism, not so much as a new system of thought, but as a re-invigorated and determined assertion of ancient Sâ*m*khya doctrines, which for a time had been thrown into the shade by the Buddhist apostasy. In this way it would become intelligible that Buddhism, though sprung from a soil saturated with Sâ*m*khya ideas, should have been anterior to that new and systematic development of Sâ*m*khya-philosophy, which we know in the Sûtras of Kapila or in the Kârikâs or even in the Tattva-samâsa; that in fact, in its elements, the Sâ*m*khya should be as decidedly pre-Buddhistic as in its final systematic form it was post-Buddhistic. That the existence side by side of two such systems as those of Kapila and Buddha, the one deemed orthodox, the other unorthodox, gave matter for reflection to the people in India we see best by a well-known verse which I quoted many years ago in my History of Ancient Sanskrit Literature (p. 102): 'If Buddha knew the law and Kapila not, what is truth? If both were omniscient, how could there be difference of opinion between the two?'

### The Yoga-Philosophy.

The Yoga-Sûtras, or the Yogânus*s*âsana[1], called also by the same name which was given to the Sâ*m*khya-Sûtras, viz. Sâ*m*khya-prava*k*ana, both being considered as expositions of the old Sâ*m*khya, may have been contained originally in some such text-book as the Tattva-samâsa. The Sûtras were published and translated by Ballantyne, 1852, a translation

[1] It is not much of an argument, but it may deserve to be mentioned, that the title given by Patañ*g*ali to the Yoga-Sûtras. Atha Yogânus*s*âsanam, 'Now begins the teaching of the Yoga,' and not Atha Yoga*g*i*g*ñâsâ, reminds us of the title which the grammarian Patañ*g*ali gives to his Mahâbhâshya, Atha *S*abdânus*s*âsanam, 'Now begins the teaching of Words or of the Word.' This title does not belong to Pâ*n*ini's Sûtras, but to the Mahâbhâshya; and it is curious that such a compound as *S*abdânus*s*âsanam would really offend against one of Pâ*n*ini's rules (II, 2, 14). According to Pâ*n*ini there ought to be no such compound, and though he does not give us the reason why he objects to this and other such-like compounds, we can easily see that Sanskrit did not sanction compounds which might be ambiguous, considering that Word-teaching might be taken in the sense of teaching coming from words as well as teaching having words for its object. It is true that this apparent irregularity might be removed by a reference to another rule of Pâ*n*ini (II, 3, 66), yet it is curious that the same, if only apparent, irregularity should occur both in the Mahâbhâshya and in the Yoga-Sûtras, both being ascribed to Patañ*g*ali.

continued by Govindadeva-sâstrin in the Pandit, vol. III, Nos. 28–68. A more useful edition, but not always quite correct translation, was given by Rajendralal Mitra in the Bibliotheca Indica, 1883, 'Yoga Aphorisms of Patañgali, with the commentary of Bhoga Râgâ.' Vigñâna-Bhikshu, whose commentary on Kapila's Sâmkhya-Sûtras was mentioned before[1], and who is chiefly known by his Yoga-vârttika, is the author also of the Yoga-sâra-samgraha, an abstract of the Yoga, which has been edited and translated by Gangânâtha Jha, Bombay, 1894, and may be consulted with advantage by students of philosophy. Colebrooke's essay on the Yoga, like all his essays, is still most useful and trustworthy; and there are in German the excellent papers on the Sâmkhya and Yoga by Professor Garbe in Bühler's *Grundriss*. Garbe speaks well of a dissertation by P. Markus, *Die Yoga-philosophie nach dem Râjamârtanda dargestellt*, which, however, I have not been able to obtain.

### Misconception of the Objects of Yoga.

It was almost impossible that the Yoga-philosophy, as represented by European scholars, should not

---

[1] Other works ascribed to the same author are:—

The Brahma-mîmâmsâ-bhâshya, called Vigñânâmrita.

The Sâmkhya-kârikâ-bhâshya, ascribed to him, but really composed by Gaudapâda (see Gangânâtha, p. 2).

The Yoga-vârttika.

The Îsvara-gîtâ-bhâshya, from the Kûrma-purâna.

The Prasnopanishad-âloka.

An explanation of Prasastapâda's commentary on the Vaiseshika-Sûtras, called Vaiseshika-vârttika.

There are printed editions of the Sâmkhya-pravakana-bhâshya, the Yoga-vârttika, and the Sâmkhya-sâra.

have suffered from its close association with the Sâ*m*khya, properly so called. All its metaphysical antecedents were there. Yoga is indeed, as the Brâhmans say, Sâ*m*khya, only modified, particularly in one point, namely, in its attempt to develop and systematise an ascetic discipline by which concentration of thought could be attained, and by admitting devotion to the Lord God as part of that discipline. Whether this was done, as is generally supposed, from mere theological diplomacy is a question we should find difficult to answer, considering how little we know of the personal character of Patañ*g*ali or of the circumstances under which he elaborated his theistic Sâ*m*khya-philosophy. There is an entire absence of animosity on his part, such as our own philosophers would certainly have displayed in accusing another philosopher of atheism and in trying to amend his system in a theistic direction. No doubt there must always have been a majority in favour of a theistic philosophy of the universe as against an atheistic, but whether Patañ*g*ali may be fairly accused of having yielded to the brutal force of numbers, and curried favour with the many against the few is quite another question. It is certainly extraordinary to see the perfect calmness with which, with very few exceptions, Kapila's atheism is discussed, and how little there is of the *ad populum* advocacy in support of a belief in God and a personal God. Nor does Kapila, like other atheistic philosophers, display any animosity against the Divine idea and its defenders. He criticises indeed the usual arguments by which theists make and unmake their God, if they represent Him as the creator and ruler of the world, and charge him at the same time with cruelty, by making him responsible for the origin of evil also. But all this is done by Kapila in a calm and what one might almost call a businesslike manner; and in answering Kapila's arguments, Patañ*g*ali also preserves the same Samatva or even temper. He imputes no *motives* to his antagonist, nor does he anywhere defend himself against any possible suspicion that in showing the necessity of a personal God, an Î*s*vara, he was defending the interests of the Brâhman priesthood. After all, Î*s*vara was not even a popular name for God, or the name of any special god, though it occurs as a name of Rudra, and in later times was applied even to such gods as Vish*n*u and *S*iva, after they had been divested of much of their old mythological trappings.

### Devotion to Î*s*vara, Misconceptions.

In this respect also we have something to learn from Hindu philosophers. Considering the importance of the subject, it is useful to see how little heat was expended on it either by Kapila or by Patañ*g*ali. If we remember how the two philosophies were in popular parlance distinguished from each other as Sâ*m*khya with and Sâ*m*khya without a Lord, we should have expected to see this question treated in the most prominent place. Instead of which we find Patañ*g*ali, at the end of the first chapter, after having described the different practices by which a man may hope to become free from all worldly fetters, mentioning simply as one of many expedients, I, 23, 'Devotion to the Lord,' or, as it is generally translated 'devotion to God.' Devotion or Pra*n*idhâna (lit. placing oneself forward and into) is explained by Bhoga as one of the forms of resignation, as worship of Him, and as the surrender of all one's actions to Him. If a man, without wishing for any rewards consisting in worldly enjoyments, makes over all his cares to Îsvara as the highest guide, that, we are told, is Pranidhâna. Patañgali then goes on, 'As it has been said that Samâdhi or complete absorption can be obtained through devotion to the Lord, the next that has to be explained in order, is the nature of that Lord, the proof, the majesty, the name of Him, the order of His worship, and the fruit thereof.' In I, 24 Patañgali goes on to say: 'Îsvara, the Lord, is a Purusha (Self) that has never been touched by sufferings, actions, rewards, or consequent dispositions.' The commentary adds: 'Sufferings are such as Nescience, Avidyâ, &c.; actions are either enjoined, forbidden, or mixed; rewards are the ripened fruits of actions manifested in birth (genus, caste) and life, while dispositions (Âsaya, Anlage) are so-called because they lie in the soil of the mind till the fruit has ripened, they are instincts (Samskâra) or impressions (Vâsanâ). If the Lord is called a Purusha, that means that He is different from all other Purushas (Selves), and if He is called Lord, that means that He is able by His work alone to liberate the whole world. Such power is due to the constant prevalence of goodness (a Guna) in Him, who has no beginning, and this prevalence of goodness arises from His eminent knowledge. But the two, knowledge and power, are not dependent on each other, for they are eternally abiding in the very *substance* of Îsvara. His very relation to that goodness is without beginning, because the union of Prak*ri*ti and Purusha, that is, the creation would, from a Yoga point of view, have been impossible without the will of such an Îs*v*ara. While the *K*itta or mind in ordinary Purushas or Selves undergoes, while in the body, modifications tending towards happiness, unhappiness, and delusion, and, if remaining without blemish, good, and full of virtue, becomes conscious of the incidence of the pictures mirrored on the mind, it is not so with Îs*v*ara. His highest modification is of goodness alone, and he remains steadfast in enjoyment through eternal union with it. Therefore he alone is Îs*v*ara, eminent above all other Purushas. Again, even for one who has gained freedom, a return of sufferings, &c., is possible, and has to be guarded against by such means as are inculcated in the Yoga; but he, the Îs*v*ara, as he is always such as he is, is not like a man who has gained freedom, but he is by nature free. Nor should one say that there may be many such Îs*v*aras. Though there be equality of Purushas, *quâ* Purushas, yet as their aims are different, such a view would be impossible. And though there be a possibility of more or less, yet the most eminent would always be the Îs*v*ara or the Lord, he alone having reached the final goal of lordship.'

The Pâta*ñg*ala-bhâshya dwells very strongly on this difference between the liberated soul and the Lord; for 'the liberated or isolated souls,' it says, 'attain their isolation by rending asunder the three bonds, whereas in regard to Îs*v*ara there never was and never can be such bondage. The emancipated implies bondage, but this can never be predicated of the Lord.'

We need not point out here the weak points of this argument, and the purely relative character of the greatness and separateness claimed for the Îsvara, as compared with other Purushas, but it may be well to try to compare our own ideas of God, when put into clear and simple language, with the ideas here propounded. Patañgali seems to me to come very near to the Homoiousia of man with God, though he does not go quite as far as the Vedântin who claims for the Âtman perfect Homoousia with Brahman. His Îsvara may be *primus inter pares*, but as one of the Purushas, he is but one among his peers. He is a little more than a god, but he is certainly not what we mean by God.

### What is Îsvara?

As Kapila had declared that the existence of such a being as Îsvara did not admit of proof, Patañgali proceeds in the next Sûtra to offer what he calls his proofs, by saying: 'In Him the seed of the omniscient (or omniscience) attains infinity.' It would be difficult to discover in this anything like a proof or a tenable appeal to any Pramâna, without the help of the commentary. But Bhoga explains that what is meant here is that there are different degrees of all excellences, such as omniscience, greatness, smallness, and other Aisvaryas, and that therefore there must be for all of them a point beyond which it is impossible to go. This Niratisaya point, this *non plus ultra* of excellence, is what is claimed for Îsvara or the Lord.

Though this could hardly be considered as a convincing argument of the existence of a Being endowed with all such transcendent excellences as are here postulated, it shows at all events an honest intention on the part of Patañ*g*ali. Patañ*g*ali's argument reminds us to a certain extent of the theistic argument of Cleanthes and Boethius. What he means is that where there is a great and greater, there must also be a greatest, and this is Îśvara, and that where there is good and better, there must be best.

Nor does he flinch in trying to answer the questions which follow. The question is supposed to have been asked, how this Îśvara, without any inducement, could have caused that union and separation of himself and Prak*ri*ti which, as we saw, is only another name for creation. The answer is that the inducement was his love of beings, arising from his mercifulness, his determination being to save all living beings at the time of the Kalpapralayas and Mahâpralayas, the great destructions and reconstructions of the world. This, of course, would not have been admitted by Kapila.

Next Patañ*g*ali proceeds to explain the majesty of Îśvara by saying, in I, 26,—

'He is the superior (Guru) even of the former ones, being himself not limited by time.'

By the former ones are meant, as we are told, the ancients, the first creators, such as Brahmâ and others, and by superior is meant instructor and guide, so that it would seem difficult to assign a higher position to any divine being than by placing him thus above Brahmâ and other accepted builders of the world. Next follows his name, I, 27:—

'His name is Pra*n*ava.'

Pra*n*ava might etymologically mean breathing forth or glory. It is assigned as a name to the sacred syllable Om, possibly a relic of a time beyond our reach. It is said to have been the name of Îsvara from all eternity, just as the name of father or son. This may be true, but it does not satisfy us. However old the name Pra*n*ava and the syllable Om may have been, they must have had a beginning, but in spite of all the theories of the Brâhmans, there is not one in the least satisfactory to the scholar. Om is their sacred syllable, which has to be repeated a hundred or a thousand times in order to draw the mind away from all disturbing impressions and to concentrate it on the Supreme Being. But why it is so we cannot tell. It may be a mere imitation of the involuntary outbreathing of the deep vowel o, stopped by the labial nasal, and then drawn in; or it may be the contraction of a pronominal stem Avam, 'that,' corresponding to Ayam, 'this,' and it is certainly used in the sense of Yes, much as *hoc illud* was used in French when contracted to *oui*. But however that may be, it is called Pra*n*ava, praise or breathing forth, and cannot be explained any further etymologically. It is a name, as Bho*g*a says, not made by anybody, and if it has any historical or etymological justification, this is at all events not known to us. Still we cannot go quite so far as Rajendralal Mitra, who sees in it an Indianised form of the Hebrew *Amen*! First of all, Amen does not mean God, and how should such a word have reached India during the Brâhma*n*a period?

Patañ*g*ali continues by telling us in Sûtra I, 38, that repetition of the syllable Om and reflection on its meaning are incumbent on the student of Yoga. And this, as Bho*g*a adds, as a means to concentrate our thoughts, and to attain to Samâdhi, the chief end of the whole Yoga-philosophy. In that sense he adds, I, 29 :—

'Thence also obtainment of inward-turned thought, and absence of obstacles.'

Inward-turned thought (Pratyak*k*etanâ) is explained as a turning away of our senses from all outward objects, and turning them back upon the mind. The obstacles to Samâdhi are mentioned in the next Sûtra, I, 30, as

'Disease, languor, doubt, carelessness, idleness, worldliness, error, not having a settled standpoint, and not keeping it; these are the obstacles causing unsteadiness of mind.'

I, 31. 'With them arise pain, distress, tremor of limbs, and disturbance of the regular inbreathing and outbreathing.'

I, 32. 'To prevent all this, there is constant fixing of the mind on one subject (Tattva).'

I, 33. 'And likewise from a reviving friendliness, pity, complacency, and indifference towards objects of happiness, unhappiness, virtue and vice, there arises serenity of mind.'

The commentator adds, 'If one sees happy people, one should not envy them; if one sees unhappiness, one should think how it could be removed; if one sees virtuous people, one should rejoice and not say, Are they really virtuous? if one sees vicious people, one should preserve indifference, and show neither approval nor aversion. Thus does the mind become serene and capable of Samâdhi. But all these are only outward helps towards fixing the mind on one subject, and of thus in time obtaining Samâdhi.'

I have given this extract in order to show how subordinate a position is occupied in Patañ*g*ali's mind by the devotion to Î*s*vara. It is but one of the many means for steadying the mind, and thus realising that Viveka or discrimination between the true man (Purusha) and the objective world (Prak*ri*ti). This remains in the Yoga as it was in the Sâ*m*khya, the *summum bonum* of mankind. I do not think, therefore, that Rajendralal Mitra was right when in his abstract of the Yoga (p. lii) he represented this belief in one Supreme God as the first and most important tenet of Patañ*g*ali's philosophy. 'The leading tenets of the Yogins,' he says, 'are first, that there is a Supreme Godhead who is purely spiritual, or all soul, perfectly free from afflictions, works, deserts, and desires. His symbol is Om, and He rewards those who are ardently devoted to Him by facilitating their attainment of liberation; but He does not directly grant it. Nor is He the father, creator, or protector of the universe, with which He is absolutely unconnected.'

Rajendralal Mitra does not stand alone in this opinion, and the very name of Se*s*vara-Sâ*m*khya, theistic Sâ*m*khya, given to the Yoga, would seem to speak in his favour. But we have only to look at the Sûtras themselves to see that originally this belief in a personal God was by no means looked upon as the most characteristic feature of Patañ*g*ali's system.

Rajendralal Mitra is right, however, in stating the tenet, second in importance, to have been that there are countless individual souls or Purushas which animate living beings, and are eternal. They are pure and immutable; but by their association with the universe they become indirectly the experiencers of joys and sorrows, and assume innumerable embodied forms in the course of an ever-recurring metempsychosis.

The Îsvara, with the Yogins, was originally" no more than one of the many souls, or rather Selves or Purushas, but one that has never been associated with or implicated in metempsychosis, supreme in every sense, yet of the same kind as all other Purushas." The idea of other Purushas obtaining union with him could therefore never have entered Patañ*g*ali's head. According to him, the highest object of the Yogin was freedom, aloneness, aloofness, or self-centredness. As one of the useful means of obtaining that freedom, or of quieting the mind previous to liberating it altogether, devotion to the Îsvara is mentioned, but again as one only out of many means, and not even as the most efficacious of all. In the popular atmosphere of India this belief in one Supreme Being may have been a strong point in favour of Patañ*g*ali's system, but from a philosophical point of view, Patañ*g*ali's so-called proofs of the existence of God would hardly stand against any criticism. They are mere *πάρεργα*, or side issues. We must remember that Kapila had committed himself to no more than that it is impossible to prove the existence of Îsvara, this Îsvara not being synonymous with God, in the highest sense of the word, but restricted to a personal creator and ruler of the world. Such a confession of an inability to prove the existence of an Îsvara does not amount to atheism, in the current sense of that word, and thus only can we explain the fact that Kapila himself was considered orthodox by friends and foes. In the Vedânta-philosophy the question of the real existence of a personal Îsvara never arises, though we know how saturated that philosophy is with a belief in the existence of Brahman, the absolute Divine Essence of which the active or personal Îsvara or the Lord is but a passing manifestation, presented by Brahmâ, masc., a mere phase of Brahman, neuter. The Sâ*m*khya, in attempting to explain the universe, such as it is, both in its subjective and objective character, has no need to call in the assistance of a personal Îsvara. What we mean by the objective world is, according to Kapila, the work or outcome of Prak*r*iti, when animated by Purusha, not of Brahman. His system is therefore without a creator or personal maker of the world, but if we called it therefore atheistic, we should have to apply the same name to Newton's system of the world and Darwin's theory of evolution, though we know that both Newton and Darwin were thoroughly religious men. Darwin himself went so far as to maintain most distinctly that his system of nature required a Creator who breathed life into it in the beginning, and even those Darwinians who look upon this admission of Darwin's as a mere weakness of the moment, would strongly object to be called irreligious or atheists. Kapila might easily have used the very words of Darwin, and this is very much what Patañ*g*ali actually did in his Yoga-Sûtras. His supreme Purusha, afterwards raised into an Âdi-Purusha, or First Being, satisfied the human craving after a First Cause, and, so far as I can see, it was this natural craving rather than any vulgar wish to curry favour with the orthodox party in India that led to Patañ*g*ali's partial separation from Kapila. We certainly need not suppose that the recognition of Kapila's orthodoxy was a mere contrivance of theological diplomacy on the part of the Brâhmans, and that these defenders of the faith were satisfied with an insincere recognition of the supreme authority of the Vedas. I confess that with what we know of the religious life of India and the character of the Brâhmans at all times, it seems to me very difficult to admit the idea of such a compromise. Besides, Kapila appeals, as we saw, to the Veda in good earnest, particularly when it supports his own views, as in V, 12, when he wants to prove 'that the world arises from primitive matter,' and appeals to the Veda, that is, to such passages as *S*vetâ*s*vatara Upanishad IV, 5, and B*ri*had. Âr. Up. I, 4, 7, that can be made to support his view. The two oldest representatives of the Sâ*m*khya-philosophy, the Tattva-samâsa and the Kârikâs[1], do not even allude to the difficulty arising from the Î*s*vara question, which seems to me an important argument in favour of their antiquity. The charge of atheism became more popular in later times, so that in the Padma-purâ*n*a the charge of atheism is brought not against the Sâ*m*khya only, but against the Vai*s*eshika and Nyâya-philosophies also, nay even against the Pûrva-Mîmâ*m*sâ. Two systems only escape this charge, the Uttara-Mîmâ*m*sâ and the Yoga; and in the case of the Uttara-Mîmâ*m*sâ, its explanation by *S*a*m*kara is stigmatised as no better than Buddhism, because it perverts the meaning of passages of the Veda, which teach the identity of the individual soul with the highest

---

[1] Hall, Preface to Sâ*m*khya-sâra, p. 39, note, and Introduction to Sâ*m*khya-prava*k*ana.

soul (Brahman without qualities), and recommends the surrender of good works, and complete indifference towards this world and the next.

### Kapila's Real Arguments.

But it is but fair that we should hear what Kapila himself has to say. And here it is important again to observe that Kapila does not make a point of vehemently denying the existence of an Îsvara, but seems likewise to have been brought to discuss the subject, as it were by the way only, while engaged in discussing the nature of sensuous perception (I, 89). He had been explaining perception as cognition arising from actual contact between the senses and their respective objects. And here he is stopped by the inevitable opponent who demurs to this definition of perception, because it would not include, as he says, the perceptions of the Yogins. Kapila replies that these visions of the Yogins do not refer to external objects, and that, without denying their reality, he is dealing with the perceptions of ordinary mortals only. But the controversy does not end here. Another opponent starts up and maintains that Kapila's definition of perception is faulty, or at all events not wide enough because it does not include the perception of the Îsvara or Lord. It is then that Kapila turns round on his opponent, and says that this Îsvara, this, as it is pretended, perceptible Îsvara, has never been proved to exist at all, has never been established by any of the three legitimate instruments of knowledge or Pramâ*n*as. This may seem to us to amount to a denial of an Îsvara, but Vi*g*ñâna-Bhikshu remarks with a great deal of truth, that if Kapila had wished to deny the existence of God, he would have said Îsvarâbhâvât, and not Îsvarâsiddhe*h*, that is, because Îsvara does not exist, and not, as he says, because Îsvara has not been proved to exist. Anyhow this is not the tone of a philosopher who wants to preach atheism, and in what follows we shall see that it is the manner rather than the matter of the proof of an Îsvara which is challenged by Kapila and defended by his antagonist. Taking his stand on the ground that the highest blessedness or freedom consists in having renounced all activity, because every activity presupposes some kind of desire, which is of evil, he says 'that every proof in support of an Îsvara as a maker or Lord, a Sat-kara, would break down. For if he were supposed to be above all variance and free, he could not have willed to create the world; if he were not so, he would be distracted and deluded and unfit for the supreme task of an Îsvara.' Then follows a more powerful objection, based on the fact that the Veda speaks of an Îsvara or Lord, and therefore he must exist. Kapila does not spurn that argument, but, as he has recognised once for all the Veda as a legitimate source of information, he endeavours to prove that the Vedic passages relied on in support of the existence of a maker of the world, have a different purpose, namely the glorification of a liberated Self or Purusha, or of one who by devotion has attained supernatural power (I, 95). This is explained by Aniruddha as referring either to a Self which is almost, though not altogether, free, because if altogether free, it could have no desire, nor even the desire of creation; or to a Yogin who by devotion has obtained supernatural powers. Vigñâna-Bhikshu goes a step further, and declares that it refers either to a Self that has obtained freedom from all variance and disturbance, or to the Self that is and has remained free from all eternity, that is, to the Âdi-purusha, the First Self, who in the theistic Yoga-philosophy takes the place of the Creator, and who may, for all we know, have been the origin of the later Purushottama.

Aniruddha thereupon continues that it might be said that without the superintendence of some such intelligent being, unintelligent Prakriti would never have acted. But this also he rejects, if it is meant to prove the existence of an active creator, because the superintendence of the Purusha of the Sâmkhyas over Prakriti is not an active one, but arises simply from proximity, as in the case of a crystal (I, 96). What he means is that in the Sâmkhya the Purusha is never a real maker or an agent. He simply reflects on Prakriti, or the products of Prakriti are reflected on him; and as anything reflected in a crystal or a mirror seems to move when the mirror is moved, though it remains all the time quite unmoved, thus the Purusha also seems to move and to be an agent, while what is really moving, changing, or being created is Prakriti. The Purusha therefore cannot be called superintendent, as if exercising an active influence over Prakriti, but Prakriti is evolved up to the point of Manas under the eyes of Purusha, and the Purusha does no more than witness all this, wrongly imagining all the time that he is himself the creator or ruler of the world. In support of this Aniruddha quotes a passage from the Bhagavad-gîtâ (III, 27): 'All emanations of Prakriti are operated by the Gunas;

but the Self deluded by Aha*m*kâra imagines that he is the operator.'

Another objection is urged against the Sâ*m*khya view that the Purusha is not a doer or creator, namely that, in that case, a dead body also might be supposed to perform the act of eating. But no, he says, such acts are performed not by a dead or inactive Âtman, as little as a dead body eats. It is the individual Purusha (*G*îva) that performs such acts, when under the influence of Prak*ri*ti (Buddhi, Aha*m*kâra, and Manas), while the Âtman or Purusha remains for ever unchanged.

A last attempt is made to disprove the neutrality or non-activity of the Âtman, that is, the impossibility of his being a creator, namely the uselessness of teaching anything, supposing the Self to be altogether without cognition. To this the answer is that though the Âtman is not cognitive, yet the Manas is. The Âtman reflects on the Manas, and hence the illusion that he himself cognises, while in reality he does no more than witness the apprehension of the Manas. Thus when it is said, 'He is omniscient and omnipotent,' *he* (in spite of the gender) is meant for Prak*ri*ti, as developed into Manas, and not for the Purusha who in reality is a mere witness of such omniscience and omnipotence (III, 56), deluded, for a time, by Prak*ri*ti.

### The Theory of Karman.

In another place where the existence of an Îsvara, or active ruler of the world, is once more discussed in the Sâ*m*khya-Sûtras, the subject is again treated not so much for its own sake, as in order to settle the old question of the continuous effectiveness of works (Karman). The reward of every work done, according to Kapila, does not depend on any ruler of the world; the works themselves are working on for evermore. If it were otherwise, we should have to ascribe the creation of the world, with all its suffering, to a Lord who is nevertheless supposed to be loving and gracious.

Mâdhava in his Sarva-darsana-sa*m*graha (translated by Cowell and Gough, p. 228) uses the same argument, saying: 'As for the doctrine of "a Supreme Being who acts from compassion," what has been proclaimed by beat of drum by the advocates of His existence, this has wellnigh passed away out of hearing, since the hypothesis fails to meet either of the two alternatives. For does He act thus *before* or *after* creation? If you say before, we reply that as pain cannot arise in the absence of bodies, &c., there will be no need, as long as there is no creation, for any desire to free living beings from pain (which is the main characteristic of compassion); and if you adopt the second alternative, you will be reasoning in a circle, as on the one hand you will hold that God created the world through compassion, and on the other hand that He compassionated it after He had created it.'

And again, as every activity presupposes desire, the Lord, whether working for Himself or for others, would *ipso facto* cease to be free from desires. This argument is examined from different points of view, but always leads to the same result in the end; that is to say, to the conviction that the highest state of perfection and freedom from all conditions is really far higher than the ordinary conception of the status of the popular Hindu deities, higher even than that of an Îsvara, if conceived as a maker and ruler of the universe. This concept of the liberated Purusha or Âtman has in fact superseded the concept of the Îsvara, and to have made this quite clear would have been, on the part of Kapila, by far the most effective defence against the charge of atheism. The conscience of Kapila and of the ancient Sâ*m*khyas was evidently satisfied with a belief in a Purusha in which the old concepts of the divine and the human had been welded into one, without claiming even the aid of an Âdi-purusha, a first Purusha, which was a later expedient.

Nor must it be forgotten that other philosophies also besides the Sâ*m*khya have been suspected or openly accused of atheism for the same reason. It is easy to understand why almost every philosophy, whether Indian or European, if it endeavours to purify, to dehumanise, and to exalt the idea of the Godhead, can hardly avoid the suspicion of denying the old gods, or of being without a belief in the God of the vulgar. It is well known that on that ground even the early Christians did not escape the suspicion of atheism.

Even *G*aimini's Pûrva-Mîmâ*m*sâ, though based on the belief that the Veda is of superhuman origin, and though entirely devoted to the interpretation of the Vedic sacrifice, has been charged with atheism, because it admitted the independent evolution of works, which was supposed to imply a denial of God; nor did the Nyâya and Vaiseshika systems, as we saw, escape the same suspicion. It may be that the recognition of the authority of the Veda was considered sufficient to quiet the theological conscience; but there is certainly, so far as I can see, no passage in the Nyâya and Vaiseshika-Sûtras where an Îsvara is clearly denied or postulated, either as the author or as the controller of the infinitesimally small elements or atoms of which the world is by them supposed to consist. There is one passage in the Nyâya-Sûtras in which the question of a divine Lord is discussed in the usual way, namely Book V, Sûtras 19–21, but otherwise we hear nothing of what the Îsvara is meant to be or to do.

These attacks, as met by the Nyâya philosophers, may be looked upon as purely academic, but the tone in which they are met, for instance, by later philosophers such as Mâdhava in his Sarva-darsana-samgraha, shows that they at all events took them seriously. As specimens of Indian casuistry some extracts from Mâdhava's chapter on the Nyâya may here be of interest. I quote from the translation by Cowell and Gough (p. 171): 'It is quite true,' he says, 'that none of the three Pramânas can prove the existence of a Supreme Being. Perception cannot, because the Deity, being devoid of form, must be beyond the senses. Inference cannot, because there is no universal proposition or middle term that could apply. The Veda cannot, because we Naiyâyikas have ourselves proved it to be non-eternal. All this we admit to be quite true, that is, we admit that a Supreme Îsvara cannot be established by proof. But is there not, on the other side, the old argument that the mountains, seas, &c., must have had a maker, because they possess the nature of being effects, quite as much as a jar (or, as we should say, a watch)? And that they are effects can easily be proved by the fact that they possess parts, these parts existing in intimate relation, and again by the fact that they possess a limited magnitude half-way between what is infinitely great and infinitesimally small. Nor has any proof ever been produced on the opposite side to show that the mountains had no maker. For if any one should argue that the mountains cannot have had a maker because they were not produced by a body, just as the eternal ether—this pretended inference would no more stand examination than the young fawn could stand the attack of the full-grown lion, for you have not even shown that what you say about the eternal ether is a real fact. We therefore abide by our old argument that the mountains have the nature of effects, and if they had no maker, they could not be effects, that is, produced, not by themselves alone, but by concurrent causes, one of them being a maker. A maker is a being possessed of a combination of volition, desire to act, a knowledge of proper means, setting in motion all other causes, but itself moved by none (the Aristotelian κινοῦν ἀκίνητον).'

But though yielding to this argument, the objector asks next, what object this maker or Îsvara could have had in view in creating the world. A feeling of compassion, if he had any, should surely have induced him to create all living beings happy, and not laden with misery, since this militates against his compassion. Hence he concludes that it would not be fitting to admit that God created the world. Hereupon the Nyâya philosopher becomes very wroth and exclaims: 'O thou crest-jewel of the atheistic school, be pleased to close for a moment thy envy-dimmed eyes, and to consider the following suggestions. His action in creating is indeed caused by compassion only, but the idea of a creation which shall consist of nothing but happiness is inconsistent with the nature of things, since there cannot but arise eventual differences from the different results which will ripen from the good and evil actions (Karman) of the beings who are to be created.'

In answer to this, the atheistic opponent returns once more to the authority of the Veda and says: 'But then, how will you remedy your deadly sickness of reasoning in a circle [for you have to prove the Veda by the authority of God, and then again God's existence by the Veda].'

But the theistic interpreter and defender of the Nyâya is not silenced so easily, and replies: 'We defy you to point out any reasoning in a circle in our argument. Do you suspect this "reciprocal dependence of each" which you call "reasoning in a circle," in regard to their being produced or in regard to their being known? It cannot be the former, for though the production of the Veda is dependent on God, still as God Himself is eternal, there is no possibility of *His* being produced; nor can it be in regard to their being known, for even if our knowledge of God were dependent on the Veda, the Veda might be learned from some other source; nor, again can it be in regard to the knowledge of the non-eternity of the Veda, for the non-eternity of the Veda is easily perceived by any Yogin endowed with transcendent faculties (Tîvra, &c.).

Therefore, when God has been rendered propitious by the performance of duties which produce His favour, the desired end, liberation, is obtained; thus everything is clear.'

Everything may be clear to one accustomed to the Indian way of arguing; but from our point of view it would certainly seem that, though the Nyâya does not teach the non-existence of an Îsvara, it is not very successful in proving by its logic the necessity of admitting a maker or ruler of the world, that is, an Îsvara.

### The Four Books of Yoga-Sûtras.

If now we turn to the Yoga-Sûtras of Patañ*g*ali we find that the first book, the Samâdhi-pâda, is devoted to an explanation of the form and aim of Yoga, and of Samâdhi, meditation or absorption of thought; the second, the Sâdhana-pâda, explains the means of arriving at this absorption; the third, Vibhûti-pâda, gives an account of the supernatural powers that can be obtained by absorption and ascetic exercises; while the fourth, the Kaivalya-pâda, explains Kaivalya to be the highest object of all these exercises, of concentration of thought, and of deep absorption and ecstasy. Kaivalya, from Kevala, alone, means the isolation of the soul from the universe and its return to itself, and not to any other being, whether Îsvara, Brahman, or any one else.

That this is the right view of the case is confirmed by the remarks made by Vi*g*ñâna-Bhikshu in his Yoga-sâra-sa*m*graha, p. 18. Here we are told that even when there is some imperfection in the employment of the above means (faith, energy, memory, absorbing meditation, and knowledge), the two results (absorption and liberation) can be brought very near by the grace of the Parama-Îsvara, the Highest Lord, and secured by devotion to Him.

By Parama-Îsvara or the Highest Lord is here meant that particular Purusha (Self) who was never touched by the five troubles, nescience and the rest, nor by virtue or vice and their various developments, or by any residue (results of former deeds) in general. Vig*ñ*âna-Bhikshu abstains from saying much more on the Lord, because, as he says, he has treated of this Being very fully in his remarks on the Brahma-Sûtras I, 1. He probably refers to his commentary on the Vedânta; and he is evidently quite convinced that, however different the roads followed by the Vedântins and Sâ*m*khya-yogins may be, the Divine idea of both schools is much the same. He only adds that the powers and omniscience of the Îsvara are equalled or excelled by none, that he is the spiritual chief and father of all the gods, such as Brahmâ, Vish*n*u, and Hara, that he imparts spiritual vision (*Gñâna-kakshus*) through the Vedas, and that he is the inner guide, and called Pra*n*ava. Devotion to Him is said to consist in contemplation and to end in direct perception. Steadfastness with regard to Îsvara is represented as the principal factor in abstract meditation and in liberation, because it leads to greater nearness to the final goal, steadiness with regard to the human self being secondary only. This devotion to Îsvara is also declared to put an end to all the impediments, such as illness, &c. (I, 30); and a passage is quoted from the Sm*ri*ti, 'For one desiring liberation the most comfortable path is clinging to or resting on Vish*n*u; otherwise, thinking only with the mind, a man is sure to be deceived.'

### True Object of Yoga.

It is clear throughout the whole of this chapter on Îsvara that devotion to him is no more than one of the means, though, it may be, a very important one, for the attainment of liberation, the highest goal of the Yoga. But it is not that highest goal itself, but only a means towards it, nor could it be accepted as the most important feature of the Yoga. The really important character of the Yoga consists in its teaching that, however true the Sâ*m*khya-philosophy may be, it fails to accomplish its end without those practical helps which the Yoga-philosophy alone supplies. The human mind, though fully enlightened as to its true nature, would soon be carried away again by the torrent of life; the impressions of the senses and all the cares and troubles of every-day life would return, if there were no means of making the mind as firm as a rock. Now this steadying of the mind, this Yoga, is what Pata*ñg*ali is chiefly concerned with.

### *K*itta.

We saw that in the second Sûtra he explained Yoga as *K*itta-v*ri*tti-nirodha, that is, restraining or steadying the actions and distractions of thought. V*ri*tti, which I translate by action, has also been rendered by movement or function; while *K*itta, which I give as thought, has often been translated by mind or the thinking principle. It is curious that the Yoga should have employed a word which, as far as I know, was not a recognised technical term of the Sâ*m*khya. In the Sâ*m*khya the term would be Manas, mind, but

Manas in a state of activity, and, of course, as a development of Aha*m*kâra and Buddhi. It has to be taken here as a psychological term, as a name for thought, as carried on in real life, and indirectly only of the instrument of thought. As I had to use mind for Manas in the Sâ*m*khya-philosophy, it would be difficult to find a better rendering of the word when used by Yoga philosophers. Of course Manas is always different from Buddhi, in so far as it is a modification of Buddhi, which itself has passed through Aha*m*kâra or the differentiation of subjectivity and objectivity. But for practical purposes, what is meant by *K*itta is simply our thought or our thinking, and though mind, with us also, has been defined very differently by different philosophers, and is used most promiscuously in common parlance, its etymological relationship with Manas pointed it out as the most convenient rendering of Manas, provided always that we remember its being a technical term of the Yoga-philosophy, as we have to do whenever we render Prak*r*iti by nature. Nirodha, restraint, does not mean entire suppression of all movements of thought, but at first concentration only, though it leads in the end to something like utter vacuity or self-absorption. In all the functions of the Manas, it must be remembered that the real self-conscious seer or perceiver is, for the time being, the Purusha or Self. It is he who is temporarily interested in what is going on, though not absorbed in it except by a delusion only. Like the moon reflected in the ripples of the waters, the Self appears as moving in the waves which break against it from the vast ocean of Prak*r*iti, but in reality it is not moving.

We saw that the mind, when receiving impressions from the outer world, was supposed in Hindu philosophy to assume for the time being the actual form of the object perceived, but, when once perfect in Yoga, it perceives nothing but itself.

### Functions of the Mind.

The principal acts and functions of the mind are described as right notion, wrong notion, fancy, sleep, and remembering, and they may be either painful or not.

Right notions are brought about by the three Pramâ*n*as, so well known from different systems of Indian philosophy, as sensuous perception, inference, and testimony, Vedic or otherwise. It is significant that Patañ*g*ali should have used Âgama instead of the Âptava*k*ana of the Sâ*m*khya, for Âgama means distinctly the Veda, and thus would establish once for all what is called the orthodox character of the Yoga.

Wrong notions require no explanation. They are illustrated by our mistaking mother-of-pearl for silver, a rope for a snake, &c. A state of doubt also when we are uncertain whether what we see at a distance is a man or the trunk of tree, is classed among wrong notions.

Fancy is explained as chiefly due to words; and a curious instance of fancy is given when we speak of the intelligence of the Self or Purusha, or of the head of Râhu, the fact being that there is no intelligence belonging to Self, but that the Self is altogether intelligence, just as Râhu, the monster that is supposed to swallow the moon, is not a being that has a head, but is a head and nothing else.

Sleep is defined as that state (V*ri*tti) of the mind which has nothing for its object. The commentator, however, explains that in sleep also a kind of perception must take place, because, otherwise, we could not say that we had slept well or badly.

Remembering is the not wiping out of an object that has once been perceived. While true perception, false perception, and fancy take place in a waking state, a dream, which is a perception of vivid impressions, takes place in sleep, while sleep itself has no perceptible object. Remembering may depend on true or false perceptions, on fancy, and even on dreams.

### Exercises.

Now all these actions or functions have to be restrained, and in the end to be suppressed, and this is said to be effected by exercises (Abhyâsa) and freedom from passions (Vairâgya), I, 12.

Indian philosophers have the excellent habit of always explaining the meaning of their technical terms. Having introduced for the first time the terms exercise and freedom from passion, Patañ*g*ali asks at once: 'What is Abhyâsa or exercise?' Abhyâsa is generally used in the sense of repetition, but he answers that he means hereafter to use this term in the sense of effort towards steadiness (Sthiti) of thought. And if it be asked what is meant by steadiness or Sthiti, he declares that it means that state of the mind, when, free from all activity (V*ri*tti), it remains in its own character, that is, unchanged. Such effort must be continuous or repeated, as implied by the term Abhyâsa (I, 13).

This Abhyâsa is said to become firmly grounded, if practised for a long time thoroughly and unintermittingly (I, 14).

### Dispassion, Vairâgya.

Next follows the definition of dispassion (Vairâgya), as the consciousness of having overcome (the world) on the part of one who has no longer any desire for any objects whatsoever, whether visible or revealed (I, 15).

Here visible (D*r*ish*t*a) stands for perceptible or sensuous objects, while Ânus*r*âvika may be translated by revealed, as it is derived from Anus*r*ava, and this is identical with *S*ruti or Veda. Perhaps Anu*s*rava is more general than Veda, including all that has been handed down, such as the stories about the happiness of the gods in paradise (Devaloka), &c. The consciousness of having subdued or overcome all such desires and being no longer the slave of them, that, we are told, is Vairâgya or dispassionateness, and that is the highest point which the student of Yoga-philosophy hopes to reach.

It is interesting to see how deeply this idea of Vairâgya or dispassionateness must have entered into the daily life of the Hindus. It is constantly mentioned as the highest excellence not for ascetics only, but for everybody. It sometimes does not mean much more than what we mean by the even and subdued temper of the true gentleman, but it signifies also the highest unworldliness and a complete surrender of all selfish desires. A very good description of what Vairâgya is or ought to be is preserved to us in the hundred verses ascribed to Bhart*r*ihari (650 A.D.), which are preceded by two other centuries of verses, one on worldly wisdom and the other on love. Many of these verses occur again and again in other works, and it is very doubtful whether Bhartrihari was really the original author of them all, or whether he only collected them as Subhâshitas [1]. Anyhow they show how the philosophy of Vairâgya had leavened the popular mind of India at that distant time, nor has it ceased to do so to the present day. It was perhaps bold, after Bhartrihari, to undertake a similar collection of verses on the same subject. But as the Vairâgya-sataka of Gainâkârya seems in more recent times to have acquired considerable popularity in India, a few extracts from it may serve to show that the old teaching of Patañgali and Bhartrihari has not yet been forgotten in their native country.

'Death follows man like a shadow, and pursues him like an enemy; perform, therefore, good deeds, so that you may reap a blessing hereafter.'

'Frequent enjoyment of earthly prosperity has led to your sufferings. Pity it is that you have not tried the "Know Yourself."'

'Live in the world but be not of it, is the precept taught by our old Rishis, and it is the only means of liberating yourself from the world.'

'The body is perishable and transitory, while the Self is imperishable and everlasting; it is connected with the body only by the link of Karman; it should not be subservient to it.'

'If, through sheer negligence, you do nothing good

---

[1] His work is actually called Subhâshita-trisatî, see Report of Sanskrit and Tamil MSS., 1896–97, by Seshagiri Sastri, p. 7.

for your fellow creatures, you will be your own enemy, and become a victim to the miseries of this world.'

'Better to do less good, with purity of heart, than to do more with jealousy, pride, malice, or fraud. Little, but good and loving work, is always valuable, like a pure gem, the essence of a drug, or pithy advice.'

'If you are unable to subject yourself physically to penances, to undergo austerities, and engage in deep contemplation, the proper course to liberate your soul from the hard fetters of Karman would be to keep the passions of your heart under control, to check your desires, to carry out your secular affairs with calmness, to devote yourself to the worship of God, and to realise in yourself the "Permanent Truth," bearing in mind the transitory nature of the universe.'

'To control your mind, speech, and body, does not mean to be thoughtless, silent or inactive, like beasts or trees; but, instead of thinking what is evil, speaking untruth, and doing harm to others, mind, speech, and body should be applied to good thoughts, good words, and good deeds.'

Dispassionateness, as here taught for practical purposes chiefly, reaches its highest point in the eyes of the Yoga-philosopher, when a man, after he has attained to the knowledge of Purusha, has freed himself entirely from all desire for the three Gu*n*as (or their products). This is at least what Patañ*g*ali says in a somewhat obscure Sûtra (I, 11)[1]. This Sûtra seems intended to describe the highest state within reach of the true Vairâgin, involving

[1] Garbe, Grundriss, p. 49.

indifference not only to visible and revealed objects, but likewise towards the Gu*n*as, that is, if I am not mistaken, the twenty-four Tattvas, here called Gu*n*as[1], because determined by them. The knowledge of the Purusha implies the distinction between what is Purusha, the Self, and what is not, and therefore also between Purusha and the Gu*n*as of Prak*ri*ti. Vi*g*ñâna-Bhikshu explains it by Âtmânâtmavivekasâkshâtkârât, i.e. from realising the difference between what is Self and what is not Self, and not as a possessive compound: the sense, however, remaining much the same. It is curious that Rajendralal Mitra should have rendered Purushakhyâte*h* by 'conducive to a knowledge of God.' From a purely philosophical point of view Purusha may be translated by God, but such a translation would be misleading here, particularly as the Sûtra 23, on the devotion to the Lord, follows so soon after. It would have been better also to translate 'arising from,' than 'conducive to.'

### Meditation With or Without an Object.

Patañ*g*ali next proceeds (I, 17) to explain an important distinction between the two kinds of meditative absorption (Samâdhi), which he calls Sampra*g*ñâtâ

---

[1] These Gu*n*as are more fully described in II, 19, where we read that the four Gu*n*as or Gu*n*aparvâ*n*i are meant for (1) Visesha, i.e. the gross elements and the organs; (2) Avisesha, i.e. the subtle elements and the mind; (3) the Li*m*gamâtra, i.e. Buddhi; (4) the Ali*m*ga, i.e. Prak*ri*ti as Avyakta. In the commentary to I, 45, the same classes of Gu*n*as are described as Ali*m*ga, a name of Pradhâna, Visish*t*ali*m*ga, the gross elements (Bhûtâni); Avisish*t*ali*m*ga, the subtle essences and the senses; Li*m*gamàtra, i.e. Buddhi, and Ali*m*ga, that is, the Pradhâna.

and Asampra*gñ*âtâ. This seems to mean that there is one kind of meditation when our thoughts are directed and fixed on a definite object, and another when there is no definite object of meditation left. Here the spirit of minute distinction shows itself once more, for though these two kinds of meditation may well be kept apart, and the former be considered as preliminary to the latter, the numerous subdivisions of each hardly deserve our notice. We are told that what is called conscious meditation may have for its object either one or the other of the twenty-four Tattvas or the Î*s*vara, looked upon as one of the Purushas. The twenty-four Tattvas are called unconscious, the twenty-fifth or Purusha is conscious. When meditation (Bhâvanâ) has something definite for its object it is called not only Pra*gñ*âta, known, or, as referred to the subject, knowing, but also Savî*g*a, literally with a seed, which I am inclined to take in the sense of having some seed on which it can fix, and from which it can develop. The Asampra*gñ*âta-samâdhi, or meditation without a known object, is called Avî*g*a, not having a seed from which to spring or to expand. Native commentators, however, take a different view.

Those who in their Samâdhi do not go beyond the twenty-four Tattvas, without seeing the twenty-fifth, the Purusha, but at all events identify themselves no longer with the body, are called Videhas, bodyless; others who do not see the Purusha yet, but only existence, are called Prak*ri*tilayas, absorbed in Prak*ri*ti.

This again is not quite clear to me, but it is hardly necessary that we should enter into all the intricate subdivisions of the two kinds of meditation, such as Savitarkâ, argumentative, Savi*k*ârâ, deliberative, Sânandâ, joyous, and Sâsmitâ [1], with false conceit. They may become important in a more minute study of the Yoga, but they can hardly be of interest to speculative philosophers except so far as they furnish another proof of a long continued study of the Yoga-philosophy in India before the actual composition of the Sûtras.

The Asampra*gñ*âta-samâdhi, or meditation without a known object, or, it may be, unconscious meditation, is explained as being preceded by a repetition of negative perception, and as the end of all previous impressions. I, 18.

This Sûtra has been differently explained by different European and native commentators. It may mean that there is a residue of previous impressions, or that there is not. The Sa*m*skâras, which I have rendered by previous impressions, are everything that has given to the mind its peculiar character, its flavour, so to say, or its general disposition,

> 'Quo semel est imbuta recens servabit odorem
> Testa diu.'

It may be intended that these Sa*m*skâras are either all wiped out, or that there is but a small residue of them, manifested in the final act of the stopping all functions of the mind.

In summing up what has been said about the different kinds of Samâdhi, Patañ*g*ali says (I, 19) once more that in the case of the Videhas and Prak*ri*ti-

[1] Asmitâ is different from Aha*m*kâra, and means the misconception that I am (Asmi) what I am not, such as Prak*ri*ti, Buddhi, Aha*m*kâra, Manas, &c.

layas (as explained before, p. 448) the object or, if you like, the cause of Samâdhi is the real world (Bhava), but that for other Yogins there are preliminary conditions or steps to Samâdhi, namely, faith, energy, memory, concentration, and knowledge succeeding each other. Every one of these Samâdhis is again carefully defined, and some more helps are mentioned in the next Sûtra (I, 21), where we read that Samâdhi may be said to be near or within reach when the zeal or the will is strong. These strong-willed or determined aspirants are again divided (I, 22) according as the means employed by them are mild, moderate, or excessive. Thus we get nine classes of Yogins, those who employ mild means, with mild, with moderate, or with excessive zeal; those who employ moderate means, with mild, with moderate, or with excessive zeal; and those who employ excessive means with mild, with moderate, or with excessive zeal.

Such divisions and subdivisions which fully justify the name of Sâ*m*khya, enumeration, make both the Sâ*m*khya- and Yoga-philosophies extremely tedious, and I shall in future dispense with them, though they may contain now and then some interesting observations.

**Îsvara Once More.**

After an enumeration of all these means of Yoga to be employed by the student, follows at last the famous Sûtra I, 23, which has always been supposed to contain, in answer to Kapila, the proof of the existence of a Deity, and which I translated before by 'Devotion to the Lord.' The commentator calls it simply an easy expedient, an alternative. Nor is it right, with Rajendralal Mitra, to translate this

Sûtra at once by 'Devotion to God.' Îsvara, as we saw, is not God in the sense in which Brahmâ might be called so. He is a God, the highest God, but always one of many Purushas; and though he was looked upon as holy (I, 25) and omniscient, he never seems to have risen to the rank of a Creator, for which there is really no room in the Sâmkhya system. Though it is true, no doubt, that the orthodox Yogins derived great comfort from this Sûtra as shielding Patañgali against the charge of atheism, it would be impossible to look upon it as a real proof in support of the existence of God, or as more than a somewhat forced confession of faith.

### Other Means of Obtaining Samâdhi.

The benefits arising from this devotion to the Lord are not essentially different from those that are to be obtained from other Upâyas or means of attaining Samâdhi, as may be seen from Sûtras I, 29 to I, 35 translated before. Nor is this devotion even the last or the highest Upâya, for Patañgali goes on immediately after to mention other means equally conducive to concentrated meditation or absorption in the thought of one object. Expedients, such as the expulsion and retention of the breath, follow next, the so-called Prânâyâmas, which we can well believe, may have been really useful as contrivances to draw away the thoughts from all subjects except the one chosen for meditation, generally one of the Tattvas. But this opens far too large a subject for our purpose in this place. We approach here to the pathological portion of the Yoga, the so-called Hatha or Kriyâ-yoga, a subject certainly far more important than has generally been supposed, but a subject for students of pathology rather than of philosophy, unless, as is now the fashion, we include the so-called physico-psychological experiments under the name of philosophy. One thing may certainly be claimed for our Sûtras; they are honest in their statements as to the discipline that can be applied to the mind through the body, and even if they could be proved to have been mistaken in their observations, their illusions do not seem to me to have been mere frauds, at least in the days of Patañ*g*ali, though it is far from my purpose to undertake a defence of all the doings and sayings of modern Yogins or Mahâtmans.

Next to the moderation or restraint of the breathing, follow descriptions of how the mind, by being directed to the tip of the nose, cognises a heavenly odour, and the same with all the other senses, which therefore are supposed to have no longer any inclination towards outward objects, having everything they want in themselves. We are next told of the perception of an inward luminous and blessed state, which produces a steadiness and contentedness of the mind when directed towards objects which no longer appeal to the passions (I, 37). No wonder that even objects seen in dreams or in sleep are supposed to answer the same purpose, that is, to fix the attention. In fact any object may be chosen for steady meditation, such as the moon without, or our heart within, provided always that these objects do not appeal to our passions.

All these are means towards an end, and there can be no doubt that they have proved efficacious; only, as so often happens, the means have evidently encroached in this case also, on the aims, and to such an extent that Yoga has often been understood to consist in these outward efforts rather than in that concentration of thought which they were meant to produce, and which was to lead on to Kaivalya or spiritual separateness and freedom. This true Yoga is often distinguished as Râ*g*a-yoga or royal Yoga from the other called Kriyâ-yoga or working Yoga, which is sometimes called Ha*th*a-yoga, though it is not clear why. Though some of these bodily exercises are represented as serving as a kind of staircase on which the mind ascends step by step, we are told at other times that any step may be useful, and that some may be skipped or taken for passed.

Now, if we ask what is the result of all this, we are told in Sûtra 41 that a man who has put an end to all the motions and emotions of his mind, obtains with regard to all objects of his senses conformation grounded in them (*sic*), or steadiness and consubstantiation, the idea being that the mind is actually modified or changed by the objects perceived (I, 41). As a crystal, when placed near a red flower, becomes really red to our eyes, in the same way the mind is supposed to become tinged by the objects perceived. This impression remains true as grounded in the object, and our mind should always be centred on one object of meditation.

Having mentioned in a former Sûtra that Samâdhi (here called Samâpatti) may be either Savitarkâ or Savi*k*ârâ, he now explains (I, 42) that when meditation is mixed with uncertainties as to word, meaning, or knowledge, it is called Savitarkâ. Thus, supposing that our meditation was centred on a cow, the question would be whether we should meditate on the sound cow, Sk. Go, or on the meaning of it (Begriff), that is the genus cow, or the idea or picture (Vorstellung) conveyed by it. Such a meditation would be called Savitarkâ. Its opposite is Nirvitarkâ when all memory vanishes and the meaning alone, without any form, remains, or, as the commentator puts it, though not much more clearly, when the knowing mind (Pra*g*ñâ), tinged with the form of its object, forgets its own subjective form of knowing, and becomes, as it were, one in form with the object.

After Samâdhi, both Savitarkâ and Nirvitarkâ, has been described, the next division is into Savi*k*ârâ and Nirvi*k*ârâ. They are defined as having reference to subtle objects (I, 44), that is, to the Tanmâtras, essences, and the senses, and thus we learn that the former, the Savitarkâ Samâdhi, had to deal with material objects only. Subtle objects include Prak*ri*ti also, and there is nothing subtle beyond it, for the Purusha is neither subtle nor non-subtle.

If we look upon the Nirvi*k*ârâ Samâdhi as the highest of the Samâdhis, then there would follow on the completion of that meditation contentment or peace of the Self (Âtman). Knowledge in this state is called *Ri*tambharâ, right or truth-bearing, quite different from the knowledge which is acquired by inference or by revelation. And from this knowledge springs a disposition which overcomes all former dispositions and renders them superfluous.

### Samâdhi Apra*g*ñâtâ.

This knowledge therefore would seem to be the highest goal of the true Yogin; but no, there is still something beyond knowledge, and that is what was called before Apra*g*ñâtâ Samâdhi, meditation without any object, or pure ecstasy. This restores the Purusha to his own nature, after he has been delivered from all the outside disturbances of life, and particularly from the ignorance that caused him to identify himself for awhile with any of the works of Prak*ri*ti (Asmitâ).

### Kaivalya, Freedom.

This short account of what is contained in the first chapter of the Yoga-Sûtras contains almost all that can be of interest to European philosophers in the system of Patañ*g*ali, and it is not impossible that it may have originally formed a book complete in itself. It shows us the whole drift of the Yoga in its simplest form, beginning with the means of steadying and concentrating the mind on certain things, and more particularly on the twenty-four Tattvas, as taken over from the Sâ*m*khya, and leading on to a description of meditation, no longer restricted to any of the Tattvas, which is tantamount to a meditation which does not dwell on anything that can be offered by an ideal representation of what is called the real world. It is really meditation of each Purusha on himself only, as distinct from all the Tattvas of Prak*ri*ti. This is Kaivalya or the highest bliss in the eyes of the true Yogin, and it may well be called the highest achievement of *G*ñâna-yoga, i.e. Yoga carried on by thought or by the will alone. Outward helps, such as the Prâ*n*âyâma, the in- and out-breathing, are just alluded to, but that is almost the only allusion to what in later times came to be the most prominent part of the practical or Kriyâ-yoga, namely, the postures and other ascetic performances (Yogâṅgas), supposed to prepare the mind for its own higher efforts. The above-mentioned Îsvara-pra*n*idhâna, 'Devotion to the Lord,' is classed here as simply one of the Yogâṅgas or accessories of Yoga, together with purification, contentment, penance, and mumbling of prayers (II, 32), showing how little of real philosophical importance was ascribed to it by Patañ*g*ali. It helps towards Samâdhi, meditation, it is a kind of worship (Bhakti-vi*s*esha) addressed to Bhagavat; but that is all the commentator has to say in recommendation of it. There is nothing to show that Patañ*g*ali imagined he had thereby given a full and satisfactory answer to the most momentous of all questions, the existence or non-existence of an individual Creator or Ruler of the world.

It is quite possible that some of my readers will be disappointed by my having suppressed fuller details about these matters, but it seems to me that they really have nothing to do with philosophy in the true sense of the word; and those who take an interest in them may easily consult texts of which there exist English translations, such as the second and third books of the Yoga-Sûtras, and better still the Ha*th*aprayoga, translated by Shrinivas Jyângar, Bombay, 1893; On the Vedântic Râj-Yoga, by Sabhâpati Svâmi, edited by Siris Chandra Basu, Lahore, 1880; the Ghera*nd*a-sa*m*hitâ, Bombay, 1895, and several more. There is also a very useful German translation by H. Walter, 'Svâtmârâma's Ha*th*a-yoga-pradîpikâ, München, 1893.

### Yogâṅgas, Helps to Yoga.

It is true that considerable antiquity is claimed for some of these Yogâṅgas, or members of Yoga.

*S*iva himself is reported to have been their author, and names such as Vasish*th*a and Yâ*gñ*avalkya are quoted as having described and sanctioned eighty-four postures, while Gorakshanâtha reckoned their true number as 8,400,000[1]. I take a few specimens from Rajendralal Mitra's Yoga Aphorisms, p. 103:—

'1. Padmâsana. The right foot should be placed on the left thigh, and the left foot on the right thigh; the hands should be crossed, and the two great toes should be firmly held thereby; the chin should be bent down on the chest, and in this posture the eyes should be directed to the tip of the nose. It is called Padmâsana, lotus-seat, and is highly beneficial in overcoming all diseases.

2. Vîrâsana. Place each foot under the thigh of its side, and it will produce the heroic posture Vîrâsana.

3. Bhadrâsana. Place the hands in the form of a tortoise in front of the scrotum, and under the feet, and there is Bhadrâsana, fortunate-seat.

4. Svastikâsana. Sitting straight with the feet placed under the (opposite) thighs is called Svastikâsana, cross-seat.

5. Da*nd*âsana. Seated with the fingers grasping the ankles brought together and with feet placed extended on the legs, stick-seat.'

This will, I believe, be considered enough and more than enough, and I shall abstain from giving descriptions of the Mudrâs (dispositions of upper limbs), of the Bandhas or bindings, and of the rules regarding the age, sex, caste, food and dwelling of the performer of Yoga. To most people these

---

[1] See Rajendralal Mitra, Yoga Aphorisms, p. 102.

minute regulations will seem utterly absurd. I do not go quite so far, for some of these facts have, in a general way, been recorded and verified so often that we can hardly doubt that these postures and restraints of breathing, if properly practised, are helpful in producing complete abstraction (Pratyâhâra) of the senses from their objects, and a complete indifference of the Yogin towards pain and pleasure, cold and heat, hunger and thirst[1]. This is what is meant by the complete subjugation of the senses (Paramâ va*s*yatâ indriyâ*n*âm, II, 55) which it is the highest desire of the Yogin to realise, and this not for its own sake, but as an essential condition of perceiving the difference between the Purusha, the seer, and Prak*ri*ti, the spectacle, presented to Purusha through the agency of the Manas as developed from Prak*ri*ti. Professional students of hypnotism would probably be able to account for many statements of the followers of Kriyâ-yoga, which to a reader without physiological knowledge seem simply absurd and incredible.

### Vibhûtis, Powers.

The third chapter of Patañ*g*ali's Yoga-Sûtras is devoted to a description of certain powers which were supposed to be obtainable by the Yogin. They are called Vibhûtis, or simply Bhûtis, Mahâsiddhis, *Ri*ddhis, or Ai*s*varyas. Here also we are able to watch the transition from rational beginnings to irrational exaggerations, the same tendency which led from intellectual to practical Yoga. That transition is clearly indicated in the Yogâṅgas or

[1] Cf. N. C. Paul, Yoga-Philosophy.

accessories of Yoga. In II, 29 we find eight of these accessories mentioned, viz. restraints (Yama), subduing (Niyama), postures (Âsana), regulation of breathing (Prânâyâma), abstraction (Pratyâhâra), firmness (Dhâranâ), contemplation (Dhyâna), and absorption (Samâdhi), but in III, 4 three only are chosen as constituting Samyama, firmness, namely Dhâranâ, Dhyâna, and Samâdhi, the other five being treated as merely outward helps. Dhâranâ, firmness in holding, is explained (III, 1) as the confinement of the Manas to one place, and this place is said to be the tip of the nose, the navel, the ether, the sky or some other place. By this all other Vrittis or motions of the Manas are stopped, and the mind can be kept fixed on one object. The next, Dhyâna, is contemplation of the one object to the exclusion of all others; while the third, real Samâdhi, absorption, arises when the mind, lost in its work, illuminates one object only. This Samâdhi, of which absorption or meditation is a very poor rendering, is explained etymologically as that by which the mind, Samyag âdhîyate, is thoroughly collected and fixed on one point without any disturbing causes (III, 3).

### Samyama and Siddhis.

The Samyama, which comprises the three highest helps to Yoga, is called internal (III, 7) in contradistinction from the other helps, but, in itself, it is still but an outside help of the so-called objectless (Nirvîga) state (III, 8). It is difficult to find a word for Samyama, firm grasp being no more than an approximative rendering. It is this Samyama, however, which leads on to the Siddhis, or perfections.

These are at first by no means miraculous, though they become so afterwards, nor are they the last and highest goal of Yoga-philosophy, as has often been supposed both by Indian and by European scholars. Patañ*g*ali, before explaining these Siddhis, endeavours to show that every thing exists in three forms, as not yet, as now, and as no more, and that it is possible from knowing one to know the other states. Thus a jar is not yet, when it exists only as clay; it is now, when it is the visible jar, and it is no more, when it has been broken up and reduced to dust again. So in all things, it is said, the future may be known from the present and the present accounted for by the past. This is expressed by Patañ*g*ali in Sûtra III, 16. So far all is clear; but it is difficult to see why Sa*m*yama is required for this, and how it is to be applied to what is called the threefold modification. Knowledge of the past from the present, or of the future from the present, is hardly miraculous yet; though, when we are told that a Yogin by means of Sa*m*yama knows what is to come and what is past, it sounds very much like a claim of the gift of prophecy, and certainly became so in time. The same applies in a still higher degree to the achievements by means of Sa*m*yama claimed by the Yogins in the following Sûtras. Here (III, 17) because a man has learned to understand the meanings and percepts indicated by words, a Yogin by applying Sa*m*yama to this gift, is supposed to be able to understand the language of birds and other animals. In fact we get more and more into superstitions, by no means without parallels in other countries, but for all that, superstitions which have little claim on the attention of the philosopher, however interesting they may appear to the pathologist. Then follow other miraculous gifts all ascribed to Samyama, such as a knowledge of former existences, a knowledge of another's mind, or thought-reading, though not of the merely casual objects of his thoughts, a power of making oneself invisible, a fore-knowledge of one's death, sometimes indicated by portents. By Samyama with respect to kindness, a man may make himself beloved by everybody. This is again natural, but soon after we are landed once more in the supernatural, when we are told that he may acquire the strength of an elephant, may see things invisible to ordinary eyes, may, by meditating on the sun, acquire a knowledge of geography, by meditating on the moon, a knowledge of astronomy, by meditating on the Polar star, a knowledge of the movements of the heavenly bodies, and by meditating on the navel, a knowledge of anatomy. He may actually suppress the feelings of hunger and thirst, he may acquire firmness, see heavenly visions, in fact know everything, if only he can bring his will or his Samyama to bear on the things which produce such effects. More of these Siddhis are mentioned from IV, 38 to 49, such as the soul entering another body, ascension to the sky, effulgence, unlimited hearing, lightness like that of cotton, conquest of all elements, conquest of the organs, conquest of time, omniscience, &c. These matters, though trivial, could not be passed over, whether we accept them as mere hallucinations to which, as we know, our senses and our thinking organ are liable, or whether we try to account for them in any other way. They form an essential part of the Yoga-philosophy, and it is certainly noteworthy, even from a philosophical point of view, that we find such vague and incredible statements side by side with specimens of the most exact reasoning and careful observation.

### Miracles.

In reading the accounts of the miracles performed by Yogins in India we have in fact the same feeling of wonderment which we have in reading of the miracles performed by the Neo-platonists in Alexandria. The same writer who can enter into the most abstruse questions of philosophy[1] will tell us with perfect good faith how he saw his master sitting in the air so many feet above the ground. One instance of the miracles supposed to have been wrought by a Yogin in India must suffice. A writer with whom I have been in correspondence, the author of a short life of his teacher, Sabhâpati Svâmy, born in Madras in 1840, relates not only visions which the young student had—these might be accounted for like other visions—but miracles which he performed in the presence of many people. We are told that it was in the twenty-ninth year of his age that Sabhâpati, thirsting for Brahma*gñ*âna or knowledge of Brahman, had a vision of the Infinite Spirit, who said to him: 'Know, O Sabhâpati, that I the Infinite Spirit am in all creations, and all the creations are in me. You are not separate from me, neither is any soul distinct from me: I reveal this directly to you, because I see that you are holy and sincere. I accept you as my disciple, and bid you rise and go to the Agastya Â*s*rama, where you will find me in the shape of Rishis and

---

[1] M. M., Theosophy, Lect. xiii.

Yogins.' After that, in the dead of the night, for it was one o'clock in the morning when he saw the divine vision, Sabhâpati left his wife and two sons, went out of his house and travelled all the night till he reached the temple of Mahâdeva, also called Veda*s*re*n*i-Svayambhu-sthalam, seven miles from Madras. There he sat for three days and three nights immured in deep contemplation, and was again commanded in a vision to proceed to the Âgastya Â*s*rama. After many perils he at last reached that Â*s*rama and found there, in a large cave, a great Yogin, two hundred years old, his face benign and shining with divinity. The Yogin had been expecting him ever since Mahâdeva had commanded him to proceed to the Âgastya Â*s*rama. He became his pupil, acquired Brahma*gñ*âna and practised Samâdhi till he could sit several days without any food. After seven years his Guru dismissed him with words that sound strange in the mouth of a miracle-monger: 'Go my son, and try to do good to the world by revealing the truths which thou hast learned from me. Be liberal in imparting the truths that should benefit the G*ri*hasthas (householders). But beware lest thy vanity or the importunity of the world lead thee to perform miracles and show wonders to the profane.' Sabhâpati seems afterwards to have taught in some of the principal cities and to have published several books, declining, however, to perform any miracles. In 1880 he was still living at Lahore. But though he himself declined to perform any of the ordinary miracles, he has left us an account of a miracle performed by one of the former members of his own Â*s*rama. About 180 years ago a Yogin passed through Mysore and visited the Râjah who received him with great reverence and hospitality. Meanwhile the Nabob of Arcot paid a visit to Mysore, and they all went with the Yogin to his Âsrama. The Nabob, being a Mussulman, asked: 'What power have you that you arrogate to yourself divine honour, and what have you that you call yourselves divine persons?' A Yogin answered, 'Yes, we possess the full divine power to do all that God can do;' and the Yogin took a stick, gave divine power to it, and threw it in the sky. The stick was transformed into millions of arrows, and cut down the branches of the fruit trees to pieces, thunder began to roar in the air, and lightning began to flash, a deep darkness spread over the land, clouds overcast the sky, and rain began to fall in torrents. Destruction was impending; and in the midst of this conflict of the elements, the voice of the Yogin was heard to say: 'If I give more power, the world will be in ruins.' The people implored the Yogin to calm this universal havoc. He willed, and the tempest and the thunder, and the rain and the wind, and the fire and all were stopped, and the sky was as serene and calm as ever[1].'

I do not say that the evidence here adduced would pass muster in a Court of Law. All that strikes me in it is the simplicity with which everything is told, and the unhesitating conviction on the part of those who relate all this. Of course, we know that such things as the miracle here related are impos-

[1] Om, a treatise on Vedântic Raj Yoga Philosophy, by the Mahâtma Giana Guroo Yogi Sabhâpati Sovarni, edited by Siris Chandra Basu, Student, Government College, Lahore, 1880.

sible, but it seems almost as great a miracle in human nature that such things should ever have been believed, and should still continue to be believed. This belief in miracles evidently began with small beginnings, with what Patañ*g*ali describes as a foretelling of the future by a knowledge of the present or the past. What could be foretold might soon be accepted as the work of the prophet who foretold it, and from prophecy even of recurrent events, there is but a step to prophesying other events also, whether wished for, feared, or expected. Prophets would soon begin to outbid prophets, and the small ball of superstition would roll on rapidly till it became the avalanche which we know it to be, and to have been at all times and in all countries.

Apart from that, however, we must also remember that the influence of the mind on the body and of the body on the mind is as yet but half explored; and in India and among the Yogins we certainly meet, particularly in more modern times, with many indications that hypnotic states are produced by artificial means and interpreted as due to an interference of supernatural powers in the events of ordinary life. But all this is beyond our province, however interesting it may be to modern psychologists, and it was only in order to guard against being supposed to be unwilling even to listen to the statements of those who believe in Kriyâyoga that I have given so much space to what I cannot help considering as self-deception, leading in many cases to a systematic deception of others.

Yoga, in its early stages, knew little or nothing of all this. It was truly philosophical, and the chief object it had in view was to realise the distinction between the experiencer and the experienced, or as we should call it, between subject and object. We are told again and again that our ordinary, though false, experience arises from our not distinguishing between these two heterogeneous factors of our consciousness, and Yoga, when perfect, represented the achievement of this distinction, the separation or deliverance of the subject from all that is or ever was objective in him ; the truth being that the Purusha never can be the immediate experiencer or perceiver of pain or pleasure, but can only see them as being reflected on the Manas or mind, this mind not being, in truth, his, the Purusha's, but simply the working of Prak*ri*ti, the ever objective. In enumerating the means by which this distinction can be realised, Patañ*g*ali always gives the preference to efforts of thought over those of the flesh. If he does not discard the latter altogether, we ought to remember that only by practical experiments could we possibly gain the right to reject them altogether.

### True Yoga.

But though Patañ*g*ali allows all these postures and tortures as steps towards reaching complete abstraction and concentration of thought, he never forgets his highest object, nay he allows that all the Siddhis, or miraculous powers, claimed by the Yogins, are useless and may even become hindrances (III, 37) in the career of the true aspirant after Viveka, distinction, Moksha, freedom, and Kaivalya, aloneness. One sometimes doubts whether all the Sûtras can really be the work of one and the same mind. Thus while in the course of Patañ*g*ali's speculations, we could not but give him credit for never trying to locate the mind or the act of perceiving and conceiving in the brain, or in something like the pineal gland, we find him suddenly in III, 34, claiming the muscle of the heart as the seat of the consciousness of thought (H*ri*daye *K*ittasa*m*vit). While the human body as such is always regarded as dark and as unclean, so that the Yogin shrinks from contact with his own, much more from contact with other bodies, we are suddenly told (III, 46) that by Sa*m*yama or restraint, colour, loveliness, strength and adamantine firmness may be gained for the body.

However, the general drift of the Yoga remains always the same, it is to serve as a Târaka (III, 54), as a ferry, across the ocean of the world, as a light by which to recognise the true independence of the subject from any object; and as a preparation for this, it is to serve as a discipline for subduing all the passions arising from worldly surroundings. In the last Sûtra of the third book, Patañ*g*ali sums up what he has said by a pregnant sentence (III, 55): 'Kaivalya (aloneness) is achieved when both the mind and the Self have obtained the same purity.' This requires some explanation. Instead of Mind, Patañ*g*ali says simply Sattva, which the commentator renders by *K*ittasattva, and defines as the entering of thought (*K*itta) into its own causal form, after the removal of the misconception of activity. This seems not quite exact, for if we took Sattva as the Gu*n*a Sattva, we should be told that a Gu*n*a cannot have a cause, while the Manas has a cause, and is to be reabsorbed into its cause or causes (Aha*m*kâra, Buddhi, Prak*ri*ti), as soon as its Guna, here the Sattva, has become perfectly Sânta or quieted.

### The Three Gunas.

I have tried to explain the meaning of the three Gunas before, but I am bound to confess that their nature is by no means clear to me, while, unfortunately, to Indian philosophers they seem to be so clear as to require no explanation at all. We are always told that the three Gunas are not qualities, but something substantial (Dravyâni). In everything that springs from nature, and therefore in the Manas also, there are these three Gunas (IV, 15) striving for mastery[1]. Sattva of the mind is goodness, light, joy, and its purification means its not being overcome by the other two Gunas of Ragas, passion, or Tamas, darkness (II, 47). From this purification springs first Saumanasya, serenity, from this Ekâgratâ, concentration, from this Indriyagaya, subjugation of the organs of sense, and from this at last Âtmadarsanayogyatâ, fitness for beholding the Self, or in the case of the Purusha, fitness for beholding himself, which is the same as Kaivalya, aloneness.

In the fourth and last chapter Patañgali recurs once more to the Siddhis, perfections, natural or miraculous, and tells us that they may be due not only to Samâdhi, meditation in its various forms, but also to birth, to drugs, to incantations, and to heat

---

[1] Yathârthas trigunas tathâ kittam api trigunam, 'As the object is threefold, the thought also is threefold.' The mind in fact is doubly affected by the Gunas, first as having them or being them, then as being tinged once more by the Gunas of the objects perceived (IV, 16).

(Tapas) or ardour of asceticism, &c. By birth is meant not only birth in this or in a future life, as a Brâhman or Sûdra, but also rebirth, such as when Nandîsvara, a Brâhman, became a Deva, or when Visvâmitra, from being a Kshatriya, became by penance a Brâhman. This is accounted for as being simply a removal of hindrances, as when a husbandman, wishing to irrigate his field, pierces the balk of earth that kept the water from flowing in.

### Samskâras and Vâsanâs.

Though, as a rule, whatever a man does has its results, whether good or bad, the act of a Yogin, we are told, is neither black nor white, it produces no fruit, because it is performed without any desire.

As the results of actions we have Vâsanâs, impressions, or Samskâras, dispositions. They show themselves either in what remains, often dormant, and is then called memory [1], or in the peculiar genus, of man, bird, cow, Brâhman or Sûdra, in the locality and in the time when a man is born. These remainders never cease, so that the animal propensities may lie dormant for a time in a Brâhman, but break out again when he enters on a canine birth. They are not said to be without beginning, because desires and fears can only arise when there are objects to be feared or desired (IV, 10). Impressions are caused by perceptions, perceptions spring from desire, desire from nescience. The result of them all is the body with its instincts, their habitat the mind, their support, or that on which they lean,

[1] This kind of memory comes very near to what we call instinct, propensity, or untaught ability.

the same as the support of perception, i. e. the objective world. Hence it is said that they sprout, like seeds, but that by Knowledge and Yoga they can be annihilated also like seeds, when roasted. In connexion with this the question is discussed, how anything can ever be completely destroyed, how what exists can be made not to exist, and how what does not exist can be made to exist. I doubt, however, whether Rajendralal Mitra can be right (III, 9, IV, 12) when he discovers here something like the theory of ideas or *logoi* in the mind of Patañ*g*ali, and holds that the three ways or Adhvans in which objects present themselves to the mind, or affect the mind, as past, present and future, correspond to the admission of *universalia ante rem*, the ideas or types, the *universalia in re*, the essence, and the *universalia post rem*, the concepts in our minds. I confess I hardly understand his meaning. It should never be forgotten that the mind is taken by Patañ*g*ali as by itself unconscious (not as Svâbhâsa, self-illuminated, IV, 18) and as becoming conscious and intelligent for a time only by the union between it and the Purusha, who is pure intelligence. The Manas only receives the consciousness of perception which comes in reality from the Purusha, so that here we should have the etymological, though somewhat fanciful, definition of consciousness (*con-scientia*) as well as of the Sanskrit Sa*m*-vid, i. e. knowing along with the mind, i.e. apprehending the impressions of the mind (Svabuddhi-Sa*m*vedanam). But though *K*itta is the work of the Manas, not directly of the Buddhi, this *K*itta, when seen by the seer (Purusha) on one side and tinged with what is seen on the other, may be spoken of as the thought of the Purusha, though it is so by a temporary misconception only. This *K*itta again is coloured by many former impressions (Vâsanâ). It may be called the highest form of Prak*ri*ti, and as such it serves no purpose of its own, but works really for another, the Purusha, whom it binds and fascinates for a time with the sole purpose, we are told, of bringing him back to a final recognition of his true Self (IV, 24).

### Kaivalya.

If that is once achieved, the Purusha knows that he himself is not experiencer, neither knower nor actor; and the Manas or active mind, when beginning to feel the approach of Kaivalya, turns more and more inward and away from the world, so as not to interfere with the obtainment of the highest bliss of the Purusha. Yet there is always danger of a relapse in unguarded moments or in the intervals of meditation. Old impressions may reassert themselves, and the mind may lose its steadiness, unless the old Yoga-remedies are used again and again to remove all impediments. Then at last, perfect discrimination is rewarded by what is called by a strange term, Dharmamegha, the cloud of virtue, knowledge and virtue being inseparable like cause and effect. All works and all sufferings have now ceased, even what is to be known becomes smaller and smaller, the very Gu*n*as, i.e. Prak*ri*ti, having done their work, cease troubling; Purusha becomes himself, is independent, undisturbed, free, and blessed.

### Is Yoga Nihilism?

This is the end of the Yoga-philosophy, and no wonder that it should have been mistaken for complete nihilism by Cousin and others. But first of all, the play of Prak*ri*ti, though it has ceased for our Purusha, who has gained true knowledge, is supposed to be going on for ever for the benefit of other innumerable Purushas; and as long as there are any spectators, the spectacle of Prak*ri*ti will never cease. Secondly, the Purusha, though freed from illusion, is not thereby annihilated. He is himself, apart from nature, and it is possible, though it is not distinctly stated, that the Purusha in his aloneness may continue his life, like the *G*îvan-mukta of the Vedânta, maintaining his freedom among a crowd of slaves, without any fear or hope of another life, unchanged himself in this ever-changing Sa*m*sâra. However, we need not attempt to supply what Patañ*g*ali himself has passed over in silence. The final goal whether of the Yoga, or of the Sâ*m*khya, nay even of the Vedânta and of Buddhism, always defies description. Nirvâ*n*a in its highest sense is a name and a thought, but nothing can be predicated of it. It is 'what no eye has seen and what has not entered into the mind of man.' We know that it is; but no one can say what it is, and those who attempt to do so are apt to reduce it to a mere phantasmagoria or to a nothing.

Though I hope that the foregoing sketch may give a correct idea of the general tendency of the Yoga-philosophy, I know but too well that there are several points which require further elucidation, and on which even native expositors hold different opinions. What we must guard against in all these studies is rejecting as absurd whatever we cannot understand at once, or what to us seems fanciful or irrational. I know from my own experience how often what seemed to me for a long time unmeaning, nay absurd, disclosed after a time a far deeper meaning than I should ever have expected.

The great multitude of technical terms, though it may be bewildering to us, could not be entirely suppressed, because it helps to show through how long and continuous a development these Indian systems of thought must have passed, before any attempt was made, as it was by Patañ*g*ali and others, to reduce them to systematic order. There remains with me a strong conviction that Indian philosophers are honest in their reasonings, and never use empty words. But there remains much to be done, and I can only hope that if others follow in my footsteps, they will in time make these old bones to live again. These ancient sages should become fellow-workers and fellow-explorers with ourselves in unknown continents of thought, and we ought not to be afraid to follow in their track. They always have the courage of their convictions, they shrink from no consequences if they follow inevitably from their own premisses. This is the reason why I doubt whether the admission of an Îsvara or lord by Patañ*g*ali, in contradistinction to Kapila who denies that there are any arguments in support of such a being, should be put down as a mere economy or as an accommodation to popular opinion. Indian philosophers are truthful, and Patañ*g*ali (II. 36) says in so many words that *truth is better than sacrifice* [1]. They may err, as Plato has erred and even Kant, but they are not *decepti deceptores*, they do not deceive or persuade themselves, nor do they try to deceive others.

---

[1] Satyapratish*th*âyâm kriyâphalâsrayatvât.

# CHAPTER VIII.

## NYÂYA AND VAI*S*ESHIKA.

### Relation between Nyâya and Vai*s*eshika.

WHILE in the systems hitherto examined, particularly in the Vedânta, Sâ*m*khya, and Yoga, there runs a strong religious and even poetical vein, we now come to two systems, Nyâya and Vai*s*eshika, which are very dry and unimaginative, and much more like what we mean by scholastic systems of philosophy, businesslike expositions of what can be known, either of the world which surrounds us or of the world within, that is, of our faculties or powers of perceiving, conceiving, or reasoning on one side, and the objects which they present to us, on the other.

It should be remembered that, like the Sâ*m*khya and Yoga, and to a certain extent like the Pûrva and Uttara-Mîmâ*m*sâ, the Nyâya and Vai*s*eshika also have by the Hindus themselves been treated as forming but one discipline. We possess indeed a separate body of Nyâya-Sûtras and another of Vai*s*eshika-Sûtras, and these with their reputed authors, Gotama and Ka*n*âda, have long been accepted as the original sources whence these two streams of the ancient philosophy of India proceeded. But we know now that the literary style which sprang up naturally in what I called the Sûtra-period, the period to which the first attempts at a written in place of a purely mnemonic literature may have to be ascribed, was by no means restricted to that ancient period, but continued to be so well imitated in later times that we find it used with great success not only in the Sâmkhya-Sûtras, which are later than Mâdhava (1350 A.D.), but in more modern compositions also. It should always be borne in mind that the Sûtras ascribed to Gotama and Kanâda presuppose a long previous development of philosophical thought, and instead of regarding the two as two independent streams, it seems far more likely that there existed at first an as yet undifferentiated body of half philosophical half popular thought, bearing on things that can be known, the Padârthas, i.e. *omne scibile*, and on the means of acquiring such knowledge, from which at a later time, according to the preponderance of either the one or the other subject, the two systems of Vaiseshika and Nyâya branched off. These two systems shared of course many things in common, and hence we can well understand that at a later time they should have been drawn together again and treated as one, as we see in Sivâditya's Saptapadârthî (about 1400 A.D.), in the Bhâshâ-Parikkheda, with its commentary the Muktâvali, in the Tarkasamgraha, the Tarkakaumudî, the Tarkâmrita, &c. For practical purposes it is certainly preferable that we should follow their example and thus avoid the necessity of discussing the same subjects twice over. There may have been an old Tarka, very like our Tarkasamgraha, the one before the bifurcation of the old system of Ânvîkshikî, the other after the confluence of the two. But these are as yet conjectures only, and may have to remain mere conjectures always, so that, in the present state of our knowledge, and depending, as we have to do, chiefly on the existing Sûtras as the authorities recognised in India itself, we must not attempt a historical treatment, but treat each system by itself in spite of unavoidable repetitions.

A very zealous native scholar, Mahâdeo Râjârâm Bodas, in the Introduction to his edition of the Tarkasa*m*graha, has indeed promised to give us some kind of history of the Nyâya-philosophy in India. But unfortunately that period in the historical development of the Nyâya which is of greatest interest to ourselves, namely that which preceded the composition of the Nyâya-Sûtras, had by him also to be left a blank, for the simple reason that nothing is known of Nyâya before Gotama. The later periods, however, have been extremely well treated by Mr. Bodas, and I may refer my readers to him for the best information on the subject. Mr. Bodas places the Sûtras of Gotama and Ka*n*âda in the fifth or fourth cent. B.C.; and he expresses a belief that the Vai*s*eshika, nay even the Sâ*m*khya, as systems of thought, were anterior to Buddha, without however adducing any new or certain proofs.

### Dignâga.

Dates are the weak points in the literary history of India, and, in the present state of our studies, any date, however late, should be welcome. In former years to assign the Kapila-Sûtras to the fourteenth or even fifteenth century A.D., would have seemed downright heresy. Was not Kâlidâsa himself assigned to a period long before the beginning of our era? It seems now generally accepted that Kâlidâsa really belonged to the sixth century A.D., and this date of Kâlidâsa may help us to a date for the Sûtras of Gotama, valuable to us, though it may be despised by those who imagine that the value of Sanskrit literature depends chiefly on its supposed remote antiquity. I have pointed out[1] that, according to native interpreters, Kâlidâsa alluded to the logician Dignâga in a verse of his Meghadûta[2]. We may suppose therefore that Dignâga was considered a contemporary of Kâlidâsa. Now Dignâga is said by Vâ*k*aspati Mi*s*ra, in his Nyâya-vârttika-tâtparya-*t*îkâ, to have interpreted the Nyâya aphorisms of Gotama in a heterodox or Buddhist sense, while Uddyotakara wrote his commentary to refute his interpretation and to restore that of Pakshilasvâmin. If Vâ*k*aspati Mi*s*ra is right, we should be allowed to place Dignâga in the sixth century, and assign the same or rather an earlier date to the Sûtras of Gotama, as explained by him and other Nyâya philosophers. So late a date may not seem to be worth much, still I think it is worth having. Several other dates may be fixed by means of that of Dignâga as I tried to show in the passage quoted above (India, pp. 307 seq.).

A more comprehensive study of Buddhist literature may possibly shed some more light on the chronology of the later literature of the Brâhmans, if I am right in supposing that in the beginning the followers of Buddha broke by no means so entirely, as has generally been supposed, with the literary traditions of the Brâhmans. It is quite intelligible

---

[1] India, p. 307.

[2] See also Prof. Sati*s* Chandra Vidyâbhûsha*n*a in Journal of Buddhist Text Society, IV, parts iii, and iv, p. 16.

why among the various systems of Hindu philosophy the Buddhists should have paid little attention to the two Mîmâmsâs, concerned as they both were with the Veda, an authority which the Buddhists had rejected. But there was no reason why the Buddhists should forswear the study of either the Nyâya or Vaiseshika systems, or even the Sâmkhya system, though making their reserves on certain points, such as the existence of an Îsvara, which was admitted by the Nyâyas, but denied by Buddha. We know that at the court of Harsha, Brâhmans, Bauddhas, and Gainas were equally welcome (India, pp. 307 seq.). We know from Chinese travellers such as Hiouen-thsang that Vasubandha, for instance, before he became a Buddhist, had read with his master, Vinayabhadra or Samghabhadra [1], not only the books of the eighteen schools which were Buddhist, but also the six Tîrthya philosophies, clearly meant for the six Brâhmanic systems of philosophy. This Vasubandha, as a very old man, was actually the teacher of Hiouen-thsang, who travelled in India from 629 to 648 A.D. Therefore in Vasubandha's time all the six systems of Indian philosophy must have been in existence, in the form of Sûtras or Kârikâs. For we possess, in one case at least, a commentary by Pakshila-svâmin or Vâtsyâyana on the Nyâya-Sûtras, the same as those which we possess, and we know that the same Sûtras were explained afterwards by Dignâga, the Buddhist. This Buddhist commentary was attacked by Uddyotakara, a Brâhman, of the sixth century, while in the beginning of the seventh century Dharmakîrtti,

[1] See also Journal of Buddhist Text Society, 1896, p. 16.

a Buddhist, is said to have defended Dignâga[1] and to have criticised Uddyotakara's Nyâyavârttika. In the ninth century Dharmottara, a Buddhist, defended Dharmakîrtti's and indirectly Dignâga's interpretation of the Nyâya-Sûtras, and it was not till the tenth century that Vâ*k*aspati Mi*s*ra finally re-established the Brâhmanic view of the Nyâya in his Nyâya-vârttika-tâtparya-*t*ikâ. This would coincide with the period of the Brâhmanic reaction and the general collapse of Buddhism in India, and thus place before us an intelligible progress in the study of the Nyâya both by Brâhmans and Buddhists from the sixth to the tenth century, while the revival of the Nyâya dates from Ga*m*ge*s*a Upâdhyâya who lived in the fourteenth century at Mithila.

Thanks to the labours of Sarat Chandra Dâs and Satî*s* Chandra Vidyâbhûsha*n*a, we have lately gained access to some of the Sûtras of the Buddhist schools of philosophy, which are full of interest. Of the four great schools of the Buddhists, the Mâdhyamika, Yogâ*k*âra, Sautrântika, and Vaibhâshika, the first or Mâdhyamika now lies before us in the Mâdhyamika V*ri*tti by *K*andra-Kîrtti, and there is every hope that other philosophical treatises also, for instance, the Nyâya-samu*kk*aya, may be made accessible to us by the labours of these indefatigable scholars.

The Sûtras or rather Kârikâs of the Mâdhyamika school must, of course, be distinguished from the system of thought which they are meant to explain.

---

[1] Though none of Dignâga's writings have as yet been discovered, *S*rî Sarat Chandra states that there is in the library of the Grand Lama a Tibetan translation of his Nyâya-samu*kk*aya (Journal of Buddhist Text Society, part iii, 1896, p. 17).

The characteristic feature of that system is the *S*ûnya-vâda, or nihilism, pure and simple. As such it is referred to and refuted in Gotama's Nyâya-Sûtras IV, 37 to 40, in Kapila's Sâ*m*khya-Sûtras I, 43, 44, in Bâdarâya*n*a's Vedânta-Sûtras II, 2, 28, where *S*a*m*kara distinctly refers the doctrine that we know no objects, but only our perceptions of them, to Sugata or Buddha. The author of the Pa*ñk*adas*î* quotes the Mâdhyamikas by name as the teachers of universal nihilism (Sarva*m* *S*ûnyam).

If Nâgâr*g*una was really the author of the Mâdhyamika-Sûtras, as we now possess them, they would carry us back to about the first century A.D., and we should have in his Kârikâs, as explained by *K*andra-Kîrtti, the oldest document of systematic philosophy in India, which will require very careful examination. Though it is different, no doubt, from all the six systems, it nevertheless shares in common with them many of the ideas and even technical terms. If it teaches the *S*ûnyatva or emptiness of the world, this after all is not very different from the Vedântic Avidyâ, and the Sâ*m*khya Aviveka, and if it teaches the Pratîtyatva of everything, that need be no more than the dependence of everything on something else[1]. The distinction made by the Mâdhyamikas between what is Pâramârthika, real in the highest sense, and Sâ*m*v*ri*tika, veiled, is much the same as the distinction of the later Vedânta between what is really real (Paramârtha-

[1] Pratîtya in Pratîtya-samutpâda and similar words may best be rendered by dependent or conditioned. A son, for instance, is a son, Pitaram Pratîtyâ, dependent on a father, and a father is impossible without a son. In the same way everything is dependent on something else.

ta*h*), and what is Vyavahârika, phenomenal or the result of Mâyâ, sometimes called Sa*m*v*ri*ti, the veil that covers the Nirgu*n*a Brahman or the Tad, which again is not very different from what the Buddhists meant originally by *S*ûnya, empty, for they hold that even the *S*ûnya is not altogether nothing. Many of the technical terms used by the Mâdhyamikas are the same as those with which we are acquainted in the other systems. Du*h*kha, pain, for instance, is divided into Âdhyatmika, intrinsic, Âdhibhautika, extrinsic, and Âdhidaivika, divine or supernatural. We meet with the five perceptions of colour, taste, smell, touch, and sound, and with their five causes, light, water, earth, air, and ether, and we also have the well-known idea that Manas, mind, forms the sixth sense. What is peculiar to the Buddhists is that to them neither the objects of sense nor the sensations point to an underlying substance or reality.

We owe a great debt of gratitude to both Sarat Chandra Dâs and *S*rî Satî*s* Chandra Vidyâbhûsha*n*a for their labours in Tibet, and we look forward to many valuable contributions from their pen, more particularly for retranslations from Tibetan.

Whether Buddhist philosophy shares more in common with the Sâ*m*khya than with the Nyâya and Vai*s*eshika seems to me as doubtful as ever. The fundamental position of the Sâ*m*khya, as Satkârya-vada, is the very opposite of the Buddhist view of the world.

### Bibliography.

It was in 1852 that published my first contributions to a study of Indian philosophy in the *Zeitschrift der Deutschen Morgenländischen Gesellschaft*. These papers did not extend, however, beyond the Vai*s*eshika and Nyâya-philosophy as treated in the Tarkasa*m*graha, and more urgent occupations connected with the edition of the Rig-veda prevented me at the time from finishing what I had prepared for publication on the other systems of Indian philosophy. Though, of course, much new and important material has come to light in the meantime, particularly through the publications of the Vai*s*eshika-Sûtras in the *Bibliotheca Indica*, through the complete translation of them by A. E. Gough, 1873, and through the comprehensive researches of European scholars, such as Professors Deussen and Garbe, I found that there was not much to alter in my old account of Gotama's and Ka*n*âda's philosophies, as given in the German Oriental Journal, and in my paper on Indian Logic contributed to the late Archbishop Thomson's Laws of Thought. Indian philosophy has this great advantage that each tenet is laid down in the Sûtras with the utmost precision, so that there can be little doubt as to what Ka*n*âda or Gotama thought about the nature of the soul, the reality of human knowledge, the relation between cause and effect, the meaning of creation, and the relation between God or the Supreme Being and man. Thus it may be understood why even papers published so long ago as 1824, such as J. Colebrooke's papers on the Nyâya and Vai*s*eshika and the other systems of Indian philosophy, may still be recommended to all who want trustworthy information on Indian philosophy. These essays have sometimes been called antiquated, but there is a great difference between what is old and what is antiquated. The difficulty in giving an account of these systems for the benefit of European readers consists far more in deciding what may be safely omitted, so as to bring out the salient points of each system, than in recapitulating all their tenets.

Books in which the Nyâya and Vaiseshika-systems may be studied by those who are unacquainted with Sanskrit are, besides the papers of Colebrooke:—

Ballantyne, The Aphorisms of the Nyâya-Philosophy by Gautama, Sanskrit and English, Allahabad, 1850. (Gautama is the same as Gotama, only that by a tacit agreement Gotama has generally been used as the name of the philosopher, Gautama as that of Buddha, both belonging, it would seem, to the family of the Gautamas or Gotamas, the MSS. varying with regard to the vowel.)

A. E. Gough, The Vaiseshika Aphorisms of Ka*n*âda, translated, Benares, 1873.

Manilal Nabubhai Dvivedi, The Tarka-Kaumudî, being an introduction to the principles of the Vai*s*eshika and Nyâya-philosophies by Laugâkshi Bhâskara, Bombay, 1886. This is the same author to whom we owe a valuable edition of the Yogasâra-sa*m*graha.

Windisch, Über das Nyâya-bhâshya, Leipzig, s. a.

Ke*s*ava *S*âstri, The Nyâya-dar*s*ana with the commentary of Vâtsyâyana, in the Pundit, 1877, pp. 60, 109, 311, 363 (incomplete); see also *Bibliotheca Indica*.

Mahâdeo Râjârâm Bodas, The Tarkasa*m*graha of Annambha*tt*a, with the author's Dîpikâ and Govardhana's Nyâya-bodhinî, prepared by the late Rao Bahadur Ya*s*avanta Vâsadeo Âthalya, and published with critical and explanatory notes, Bombay, 1897. This book reached me after these chapters on the Nyâya and Vai*s*eshika were written, but not too late to enable me to profit by several of his explanations and criticisms, before they were printed.

### Nyâya-Philosophy.

Though Nyâya has always been translated by logic, we must not imagine that the Nyâya-Sûtras are anything like our treatises on formal logic. There is, no doubt, a greater amount of space allowed to logical questions in these than in any of the other systems of Indian philosophy; but originally the name of Nyâya would have been quite as applicable to the Pûrva-Mîmâ*m*sâ, which is actually called Nyâya in such works, for instance, as Sâya*n*a's Nyâya-mâlâ-vistara, published by Goldstücker. Nor is logic the sole or chief end of Gotama's philosophy. Its chief end, like that of the other Dar*s*anas, is salvation, the *summum bonum* which is promised to all. This *summum bonum* is called by Gotama Ni*hs*reyasa, literally that which has nothing better, the *non plus ultra* of blessedness. This blessedness, according to the ancient commentator Vatsyâyana, is described as consisting in renunciation with regard to all the pleasures of this life, and in the non-acceptance of, or indifference to any rewards in the life to come; as being in fact what Brahman is, without fear, without desire, without decay, and without death. Even this Brahmahood must not be an object of desire, for such desire would at once produce a kind of bondage, and prevent that perfect freedom from all fear or hope, which is to follow by itself, but should never be yearned for. This perfect state of freedom, or resignation, can, according to Gotama, be realised in one way only, namely, by knowledge, and in this case, by a knowledge of the sixteen great topics of the Nyâya-philosophy.

### Summum Bonum.

In this respect all the six systems of philosophy are alike, they always promise to their followers or their believers the attainment of the highest bliss that can be obtained by man. The approaches leading to that bliss vary, and the character also of the promised bliss is not always the same; yet in each of the six systems philosophy is recommended not, as with us, for the sake of knowledge, but for the highest purpose that man can strive after in this life, that is, his own salvation.

We saw that the Vedânta recognised true salvation or Moksha in the knowledge of Brahman, which knowledge is tantamount to identity with Brahman. This Brahman or God is, as the Upanishads already declare, invisible, and far beyond the reach of the ordinary faculties of our mind. But he can be learnt from revelation as contained in the Veda, and as *S*vetaketu was taught 'Tat tvam asi,' 'Thou art it,' every Vedântist is to learn in the end the same lesson, and to realise his identity with Brahman, as the fulfilment of all desires, and the surcease of all suffering (Du*h*khânta).

The end of all suffering is likewise the object of the Sâ*m*khya-philosophy, though it is to be reached by a different road. Kapila, being a dualist, admits an objective substratum by the side of a subjective spirit or rather spirits, and he sees the cause of all suffering in the spirits' identifying themselves with what is purely objective or material. He therefore recognises the true means of destroying all bondage and regaining perfect freedom of the spirit in our distinguishing clearly between spirit and matter, between subject and object, between Purusha and Prak*ri*ti. Kaivalya, or aloneness, is the right name for that highest state of bliss which is promised to us by the Sâ*m*khya-philosophy.

The Yoga-philosophy holds much the same view of the soul recovering its freedom, but it insists strongly on certain spiritual exercises by which the soul may best obtain and maintain peace and quietness, and thus free itself effectually from the illusions and sufferings of life. It also lays great stress on devotion to a Spirit, supreme among all the other spirits, whose very existence, according to Kapila, cannot be established by any of the recognised means of real knowledge, the Pramâ*n*as.

Of the two Mîmâ*m*sâs we have seen already that the Brahma-Mîmâ*m*sâ or the Vedânta recognises salvation as due to knowledge of the Brahman, which knowledge produces at once the recognition of oneself as in reality Brahman (Brahmavid Brahma eva bhavati, 'He who knows Brahman is Brahman indeed'). It is curious to observe that, while the Sâ*m*khya insists on a distinction between Purushas, the subjects, and Prak*ri*ti, all that is objective, as the only means of final beatitude, the Vedânta on the contrary postulates the surrendering of all distinction between the Self and the world, and between the Self and Brahman as the right means of Moksha. The roads are different, but the point reached at last is much the same.

The other Mîmâ*m*sâ, that of *G*aimini, diverges widely from that of Bâdarâya*n*a. It lays its chief stress on works (Karman) and their right performance, and holds that salvation may be obtained through the performance of such works, if only they are performed without any desire of rewards, whether on earth or in heaven.

Lastly, the Nyâya and Vaiseshika systems, though they also aim at salvation, are satisfied with pointing out the means of it as consisting in correct knowledge, such as can only be obtained from a clear apprehension of the sixteen topics treated by Gotama, or the six or seven categories put forward by Ka*n*âda. These two philosophies, agreeing as they do among themselves, seem to me to differ very characteristically from all the others in so far as they admit of nothing invisible or transcendent (Avyakta), whether corresponding to Brahman or to Prak*ri*ti. They are satisfied with teaching that the soul is different from the body, and they think that, if this belief in the body as our own is once surrendered, our sufferings, which always reach us through the body, will cease by themselves.

But while we can understand that each of the six systems of Indian philosophy may succeed in removing pain, it is very difficult to see in what that actual happiness was supposed to consist which remained after that removal.

The Vedânta speaks of Ânanda, or bliss, that resides in the highest Brahman; but the happiness to be enjoyed by the souls near the throne of Brahman, and in a kind of paradise, is not considered as final, but is assigned to a lower class only. That paradise has no attraction, and would give no real satisfaction to those who have reached the knowledge of the Highest Brahman. Their blissful knowledge is described as oneness with Brahman, but no details are added. The bliss held out by the Sâ*m*khyas also is very vague and indefinite. It can arise only from the Purusha himself, if left entirely to himself, far from all the illusions and disturbances arising from objective nature, or the works of Prak*ri*ti.

Lastly, the Apavarga (bliss) of the Nyâya and Vai*s*eshika systems seems entirely negative, and produced simply by the removal of false knowledge. Even the different names given to the supreme bliss promised by each system of philosophy tell us very little. Mukti and Moksha mean deliverance, Kaivalya, isolation or detachment, Ni*hs*reyasa, *non plus ultra*, Am*ri*ta, immortality, Apavarga, delivery. Nor does the well-known Buddhist term Nirvâ*n*a help us much. We know indeed from Pâ*n*ini (VIII, 2, 50) that the word was pre-Buddhistic and existed in his time. He tells us that, if used in the sense of 'blown out,' the right form would be Nirvâta*h*, such as Nirvâto vâta*h*, 'the wind has ceased to blow,' but Nirvâ*no*-*gñih*, 'the fire is gone out.' We cannot prove, however, that Nirvâ*n*a was used as the technical term for the *summum bonum* in Pâ*n*ini's time, and it does not seem to occur in the classical Upanishads. Its occurring as the title of one of the modern Upanishads makes it all the more likely that it was borrowed there from Buddhistic sources. There is one passage only, in the shorter text of the Maitreya[1] Upanishad where Nirvâ*n*am anu*s*âsanam occurs, possibly meant for Nirvâ*n*ânu*s*âsanam, the teaching of Nirvâ*n*a. What should be clearly understood is that in the early Buddhistic writings also, Nirvâ*n*a does not yet mean a complete blowing out of the individual soul,

---

[1] Sacred Books of the East, XV, p. 61.

but rather the blowing out and subsiding of all human passions and the peace and quietness which result from it. The meaning of complete annihilation was a later and purely philosophical meaning attached to Nirvâ*n*a, and no one certainly could form an idea of what that Nirvâ*n*a was meant to be in the Buddhist Nihilistic or *S*ûnyatâ-philosophy. I doubt even whether the Upanishads could have given us a description of what they conceived their highest Mukti or perfect freedom to be. In fact they confess themselves (Taitt. Up. II, 4, 1) that 'all speech turns away from the bliss of Brahman, unable to reach it[1],' and when language fails, thought is not likely to fare better.

### Means of Salvation.

Turning now to the means by which the Nyâya-philosophy undertakes to secure the attainment of the *summum bonum* or Apavarga, we find them enumerated in the following list:—

### The Sixteen Topics or Padârthas.

(1) Pramâ*n*a, means of knowledge; (2) Prameya, objects of knowledge; (3) Sa*m*saya, doubt; (4) Prayo*g*ana, purpose; (5) D*r*ish*t*ânta, instance; (6) Siddhânta, established truth; (7) Avayava, premisses; (8) Tarka, reasoning; (9) Nir*n*aya, conclusion; (10) Vâda, argumentation; (11) *G*alpa, sophistry; (12) Vita*nd*â, wrangling, cavilling; (13) Hetvâbhâsa, fallacies; (14) *Kh*ala, quibbles; (15)

---

[1] See a very learned article on Nirvâ*n*a by Professor Satis Chandra Vidyâbhûsha*n*a, in the Journal of the Buddhist Text Society, VI, part i, p. 22.

*G*âti, false analogies; (16) Nigrahasthâna, unfitness for arguing.

This may seem a very strange list of the topics to be treated by any philosophy, particularly by one that claims the title of Nyâya or logic. It is clear that in reality the chapters on Pramâ*n*a or means of knowledge, and Prameya, objects of knowledge, comprehend the whole of philosophy.

### Means of Knowledge.

The four Pramâ*n*as, according to Gotama, are Pratyaksha, sensuous perception, Anumâna, inference, Upamâna, comparison, and *S*abda, word.

Perception comes first, because inference can only begin to do its work after perception has prepared the way, and has supplied the material to which inference can be applied. Comparison is no more than a subordinate kind of inference, while the *S*abda or the word, particularly that of the Veda, depends again, as we should say, on a previous inference by which the authority of the word, more particularly the revealed word, has first been established. Imperfect as this analysis of our instruments of knowledge may seem, it seems to me highly creditable to Indian philosophers that they should have understood the necessity of such an analysis on the very threshold of any system of philosophy. How many misunderstandings might have been avoided if all philosophers had recognised the necessity of such an introductory chapter. If we must depend for all our knowledge, first on our senses, then on our combinatory and reasoning faculties, the question whether revelation falls under the one or the other, or whether it can claim an independent authority, can far more easily be settled than if such questions are not asked *in limine*, but turn up casually whenever transcendental problems come to be treated.

### Objects of Knowledge.

The objects of knowledge, as given by the Nyâya, comprehend *omne scibile*, such as body, soul, organs of sense, qualities, cognition, mind, will, fault, death, enjoyment, pain, and final freedom. These objects are afterwards discussed singly, but have of course little to do with logic. Doubt and purpose mark the first steps towards philosophical discussion, instances and established truths supply materials, while premisses and reasoning lead on to the conclusion which disputants wish to reach. From Nos. 10 to 16, we have rules for dialectic rather than for logic. We are taught how to meet the artifices of our antagonists in a long argumentation, how to avoid or to resist sophistry, wrangling, fallacies, quibbles, false analogies, and downright misstatements, in fact, how to defend truth against unfair antagonists.

If from our point of view we deny the name of logic to such problems, we should be perfectly justified, though a glance at the history of Greek philosophy would show us that, before logic became an independent branch of philosophy it was likewise mixed up with dialectic and with questions of some more special interest, the treatment of which led gradually to the elaboration of general rules of thought, applicable to all reasoning, whatever its subject may be.

It is quite clear that these sixteen topics should

on no account be rendered, as they mostly have been, by the sixteen categories. Categories are the *praedicabilia*, or whatever can be predicated, and however much the meaning of this term may have been varied by European philosophers, it could never have been so far extended as to include wrangling, fallacies, quibbles and all the rest. We shall see that the six or seven Padârthas of the Vaiseshikas correspond far more nearly to the categories of the Aristotelian and afterwards of European philosophy in general.

### Padârtha, Object.

Nothing shows so well the philosophical character of the Sanskrit language than this very word Padârtha, which has been translated by category. It means in ordinary Sanskrit simply a thing, but literally it meant Artha, the meaning, the object, Pada, of a word. What we should call objects of thought, they called far more truly objects of words, thus showing that from the earliest times they understood that no thought was possible except in a word, and that the objects of our knowledge became possible only after they had been named. Their language passed through an opposite process to that of Latin. Latin called every kind of knowledge or all known things *gnomina*, from *g)nosco*, to know; but after a time, and after the initial *g* had been dropped, as we drop it involuntarily in *gnat*, their *gnomina* became *nomina*, and were then supposed to be something different from the old and forgotten *gnomina*; they became *nomina*, i. e. mere names.

### Six Padârthas of Vaiseshika.

According to the Vaiseshikas, we have six Padârthas, i. e. six general meanings, categories or predicates, to which all words i. e. all things can be referred. All known things must be either substances (9), qualities (24), or motions, the last meaning, however, more than mere local movement, so as to correspond in fact to our activity or even to our becoming (Werden). Knowledge (Buddhi) is here treated as one of the qualities of the soul, which itself is one of the substances, so that many things which with us belong to psychology and logic, are treated by the Vaiseshikas under this head.

The next two, the general and the particular, comprehend what is shared in common by many objects, and what is peculiar to one, and thus distinguishes it from all others.

Samavâya or intimate connection is a very useful name for a connection between things which cannot exist one without the other, such as cause and effect, parts and the whole, and the like. It comes very near to the Avinâbhâva, i. e. the Not-without-being, and should be carefully distinguished from mere conjunction or succession.

The seventh category, Abhâva, or negation, was added, it would seem, at a later time, and can be applied to previous, to present or to subsequent non-existence, or even to absolute Abhâva.

### Mâdhava's Account of Nyâya.

In order to see what, in the eyes of native scholars, the Nyâya-philosophy was meant to achieve, it may be useful to look at an account of it given by the great Mâdhavâ*k*ârya in his Sarvadar*s*ana-sa*m*graha, the compendium of all the systems of philosophy. 'The Nyâya-*s*âstra,' he says, 'consists of five books, and each book contains two daily portions or Ahnikas. In the first Ahnika of the first book the venerable Gotama discusses the definitions of nine subjects, beginning with "proof" (Pramâ*n*a), and in the second those of the remaining seven, beginning with discussion (Vâda). In the first daily portion of the second book he examines doubt (8), discusses the four kinds of proof, and refutes all objections that could be made against their being considered as instruments of right knowledge; and in the second he shows that "presumption" and other Pramâ*n*as are really included in the four kinds of "proof" already given. In the first daily portion of the third book he examines the soul, the body, the senses, and their objects; in the second, "understanding" (Buddhi) and mind (Manas). In the first daily portion of the fourth book he examines activity (Prav*r*itti), faults (Dosha), transmigration (Pretyabhâva), fruit or reward (Phala), pain (Du*h*kha), and final liberation (Apavarga); in the second he investigates the truth as to the causes of the "faults," and also the subject of "wholes" and "parts." In the first daily portion of the fifth book he discusses the various kinds of futility (*G*âti), and in the second the various kinds of objectionable proceedings (Nigrahasthâna).'

After having held out in the first Sûtra the promise of eternal salvation to all who study his philosophy properly, Gotama proceeds at once to a description of the steps by which the promised Ni*h*sreyasa, or highest happiness, is to be attained, namely by the successive annihilation of false knowledge, of faults, of activity, and, in consequence, of birth and suffering. When the last or suffering has been annihilated there follows *ipso facto* freedom, or blessedness (Apavarga), literally abstersion or purification. This process reminds us strongly of some of the links in the Pa*tikk*a Samuppâda of the Buddhists. This is generally translated by Chain of Causation, and was meant to sum up the causes of existence or of misery, the twelve Nidânas. It really means origin resting on something else. The first step is Avidyâ or that cosmic Nescience which was so fully elaborated in the Vedânta-philosophy. According to the Buddhists there follow on Avidyâ the Sa*m*khâras [1], all the varieties of existence; on these Vi*gñ*âna, sensation; on this Nâmarûpa, names and forms; on these the Sha*d*âyatana, the six organs of perception. Then follow in succession Spar*s*a, contact, Vedanâ, sensation, T*r*ish*n*â, desire, Upâdâna, attachment, Bhava, state of existence, *G*âti, birth, *G*arâmara*n*a, decay and death, *S*oka, sorrow, Parideva, lamentation, Du*h*kha, suffering, Daurmanasya, grief, and Upâyâsa, despair [2].

This chain of successive states proclaimed by Buddha has formed the subject of ever so many commentaries, none of which seems quite satisfactory. The chain of Gotama is shorter than that of Gautama, but the general likeness can hardly be mistaken. Who was the earlier of the two, Gotama or Gautama, is still a contested question, but whatever the age of our Sûtras (the sixteen topics) may

[1] Cf. Garbe, Sâ*m*khya-Philosophie, p. 269 seq.

[2] Cf. Childers, s.v.

be, a Nyâya-philosophy existed clearly before the rise of Buddhism.

### I. Pramâ*n*a.

Gotama proceeds next to examine each of the sixteen topics.

The first topic or Padârtha is Pramâ*n*a, which is said to consist of four kinds, all being means or measures of knowledge. They are in the Nyâya as in the Vai*s*eshika, (1) Pratyaksha, sense-perception; (2) Anumâna, inference; (3) Upamâna, comparison; and (4) *S*abda, word.

#### Perception or Pratyaksha.

1. Perception (Pratyaksha) is explained as knowledge produced by actual contact between an organ of sense and its corresponding object, this object being supposed to be real. How a mere passive impression, supposing the contiguity of the organs of sense with outward objects had once been established, can be changed into a sensation or into a presentation (*Vorstellung*), or what used to be called a material idea, is a question not even asked by Gotama.

#### Inference or Anumâna.

2. Inference (Anumâna), preceded by perception, is described as of three kinds, Pûrvavat, proceeding from what was before, i.e. an antecedent; *S*eshavat, proceeding from what was after, i.e. a consequent; and Sâmânyato D*r*ish*t*a, proceeding from what is constantly seen together. Though, as we saw, the *K*ârvâka rejects every kind of Anumâna or inference, he, as Vâ*k*aspati Misra remarks very acutely (Kârikâ 5), in attacking his antagonists for

their mistaken faith in inference, does really himself rely on inference, without which he could not so much as surmise that his antagonists held erroneous opinions, such erroneous opinions being never brought into contact with his organs of sense, but being supposed to exist on the strength of Anumâna.

The meaning of the three kinds of inference differs considerably according to different commentators. It is generally explained that a Pûrvavat, preceded by or possessed of a prius, refers to the mutual relation between a sign and what is signified by it, so that the observation of the sign leads to the observation or rather inference of what is universally associated with it or marked by it. This unconditional association is afterwards treated under the name of Vyâpti, literally pervasion of one thing by another. Examples will make this clearer. When we see a river rising we infer as its Pûrva or *prius* that it has rained. When we see that the ants carry their eggs, or that the peacocks are screaming, we infer as the *S*esha or posterior that it will rain. (Nyâya S. II, 5, 37). It is true that in all these cases the reason given for an inference may what is called, wander away, that is, may prove too much or too little. In that case the fault arises from the conditioned character of the Vyâpti or the pervasion. Thus the rising of a river may be due to its having been dammed up, the carrying off their eggs by the ants may have been caused by some accidental disturbance of their hill, and the screaming of the peacocks may really have been imitated by men. The fault, however, in such cases does not affect the process of inference, but the Vyâpti only; and as soon as the relation between the sign and the thing signified has been rectified, the inference will come right. Each Vyâpti, that is each inductive truth, consists of a sign (Liṅga), and the bearer of a sign (Liṅgin). The bearer of the sign is called Vyâpaka or pervading, the sign itself Vyâpya, what is to be pervaded. Thus smoke is the sign (Liṅga, Vyâpya), and fire is what pervades the smoke, is always present when there is smoke, is the *sine quâ non* of smoke, is therefore Liṅgin or Vyâpaka.

But everything depends on whether the two are either absolutely or only conditionally related. These conditions are called the Upâdhis. Thus the relation between fire and smoke is conditioned by damp firewood; and there are other cases also where fire exists without smoke, as in a red-hot iron ball.

The third kind of inference, the Sâmânyato D*r*ish*t*a, based on what is constantly seen together, is illustrated by our inferring that the sun is moving because it is seen in different places, everything that is seen in different places being known to have moved. Here the Vyâpti, on which the ancient logicians depended, had to wait till it was corrected by Copernicus.

Even a deaf man may infer the existence of sound if he sees a particular conjunction of a drumstick with a drum. It requires but a certain amount of experience to infer the presence of an ichneumon from seeing an excited snake, or to infer fire from perceiving the heat of water, nay to infer the existence of an organ of touch from our feeling any animated body. In all such cases the correctness of the inference is one thing, the truth of the conclusion quite another, the latter being always conditioned by the presence or absence of certain Upâdhis.

Different from this very natural explanation of the three kinds of Anumâna is another, according to which *S*esha is not supposed to mean subsequent effect, allowing us to infer its invariable cause, but is to be taken in the sense of what is left. This is illustrated by an example, such as 'Earth is different from all other elements, because it alone possesses the quality of smell,' that is to say, earth is left over, being separated from all other elements by its peculiar quality of smell. One might have inferred from the fact that the element of earth possesses smell, that all elements possessed the same. But this is wrong, because it is Aprasakta, i.e. does not apply. It would be no better than if we were to infer that smell must belong to other qualities and actions also, which would be simply absurd. But as earth is different from all other substances, we may infer that smell does not belong to anything that is not earth, except artificially, as in scented articles. This is the residuary inference, or method of residues.

In the same manner we are told that Pûrva, the *prius*, should not be taken in the sense of antecedent cause, but as a general concept the properties of which have been formerly comprehended as known. Thus from smoke on a hill we should infer the presence of a particular fire on the hill, falling under the general concept of fire as belonging to the genus fire.

The third, or Sâmânyato D*r*ish*t*a, inference, is illustrated by our inferring the existence of senses, which are by themselves imperceptible (Indriyâ*n*i Atîndriyâ*n*i), because we do perceive colour &c., and as no actions can take place without instruments we may infer the existence of senses as instruments for our action of seeing, &c. Sâmânyato D*r*ish*t*a thus becomes very like the seeing of a general concept. It is inference from the sensible to the supersensible.

With all respect for native commentators, both ancient and modern, I must confess that I prefer the more natural explanation of the three kinds of inference being based on cause, effect, and association, nay I find it difficult to understand why this view should have been given up by the modern Naiyâyikas.

Among these three inferences, the first and last are called Vîta or straightforward, the second Avîta, or not straightforward; but this only if we adopt the second explanation of the three kinds of Anumâna.

We shall have to deal again with Anumâna when we come to consider the seventh Padârtha, the Avayavas or Premisses, or what we should call the members of a syllogism.

### Comparison or Anumâna.

3. Next follows Comparison (Upamâna) or recognition of likeness, explained as an instrument for ascertaining what has to be ascertained by means of similarity with something well known before. For instance, having been told that a Gavaya (*bos gavaeus*) is like a cow, and seeing an animal like a cow, but not a cow, a man may infer that it is a Gavaya.

### Word or *S*abda.

4. Word (*S*abda) is explained either as a precept of one worthy to be trusted, or as a right precept. It refers, we are told, either to visible or invisible objects. It is curious to see that among the people to be trusted (Âpta) the commentator

should mention not only Rishis and Âryas, but Mle*kk*has or barbarians also, provided they are well informed. Strictly speaking the Veda would not come under *S*abda, unless it can be proved to be Âptava*k*ana, the word of one worthy to be trusted.

### II. Prameya.

The second Padârtha or topic is Prameya, that is, all that can be established by the four Pramâ*n*as, or what we should call *omne scibile*. Twelve such objects are mentioned: (1) Self or soul, (2) body, (3) senses, (4) sense-objects, (5) understanding, (6) mind, (7) activity (will), (8) faults, (9) transmigration, (10) rewards of deeds, (11) suffering, (12) final beatitude. The first six of these are called causative, the other six caused. Gotama next proceeds to define each of these Prameyas, by enumerating the characteristics peculiar to each.

1. The characteristics of the Self are desire, hatred, will, pleasure, pain, and knowing (Buddhi).

2. Body is defined as the seat of action, of the senses, and what they intimate, that is, their objects[1].

3. The senses or organs of sense are defined as those of smell, taste, sight, touch, and hearing. They are supposed to arise from the elements.

4. These elements (from which the senses draw their origin and their perceptions) are earth, water, light, air, and ether; while the objects of the senses are the qualities of earth, &c., such as odour, savour, colour, touch, and sound. It is essential to remember that of the elements the first four are both

[1] According to the commentary the sensations, and according to the next Sûtra, the qualities of the objects of sense, which alone can be perceived.

eternal and non-eternal, while the fifth, Âkâsa, which we translate by ether, is eternal only, and hence not tangible. The non-eternal substances are either inorganic, organic, or sensitive, but always related to the sense, so that the sense of light perceives or sees light only. The sense of scent perceives odour only, and so on.

5. As to Buddhi, understanding, it is by the Naiyâyikas explained as being the same as apprehension or knowledge, and as being twofold, notion, Anubhava, and remembrance, Smara*n*a.

6. Mind (Manas) is different from understanding, and is explained as that which prevents more than one notion from arising at the same time, that is to say, it prevents the rushing in of all sorts of sensuous impressions at once, and regulates them in our consciousness. It is sometimes called the gatekeeper or controller of the senses. The transformation of sensations into percepts, and of percepts into concepts, a subject little cultivated by Indian philosophers, would naturally fall to the Manas. Little attention, however, is paid by Hindu logicians to this subject, which has assumed such large proportions with us. Even the distinction between percepts, *Vorstellungen*, and concepts, *Begriffe*, has never been fully realised by Indian logicians.

Manas or mind is considered as A*n*u or an atom, and the question has been fully discussed how Manas, being A*n*u, can be united with Âtman, which is Vibhu, or infinitely great. If, with the Mîmâ*m*sakas, it were admitted that the two could unite, then there could never be any cessation of knowledge, such as we know there is in sleep, for the union of Âtman and Manas, if once effected, would be indissoluble.

It is held by the Naiyâyikas that when Manas enters a particular region of the body called Purîtat, the effect of the union of Âtman and Manas is neutralised, and sleep ensues. If Manas were supposed to be co-extensive with the body it would be Anitya, non-eternal, and be destroyed with the body, and we should lose that which retains the impressions of acts done in the body, nay we should be unable to account for a future life and the inequalities of birth in any future life; we should have to admit, in fact, effects without a cause. The Naiyâyikas hold, therefore, that the Manas is both A*n*u, infinitely small, and Nitya, eternal (Tarkakaumudî, p. 4, n. 24), while Manas, like Âtman, is eternal and numerous, differing, however, from Âtman by being atomic in dimension.

7. Activity (will) is the effort of body, of the understanding working through the mind (Manas), and of the voice.

8. Faults cause acts, and acts bear fruit, good or bad[1].

9. Pretyabhâva is transmigration.

10. Rewards are results produced by faults, in the most general sense, and by actions consequent on them, so that they are sometimes explained as consciousness of pleasure and pain.

11. Pain is characterised by vexation; and as pleasure also involves pain, both pain and pleasure are here treated together under pain. Entire deliverance from pain and pleasure is

12. Apavarga or final beatitude.

Having thus examined all that can form the

---

[1] See I, 20, Prav*ri*ttidoshaganitârtha*h* phalam.

object of our knowledge, the Pramâ*n*as or measures of knowledge, and the Prameyas, we now enter on the third of the sixteen topics.

### III. Sa*m*saya.

Sa*m*saya or doubt. Doubt, we are told, arises from our recognition of various attributes opposed to one another in one and the same object, as when we recognise in a distant object the qualities of a man and of a post. The definition given of doubt shows that the ancient logicians of India had carefully thought about the different causes of doubt, so that they were led to the admission of three or even five kinds of it.

### IV. Prayo*g*ana. V. D*r*ish*t*ânta. VI. Siddhânta.

But these disquisitions, as well as those referring to (IV) Prayo*g*ana, purpose or motive; (V) D*r*ish*t*ânta, example, familiar case; (VI) Siddhânta, tenets, contain nothing that is of peculiar interest to the historian of philosophy, except so far as they offer once more the clearest evidence of a long continued previous study of logic in the ancient schools or settlements of India.

### VII. The Avayavas, or Members of a Syllogism.

Much more important is the next subject, the so-called members, that is, the members of a syllogism. To us a syllogism and its structure are so familiar that we hardly feel surprised at meeting with it in the schools of logic in India. Yet, unless we are inclined to admit either an influence of Greek on Indian, or of Indian on Greek philosophy, neither of which has as yet been proved, the coincidences between the two are certainly startling. As to myself I feel bound to confess that I see no evidence of any direct influence, either on one side or on the other; and though I am far from denying its possibility, I keep to my conviction, expressed many years ago, that we must here also admit the existence of undesigned coincidences to a much larger extent than our predecessors were inclined to do. We must never forget that what has been possible in one country, is possible in another also.

At the time when the different systems of Indian philosophy became first known to the scholars of Europe everything that came from the East was looked upon as of extreme antiquity. There had been vague traditions of ancient Indian philosophy even before the time of Aristotle. Alexander himself, we are told, was deeply impressed with that idea, as we may gather from his desire to communicate with the gymnosophists of India.

### Indian and Greek Logic.

One of these gymnosophists or Digambaras seems to have been the famous Kalanos (Kalyâ*n*a ?), who died a voluntary death by allowing himself to be burnt before the eyes of the Macedonian army. It was readily admitted, therefore, by European scholars that the Hindu systems of philosophy, and particularly Indian Logic, were more ancient than that of Aristotle, and that the Greeks had borrowed the first elements of their philosophy from the Hindus.

The view that Alexander might actually have sent some Indian philosophical treatises to his tutor at home, and this even at a time when, as far as we know at present, manuscripts in India were still unknown, and that Aristotle might have worked them up into a system, inconceivable as it now seems to us, was taken up and warmly defended by men like Görres and others. Görres undertook to prove that the Greeks had actually retained some technical terms taken from Sanskrit. For instance, as Indian philosophers admit five elements, the fifth being called Âkâsa, ether, Görres, without giving any reference, quoted a passage from Aristotle in which he speaks of a fifth element and calls it ἀκατ-ονόματον, i. e. *akâs-nominatum*, this being probably an ingenious conjecture for ἀκατονόμαστον[1]. It is quite true that one such verbal coincidence would settle the whole question, but even that one coincidence has not yet been discovered. No doubt there were many points of coincidence between Greek and Indian logic, but none in technical terms, which, like proper names in Comparative Mythology, would have clinched the argument once for all.

But does it, on the other hand, show a higher power of historical criticism, if Niebuhr and others stood up for the opposite view and tried to derive Indian philosophy from Greece? Niebuhr is reported to have said in his Lectures on Ancient History, 'If we look at Indian philosophy we discern traces of a great similarity with that of the Greeks. Now as people have given up the hypothesis that Greek philosophy formed itself after Indian philosophy, we cannot explain this similarity except by the inter-

---

[1] Plutarch, De Placit. Philos., quotes Epicurus as to the soul being a mixture of three elements, fire, air, and water, and a fourth ἀκατονόμαστον, ὃ ἦν αὐτῷ αἰσθητικόν.

course which the Indians had with the Graeco-Macedonic kingdom of Bactra.'

Is that really so? To Niebuhr and to most Greek scholars it would naturally seem next to impossible that Greek philosophy, which can be watched from its first childhood, should have been of foreign origin, a mere importation from India. They know how Greek philosophy grew up gradually, how its growth ran parallel with the progress of Grecian poetry, religion, art, and civilisation. They feel it to be a home-grown production, as certainly as Plato and Aristotle were Greeks and not Brâhmans.

But they ought not to be surprised if Sanskrit scholars have just the same feeling with regard to Indian philosophy. They also can show how in India the first philosophical ideas, as yet in a very vague and shadowy form, show themselves in the hymns of the early poets of the Veda. They can trace their gradual development in the Brâhma*n*as and Upanishads. They can show how they gave rise to discussions, public and private, how they assumed a more and more definite form, and how at last they were fixed in different schools in that form in which they have reached us. They, too, are as certain that philosophy was autochthonous in India as that Gotama and Ka*n*âda were Brâhmans and not Greeks.

What then remains? It seems to me that until it can be proved *historically* that the Greeks could freely converse with Indians in Greek or in Sanskrit on metaphysical subjects or *vice versa*, or until technical philosophical terms can be discovered in Sanskrit of Greek, or in Greek of Sanskrit origin, it will be best to accept facts and to regard both Greek and Indian philosophy as products of the intellectual soil of India and of Greece, and derive from their striking similarities this simple conviction only, that in philosophy also there is a wealth of truth which forms the common heirloom of all mankind, and may be discovered by all nations if they search for it with honesty and perseverance.

Having once learnt this lesson we shall feel less inclined, whenever we meet with coincidences of any kind, to conclude at once that they cannot be explained except by admitting a historical contact and a borrowing on one side or the other[1]. No doubt there are the Vaiseshika categories = Padârthas, there is Dravya, substance, Guna, quality; there is genus = Sâmânya, and species = Visesha, nay, even syllogism = the Avayavas; there is induction = Vyâpti, and deduction = Upanaya, both in Sanskrit and in Greek. But why not? If they could be developed naturally in Greece, why not in India? Anyhow, we must wait and not hamper the progress of research by premature assertions.

### VIII. Tarka.

But before we enter into the intricacies of the Indian syllogism, it will be best to finish first what remains of the sixteen topics of the Nyâya. After the five members follows VIII, Tarka, which is explained as refutation, or reasoning from the fitness of the case, as when a person, though seeing smoke on a hill, does not see that there must be fire, and is

---

[1] See M. M., On Coincidences, a paper read before the Royal Society of Literature, 1896.

thereupon made to see that if the hill were without fire, it would of necessity be without smoke. It is meant to be a *reductio ad absurdum*.

### IX. Nir*n*aya.

The next topic to be considered is IX, Nir*n*aya, ascertainment.

### X–XVI. Vâda, *G*alpa, Vita*nd*â, Hetvâbhâsa, *G*âti, *Kh*ala, Nigrahasthâna.

Then follow the paragraphs connected with rhetoric or eristics rather than with logic, such as X, Vâda or argumentation, consisting of objections and answers, both disputants, however, caring for truth only; next XI, *G*alpa, sophistical wrangling or attacking what has been established, by means of fraud; XIV, *G*âti, futility, arising from false analogies; XV, *Kh*ala, quibbling; and XVI, Nigrahasthâna, unfitness for discussion. In the last five cases disputants are supposed to care for victory only, and not for truth.

If this wrangling is devoid of any attempt at really establishing an opposite opinion, it is called XII, Vita*nd*â, cavilling.

We next come to XIII, Hetvâbhâsas, or specious arguments, that is, paralogisms and sophisms. These are Savyabhi*k*âra, arguments that prove too much, Viruddha, that prove the reverse, Prakara*n*asama, that tell equally on both sides, Sâdhyasama, that stand themselves in need of proof, and Kâlâtîta, mistimed.

As to XV, *Kh*ala, fraud in using words in a sense different from what is generally understood, and XIV, *G*âti, futility arising from change of class, they have been mentioned before. It is difficult to understand why *Gâti*, i.e. birth or genus, should mean a futile argument, unless it meant originally a *transitio in alterum genus*, as when, in answer to an argument that a man is unable to travel, because he has a fever, it should be answered that he is able to travel, because he is a soldier. Here the same man is referred first to the class of those who suffer from fever, and then to that of soldiers who are always supposed to be able to march.

The last, XVI, Nigrahasthâna, unfitness for discussion, is when a man by misunderstanding or not understanding, yet continuing to talk, renders himself liable to reproof.

This may seem a long list, though in several cases there are subdivisions which have here been left out, and yet at the end of the list Gotama actually apologises and says that there are many more sorts of futility, &c., which have been passed over by him, but will have to be discussed hereafter.

### Judgments on Indian Logic.

If we were to look upon this list of the sixteen topics, as some have done, as an abstract of Gotama's whole philosophy, or with others, as his table of the categories, European philosophers would no doubt be justified in saying what Ritter said in his History of Philosophy that the exposition of the Nyâya is tedious, loose, and unmethodical. It is certainly mixed up with subjects which have nothing to do with pure logic, but so was Greek logic in its beginning, in the school of Zeno, for instance. It may be also too minute for our taste, but it cannot be called loose at the same time. It is equally unfair to charge the Nyâya and all the other systems of Indian philosophy, with being unpractical and with entirely ignoring all the problems of ethics. We must remember that philosophy in India had very different antecedents from what it had with us. We ourselves can hardly conceive a philosophy which in the end is not to be of practical usefulness, and which ignores all questions of morality. But we must learn to take philosophers as they are. Morality with the Brâhmans depends either on prescriptive *sacra* (Dharma), or on what is called Samaya, the agreement of good people. But its strongest support is a firm belief in the solidarity of life here and hereafter, and a firm conviction that nothing can ever be lost. The popular mind of India seems never to have doubted the fact that every good or every evil thought or deed will grow and bear fruit, and that no one can ever escape from the consequences of his own acts and thoughts. Whether such a belief is right or wrong is not the question, but it produced at all events a deep sense of responsibility. Instead of complaints about the injustice and cruelty of God, people were taught that what seemed undeserved misfortunes, were fully deserved, were in fact the natural consequences of previous acts, and in one respect the safest means of paying off all debts. Philosophy at the same time held out a hope that in the end this net of consequences might be broken through, and the Self, enlightened by true knowledge, return to whence it came, return to himself and be himself; that is, be again the Universal Self, free for ever from the chains and pains of this transient episode of life on earth.

That highest freedom and beatitude, according to

Indian views, depended on philosophy or knowledge; it could not be acquired by good works or good thoughts alone. This again may be right or wrong, but I can discover no looseness of reasoning in it, nor in Indian philosophy in general. We must not forget that, from a Hindu point of view, this life on earth is but an episode that may be very important in itself, but is a mere nothing compared with what lies behind and before, the eternal life of the soul. If they hold that a knowledge of the true relation between man and the world, and between man and the Author of the world, is essential to true freedom and true happiness, are they so far wrong? And what is true in the case of the Vedânta, the Sâ*m*khya and Yoga systems of philosophy, is true in a certain sense of the Nyâya also. It may be said that the fundamental points of this philosophy are contained in what can be known, Prameya, and the means of knowing, Pramâ*n*a, that is to say, it seemed necessary to Gotama to establish, first of all, the limits of the two, just as Kant began his philosophy with his Critique of Pure Reason, that is, the tracing of the limits of Pure Reason. But this being done in full detail under his sixteen headings, Gotama too, like Bâdarâya*n*a and Kapila, enters on an explanation of the process by which it was possible to destroy ignorance or Mithyâ*g*ñâna, which, as he holds, is the true cause of error or sin, 'which is the cause of activity, which is the cause of birth, which is the cause of suffering' (I, 2). This, whether right or wrong, is at all events perfectly coherent, nor does it betray any looseness of reasoning, if indirectly the whole Nyâya-philosophy is called the cause of final freedom or blessedness. Modern Nyâya is almost entirely confined to Pramâ*n*a.

### The Later Books of the Nyâya.

In this way the first book of the Nyâya-Sûtras gives us indeed a fair outline of the whole of Gotama's philosophy, while the following three books enter into a more minute examination of its details. Thus the second book treats more fully of the Pramâ*n*as, the third and fourth of the Prameyas, the fifth treats of all that comes under the head of paralogisms. Some of the questions discussed in these books show quite clearly that they must have formed the subject of lively and long-continued controversy, for though some of the objections raised may seem to us of little importance, they prove at all events the conscientiousness of the early Naiyâyikas.

### Pratyaksha, Perception.

That sensuous perception should be a Pramâ*n*a or authority would hardly seem to us to have required further proof. But Gotama or his opponent starts the question, on what ground the evidence of the senses can claim such authority, or who is the authority of its authority. This is an idea that anticipates an important element of modern philosophy. As a balance may serve to weigh a thing, but must also be weighed or tested itself, it might be said that the authority of the senses also requires to be established by another authority, and so on *ad infinitum.* In answer to this Gotama uses what seems to be an *ad hominem* argument, namely, that if there is no authority anywhere, there can be none on the side of the objector either. The objector would cut away the ground under his own feet, and thus would himself have no *locus standi* for offering any objections (II, 13).

But admitting that sensuous perception has authority just as a lamp has light to light up the things around it, the next question is whether the definition of sensuous perception, that which results from contact of sense with its object, is not incomplete, because for real perception there must be contact not only with the organs of sense, but likewise between the senses and the mind (Manas), and between the mind and the Self (Âtman). This is not denied by Gotama, he only defends himself by saying that everything cannot be said at the same time, and that his definition of perception, though it dwells only on what is essential (the contact of sense and object), does by no means exclude that between mind and Self, on the contrary takes it here for granted. He also admits that contact between sense and object does not invariably produce perception, that in fact there may be sensation without perception, as when we are so absorbed in listening to music that we do not perceive the objects around us, from want of attention. This again reminds us of modern philosophy. Even such questions as to whether there is any interval of time between our hearing the sound of a word and our realising its meaning, are alluded to by Gotama and his school, and the question whether several impressions can be taken in at the same time is negatived by a reference to the running of a pin through a number of sheets of a MS. Here the piercing seems simultaneous, yet we know that it can only be successive. Another question also which has lately occupied our psycho-physiologists, whether perception does not involve inference, is discussed by Gotama (II, 31), particularly in cases where our senses can apprehend a part only of their object when perceiving, for instance, a tree, of which one side only can be seen at the time, while the rest has to be supplied by memory or inference. This leads him on to another question whether there really is such a thing as a whole, and as we can in reality never see more than one side at a time, he tries to account for the process by which we take a part for the whole. No one, for instance, has ever seen more than one side of the moon, yet taking it as a whole, and as a globe, we postulate and are convinced that there is another side also. The illustration given by Gotama to show that a tree is a whole, namely, because when we shake one branch of it, the whole tree trembles, may seem childish to us, but it is exactly in these simple and so-called childish thoughts that the true interest of ancient philosophy seems to me to consist.

### Time—Present, Past, Future.

The next problem that occupies Gotama is that of time—of present, past, and future. The objector, and in this case, it seems, a very real objector, for it is the opinion of the Buddhists, denies that there is such a thing as present time, because the moment we see a fruit falling from a tree, we see only that it has fallen or that it has still to fall, but never that it is falling. Here the answer is that past and future themselves would be impossible, if the present did not exist, and on the objector's admitting such a possibility, Gotama remarks that in that case perception and all that springs from it would be altogether impossible, because it can only depend on what is present.

### Upamâna, Comparison.

Passing over what is said in this place about the validity of inference, because we shall have to return to it hereafter, we find Gotama bent on establishing by the side of it, by the side of Anumâna, his next instrument of knowledge, namely Upamâna, analogy or comparison. And here Gotama seems in conflict with Ka*n*âda who, as we shall see, declines to accept Upamâna, comparison, as one of the independent authoritative evidences, or, at all events, as essentially different from Anumâna, inference. We might feel tempted to conclude from this that Gotama must have been later in time than Ka*n*âda. But first of all, Ka*n*âda's name is not mentioned here nor that of his system, Vaiseshika; and secondly, we know that this question of the Pramâ*n*as had been discussed again and again in every school of Indian philosophy, so that a mere reference to the subject cannot be used as determining the seniority either of the opponent or of the defender. All we can say is that, whenever we see Upamâna appealed to as a means of valid knowledge, we know that we have to deal with followers of the Nyâya school; but the Vaiseshika, though denying it an independent place among the Pramâ*n*as, would by no means reject it, if presented as a kind of Anumâna.

### *S*abda, the Word.

We now come to the various kinds of verbal testimony. Testimony is said to be conveyed by words, and by a sentence, consisting of many words, conveying the meaning of each word in its relation to the other words. Though the meaning of words is admitted to be conventional, yet opinions differ because some consider such conventions to be eternal or divine, while others take them to be non-eternal or human. The chief authority for determining the meaning of a word is admitted to be the usage of trustworthy persons, but it is argued that as the highest authority is Brahman or God, and as the Veda is the word of Brahman, it follows that every word of the Veda possesses the highest authority. This, however, as we know, does not satisfy the Mîmâ*m*sakas, who assign eternity to the *S*abda itself, the word or the sound of a word.

In the examination of the validity of *S*abda or word, we fihd again the same question started as before, whether it deserves a place by itself, or whether it should not rather be treated as a kind of inference. Then, after Gotama has shown the difference between 'I know' and 'I infer,' between acceptance of the word of an authority (Âptopadesa) and reliance on an inference, he enters on new problems such as the association of sense with sound, a question which is intimately connected with the question of what authority is due to the Veda as the Word *par excellence.* Here we meet with a number of arguments in defence of the supreme authority of the Veda with which we are familiar from the Pûrva-Mîmâ*m*sâ, but which again, though clearly referring to *G*aimini, must not be taken to prove the anteriority of *G*aimini's Sûtras to those of Gotama's, and certainly do not enable us to admit more than the contemporaneous activity of the various schools of

Hindu philosophy during the centuries intervening between the close of the Vedic age and the rise and spread of Buddhism.

### The Eight Pramâ*n*as.

Having defended the teaching of the Nyâya, that there are four Pramâ*n*as, neither more nor less, Gotama proceeds to criticise the four additional Pramâ*n*as of the Mîmâ*m*sakas, and shows that their number is superabundant. They include, as we saw, Aitihya, tradition, not necessarily authoritative, Arthâpatti, assumption, Sambhava, probability, and even Abhâva, non-existence, because they hold that there can be knowledge arising from not-being or from absence, as when we conclude from the fact that Devadatta is not in his house, that he must have gone out. Of these four Pramâ*n*as the first is referred by Gotama to *S*abda, Word, the others to Anumâna, inference, while *K*esh*t*â, or mere gesture, as supplying knowledge, may, it is added, be classed either under Word, like written letters, or under Anumâna. The Pramâ*n*as seem to have formed a subject of prominent interest to the Nyâya philosophers; in modern times they have absorbed the whole of Nyâya.

We are told that Nâgâr*g*una, before he became a Buddhist, was a zealous student of the Nyâya-philosophy. He wrote a work, called Pramâ*n*a-samu*kk*aya, which was, however, supposed to be lost, till Sarat Chandra discovered a Tibetan version of it in the library of the Grand Lama at Lhassa (Journal of Buddhist Text Society, IV, parts iii and iv, p. 17)[1].

[1] This would prove at the same time the study of the Nyâya-philosophy in the first century of our era; see p. 480.

Here follow long discussions as to the nature of words, the difference between sound (Dhvani) and words, till we arrive again at the question whether the word is eternal, and therefore a Pramâna by itself, or not. Similar questions occur in most of the Indian philosophical systems, and as I passed them over before, it will be necessary to examine them more fully in this place, where we meet with them again as worked out by Gotama. Though they deal with such purely grammatical questions as whether a vowel such as *i* can ever be changed into the semi-vowel *y*, in fact whether any letter can ever become another letter, these disquisitions branch out very far, and we shall be surprised to see how intimately in the minds of Hindu philosophers they are connected with some of the greatest problems of philosophy, such as the existence of a Creator and the relation between the cause and the effect of our created world.

The oftener we read these discussions on the eternal character of sound, on words and their true nature, and at last on the divine, nay transcendental character of language, the more we shall feel the difference between Eastern and Western philosophy. The true problem of language has been almost entirely neglected by Greek philosophers and their disciples in Europe, for all the discussions about the φύσει or θέσει origin of language touch only the very hem of the question, as it presents itself to Indian philosophers. The way in which the problem of language is handled by them will no doubt be dismissed as childish by modern philosophers, and I do not mean to deny that some of their remarks on language are really childish. But we shall see that the whole question is treated by Hindu philosophers in a very serious and searching spirit. Students of philosophy should overlook what may seem strange to them in the manner of treatment, and always try to keep their eye on what is important and has often been overlooked even by the greatest thinkers among us. Language has been to most of us so familiar a subject that we have hardly perceived what is behind it, and have scarcely asked the questions which it has cost so much effort to Indian philosophers to answer. We have already on a former occasion examined some of the views on language, as expressed in the philosophical hymns, Brâhma*n*as, and Upanishads of the Vedic period. We have now to follow up these views as they are presented to us in a more systematic form in the Sûtra-period.

### Thoughts on Language.

If I was right in tracing the word B*ri*h, speech, in B*ri*has-pati, back to the same root as that of Brahman, the connection of the two ideas, Word and Creator, would carry us back even beyond what we call the Vedic period. At all events the idea that Brahman was the Word, and that the world was created by the Word, existed, as we saw, long before the rise of philosophical systems. It was shadowed forth in the very language of India, but it received its full development in the Sûtras only, more particularly in the Vedânta-Sûtras, to which we must return for our present purpose. We read in Sûtra I, 3, 28: 'We refute his objection on the ground that (the world) originates from the Word, as is shown both by perception and by inference.' Perception is here taken in the sense of *S*ruti, scripture, and inference in the sense of Sm*ri*ti, tradition. An objection had been started that the Veda could not be considered as eternal, if it contained names of non-eternal things, and as even the gods, the Devas, were looked upon as non-eternal, having been proved to be subject to birth and rebirth, it followed that the Veda, as containing their names, could not possibly be ante-temporal or eternal. Against this, though readily admitting the non-eternal character of the gods, the Devas, *S*a*m*kara argues, that in spite of that, the gods and other beings, nay the whole world, must be admitted to have originated from the Word or the Veda, and that this Word is Brahman. Only, he adds, it is not the individuals, nor this or that Deva, not this or that cow or horse, that had their origin in the Word, but the genus to which they belong, that is, the εἴδη (Âk*ri*tis). It is with the genus that words are connected, not with individuals, for these, as being infinite in number, are not capable of entering into that connection. Hence all individual things, and individual gods also, are allowed to have had an origin, but not the genus to which they belong, which was thought and uttered at first by Brahman. Nor must it be supposed that the Word constitutes the material cause of things; this, as shown before, lies in Brahman only, which is therefore more than the Word. The word of the Veda is simply the expression of what is permanent and eternal in all things (*universalia in rebus*), and as all individual things are created in accordance with it, they are rightly said to have their true origin in the Veda and in Brahman. This is afterwards confirmed by passages from *S*ruti and Sm*ri*ti, such as B*ri*h. Âr. Up. I, 2, 4: 'Then with his mind he united himself with Speech.' The Word therefore, or Speech, existed before creation, as we read in the Smriti also, e. g. the Mahâbhârata XII, 8534: 'He who exists by himself let first stream forth the Word, the eternal, without beginning or end, the Divine Word which we read in the Veda, whence proceeded the evolution of the world;' and again, Mahâbh. XII, 8535: 'God in the beginning created the names and forms of things, and the continuous process of their works.'

If we read such passages carefully, it is easy to see that Veda, which is identified with the words of creation, or the ideas or *logoi* of the world, was meant for more than what was afterwards called the three Vedas, the Samhitâs, and Brâhmanas. Veda stands here for *Logos* or *Sophia*, and comprehends all named concepts, necessary for the creation of all created things.

In order to show that there is nothing strange in this, *S*amkara remarks that even we ourselves, when we mean to do anything, have first to think of the word for what we mean to do. In the same manner the words of the Veda had to be present to the mind of the Creator, Pragâpati, before he could have created the things corresponding to them. And thus it is said in the Veda (Taitt. Br. II, 2, 4, 2): '"This is the earth," he said, and created the earth.' This will sound strange to many readers, as, I confess, it sounded strange to me when I first came across these thoughts, so full of Neo-platonic reminiscences, nay even to such O. T. thought as 'God spake, Let there be light, and there was light.' Of course, if we can bring ourselves to say that the *Logos* of the Alexandrian philosophers had no antecedents in early Greek philosophy[1], there would be an end of the whole question, and we should simply have to admit that Brâhmans came to Alexandria, and indoctrinated pagan and Christian philosophers with their ideas of Vâ*k* or Speech. But as every Greek scholar knows that the very opposite is the case, and I have tried to show this on several occasions, the question requires a very different solution from that proposed by Professor Weber, if indeed it admits of any. Why will people not see that it is far more scholarlike to confess our ignorance than to give an answer, however hesitatingly, and thus to discourage further research?

Hindu philosophers have treated this whole question with so much care that we can see at least that they truly cared for it, and had fully perceived its intimate connection with some of the highest problems, both religious and philosophical, which were nearest to their heart.

They begin with the beginning and try first to make it clear to themselves what *S*abda is. *S*abda means word, but it also means sound, and they therefore begin with asking what sound is. We have seen already that they actually postulated a fifth element Âkâsa, which we translate by ether, and which was meant to be the vehicle of sound and of sound only. The existence of this fifth element was altogether denied by the materialists, the Bârhaspatyas, because it is supersensible, but it was admitted as an independent element by the other schools of thought, even by the Buddhists, because

---

[1] See Anathon Aall, Geschichte der Logosidee, 1896, pp. 218 seq.

they held that air could not possibly be the vehicle of sound. Its loudness might depend on it, but not its quality. The Vaiseshika-philosophy, for instance, which takes a special interest in the question of the elements, explains sound as the object apprehended by the sense of hearing (II, 2, 21). It then declares that sound is neither substance nor action, but a quality (cf. I, 1, 6 com.), having Âkâsa or ether for its substance. The opinion that sound exists always and eternally, and is only made manifest by each speaker, which is held by the Mîmâmsakas, is rejected by Kanâda, sounds and words being accepted as momentary manifestations only of eternal sound. This is illustrated by the striking of a drum with a drumstick, where we can clearly see that sound is produced by a conjunction between a drum and a drumstick, and that it is only carried along by the air.

All these arguments are clearly directed against the Mîmâmsakas who for reasons of their own require Sabda, whether sound or word, to be eternal. It must be said, however, to their honour that they allow full credit to the Pûrvapakshin who opposes the eternal character of sounds and words. 'No,' he says[1], 'sound cannot be eternal, because we see (1) that it is a product, (2) that it passes away. (3) that it is made (the very letters being called A-kâra, Ka-kâra &c., A-making, Ka-making &c.). We see (4) that it is perceived by different persons at once, (5) that it changes (as Dadhi Atra changes to Dadhy Atra), and (6) that it is augmented by the number of those who make it. But to all these

---

[1] Cf. Ballantyne's Mîmâmsâ-Sûtras, p. 8; Muir, Orig. Sansk. Texts, III, pp. 70 seq.

difficulties the Mîmâmsaka has a ready answer. The word is eternal, he says, and though the perception of sound is the same on both sides, we are right in looking on sound as eternal and as always present, only not always manifested on account of the absence of an utterer or an exciter. The letter k, now heard, is the same which has always been heard. If it is said that sound is made, that only means that it is employed, and if it is perceived at the same time by many, the same applies to the sun. As to the modification of sound, it is not the same letter modified, but it is another letter in the place of a letter, and as to the increase of noise, that is due to the increase of the number of conjunctions and disjunctions of the air.

*G*aimini's reasons in support of the eternal character of sound are that, though the sound may vanish, it leaves its traces in the mind of the hearer or learner; that it is everywhere at the same time; that, if repeated, it is the same, and that we have no right to suppose that it is ever annihilated. If it should be supposed that sound is a mere modification of air, the answer is that the ear does not simply hear the air, but is sensitive only to what is intangible in sound, the quality. Besides, there are the definite words of the Veda which tell us of an eternal Voice.

Having thus established to his own satisfaction the eternity of sound, *G*aimini proceeds to defend the sounds or words of the Veda against all possible objections. These arguments were examined by us before, when the authorship of the Veda had to be discussed, and when it was shown that the author of the Veda could not have been a personal being, but that the Veda could only have been seen by inspired Rishis as revealed to them, not as made by them. We may therefore at once proceed to the next point, namely, to the question, as to what constitutes a word, and what according to Indian philosophers is its real character. Though these discussions are of a grammatical rather than of a philosophical character, they deserve our attention, because they show how keen an interest the ancient philosophers of India had taken in the Science of Language, and how clearly they had perceived the intimate relation between language and thought, and in consequence between the Science of Language and the Science of Thought or Philosophy.

How well the Hindus understood that the study of language forms an integral part of philosophy, we may gather from the fact that they actually admitted Pâ*n*ini, their greatest grammarian, among their representative philosophers. They had evidently perceived that language is the only phenomenal form of thought, and that, as human beings possess no means of perceiving the thoughts of others, nay even their own thoughts, except in the form of words, it was the duty of a student of thought to inquire into the nature of words before he approached or analysed the nature of what we mean by thought, naked thought, nay skinned thought, as it has been truly called, when divested of its natural integuments, the words. They understood what even modern philosophers have failed to understand, that there is a difference between *Vorstellung* (presentation or percept) and *Begriff* (concept), and that true thought has to do with conceptual words only, nay that the two, word and thought, are inseparable, and perish when separated. Mâdhava in his survey of all philosophies, assigns a place between *G*aimini's Pûrva Mîmâ*m*sâ and Kapila's Sâ*m*khya to the Pâ*n*ini Darsana, what we should call the grammatical system of Pâ*n*ini. Other systems also treat most fully of linguistic questions, as, for instance, the Pûrva-Mîmâ*m*sâ when treating of the question whether sound, the material element of words, is eternal or not.

### Spho*ta*.

Hindu philosophers have actually elaborated an idea which does not exist in any other philosophy, that of Spho*ta*. It is true that in Pâ*n*ini's own Sûtras the word Spho*ta* does not occur, but the name of a grammarian whom he quotes (VI, 1, 123), Spho*t*âyana, shows that this peculiar word Spho*ta* must have existed before Pâ*n*ini's time. Derived as it is from Sphu*t*, Spho*ta* must have meant originally what bursts forth. It has been translated by expression, notion, concept or idea, but none of these renderings can be considered as successful. It really means the sound of a word as a whole, and as conveying a meaning, apart from its component letters. The subject has been well treated by Mâdhava in his Sarva-dar*s*ana-sa*m*graha. Here, when examining the Pâ*n*ini Dar*s*ana, he shows first of all that the *S*abda or word which Pâ*n*ini professes to teach in his *S*abdânu*s*âsana, or grammar, is really the same as Brahman. 'The eternal word,' he writes, 'which is called Spho*ta*, and is without parts, is the true cause of the world,' is in fact Brahman, and he adds thereupon some lines from

Bhart*ri*hari's Brahmakâ*nd*a, where that grammarian (died 650 A.D.) says :—

'Brahman, without beginning or end, the indestructible essence of language,
Which developed in the form of things, and whence springs the creation of the world.'

What more could be said of the Neo-platonic Logos?

In answer to some who deny the existence of such a Spho*t*a, it is maintained that it is actually an object of perception, for all men, on hearing the word 'cow,' know it as distinct from the letters composing it. This shows, as we knew already from the Prâtisâkhyas, that the Hindus had elaborated the idea of letters, nay even of vowels and consonants, long before they became acquainted with the written letters of a Semitic alphabet, and I only wonder that those who believe in an ancient indigenous alphabet, should never have appealed, though vainly, to the discussions of Spho*t*a, in support of their opinion. And if it were said that cognition arises from the separate letters of a word, we ask, he says, whether these letters are supposed to produce cognition in their collective or in their separate form. It cannot be in their collective form, because each letter, as soon as pronounced, vanishes, and therefore cannot form a whole; nor can it be in their separate form, because no single letter has the power of producing cognition of the meaning of any word. As therefore the letters, whether in their single or their united form, cannot produce cognition, there must be something else by means of which knowledge is produced, and that is the Spho*t*a, the sound, distinct from the letters though revealed by them. He then quotes from Patañgali's Mahâbhâshya: 'Now what is the word Cow? It is that by which, when pronounced, there is produced in us the simultaneous cognition of dewlap, tail, hump, hoofs, and horns.' Kaiya*t*a explains this more fully by saying: 'Grammarians maintain that it is the word, as distinct from the letters, which expresses the meaning, since, if the letters expressed it, there would be no use in pronouncing the second and following ones (as the first would already have conveyed all that is wished). It is therefore something distinct from the single letters which conveys the meaning, and that is what we call the Spho*t*a.'

The objector, however, is not silenced at once. He, too, asks the question whether this Spho*t*a is manifest or non-manifest. If it required no manifestation, it would always be there, but if it requires manifestation, this could be by its letters only, when they are pronounced; and thus the same difficulties which were pointed out before as to the collective or single action of letters, would arise again. This dilemma is put forward by Bha*tt*a in his Mîmâ*m*sâ-*s*loka-vârttika: 'The grammarian who holds that Spho*t*a is manifested by the letters as they are severally pronounced and apprehended, though itself one and indivisible, does not thereby escape from a single difficulty.'

On this point Pâ*n*ini (I, 4, 14) seems to have given the right solution, by laying it down as a principle that letters can never form a word unless they have an affix at the end, while the letters, as they are apprehended, simply help to convey the meaning by means of a conventional association (θέσει). This shows that the conventional character of the relation between sound and meaning was fully recognised in India, whether that sound was called *S*abda or Spho*t*a. Nor is it enough that the letters should be the same, they must also follow each other in the same order, otherwise Vasa and Sava, Nava and Vana, &c., would carry the same meaning, which they do not.

All this was meant to show that the admission of a Spho*t*a was unnecessary; but we now get the orthodox answer, namely, that the admission of Spho*t*a is necessary, and that all the objections are no more than a catching at a straw by a drowning person, because separate letters would never be a word, as little as flowers without a string would be a wreath. And as the letters cannot combine, being evanescent as soon as they have been pronounced, we are asked to admit a Spho*t*a, and to accept the first letters, as revealing the invisible Spho*t*a, whereas the following letters serve only to make that Spho*t*a more and more manifest and explicit.

### Words express the *Summum Genus.*

After having thus in his own way established the theory of a Spho*t*a for every word, our philosophical grammarian takes another step, trying to prove that the meaning of all words is ultimately that *summum genus* (Sattâ), namely pure existence, the characteristic of which is consciousness of the supreme reality. And lest it should be thought that in that case all words would mean one and the same thing, namely Brahman or being, it is remarked that in one sense this is really so; but that, as a crystal is coloured by its surroundings, Brahman, when connected with different things and severally identified with each, stands afterwards for different species, such as cow, horse, &c., these being first of all 'existence' (Sattâ) or the highest genus, as found in individuals, and then only what they are in this phenomenal world. In support of this another passage of Bhartrihari's is quoted: 'Existence being divided, as found in cows, &c., is called this or that species by means of its connection with different objects, and on it all words depend. This they call the meaning of the stem, and the meaning of the root. This is existence, this is the great Âtman (or Brahman), expressed by affixes such as Tva, Tal, &c., which form abstract nouns, such as Go-tva, cow-hood, &c. For existence, as the *summum genus*, is found in all things, in cows, horses, &c., and therefore all words, expressive of definite meanings, rest ultimately on the *summum genus*, existence, differentiated by various thoughts or words, such as cows, horses, &c., in which it resides. If the stem-word, the Prâtipadika, expresses existence, the root expresses Bhâva, a state, or, as others say, Kriyâ, action.'

This will remind us of many of the speculations of Greek as well as medieval logicians; and it is exactly what my late friend Noiré tried to establish, that all words originally expressed action, to which I added the amendment that they expressed either an action or a status. If this true kernel of every word is by Hindu philosophers called the Great Âtman (Mahân Âtmâ), and Sattâ, the *summum genus*, we must remember that, according to the Vedânta, Brahman is the true substance of everything. This is stated again by Bhartrihari:—

'The true reality is known under its illusory forms, by words under untrue disguises; the true reality is named (for a time), like the house of Devadatta, so called for a vanishing reason (that is, only so long as Devadatta is the possessor of the house); but by the word house, pure household[1] only is expressed.'

### Words Expressive of Genera or Individuals?

But while the meaning of all words is thus admitted to be Brahman, we meet with two schools, the one of Vâ*g*apyâyana, maintaining that our ordinary words mean a genus, the other, of Vyâ*d*i, who holds that they mean individual things. Pâ*n*ini holds both views as true in grammar, for in one place, I, 2, 58, he shows that 'a Brâhman' may mean many Brâhmans, as when we say, that a Brâhman is to be honoured; in another, I, 2, 64, he states that the plural Râmas means always Râma, Râma and Râma, i.e. so many single Râmas.

### All Words mean τὸ ὄν.

The idea that all words in the end mean Brahman, the one Supreme Being, was necessitated by the very character of the Vedânta-philosophy, which admits of no duality except as the result of nescience. Hence it is said: The Supreme Being is the thing denoted by all words, and it is identical with the word; but the relation of the two, while they are ultimately identical, varies as it does in the case of the two Âtmans, the Paramâtman and the *G*îvâtman, the highest or universal, and the living or individual

[1] Read G*r*ihatvam instead of G*r*ihîtam?

soul, the difference between the two being due to Avidyâ or temporary nescience. As early as the Maitrâyana Upanishad we meet with verses to the same effect, and of an earlier date than itself, such as (VI, 22), 'Two Brahmans have to be meditated on, the Word and the Non-word, and by the Word alone is the Non-word revealed.' In this way the grammatical philosophers endeavoured to prove that grammar or exposition of words, as it was called by Patañgali (Sabdânusâsana), is, like every other system of philosophy, 'the means of final beatitude, the door of emancipation, the medicine of the diseases of language, the purifier of all sciences, the science of sciences; it is the first rung on the ladder that leads up to final bliss, and the straight royal road among all the roads that lead to emancipation.'

This may be accepted as representing the views, if not of Pânini himself, at least of his followers; and I must say that if his explanation of a word as a number of letters ending in a suffix had been accepted, there would have been no necessity for the admission of a Sphota. It was evidently not seen by the inventors of this Sphota that letters have no independent existence at all, and can be considered only as the result of a scientific analysis, and that words existed long before even the idea of letters had been formed. Letters, by themselves, have no *raison d'être*. Sphota is in fact the word before it had been analysed into letters, the breaking forth of a whole and undivided utterance, such as Go, 'cow,' conveying a meaning which does not depend on any single letter nor on any combination of them. Though from our point of view the idea of such a Sphota may seem unnecessary, we cannot help admiring the ingenuity of the ancient philosophers of India in inventing such a term, and in seeing difficulties which never attracted the attention of European philosophers. For it is perfectly true that the letters, as such, have no reality and no power, and that every word is something different from its letters, something undivided and indivisible. In such a word as Vâ*k*, Vox, we have not a combination of three letters v, â, *k*, which would be nothing, but we have an indivisible explosion, expressive of its meaning in its undivided form only, and this may be raised to the status of a word by means of a grammatical suffix which, as we should say, makes an organised whole of it. All this is true and recognised now by all students of the Science of Language, though never even suspected by the philosophers of other countries.

Still more important is the idea that all words originally meant Brahman or τὸ ὄν, and receive their special meaning from their relation to the genera or *logoi* in the mind of Brahman, as creative types. Words are not names of individuals, but always of classes or genera, and as genera they are eternal. These *logoi* existed before the creation of the world, nay, rendered that creation possible. This is the much-despised Neo-platonic philosophy, the basis of the Christian theory of creation; and that we should find it so fully elaborated in the ancient world of India is surely a surprise, and, I should add, a welcome surprise. And can we suppose that ideas which, in Greece, required so many evolutions of thought till they reached the point which they reached in Alexandria, and afterwards in Palestine, should have sprung up in India suddenly or, as it were, casually? Do we not rather see clearly here also how long and how continuous a development of thought must have taken place south of the Himâlayas before such fruits could have ripened? Would any Greek scholar dare to say that all this was borrowed from Greece? Would any Sanskrit scholar be so intrepid as to hint that the Greeks might possibly have learnt their *Logos* from the Vedic Vâ*k*? Even if we do not accept the last results of this Indian line of thought, which ended where Greek philosophy ended, and where Christian philosophy began, nay even if we should put aside as unintelligible the beginning words of the fourth Gospel, 'In the beginning was the Word,' we can at least admire the struggle which led up to this view of the world, and tried to establish the truth that there is a *Logos*, thought, that there is Rhyme and Reason in the world, and that the whole universe is full of Brahman, the Eternal and the Divine, not visible to the human eye, though visible to the human mind. That mind, according to Indian philosophy, has its true being in the Divine Mind, in which it lives and moves, in which alone it has its true Self or Âtman, which Âtman is Brahman. To have mounted to such heights, even if we have to descend again frightened and giddy, must have strengthened the muscles of human reason, and will remain in our memory as a sight never to be forgotten, even in the lower spheres in which we have to move in our daily life and amidst our daily duties. Speaking for myself, I am bound to say that I have felt an acquaintance with the general spirit of Indian philosophy as a blessing from my very youth, being strengthened by it against all the antinomies of being and thinking, and nerved in all the encounters with the scepticism and materialism of our own ephemeral philosophy. It is easy, no doubt, to discover blemishes in the form and style of Indian philosophy, I mean chiefly the Vedânta, and to cite expressions which at first sight seem absurd. But there are such blemishes and such absurdities in all philosophies, even in the most modern. Many people have smiled at the Platonic ideas, at the atoms of Democritus, or at the location of the soul in the pineal gland or in certain parts of the brain; yet all this belongs to the history of philosophy, and had its right place in it at the right time. What the historian of philosophy has to do is first of all to try to understand the thoughts of great philosophers, then to winnow what is permanent from what is temporary, and to discover, if possible, the vein of gold that runs through the quartz, to keep the gold, and to sweep away the rubbish. Why not do the same for Indian philosophy? Why not try to bring it near to us, however far removed from it we may seem at first sight. In all other countries philosophy has railed at religion and religion has railed at philosophy. In India alone the two have always worked together harmoniously, religion deriving its freedom from philosophy, philosophy gaining its spirituality from religion. Is not that something to make us think, and to remind us of the often-repeated words of Terence, *Humani nihil a me alienum puto*? A rich kernel is often covered by a rough skin, and true wisdom may be hiding where we least expect it.

### Vedânta on Sphota.

We have now to see what the other systems of philosophy have to say on this subject, for it is quite clear that the idea of a Spho*t*a, though known to them, was not accepted by all. *Sam*kara, as representing the Vedânta-philosophy, is entirely opposed to the admission of a Spho*t*a. He fully admits that earth and all the rest were created according to the words earth, &c., which were present to the mind of the Creator, but he asks, how were these words present? Beginning as usual with the Pûrvapakshin [1] or opponent, he produces as arguments in favour of the admission of a Spho*t*a, that the letters cannot convey the meaning, because as soon as they are pronounced they perish, because they differ according to the pronunciation of each speaker, because they possess neither singly nor collectively any significative power, because not even the last letter with the impression left by the preceding letter in our memory, would convey to us the sense of a word. Hence something different from the letters must be admitted, the Spho*t*a, the outburst of the whole word, presenting itself all at once as the object of our mental act of apprehension. That Spho*t*a is what is eternal, different .therefore from perishable and changeable letters, and it is that Spho*t*a from which whatever is denoted by it was produced in creation, and which in conversation conveys to others what is in our own mind, but always clothed in sound.

*Sam*kara himself, however, considers such an admission of a Spho*t*a entirely unnecessary, and, in order to prove this, he goes back and calls to

---

[1] Ved. Sûtras I, 3, 28. This is one of the cases where the Pûrvapaksha, the opponent's view, has been mistaken for *Sam*kara's own final opinion, or for the Siddhânta.

his aid an old Vedântist, Upavarsha, whom he refers to elsewhere also (III, 3, 53)[1]. This Upavarsha argues that the letters by themselves constitute the word, because though they perish as fast as they are pronounced, they are always recognised again as the same letters, not only as belonging to the same class, but as actually the same. Thus when the word cow is pronounced twice, we do not think that two words have been pronounced, but that the same word has been pronounced twice. And though two individuals may, no doubt, pronounce the same word differently, such differences are due to the organs of pronunciation, and not to the intrinsic nature of the letters. He holds that the apprehension of difference depends on external factors, but that their recognition is due only to the intrinsic nature of the letters. The sound which enters the ear (Dhvani) may be different, strong or weak, high or low, but the letters through all this are recognised as the same. And if it be said that the letters of a word, being several, cannot form the object of one mental act, this is not so, because the ideas which we have of a row, or a wood, or an army, show that things which comprise several unities can become objects of one and the same act of cognition. And if it be asked why groups of letters such as Pika and Kapi should convey different meanings, viz. cuckoo and ape, we have only to look at a number of ants, which as long as they move one after another in

---

[1] Here *S*a*m*kara charges *S*abarasvâmin, the famous commentator on the Pûrva-Mimâ*m*sâ, I, 1, 5, with having borrowed an argument from Bâdarâya*n*a.

a certain order, convey the idea of a row, but cease to do so if they are scattered about at random.

Without adducing further arguments, *Sam*kara in the end maintains that the admission of a Spho*t*a is unnecessary, and that it is simpler to accept the letters of a word as having entered into a permanent connection with a definite sense, and as always presenting themselves in a definite order to our understanding, which, after apprehending the several letters, finally comprehends the entire aggregate as conveying a definite sense. We never perceive a Spho*t*a, he argues, and if the letters are supposed to manifest the Spho*t*a, the Spho*t*a in turn would have to manifest the sense. It would even be preferable to admit that letters form a genus, and as such are eternal, but in either case we should gain nothing by the Spho*t*a that we could not have without it, by the admission of eternal words from which all non-eternal things, such as gods, cows, and horses, originated. Hence we see that, though the theory of the Spho*t*a is rejected by the Vedânta, the eternal character of the words is strenuously retained, being considered essential, as it would seem, in order to maintain the identity of Brahman and the Word, and the creation of the world by Brahman in accordance with the eternal words.

### Yoga and Sâ*m*khya on Spho*t*a.

The Yoga-philosophy accepted the theory of the Spho*t*a, nay it has been supposed to have first originated it[1], for, according to the commentary,

---

[1] Garbe, Sâ*m*khya-Philosophie, p. 111 n.

it was against the Yoga-philosophers, rather than against the Mîmâmsâ, that Kapila's objections concerning the Sphota were directed. What Kapila says about Sphota is of much the same character as what he had said about Îsvara, the Lord, namely that its existence cannot be proved, not that it does not exist. If Sphota, he says, is meant for the group of letters forming a word, then why not be satisfied with this, and simply speak of a word (Pada), as manifesting its sense? Why invent something which has never been perceived, and which exists as little apart from the letters as a forest exists apart from the trees, what is in fact entirely gratuitous (V, 57).

Nor are the letters, from Kapila's point of view, eternal (V, 58), because, as Bâdarâyana also remarked, we can witness their production; and our being able to recognise them as the same, proves no more than their belonging to one and the same genus, but not their being eternal.

It is curious to observe the elaborateness with which what seems to us a purely grammatical question is discussed in the various schools of Indian philosophy. The Sphota, however, is to Indian thinkers not merely a grammatical problem; it is distantly connected with the question of the eternity of the Veda. This eternity is denied by Kapila (Sâmkhya V, 46) because the Vedas speak of themselves as having been produced in such passages as: 'He became heated, and from him, thus heated, the three Vedas were produced.' Eternity of the Veda can therefore, according to Kapila, mean no more than an unbeginning and unbroken continuity, so that even at the beginning of a new creation the order of words in the Veda remains the same as before. But if, as Nyâya and Vaiseshika maintain, this Veda was the work of a personal being, such as Îsvara, this is declared impossible by Kapila, because, as he holds, such an Îsvara has never been proved to exist. For he holds that the Lord or Îsvara could only have been either a liberated or an unliberated Purusha. Now a liberated Purusha, such as Vishnu for instance, could not have composed this enormous Veda, because he is free from all desires, nor could an active, non-liberated Purusha have been the author, because he would not have possessed the omniscience required for such a work.

But we must not conclude that, because we know of no possible personal author, therefore the Veda is eternal, in the same way as germs and sprouts. What is called the work of a personal being always presupposes a corporeal person, and it presupposes a will. We should not call the mere breathing of a person in sleep, a personal work. But the Vedas, as we read, rise spontaneously like an exhalation from the Highest Being, not by any effort of will, but by some miraculous virtue. It must not be supposed that the words of the Veda are manifested, like the notes of birds, without any purpose or meaning. No, they are the means of right knowledge, and their innate power is proved by the wonderful effects which are produced, for instance, by medical formulas taken from the Âyur-veda. This is the same argument which was used in the Nyâya-Sûtras II, 68, as a tangible and irrefutable proof of the efficiency of the Vedas. Here all would depend on the experimental proof, and this the Hindus, ancient or modern, would find it difficult to supply; but if the Hindus were satisfied, we have no reason to find fault.

### Nyâya on Sphota.

If now we turn to the Nyâya-philosophy we find that Gotama also denies the eternity of sound, because, it is argued, we can see that it has a beginning or cause, because it is an object of sense-perception, and because it is known to be factitious. Besides, if sound were eternal, we should be able to perceive it always, even before it is uttered, there being no known barrier between the ether and our ear (II, 3, 86). This ethereal substratum of sound is, no doubt, intangible (II, 3, 104), but it is nevertheless a something perceptible by one of our senses, that of hearing, and hence it must be non-eternal. The true eternity of the Vedas consists, according to Gotama, in the unbroken continuity of their tradition, study, and employment, both in the Manvantaras and Yugas which are past and those that are still to come, whilst their authority depends on the authority of the most competent persons. This is the same with secular words [1]. This last admission would of course be strongly resisted and resented by Vedânta philosophers, but it shows at all events the freedom with which all Indian philosophers were allowed to handle the ancient Sacred Books of the country.

---

[1] Vâtsyâyana's Commentary on the Nyâya, p. 91, ed. Biblioth. Indica, Muir, O. S. T., III, p. 115.

### Vai*s*eshika on Spho*t*a.

The Vai*s*eshikas lastly do not differ much from the Naiyâyikas as to whether the Veda is eternal or not, is authoritative or not, but they follow their own way of reasoning. The very last Sûtra of the Vai*s*eshika-Sâstra, X, 2, 9, says: 'It has been declared that authoritativeness belongs to the Âmnâya (Veda) because it is uttered by Him'; and this declaration is found likewise in the third Sûtra of the first book to which the final Sûtra refers. But though this Sûtra is given twice, there attaches some uncertainty to its meaning, because, as pointed out by the native commentators, the words 'because uttered by Him,' may also be translated by 'because it declares it,' i.e. 'because it teaches duty (Dharma).' But in either case there are objections, the same as those with which we are familiar from the Pûrvapaksha in the Vedânta and Mîmâ*m*saka-Sûtras, such as self-contradictoriness, tautology, and the rest discovered by some critics in the text of the Vedas. Thereupon the eternal character, too, of the Veda is called in question, and whoever its author may have been, whether human or divine, it is doubted whether he can justly claim any authority.

In answer to this sweeping condemnation the Vai*s*eshika points out VI, 1, 1, 'that at all events there is in the Veda a construction of sentences consequent upon intelligence,' or as we should say, the Veda must at least be admitted to be the work of a rational author, and not of an author of limited intelligence, because no merely rational author could propound such a rule as 'He who desires paradise, should sacrifice.' Such matters could not be known in their causes and effects to men of limited knowledge like ourselves. Whatever we may think of this argument, it shows at all events the state of mind of the earliest defenders of revelation. They argued that, because the author must at least be admitted to have been a rational being, he could not possibly have declared things that are beyond the knowledge of ordinary rational beings, such as the rewards of sacrifices in another world, and other matters beyond the ken of experience. The Vai*s*eshikas admitted a personal author of the Veda, an Î*s*vara, but this by no means involved the eternity of the Veda. With the Vai*s*eshikas, also, the eternity of the Veda meant no more than its uninterrupted tradition (Sampradâya), but some further supports to its authority were found in the fact that, besides being the work of a rational being, in this case of Î*s*vara, the Lord, it had been accepted as the highest authority by a long line of the great or greatest men who themselves might safely be regarded, if not as infallible, at least as trustworthy and authoritative.

### Prameyas, Objects of Knowledge.

If now, after an examination of the various opinions entertained by the Nyâya and other Hindu philosophers of the significative power of words, we return to the Sûtras of Gotama, we find that, in his third book, he is chiefly concerned with the Prameyas, that is, the objects of knowledge, as established by the Pramâ*n*as ; and the first question that meets us is whether the senses or Indriyas, the instruments of objective knowledge, should be treated as different from the Âtman, the Self, or not.

### Indriyas, Senses.

Gotama holds that they are different from the Âtman; and in order to prove this, he argues, that if each sense could perceive by itself, each sense would perceive its own object only, the ear sound, the eye colour, the skin warmth, &c.; and that therefore what perceives all these impressions together, at the same time and in the same object, must be something different from the several senses, namely the Âtman, or, according to other systems, the Manas or mind.

### Sarîra, Body.

Next follows the question whether the body is the same as the Âtmán, a question which would never occur to a Vedântist. But Gotama asks it and solves it in his own way. It cannot be, he says, because, when the body has once been destroyed by being burnt, the consequences of good and evil deeds would cease to pursue the Self through an endless series of births and rebirths. A number of similar objections and answers follow, all showing how much this question had occupied the thoughts of the Nyâya philosophers. Some of them suggest difficulties which betray a very low state of philosophical reasoning, while other difficulties are such that even in our own time they have not ceased to perplex minute philosophers. We meet with the question why, with the dual organ of vision, there is no duality of perception; why, if memory is supposed to be a quality or mode of the Self, mere remembrance of an acid substance can make our mouth water. After these questions have been, if not solved, at least carefully considered, Gotama goes on to show that if the body be not Âtman, neither can Manas, mind, be conceived as the Âtman.

### Manas, Mind.

The Self is the knower, while the mind or Manas is only the instrument (Kara*n*a) of knowledge by which attention is fixed on one thing at a time. The Self is eternal, not of this life only, without beginning and therefore without end. And here a curious argument is brought in, different from the usual Indian arguments in support of our previous existence, to show that our Self does not begin with our birth on earth, because, as he says, the smile of a new-born child can only arise from memory of a previous experience. While our modern psycho-physiologists would probably see in the smiles or the cries of a new-born child a reflex action of the muscles, our Indian objector declares that such movements are to be considered as no more than the opening and closing of a lotus-flower. And when this view has been silenced by the remark that a child does not consist of the five elements only, is not in fact, as we should say, a mere vegetable, a new argument of the same character is adduced, namely the child's readiness to suck, which can only be accounted for, they say, by the child having, in a former life, acquired a desire for milk. When this again has been rejected as no argument, because we see that iron also moves towards a magnet, Gotama answers once more that a child cannot be treated like a piece of iron. And when, as a last resource, desire in general, as manifested by a child, is appealed to as showing a child's previous existence, and when this also has once more been answered by the remark that a child, like every other substance, must be possessed of qualities, Gotama finally dismisses all these objectors by maintaining that desires are not simply qualities, but can arise from experience and previous impressions (Sa*m*kalpa) only.

The consideration of the body and of the substances of which it consists, whether of earth only, or of three elements, earth, water and fire, or of four, earth, water, fire and air, or of five, because it displays the qualities of the five, is naturally of small interest in our time. The final solution only deserves our attention, in so far as it clearly shows that the Nyâya also recognised in some cases the authority of the Veda as supreme, by stating that the body is made of earth, and why? '*S*rutiprâmâ*n*yât,' 'because scripture says so.'

What follows, the discussion of sight or of the visual ray proceeding from the eye, and the question whether we possess one general sense only, or many, may contain curious suggestions for the psycho-physiologist; but there is little of what we mean by really philosophic matter in it. The qualities assigned to the objects of perception are not very different from what they are supposed to be in the other systems of philosophy, and they may be passed by here all the more because they will have to be considered more fully when we come to examine the Vaiseshika system.

More interesting is the discussion which occupies the rest of the third book. It is chiefly concerned with the nature of Self (Âtman), the mind (Manas), the difference between the two, and their relation to knowledge. Here we should remember that, according to I, 15, Buddhi (understanding), Upalabdhi (apprehension), and *Gñâna* (knowledge) are used synonymously. Though there are many manifestations of Manas, such as memory, inference, verbal testimony, doubt, imagination, dreaming, cognition, guessing, feeling of pleasure, desire, and all the rest, yet its distinguishing feature, we are told, is what we should call attention, or as Gotama explains it (I, 16), 'the preventing of knowledge arising altogether.' This is declared to be due to attention, and in many cases this would be the best rendering of Manas. Manas is therefore often called the doorkeeper, preventing sensations from rushing in promiscuously and all at once. If therefore we translate Manas by mind, we must always remember its technical meaning in Indian philosophy, and its being originally different from Buddhi, understanding, which might often be rendered by light or the internal light that changes dark and dull impressions into clear and bright sensations, perceptions, and knowledge in general, or by understanding, at least so far as it enables us to transform and understand the dull impressions of the senses.

The difference between the philosophical nomenclatures in English and Sanskrit for the Manas and its various functions is so great that a translation is almost impossible, and I am by no means satisfied with my own. It should also be remembered that the same Sanskrit term has often very different meanings in different systems of philosophy.

The Buddhi of the Nyâya philosophers, for instance, is totally different from the Buddhi of the Sâ*m*khyas. Their Buddhi is eternal, while the Buddhi of Gotama is distinctly declared to be non-eternal.

The Buddhi of the Sâ*m*khya is a cosmic principle independent of the Self, and meant to account for the existence of the light of reason in the whole universe; while in the Nyâya-philosophy it signifies the subjective activity of thought in the acquisition of knowledge, or in the lighting up and appropriating of the inert impressions received by the senses. This knowledge can come to an end and vanish by forgetfulness, while an eternal essence, like the Buddhi of the Sâ*m*khyas, though it may be ignored, can never be destroyed.

### Âtman.

In answering the question, What is knowledge, Gotama declares in this place quite clearly that real knowledge belongs to the Âtman only, the Self or the soul. It cannot belong to the senses and their objects (Indriyârtha), because knowledge abides even when the senses and what they perceive have been suppressed. Nor does knowledge belong to the Manas, which is but the instrument of knowledge, but it arises from the conjunction of Âtman (Self) with Manas (attention), and on the other side of Manas with Indriyas (senses). Manas is the instrument, and the wielder of that instrument, like the wielder of an axe, must be some one different from it; this, according to the Nyâya, can only be the Self who in the end knows, who remembers, who feels pain and pleasure, who desires and acts.

### Memory.

Memory, Sm*ri*ti, has not received from Indian philosophers the attention which it deserves. If it is treated as a means of knowledge, it falls under Anubhava, which is either immediate or mediate, and then called Sm*ri*ti. Every Anubhava is supposed to leave an impression or modification of the mind, which is capable of being revived. There is another manifestation of memory in the act of remembering or recognising, as when on seeing a man we say, This is he, or This is Devadatta. Here we have Anubhava, knowledge of this, joined with something else, namely he or Devadatta, a revived Sa*m*skâra, impression, or Sm*ri*ti. The subject of memory is more fully treated in III, 113, and the various associations which awaken memory are enumerated as follows:—

1. Attention to an object perceived;

2. Connection, as when the word Pramâ*n*a, proof, recalls Prameya, what has to be proved;

3. Repetition, as when one has learned a number of things together, one calls up the other;

4. A sign, as when a thing recalls its *sine quâ non*;

5. A mark, as when a standard reminds one of its bearer;

6. Likeness, as when one body recalls a similar body;

7. Possession, as when a property reminds us of its owner;

8. Belonging, as when royal attendants remind us of the king;

9. Relation, as when a disciple reminds us of the teacher, or kine of a bull;

10. Succession, as when the pounding of rice reminds one of sprinkling;

11. Absence, as of a wife;

12. Fellow-workers, as when one disciple reminds us of the co-disciples;

13. Opposition, as when the ichneumon recalls the snake ;

14. Pre-eminence, as when investiture with the sacred string recalls the principal agent, the Guru or teacher ;

15. Receiving, as when a gift reminds one of the giver ;

16. Covering, as when a sword reminds one of the sheath ;

17. Pleasure and pain, each of which recalls the occasioner of it ;

18. Desire and aversion, reminding us of their causes ;

19. Fear, reminding us of what is feared, such as death ;

20. Want, which makes us think of those who can supply our wants ;

21. Motion, as when a shaking branch reminds us of the wind ;

22. Affection, reminding us of a son, &c. ;

23. Merit and Demerit, which make us reflect on joys and sorrows of a former life.

Such lists are very characteristic of Hindu philosophy, and they show at the same time that it is a mistake to ascribe them exclusively to the Sâ*m*khya-philosophy. Though they do not add much to our knowledge of the fundamental tenets of Indian philosophy, they show once more how much thought had been spent in the elaboration of mere details ; and this, as we are told in this case by the commentator himself, chiefly in order to stir up the thoughts of the learners, *S*ishyavyutpâdanâya, to independent activity.

### Knowledge not Eternal.

The important point, however, which Gotama wishes to establish is this, that knowledge, though belonging to the eternal Self, is not in itself eternal, but vanishes like any other act. He also guards against the supposition that as we seem to take in more than one sensation at the same time, as in eating a cake full of different kinds of sweets, we ought to admit more than one Manas; and he explains that this simultaneousness of perception is apparent only, just as the fiery circle is when we whirl a firebrand with great rapidity, or as we imagine that a number of palm-leaves are pierced by a pin at one blow, and not in succession, one after the other. Lastly, he states that the Manas is A*n*u, infinitely small, or, as we should say, an atom.

### More Prameyas.

While the third book was occupied with the first six of the Prameyas, or objects to be known and proved, including the whole apparatus of knowledge, such as Âtman, Self or soul, Indriyas, senses, Manas, mind, central sensorium, Buddhi, understanding, and *S*arîra, body, and therefore gave rise to some important questions not only of metaphysics, but of psychology also, the fourth book which is devoted to the remaining six Prameyas, such as (7) Prav*r*itti (activity), (8) Dosha (faults), (9) Pretyabhâva (transmigration), (10) Phala (rewards), (11) Du*h*kha (pain), and (12) Apavarga (final beatitude), is naturally of a more practical character, and less attractive to the student of the problems of being and thinking. Some questions, however, are treated in it which cannot well be passed over, if we wish to give a full insight into the whole character, and the practical bearing of the Nyâya-philosophy.

Though this philosophy is supposed to represent Indian logic only, we have already seen enough of it to know that it included almost every question within the sphere of philosophy and religion, and that its chief object was the same as that of all the other systems of Indian philosophy, namely salvation.

### Life after Death.

One of the seven interesting subjects treated here is Pretyabhâva, literally existence after having departed this life, and this is proved in a very short way. As the Self has been proved to be eternal, Gotama says (IV, 10) it follows that it will exist after what is called death. Some of the objections made to this tenet are easily disposed of, but nothing is said to establish what is meant by transmigration, that is being born again in another world as either a human or as some other animal being, or even as a plant.

### Existence of Deity.

Another important subject, if it is not passed over altogether, is treated by Gotama, as it was by Kapila, incidentally only, I mean the existence of a Deity. It comes in when a problem of the Buddhists is under discussion, namely, whether the world came out of nothing, and whether the manifestation of anything presupposes the destruction of its cause. This is illustrated by the fact that the seed has to perish before the flower can appear. But Gotama strongly denies this, and reminds the opponent that if the seed were really destroyed by being pounded or burnt, the flower would never appear. Nor could it be said that the flower, if it had not existed previously, destroyed the seed, while, if it had, it would have owed its existence to the simple destruction of the seed. Therefore, he continues, as nothing can be produced from nothing, nor from an annihilated something, like a seed, the world also cannot have sprung from nothingness, but requires the admission of an Îsvara, the Lord, as its real cause. And this admission of an Îsvara, even though in the capacity of a governor rather than of a maker of the world, is confirmed by what was evidently considered by Gotama as a firmly established truth, namely, that every act of man invariably produces its result, though not by itself, but under the superintendence of some one, that is, of Îsvara. We then meet with a new argument, different from that of the Mîmâmsakas, namely that, if work done continued to work entirely by itself, the fact that some good or evil deeds of men do not seem to receive their reward would remain unaccounted for. This is certainly a curious way of proving the existence of God by the very argument which has generally been employed by those who want to prove His non-existence. Gotama's real object, however, is to refute the Buddhist theory of vacuity (Sûnya), or of Nothing being the cause of the world, and afterwards to disprove the idea that effects can ever be fortuitous. And as Gotama differs from Gautama in denying the origin of the world out of nothing, he also differs from the Sâmkhya philosophers, who hold that all things, as developed out of Prakriti, are real only so long as they are noticed by the Purusha. He holds, on the contrary, that some things are real and eternal, but others are not, because we actually see both their production and their destruction. If we were to doubt this, we should doubt what has been settled by the authority of all men, and there would be an end of all truth and untruth. This[1] is a novel kind of argument for an Indian philosopher to use, and shows that with all the boldness of their speculations they were not so entirely different from ourselves, and not entirely indifferent to the *Securus judicat orbis terrarum.*

### Cause and Effect.

If, however, we call the Nyâya-philosophy theistic, we should always remember that such terms as theistic and atheistic are hardly applicable to Indian philosophy in the sense in which they are used by Christian theologians. With us atheistic implies the denial of a supreme and absolute Being; but we saw that even the so-called atheism of the Sâ*m*khya-philosophy does not amount to that. It is simply the denial of an Î*s*vara, as an active and personal creator and ruler of the world.

And even such a personal God is not altogether denied by the Sâ*m*khyas; they only deny that He can be proved to exist by human arguments, and if He exists as such, they hold that in the eyes of philosophers He would be but a phenomenal manifestation of the Godhead, liable to change, liable even to temporary disappearance at the end of each aeon, and to reappearance at the beginning of a new aeon. It is this kind of a divine being, a personal Î*s*vara or Lord, that is taken for granted by the

---

[1] Sârvalaukikapramâtva.

Nyâya philosophers, and, it may be added at once, by the Vaiseshika philosophers also[1].

In the Tarka-Samgraha, for instance, it is distinctly stated that 'the Âtman or Self is twofold, the Gîvâtman (personal Self), and the Paramâtman (the Highest Self).' It must not be supposed, however, that Îsvara, the omniscient Lord, is Paramâtman, which is one only, while the Gîvâtman is separate for each individual body, all-pervading and eternal. Though Paramâtman is Îsvara, Îsvara is not Paramâtman, but a phenomenal manifestation of Paramâtman only. The argument which we met with before is fully stated in Gotama's Sûtras, IV, 19–21. The actions of men, it is said, do not always produce an effect. Good actions do not always produce good results, nor bad actions bad results, as they ought, if every act continued to act (Karman). Hence there must be another power that modifies the continuous acting of acts, and that can be Îsvara only. It is not denied thereby that human actions are required, and that no effects would take place without the working of human agents, only they are not the sole cause of what happens, but we require another power, an Îsvara, to account for what would otherwise be irrational results of human actions.

### Phala, Rewards.

We now come to the tenth of the Prameyas, Phala; and here the same subject is treated once more, though from a different point of view. It is

---

[1] Ballantyne, Christianity contrasted with Hindu Philosophy, p. 12; Muir, O. S. T., vol. iii, p. 133.

asked, how are effects, rewards or punishments, possible in another life? As both good and evil works are done in this life, the cause, namely these works, would have ceased to exist long before their fruit is to be gathered. This objection is met by an illustration taken from a tree which bears fruit long after it has ceased to be watered. The objector is not, however, satisfied with this, but, on the contrary, takes a bolder step, and denies that any effect either is or is not, or is or is not, at the same time. Gotama is not to be frightened by this apparently Buddhistic argument, but appeals again to what we should call the common-sense view of the matter, namely, that we actually see production and destruction before our very eyes. We can see every day that a cloth, before it has been woven, does not exist, for no weaver would say that the threads are the cloth, or the cloth the threads. And if it should be argued that the fruit produced by a tree is different from the fruit of our acts, because there is no receptacle (Â*s*raya) or, as we should say, no subject, this is met by the declaration that, in the case of good or bad acts, there is a permanent receptacle, namely the Self, which alone is capable of perceiving pain or joy in this or in any other state of existence.

### Emancipation.

After examining the meaning of pain, and expressing his conviction that everything, even pleasure, is full of pain, Gotama at last approaches the last subject, emancipation (Apavarga). He begins as usual with objections, such as that it is impossible in this life to pay all our moral debts, that certain sacrificial duties are enjoined as incumbent on us to the end of our lives, and that if it is said that a man is freed from these by old age, this does not imply that, even when he is no longer able to perform his daily duties, he should not perform certain duties, if in thought only. If, therefore, good works continue, there will be rewards for them, in fact there will be paradise, though even this would really have to be looked upon as an obstacle to real emancipation. Nothing remains but a complete extinction of all desires, and this can be effected by knowledge of the truth only. Therefore knowledge of the truth or removal of all false notions, is the beginning and end of all philosophy, and of the Nyâya-philosophy in particular. The first step towards this is the cessation of Aha*m*kâra, here used in the sense of personal feelings, such as desire for a beautiful and aversion to a deformed object. Desire therefore has to be eradicated and aversion also; but before he explains how this desire, which arises from false apprehension (Mithyâ*g*ñâna) can be eradicated, Gotama is carried back once more to a subject which had been discussed before, namely whether the objects of desire exist as wholes or as parts. And this leads him on to what is the distinguishing doctrine both of the Nyâya and of the Vai*s*eshika-philosophies, namely the admission of A*n*us or atoms. If wholes are constantly divided and subdivided, we should in the end be landed in nihilism, but this is not to be. There cannot be annihilation because the A*n*us or the smallest parts are realities (IV, 8–82), and, according to their very nature, cannot be further reduced or compressed out of being. Against this view of the existence of what we should call atoms, the usual arguments are then adduced, namely that ether (or space) is everywhere, and therefore in an atom also, and if an atom has figure or a without and a within, it is of necessity divisible. In reply, ether is said to be intangible, neither resistant nor obstructing, that is, neither occupying space against others, nor preventing others from occupying space; and in the end an appeal is made to a recognised maxim of Hindu philosophy, that there must never be a *regressio in infinitum,* as there would be in attempting to divide an atom.

### Knowledge of Ideas, not of Things.

And now the opponent, again, it would seem, a Buddhist, makes a still bolder sweep by denying the existence of any external things. All we have is knowledge, he says, not things; nothing different from our knowledge, or independent of our knowledge, can exist for us. Gotama objects to this (Vidyâmâtra) doctrine, first of all because, if it were impossible to prove the existence of any external things, it would be equally impossible to prove their non-existence. And if an appeal were made to dreams, or visions produced by a mirage, or by jugglery, it should be remembered that dreams also, like remembrances, presuppose previous perception of things; and that even in mistaking we mistake something, so that false knowledge can always be removed by true knowledge. After granting that, one more question arises, how that true knowledge, if once gained, is to be preserved, because we saw that knowledge is not eternal, but vanishes. And here the Nyâya suddenly calls the Yoga to its aid, and teaches that Samâdhi or intense meditation will prove a safe preservative of knowledge, in spite of all disturbances from without, while the Nyâya-philosophy retains its own peculiar usefulness as employed in the defence of truth against all comers, in which case even such arts as wrangling and cavilling may prove of service.

This may seem a very humble view to take with regard to a system of philosophy which at the very outset promised to its students final beatitude as the highest reward. But considering the activity of philosophical speculation, of which we have had so many indications in the ancient as well as in the modern history of India, we can well understand that philosophers, skilled in all the arts and artifices of reasoning, would secure for their system that high position which the Nyâya certainly held and still holds[1] among the recognised systems of orthodox philosophy. It would be useless to go once more over the topics from *G*âti, futility, No. XIV, to No. XVI, Nigrahasthâna, objectionable proceedings, which are fully treated in the fifth book.

### Syllogism.

There is one subject, however, which requires some more special consideration, namely the Syllogism, or the Five Members, treated as VII. This has always excited the special interest of European logicians on account of certain startling similarities which no doubt exist between it and the syllogism of Aristotle and the schoolman. But from a Hindu point of view this syllogism or even logic in general

---

[1] Cowell, Report on the Toles of Nuddea, 1867.

is by no means the chief object of the Nyâya-philosophy, nor is it its exclusive property. It has been fully discussed in the Vedânta and Sâmkhya systems, and once more in the Vaiseshika; but as it forms the pride of the Nyâya, it will find its most appropriate place here[1].

As we saw colour mentioned as the distinguishing quality of light, we found knowledge put forward as the characteristic feature of Self. The Nyâya looks upon knowledge as inseparably connected with the Self, though in the larger sense of being the cause of every conception that has found expression in language. Knowledge, according to the Nyâya, is either perception or remembrance. Perception again is twofold, right or wrong. Right perception represents a thing such as it is, silver as silver. This is called truth, Pramâ. Wrong perception represents a thing as it is not, mother-of-pearl as silver.

This right perception, according to the Nyâya-philosophy is, as we saw, of four kinds, sensuous, inferential, comparative, and authoritative, and is produced by perception, by inference, by comparison, and by revealed authority. Here we are brought back to the Pramânas again which were discussed in the beginning, but among which one, Anumâna or inference, receives here a more special treatment. We are thus obliged, in following the Sûtras, to go over some of the ground again. Different systems of philosophy differed, as we saw,

---

[1] See M. M., Appendix to Archbishop Thomson's Laws of Thought; also Die Theorie des indischen Rationalisten von den Erkenntnissmitteln, von R. Garbe, 1888.

in the number of Pramâ*n*as which they admit, according to what each considers the only trustworthy channels of knowledge.

**Pramâ*n*as in different Philosophical Schools.**

*One*, Perception : *K*ârvâkas.

*Two*, Perception and inference : Vai*s*eshikas and Buddhists.

*Three*, Perception, inference, and word (revelation) : Sâ*m*khyas.

*Four*, Perception, inference, revelation, and comparison : Naiyâyikas.

*Five*, Perception, inference, revelation, comparison, and presumption : Prabhâkara (a Mîmâ*m*saka).

*Six*, Perception, inference, revelation, comparison, presumption, and not-being : Mîmâ*m*sakas.

Others admit also Aitihya, tradition, Sambhava, equivalence, *K*esh*t*â, gesture.

After sensuous knowledge, which takes cognisance of substances, qualities, and actions, has been examined, the question arises, how can we know things which are *not* brought to us by the senses? How do we know, for instance, that there is fire which we cannot see in a mountain, or that a mountain is a volcano, when all that we do see is merely that the mountain smokes? We should remember that there were three kinds of Anumâna (Nyâya-Sûtras II, 37) called Pûrvavat, having the sign before, or as the cause, *S*eshavat, having the sign after or as the effect, and Sâmânyatod*ri*sh*t*a, seen together. In the first class the sign of past rain was the swelling of rivers; in the second the sign of coming rain was the ants carrying off their eggs; in the third the sign of the motion of the sun was its being seen in different places. Knowledge of things unseen, acquired in these three ways, is called inferential knowledge (Anumâna), and in order to arrive at it, we are told that we must be in possession of what is called a Vyâpti. This, as we saw, was the most important word in an Indian syllogism. Literally it means pervasion. Vyâpta means pervaded; Vyâpya, what must be pervaded; Vyâpaka, what pervades. This expression, to pervade, is used by logicians in the sense of invariable, inseparable or universal concomitance. Thus sea-water is always pervaded by saltness, it is inseparable from it, and in this sense Vyâpya, what is to be pervaded, came to be used for what we should call the middle term in a syllogism. Vyâpti, or invariable concomitance, may sometimes be taken as a general rule, or even as a general law, in some cases it is simply the *sine quâ non*. It is such a Vyâpti, for instance, that smoke is pervaded by or invariably connected with fire, or, as the Hindus say, that smokiness is pervaded by fieriness, not, however, fieriness by smokiness. We arrive by induction at the Vyâpti that wherever there is smoke, there is fire, but not that wherever there is fire, there is smoke. The latter Vyâpti in order to be true would require a condition or Upâdhi, viz. that the firewood should be moist. If we once are in possession of a true Vyâpti as smokiness being pervaded by fieriness, we only require what is called groping or consideration (Parâmar*s*a) in order to make the smoke, which we see rising from the mountain, a Paksha or member of our Vyâpti, such as 'wherever there is smoke, there is fire.' The conclusion then follows that this mountain which shows smoke, must have fire.

All this may sound very clumsy to European logicians, but it would have been easy enough to translate it into our own more technical language. We might easily clothe Ka*n*âda in a Grecian garb and make him look almost like Aristotle. Instead of saying that inferential knowledge arises from discovering in an object something which is always pervaded by something else, and that the pervading predicate is predicable of all things of which the pervaded predicate is, we might have said that our knowledge that S is P arises from discovering that S is M, and M is P, or with Aristotle, ὁ συλλογισμὸς διὰ τοῦ μέσου τὸ ἄκρον τῷ τρίτῳ δείκνυσιν. What Ka*n*âda calls one member of the pervasion, Paksha, e. g. the smoking mountain, might have been translated by subject or *terminus minor*; what pervades, Vyâpaka or Sâdhya, e. g. fieriness, by predicate or *terminus major*; and what is to be pervaded, Vyâpya, i. e. smokiness, by *terminus medius*. But what should we have gained by this? All that is peculiar to Indian logic would have evaporated, and the remainder might have been taken for a clumsy imitation of Aristotle. *Multa fiunt eadem, sed aliter*, and it is this very thing, this *aliter*, that constitutes the principal charm of a comparative study of philosophy. Even such terms as syllogism or conclusion are inconvenient here, because they have with us an historical colouring and may throw a false light on the subject. The Sanskrit Anumâna is not exactly the Greek συμπέρασμα, but it means measuring something by means of something else. This is done by what we may call syllogism, but what the Hindus describe as Parâmarsa or groping or trying to find in an object something which can be measured by something else or what can become the member of a pervasion. This corresponds in fact to the looking for a *terminus medius*. In Kapila's system (I, 61) the principal object of inference is said to be transcendent truth, that is, truth which transcends the horizon of our senses. Things which cannot be seen with our eyes, are known by inference, as fire is, when what is seen is smoke only. Gotama therefore defines the result of inference (I, 101) as knowledge of the connected, that is, as arising from the perception of a connection or a law. But, again, the relation of what pervades and what is pervaded is very different from what we should call the relative extension of two concepts. This will become more evident as we proceed. For the present we must remember that in the case before us the act of proving by means of Anumâna consists in our knowing that there is in the mountain something always pervaded by, or inseparable from something else, in our case, smoke always pervaded by fire, and that therefore the mountain, if it smokes, has fire.

By this process we arrive at Anumiti, the result of Anumâna, or inferential knowledge, that the mountain is a volcano. So much for the inference for ourselves. Next follows the inference for others.

### Anumâna for Others.

What follows is taken from Anna*m*bha*tt*a's Compendium. 'The act of concluding,' he says, 'is twofold, it being intended either for one's own benefit or for the benefit of others. The former is the means of arriving at knowledge for oneself, and the process is this. By repeated observation, as in the case of kitchen hearths and the like, we are reminded of a rule (Vyâpti), such as that wherever we have seen smoke, we have seen fire. We now approach a mountain and wonder whether there may or may not be fire in it. We see the smoke, we remember the rule, and immediately perceive that the mountain itself is fiery. This is the process when we reason for ourselves.

But if we have to convince somebody else of what we, by inference, know to be true, the case is different. We then start with the assertion, The mountain is fiery. We are asked, Why? and we answer, Because it smokes. We then give our reason, or the major premiss, that all that smokes is fiery, as you may see, for instance, on a kitchen hearth and the like. Now you perceive that the mountain does smoke, and hence you will admit that I was right when I said that the mountain is fiery. This is called the five-membered form of exposition, and the five members are severally called [1],—

(1) Assertion (Prati*gñ*â), the mountain has fire;

(2) Reason (Hetu [2]), because it has smoke;

(3) Instance (Udâhara*n*a or Nidar*s*ana), look at the kitchen hearth, and remember the Vyâpti between smoke and fire;

(4) Application (Upanaya), and the mountain has smoke;

(5) Conclusion (Nigamana), therefore it has fire [3].'

---

[1] Nyâya-Sûtras I, 32.

[2] Synonyms of Hetu are Apade*s*a, Li*m*ga, Pramâ*n*a, and Kara*n*a. Vai*s*eshika-Sûtras IX, 2, 4.

[3] The Vai*s*eshika terms are (1) Prati*gñ*â, (2) Apade*s*a, (3) Nidar*s*ana, (4) Anusa*m*dhâna, (5) Pratyâmnâya.

In both cases the process of inference is the same, but the second is supposed to be more rhetorical, more persuasive, and therefore more useful in controversy.

What is called by Anna*m*bha*tt*a the conclusion for oneself, corresponds *totidem verbis* to the first form of Aristotle's syllogism :—

All that smokes is fiery,
The mountain smokes ;
Therefore the mountain is fiery.

We must not forget, however, that whatever there is of formal Logic in these short extracts, has but one object with Gotama, that of describing knowledge as one of the qualities of the Self, and as this knowledge is not confined to sensuous perceptions, Gotama felt it incumbent on him to explain the nature and prove the legitimacy of the inferential kind of knowledge also. It is not so much logic as it is noëtic that interested Ka*n*âda. He was clearly aware of the inseparability of inductive and deductive reasoning. The formal logician, from the time of Aristotle to our own, takes a purely technical interest in the machinery of the human mind, he collects, he arranges and analyses the functions of our reasoning faculties, as they fall under his observation. But the question which occupies Gotama is, How it is that we know any thing which we do not, nay which we cannot perceive by our senses, in fact, how we can justify inferential knowledge. From this point of view we can easily see that neither induction nor deduction, if taken by itself, would be sufficient for him. Deductive reasoning may in itself be most useful for forming Vyâptis, it may give a variety of different aspects to our knowledge, but it can never add to it. And if on one side Gotama cannot use deduction, because it teaches nothing new, he cannot on the other rely entirely on induction, because it cannot teach anything certain or unconditional.

The only object of all knowledge, according to Gotama, is absolute truth or Pramâ. He knew as well as Aristotle that ἐπαγωγή in order to prove the ὅλως must be διὰ πάντων, and that this is impossible. Knowledge gained by epagogic reasoning is, strictly speaking, always ἐπὶ τὸ πόλυ, and not what Gotama would call Pramâ. The conclusion, f.i., at which Aristotle arrives by way of induction, that animals with little bile are long-lived, might be called a Vyâpti. He arrives at it by saying that man, horse, and mule (C) are long-lived (A); man, horse, and mule (C) have little bile (B); therefore all animals with little bile are long-lived. Gotama does not differ much from this, but he would express himself in a different way. He would say, wherever we see the attribute of little bile, we also see the attribute of long life, as for instance in men, horses, mules, &c. But there he would not stop. He would value this Vyâpti merely as a means of establishing a new rule; he would use it as a means of deduction and say, 'Now we know that the elephant has little bile, therefore we know also that he is long-lived.' Or to use another instance, where Aristotle says that all men are mortal, Ka*n*âda would say that humanity is pervaded by mortality, or that we have never seen humanity without mortality; and where Aristotle concludes that kings are mortal because they belong to the class of men, Gotama, if he argued for himself only, and not for others, would say that kinghood is pervaded by manhood and manhood by mortality, and therefore kings are mortal.

It would be easy to bring objections against this kind of reasoning, and we shall see that Indian philosophers themselves have not been slow in bringing them forward, and likewise in answering them. One thing can be said in favour of the Indian method. If we go on accumulating instances to form an induction, if, as in the afore-mentioned case, we add horses, mules, men, and the like, we approximate no doubt more and more to a general rule, but we never eliminate all real, much less all possible, exceptions. The Hindu, on the contrary, by saying, 'Wherever we have seen the attribute of little bile, we have observed long life,' or better still, 'We have never observed long life without the attribute of little bile,' and by then giving a number of mere instances, and these by way of illustration only, excludes the reality, though not the possibility, of exceptions. He states, as a fact, that wherever the one has been, the other has been seen likewise, and thus throws the *onus probandi* as to any case to the contrary upon the other side. The Hindu knows the nature of induction quite well enough to say in the very words of European philosophers, that because in ninety-nine cases a Vyâpti[1] or rule has happened to be true, it does not follow that it will be so in the hundredth case. If it can be proved, however, that there never has been an instance where smoke was seen without fire, the mutual inherence and inseparable connection of

---

[1] '*S*atasa*h* saha*k*aritayor api vyabhi*k*âropalabdhe*h*.' Anumânakha*nd*a of Tattva*k*intâma*n*i.

smoke and fire is more firmly established than it would be by any number of accumulated actual instances where the two have been seen together.

The conditions (Upâdhis) under which it is allowable to form a Vyâpti, that is to say, to form a universal rule, have greatly occupied the thoughts of Hindu philosophers. Volumes after volumes have been written on the subject, and though they may not throw any new light on the origin of universals, they furnish at all events a curious parallel to the endeavours of European philosophers in defence both of inductive and deductive thinking.

It seems hardly time as yet to begin to criticise the inductive and the deductive methods as elaborated by Hindu philosophers. We must first know them more fully. Such objections as have hitherto been started were certainly not unknown to Gotama and Ka*n*âda themselves. In accordance with their system of Pûrvapaksha and Uttarapaksha, every conceivable objection was started by them and carefully analysed and answered. Thus it has been pointed out by European philosophers that the proposition that wherever there is smoke there is fire, would really lose its universal character[1] by the introduction of the instance, 'as on the kitchen hearth.' But the Hindu logicians also were perfectly aware of the fact that this instance is not essential to a syllogism. They look upon the instance simply as a helpful reminder for

---

[1] Ritter, History of Philosophy, IV, p. 365, says that 'two members of Ka*n*âda's argument are evidently superfluous, while, by the introduction of an example in the third, the universality of the conclusion is vitiated.'

controversial purposes, as an illustration to assist the memory, not as an essential part of the process of the proof itself. It is meant to remind us that we must look out for a Vyâpti between the smoke which we see, and the fire which is implied, but not seen. It is therefore in rhetorical syllogisms or syllogisms for others only that the instance has its proper place. In Sûtra I, 35 Gotama says, 'The third member or example is some familiar case of the fact which, through its having a character which is invariably attended by that which is to be established, establishes (in conjunction with the reason) the existence of that character which is to be established.' It is Indian rhetoric therefore far more than Indian logic that is responsible for the introduction of this third member which contains the objectionable instance; and rhetoric, though it is not logic, yet, as Whately says, is an offshoot of logic.

The fact is that Gotama cares far more for the formation of a Vyâpti, pervasion, than for the manner in which it may serve hereafter as the basis of a syllogism, which must depend on the character of the Vyâpti. A Vyâpti was considered as threefold in the school of Gotama, as Anvaya-vyatireki, Kevalânvayi, and Kevala-vyatireki. The first, the Anvaya-vyatireki, present and absent, is illustrated by such a case as, Where there is smoke, there is fire, and where fire is not, smoke is not. The second, or Kevalânvayi, i. e. present only, is illustrated by such a case as, Whatever is cognisable is nameable, where it is impossible to bring forward anything that is not cognisable. The third case, or Kevala-vyatireki, is illustrated by a case such as, Earth is different from the other elements, because it is odorous. Here we could not go on and say, all that is different from the other elements has odour, because the only case in point (Udâhara*n*a) would again be earth. But we have to say, what is not different from the other elements is not odorous, as water (by itself). But this earth is not so, is not inodorous, and therefore it is not not-different from the other elements, but different from them, *q. e. d.*

Much attention has also been paid by Hindu philosophers to the working of the Upâdhis or conditions assigned to a Vyâpti. Thus in the ordinary Vyâpti that there is smoke in a mountain, because there is fire, the presence of wet fuel was an Upâdhi, or indispensable condition. This Upâdhi pervades what is to be established (Sâdhya-vyâpaka), in this case, fire, but it does not pervade what establishes (Sâdhana-vyâpaka), i. e. smoke, because fire is not pervaded by or invariably accompanied by wet fuel, as, for instance, in the case of a red-hot iron ball, where we have really fire without smoke. Hence it would not follow by necessity that there is fire because there is smoke, or that there is no fire because there is no smoke. How far the Indian mind may go in these minutiae of reasoning may be seen from the following instance given by Dr. Ballantyne in his Lectures on the Nyâya-philosophy, founded chiefly on the Tarka-sa*m*graha, p. 59 :—

'To be the constant accompanier of what is to be established (Sâdhya-vyâpakatva) consists in the not being the counter-entity (Apratiyogitva) of any absolute non-existence (Atyantâbhâva) having the same subject of inhesion (Samânâdhikara*n*a) as that which is to be established. To be not the constant accompanier of the argument (Sâdhanâ-vyâpakatva) consists in the being the counter-entity (Pratiyogitva) of some absolute non-existence [not impossibly] resident in that which possesses [the character tendered as an] argument.'

The credit of this translation belongs not to me, but to the late Dr. Ballantyne, who was assisted in unravelling these cobwebs of Nyâya logic by the Nyâya-Pandits of the Sanskrit College at Benares. Such native aid would seem to be almost indispensable for such an achievement.

## CHAPTER IX.

### VAISESHIKA PHILOSOPHY.

#### Date of Sûtras.

It is fortunate that with regard to the Vaiseshika philosophy, or rather with regard to the Vaiseshika-Sûtras, we are able to fix a date below which their composition cannot be placed. In the year 1885 Professor Leumann, well known by his valuable researches in *G*aina literature, published an article, 'The old reports on the schisms of the *G*ainas,' in the *Indische Studien*, XVII, pp. 91–135. Among the various heresies there mentioned, the sixth, we are told, p. 121, was founded by the author of the Vaisesiya-sutta of the Chaulû race, and hence called Chaulûga[1]. If there could be any doubt that this is meant for the Vaiseshika-Sûtras it would at once be dispersed by the 144 so-called points of that system, as mentioned by the author, *G*inabhadra. *G*inabhadra's date is fixed by Professor Leumann in the eighth century A.D., and is certainly not later. This, it is true, is no great antiquity, still, if we consider the age of our Sâ*m*khya-Sûtras, referred now to the thirteenth century A.D., even such a date, if only certain, would be worth having. But we can make another step backward. Haribhadra, originally a

[1] Could this be meant for Aulûka?

Brâhman, but converted to *G*ainism, has left us a work called the Sha*d*d*a*rsanasamu*kk*aya-sûtram, which contains a short abstract of the six Dar*s*anas in which the Vai*s*eshika-dar*s*ana is described as the sixth, and in that description likewise we meet with the most important technical terms of the Vai*s*eshika. This short but important text was published in the first volume of the *Giornale della Società Asiatica Italiana*, 1887, and Sanskrit scholarship is greatly indebted to Professor C. Puini for this and other valuable contributions of his to *G*aina literature. The author, Haribhadra, died in 1055 of the Vîra-era, i.e. 585 Sa*m*vat, that is 528 A.D. This would give us an attestation for the Vai*s*eshika-Sûtras as early as that of the Sâ*m*khya-kârikâs, if not earlier, and it is curious to observe that in Haribhadra's time the number six of the Dar*s*anas was already firmly established. For, after describing the (1) Bauddha, (2) Naiyâyika, (3) Sâ*m*khya, (4) *G*aina, (5) Vai*s*eshika, and (6) *G*aiminîya systems, he remarks, that if some consider the Vai*s*eshika not altogether different from the Nyâya, there would be only five orthodox systems (Âstika), but that in that case the number six could be completed by the Lokâyita (*sic*) system which he proceeds to describe, but which, of course, is not an Âstika, but a most decided Nâstika system of philosophy. It is curious to observe that here again the Vedânta-philosophy, and the Yoga also, are passed over in silence by the *G*ainas, though, for reasons explained before, we have no right to conclude from this that these systems had at that time not yet been reduced to a systematic form like the other four Dar*s*anas. What we learn from this passage is that early in the sixth century A.D. the Nyâya,

Sâmkhya, Vaiseshika, and Pûrva-Mîmâmsâ systems of philosophy formed the subject of scientific study among the *G*ainas, and we may hope that a further search for *G*aina MSS. may bring us some new discoveries, and some further light on the chronological development of philosophical studies in India.

### Dates from Tibetan Sources.

Whenever we shall know more of the sources from which Tibetan writers derived their information about Indian literary matters, more light may possibly come from thence on the dates of the Indian philosophical systems of thought also. It is true that the introduction of Buddhism into Tibet dates from the eighth century only, but the translators of Sanskrit originals, such as *S*ânti Rakshita, Padma Sambhava, Dharmakîrti, Dîpamkara *S*rî*g*ñâna and others, may have been in possession of much earlier information. In an account [1] of King Kanishka (85–106 A.D.) and his Great Council under Vasumitra and Pûrnaka, we read that there was at that time in Kashmir a Buddhist of the name of Sûtra who maintained a large Buddhist congregation headed by a sage Dharmarakshita, and he is said to have belonged to the Vaiseshika school [2]. This would prove the existence of the Vaiseshika philosophy in the first century A.D., a date so welcome that we must not allow ourselves to accept it till we know what authority there was for the Tibetan writers to adopt it. It is taken from Sumpâhi Choïjûng, and the same authority states that after the death of

---

[1] Journal of Buddhist Text Society, vol. I, p. 1 seq.

[2] Ibid., vol. I, part 3, p. 19.

Kanishka, a rich householder of the name of Jati who lived at A*s*vaparanta in the north, invited Vasunetra, a monk of the Vai*s*eshika school, from Maru in the west, and another, Gosha Sa*m*gha from Bactria, and supported the native clergy, consisting of three hundred thousand monks, for a period of ten years.

### Ka*n*âda.

Although Nyâya and Vai*s*eshika have been often treated as sister philosophies, we must, after having examined Gotama's philosophy, give, for the sake of completeness, at least a general outline of Ka*n*âda's system also. It does not contain much that is peculiar to it, and seems to presuppose much that we found already in the other systems. Even the theory of A*n*us or atoms, generally cited as its peculiar character, was evidently known to the Nyâya, though it is more fully developed by the Vai*s*eshikas. It begins with the usual promise of teaching something from which springs elevation or the *summum bonum*, and that something Ka*n*âda calls Dharma or merit. From a particular kind of merit springs, according to Ka*n*âda, true knowledge of certain Padârthas, or categories, and from this once more the *summum bonum*. These categories, of which we spoke before as part of the Nyâya-philosophy, embrace the whole realm of knowledge, and are: (1) substance, Dravya; (2) quality, Gu*n*a; (3) action, Karman; (4) genus or community, Sâmânya, or what constitutes a genus; (5) species or particularity, Vi*s*esha, or what constitutes an individual; (6) inhesion or inseparability, Samavâya; (7) according to some, privation or negation, Abhâva. These are to be considered by means of their mutual similarities and dissimilarities, that is, by showing how they differ and how far they agree. Here we have, indeed, what comes much nearer to Aristotle's categories than Gotama's Padârthas. These categories or predicaments were believed to contain an enumeration of all things capable of being named, i. e. of being known. If the number of Aristotle's categories was controverted, no wonder that those of Ka*n*âda should have met with the same fate. It has always been a moot point whether Abhâva, non-existence, deserves a place among them, while some philosophers were anxious to add two more, namely, *S*akti, potentia, and Sâd*ris*ya, similitude.

### Substances.

I. The substances, according to the Vai*s*eshikas, are: (1) earth, P*ri*thivî; (2) water, Âpa*h*; (3) light, Te*g*as; (4) air, Vâyu; (5) ether, Âkâ*s*a; (6) time, Kâla; (7) space, Di*s*; (8) self, Âtman; (9) mind, Manas. These substances cannot exist without qualities, as little as qualities can exist without substances. The four at the head of the list are either eternal or non-eternal, and exist either in the form of atoms (A*n*us) or as material bodies. The non-eternal substances again exist as either inorganic, organic, or as organs of sense. The impulse given to the atoms comes from God, and in that restricted sense the Vai*s*eshika has to be accepted as theistic. God is Âtman in its highest form. In its lower form it is the individual soul. The former is one, and one only, the latter are innumerable.

### Qualities.

II. The principal qualities of these substances are: (1) colour, Rûpa, in earth, water, and light; (2)

taste, Rasa, in earth and water; (3) smell, Gandha, in earth; (4) touch, Sparsa, in earth, water, light, and air; (5) number, Samkhyâ, by which we perceive one or many; (6) extension or quantity, Parimâna; (7) individuality or severalty, Prithaktva; (8) conjunction, Samyoga; (9) disjunction, Viyoga; (10) priority, Paratva; (11)[1] posteriority, Aparatva; (12) thought, Buddhi; (13–14) pleasure and pain, Sukha-duhkha; (15–16) desire and aversion, Ikkhâ-dveshau; (17)[2] will, effort, Prayatna.

### Actions.

III. The principal actions affecting the substances are: (1) throwing upwards, Utkshepana; (2) throwing downwards, Avakshepana (or Apa); (3) contracting, Âkuñkana; (4) expanding, Utsârana (or Pras-); (5) going, Gamana. These actions or movements are sometimes identified with or traced back to the Samskâras, a word difficult to translate, and which has been rendered by dispositions and instincts, as applied to either animate or inanimate bodies. These Samskâras[3] have an important position both in the Sâmkhya- and in the Bauddha-philosophies. In the Tarkadîpikâ Samskâra is rendered even by Gâti (gâtih samskârâtmikâ bhavati), i.e. nature or inborn peculiarity; and in the Tarkasamgraha it is

---

[1] Here follow in some lists as 11 to 15, gravity, fluidity, viscidity, and sound. The remaining Gunas are said to be perceptible by the mental organ only, not by the organs of sense.

[2] Here again some authorities add Dharma, virtue, and Adharma, vice, Samskâra, faculty or disposition, and Bhâvanâ, imagination.

[3] See Garbe, Sâmkhya, p. 269 seq.

represented as threefold (Vega*h*, Bhâvanâ, and Sthitisthâpaka*h*).

In the Sûtras which follow, Ka*n*âda tries to point out certain features which the three categories of substance, quality, and action share in common, and others which are peculiar to two, or to one only. In the course of this discussion he has frequently to dwell on the effects which they produce, and he therefore proceeds in the next lesson to examine the meaning of cause and effect, and likewise of genus, species, and individuals. It may be that the name of Vai*s*eshika was given to Ka*n*âda's philosophy from the differences, or Vi*s*eshas, which he establishes between substances, qualities, and actions, or, it may be, from Vi*s*esha as a name of individual things, applicable therefore to atoms. But this, in the absence of decisive evidence, must for the present remain undetermined.

### Cause.

As to cause and effect, Ka*n*âda remarks that cause precedes the effect, but that, in order to be a true cause, it must be a constant antecedent, and the effect must be unconditionally subsequent to it. There is an important and often neglected difference between Kăra*n*a and Kâra*n*a. Kăra*n*a, though it may mean cause, is properly the instrumental cause only, or simply the instrument. An axe, for instance, is the Kăra*n*a, or instrument, in felling a tree, but it is not the Kâra*n*a, or cause. Causes, according to Ka*n*âda, are threefold, intimate, non-intimate, and instrumental. The threads, for instance, are the intimate cause of the cloth, the sewing of the threads the non-intimate, and the shuttle the instrumental cause.

### Qualities Examined.

In the second book Ka*n*âda examines the qualities of earth, water, &c. He, like other philosophers, ascribes four qualities to earth, three to water, two to light, one to air (Âkâ*s*a). These are the principal and characteristic qualities, but others are mentioned afterwards, making altogether fourteen for earth, such as colour, taste, smell, touch, number, extension, individuality, conjunction, disjunction, genus, species, gravity, fluidity, and permanence (II, 1, 31). Qualities ascribed to Î*s*vara, or the Lord, are number, knowledge, desire, and volition. In the case of air, which is invisible, he uses touch as a proof of its existence, also the rustling of leaves; and he does this in order to show that air is not one only. Curiously enough Ka*n*âda, after explaining that there is no visible mark of air (II, 1, 15) but that its existence has to be proved by inference and by revelation (II, 1, 17), takes the opportunity of proving, as it were, by the way, the existence of God (II, 1, 18) by saying that 'work and word are the signs of the substantial existence of beings different from ourselves.' This, at least, is what the commentators read in this Sûtra, and they include under beings different from ourselves, not only God, but inspired sages also. It seems difficult to understand how such things as earth and the name of earth could be claimed as the work of the sages, but, as far as God is concerned, it seems certain that Ka*n*âda thinks he is able to prove His existence, His omnipotence and omniscience by two facts, that His name exists, and that His works exist, perceptible to the senses.

Immediately afterwards, Ka*n*âda proceeds to

prove the existence of Âkâsa, ether, by showing that it must exist in order to account for the existence of sound, which is a quality, and as such requires the substratum of an eternal and special substance, as shown before. The question of sound is treated again more fully II, 2, 21–37.

A distinction is made afterwards between characteristic and adventitious qualities. If a garment, for instance, is perfumed by a flower, the smell is only an adventitious quality of the garment, while it is characteristic in the case of earth. Thus heat is characteristic of light, cold of water, &c.

### Time.

Time, which was one of the eternal substances, is declared to manifest its existence by such marks as priority, posteriority, simultaneity, slowness, and quickness. The arguments in support of the substantiality of air and ether apply to time also, which is one, while its division into past, present, and future, hibernal, vernal, and autumnal, is due to extrinsic circumstances, such as the sun's revolutions. Time itself is one, eternal, and infinite.

### Space.

Space, again, is proved by our perceiving that one thing is remote from or near to another. Its oneness is proved as in the case of time; and its apparent diversity, such as east, south, west, and north, depends likewise on extrinsic circumstances only, such as the rising and setting of the sun. Like time it is one, eternal, and infinite.

So far Ka*n*âda has been chiefly occupied with external substances, their qualities and activities, and he now proceeds, according to the prescribed order, to consider the eighth substance, viz. Âtman, the Self, the first in the list of his sixteen Padârthas. Like Gotama, Ka*n*âda also argues that the Âtman must be different from the senses, because while the senses apprehend each its own object only—(1) the sense of hearing, sound; (2) the sense of smelling, odour; (3) the sense of tasting, savour; (4) the sense of seeing, colour; (5) the sense of feeling, touch; it follows that there must be something else to apprehend them all, the work which in other philosophies was ascribed to Manas, at least in the first instance. Besides, the organs of sense are but instruments, and as such unconscious, and they require an agent who employs them. If we see a number of chariots skilfully driven, we know there must be a charioteer, and we know also that chariots and horses are different from the charioteer. The same applies to the senses of the body and to the Self, and shows that the senses by themselves could not perform the work that results in cognition. In defending this argument against all possible objections, Ka*n*âda, following the example of Gotama, is drawn away into a discussion of what is a valid and what is an invalid argument, and more particularly into an examination of what is a Vyâpti, or an invariable concomitance, fit to serve as a true foundation for a syllogism.

### Manas.

But he soon leaves this subject, and, without finishing it, proceeds to a consideration of Manas, the ninth and last of the Dravyas or substances.

This, too, is to him much the same that it was to Gotama, who treats it as the sixth of the Prameyas. In this place, as we saw, Manas might be translated by attention rather than by mind.

### A*n*us or Atoms.

What is thought to be peculiar to Ka*n*âda, nay the distinguishing feature of his philosophy, is the theory of A*n*us or atoms. They take the place of the Tanmâtras in the Sâ*m*khya-philosophy. Though the idea of an atom is not unknown in the Nyâya-philosophy (Nyâya-Sûtras IV, 2, 4–25), it is nowhere so fully worked out as in the Vai*s*eshika. Ka*n*âda argued that there must be somewhere a smallest thing, that excludes further analysis. Without this admission, we should have a *regressus ad infinitum*, a most objectionable process in the eyes of all Indian philosophers. A mountain, he says, would not be larger than a mustard seed. These smallest and invisible particles are held by Ka*n*âda to be eternal in themselves, but non-eternal as aggregates. As aggregates again they may be organised, organs, and inorganic. Thus the human body is earth organised, the power of smelling is the earthly organ, stones are inorganic.

It is, no doubt, very tempting to ascribe a Greek origin to Ka*n*âda's theory of atoms. But suppose that the atomic theory had really been borrowed from a Greek source, would it not be strange that Ka*n*âda's atoms are supposed never to assume visible dimensions till there is a combination of three double atoms (Trya*n*uka), neither the simple nor the double atoms being supposed to be visible by themselves. I do not remember anything like this in Epicurean authors, and it seems to me to give quite an independent character to Kaṇâda's view of the nature of an atom.

We are told that water, in its atomic state, is eternal, as an aggregate transient. Beings in the realm of Varuṇa (god of the sea) are organised, taste is the watery organ, rivers are water inorganic.

Light in its atomic state is eternal, as an aggregate transient. There are organic luminous bodies in the sun, sight or the visual ray is the luminous organ, burning fires are inorganic.

Air, again, is both atomic and an aggregate. Beings of the air, spirits, &c., are organised air; touch in the skin is the aërial organ, wind is inorganic air. Here it would seem as if we had something not very unlike the doctrine of Empedocles, *Γαίῃ μὲν γὰρ γαῖαν ὀπώπαμεν, ὕδατι δ' ὕδωρ Αἰθέρι δ' αἰθέρα δῖον, ἀτὰρ πυρὶ πῦρ ἀΐδηλον.* But though we may discover the same thought in the philosophies of Kaṇâda and Empedocles, the form which it takes in India is characteristically different from its Greek form.

Ether is always eternal and infinite. The sense of hearing is the ethereal organ: nay, it is supposed by some that ether is actually contained in the ear.

As to atoms, they are supposed to form first an aggregate of two, then an aggregate of three double atoms, then of four triple atoms, and so on. While single atoms are indestructible, composite atoms are by their very nature liable to decomposition, and, in that sense, to destruction. An atom, by itself invisible, is compared to the sixth part of a mote in a sunbeam.

### Sâmânya.

IV. As to Sâmânya, community, or, as we should say, genus, the fourth of Ka*n*âda's categories, it is supposed to be eternal, and a property common to several, and abiding in substance, in quality, and in action. It is distinguished by degrees, as high and low; the highest Sâmânya, or, as we should say, the highest genus (*G*âti) is Sattâ, mere being, afterwards differentiated by Upâdhis, or limitations, and developed into ever so many subordinate species. The Buddhist philosophers naturally deny the existence of such a category, and maintain that all our experience has to do with single objects only.

### Vi*s*esha.

V. These single objects are what Ka*n*âda comprehends under his fifth category of Vi*s*esha, or that which constitutes the individuality or separateness of any object. This also is supposed to abide in eternal substances, so that it seems to have been conceived not as a mere abstraction, but as something real, that was there and could be discovered by means of analysis or abstraction.

### Samavâya.

VI. The last category, with which we have met several times before, is one peculiar to Indian philosophy. Samavâya is translated by inhesion or inseparability. With Ka*n*âda also it is different from mere connection, Sa*m*yoga, such as obtains between horse and rider, or between milk and water mixed together. There is Samavâya between threads and cloth, between father and son, between two halves and a whole, between cause and effect, between substances and qualities, the two being interdependent and therefore inseparable.

Though this relationship is known in non-Indian philosophies, it has not received a name of its own, though such a term might have proved very useful in several controversies. The relation between thought and word, for instance, is not Sa*m*yoga, but Samavâya, inseparableness.

### Abhâva.

VII. In addition to these six categories, some logicians required a negative category also, that of Abhâva or absence. And this also they divided into different kinds, into (1) Prâgabhâva, former not-being, applying to the cloth before it was woven; (2) Dhva*m*sa, subsequent non-being, as when a jar, being smashed, exists no longer as a jar; and (3) Atyantâbhâva, absolute not-being, an impossibility, such as the son of a barren woman; (4) Anyonyâbhâva, reciprocal negation, or mutual difference, such as we see in the case of water and ice.

It may seem as if the Vai*s*eshika was rather a disjointed and imperfect system. And to a certain extent it is so. Though it presupposes a knowledge of the Nyâya-system, it frequently goes over the same ground as the Nyâya, though it does not quote *verbatim* from it. We should hardly imagine that the Vai*s*eshika-Sûtras would argue against Upamâna, or comparison, as a separate Pramâ*n*a, in addition to Pratyaksha (sense) and Anumâna (inference), unless in some other school it had been treated as an independent means of knowledge; and this school was, as we saw, the Nyâya, which is so far shown to be anterior to the Vai*s*eshika-philosophy. Ka*n*âda denies by no means that comparison is a channel through which knowledge may reach us, he only holds that it is not an independent channel, but must be taken as a subdivision of another and larger channel, viz. Anumâna or inference. He probably held the same opinion about *S*abda, whether we take it in the sense of the Veda or of an utterance of a recognised authority, because the recognition of such an authority always implies, as he rightly holds, a previous inference to support it. He differs in this respect from the *K*ârvâka secularist, who denies the authority of the Veda outright, while Ka*n*âda appeals to it in several places.

A similar case meets us in Gotama's Nyâya-Sûtras (I, 16). Here, apparently without any definite reason, Gotama tells us in a separate aphorism that Buddhi (understanding), Upalabdhi (apprehension), and *G*ñâna (knowing) are not different in meaning. Why should he say so, unless he had wanted to enter his protest against some one else who had taught that they meant different things? Now this some one else could only have been Kapila, who holds, as we saw, that Buddhi is a development of Prak*ri*ti or unintelligent nature, and that conscious apprehension (Sa*m*vid) originates with the Purusha only. But here again, though Gotama seems to have had the tenets of the Sâ*m*khya-school in his eye, we have no right on this ground to say that our Sâ*m*khya-Sûtras existed before the Nyâya-Sûtras were composed. All we are justified in saying is that, like all the other systems of Indian philosophy, these two also emerged from a common stratum in which such opinions occupied the minds of various thinkers long before the final outcome settled down, and was labelled by such names as Sâ*m*khya, or Nyâya, Kapila, or Gotama, and long, of course, before the Sâ*m*khya-Sûtras, which we now possess, were constructed.

### The Six Systems.

It must have been observed how these six, or, if we include the Bârhaspatya, these seven systems of philosophy, though they differ from each other and criticise each other, share nevertheless so many things in common that we can only understand them as products of one and the same soil, though cultivated by different hands. They all promise to teach the nature of the soul, and its relation to the Godhead or to a Supreme Being. They all undertake to supply the means of knowing the nature of that Supreme Being, and through that knowledge to pave the way to supreme happiness. They all share the conviction that there is suffering in the world which is something irregular, has no right to exist, and should therefore be removed. Though there is a strong religious vein running through the six so-called orthodox systems, they belong to a phase of thought in which not only has the belief in the many Vedic gods long been superseded by a belief in a Supreme Deity, such as Pra*g*âpati, but this phase also has been left behind to make room for a faith in a Supreme Power, or in the Godhead which has no name but Brahman or Sat, 'I am what I am.' The Hindus themselves make indeed a distinction between the six orthodox systems. They have no word for orthodox; nay, we saw that some of these systems, though atheistic, were nevertheless treated as permissible doctrines, because they acknowledged the authority of the Veda. Orthodox might therefore be replaced by Vedic; and if atheism seems to us incompatible with Vedism or Vedic orthodoxy, we must remember that atheism with Indian philosophers means something very different from what it means with us. It means a denial of an active, busy, personal or humanised god only, who is called Îsvara, the Lord. But behind him and above him Hindu philosophers recognised a Higher Power, whether they called it Brahman, or Paramâtman, or Purusha. It was the denial of that reality which constituted a Nâstika, a real heretic, one who could say of this invisible, yet omnipresent Being, Na asti, 'He is not.' Buddha therefore, as well as B*ri*haspati, the *K*ârvâka, was a Nâstika, while both the Yoga and the Sâ*m*khya, the former Sesvara, with an Îsvara, the other Anîsvara, without an Îsvara, the one theistic, the other atheistic, could be recognised as orthodox or Vedic.

The Hindus themselves were fully aware that some of their systems of philosophy differed from each other on essential points, and that some stood higher than others. Madhusûdana clearly looked upon the Vedânta as the best of all philosophies, and so did *S*a*m*kara, provided he was allowed to interpret the Sûtras of Bâdarâya*n*a according to the principles of his own unyielding Monism. Madhusûdana, as we saw, treated the Sâ*m*khya and Yoga by themselves as different from the two Mîmâ*m*sâs, Nyâya and Vaiseshika, and as belonging to Sm*ri*ti rather than to *S*ruti. Vi*gñ*âna-Bhikshu, a philosopher of considerable grasp, while fully recognising the difference between the six systems of philosophy, tried to discover a common truth behind them all, and to point out how they can be studied together, or rather in succession, and how all of them are meant to lead honest students into the way of truth.

In his Preface to the Sâ*m*khya-Sûtras, so well edited and translated by Professor Garbe, Vi*gñ*âna-Bhikshu says: "If we read in the B*ri*hadâra*n*yaka Upanishad II, 4, 5, and IV, 5, 6, that the Self must be seen, must be heard, must be pondered and meditated on, hearing and the rest are evidently pointed out as means of a direct vision of the Self, by which the highest object of man can be realised. If it is asked how these three things can be achieved, Sm*ri*ti or tradition answers: 'It must be heard from the words of the Veda, it must be pondered on with proper arguments, and, after that, it must be meditated on continuously. These are the means of the vision of the Self.'

'Meditated on,' that is, by means proposed in Yoga-philosophy. Three things are known from passages of the Veda, (1) the highest object of man, (2) knowledge essential for its attainment, (3) the nature of the Âtman or Self which forms the object of such knowledge. And it was the purpose of the Exalted, as manifested in the form of Kapila, to teach, in his six-chaptered manual on Viveka or distinction between Purusha and Prak*ri*ti, all the arguments which are supported by *S*ruti.

If then it should be objected that we have already a logical treatment of these subjects in the Nyâya and Vai*s*eshika systems, rendering the Sâ*m*khya superfluous, and that it is hardly possible that both—the Sâ*m*khya as well as the Nyâya and Vai*s*eshika—could be means of right knowledge, considering that each represents the Self in a different form, the Nyâya and Vai*s*eshika as with qualities, the Sâ*m*-

khya as without, thus clearly contradicting each other, we answer No, by no means! Neither is the Sâ*m*khya rendered superfluous by the Nyâya and Vai*s*eshika, nor do they contradict each other. They differ from each other so far only as Nyâya and Vai*s*eshika treat of the objects of empirical knowledge, but the Sâ*m*khya of the highest truth. The Nyâya and Vai*s*eshika, as they follow the common-sense view that it is the Self that feels joy and pain, aim at no more than at the first steps in knowledge, namely at the recognition of the Âtman as different from the body, because it is impossible to enter *per saltum* into the most abstruse wisdom. The knowledge of those preliminary schools which is attained by simply removing the idea that the Self is the body is no more than an empirical comprehension of facts, in the same manner as by a removal of the misapprehension in taking a man at a distance for a post, there follows the apprehension that he has hands, feet, &c., that is, a knowledge of the truth, yet purely empirical. If therefore we read the following verse from the Bhagavad-gîtâ III, 29:—

'Those who are deceived by the constituent Gu*n*as of Prak*ri*ti, cling to the workings of the Gu*n*as (Sattva, Ra*g*as, and Tamas). Let therefore those who know the whole truth take care not to distract men of moderate understanding who do not as yet know the whole truth;'

—we see that here the followers of the Nyâya and Vai*s*eshika systems, though they hold to the false belief that the Self can be an agent, are not treated as totally in error, but only as not knowing the whole truth, if compared with the Sâ*m*khyas, who know the whole truth. Even such knowledge as they possess, leads step by step by means of the lower impassiveness (Apara-vairâgya) to liberation; while the knowledge of the Sâ*m*khyas only, as compared with the lower knowledge, is absolute knowledge, and leads by means of higher impassiveness (Paravairâgya) straight to liberation. For it follows from the words quoted from the Bhagavad-gîtâ that he only who knows that the Self is never an agent, can arrive at the whole truth, and from hundreds of true Vedic texts, such as B*ri*h. Âr. Up. IV, 3, 22: 'Then he has overcome all the sorrows of the heart'; thinking that desires, &c., belong to the internal organ (Manas) only; or B*ri*h. Âr. Up. IV, 3, 7: 'He, remaining the same (the Self), wanders through both worlds, as if thinking, and as if moving (but not really)'; or B*ri*h. Âr. Up. IV, 3, 16: 'And whatever he may have seen there he is not followed (affected) by it'; and likewise from hundreds of similar passages in the Sm*ri*ti, such as Bhag. III, 27: 'All works are performed by the constituents of matter (the Gu*n*as of Prak*ri*ti); he only who is deceived by Aha*m*kâra or subjectivation imagines that he is the agent'; and such as V. P. VI, 7, 22: 'The Self consists of bliss (Nirvâ*n*a) and knowledge only, and is not contaminated (by the Gu*n*as). The qualities (Gu*n*as) are full of suffering, not of knowledge, and they belong to Prak*ri*ti, not to the Self'—from all such passages we say that it is clear that the knowledge proclaimed by Nyâya and Vai*s*eshika with regard to the highest subject is overcome.

By this, however, we do not mean to say that Nyâya and Vai*s*eshika are not means of right knowledge, for their teaching is not superseded by the Sâ*m*khya so far as regards that portion which treats of the difference between Self and the material body. Here we must follow the principle (laid down in the Pûrva-Mîmâ*m*sâ), that what a word (chiefly) aims at, that is its meaning; (and apply it to the systems of philosophy). The Nyâya simply repeats the popular idea that joy pertains to the Self, without referring to any further proofs; and this chapter therefore is not to be considered as really essential (or as what the Nyâya chiefly aims at).

But admitting that there is here no difference between Nyâya-Vai*s*eshika and the Sâ*m*khya systems, is there not a clear contradiction between the Sâ*m*khya on one side and the Brahma-Mîmâ*m*sâ (Vedânta) and the Yoga on the other? The former denies the existence of an eternal Î*s*vara, the two others maintain it. Surely it cannot be said that here also the contradiction between these systems, the atheistic and theistic, can be removed by simply admitting, as before, two points of view, the metaphysical and the empirical, as if the theistic doctrine existed only for the sake of the worship of the multitude. Such a decision would here be impossible. The atheistic view that an Î*s*vara is difficult to know and therefore non-existent, may well have been merely repeated by the Sâ*m*khyas, as a popular idea, and in order to put an end to the desire of men for acquiring a divine status and divine honours (by means of penance, &c.), as in the case of the Naiyâyikas when they say that the Self possesses qualities (which must be taken as merely a provisional remark). In the Veda or elsewhere Î*s*vara, the anthropomorphic deity, is never explicitly denied, so that one could say that theism should be taken as the common popular view only.

In spite of all this we hold that here too these different views are really due to empirical or to metaphysical conceptions.

For as works like the Bhagavad-gîtâ (XVI, 8) when saying:—

'Those say that the world is unreal, without support, without an Îsvara,'

condemn the atheistic doctrine, we may very well suppose that the Sâmkhyas simply repeated a common popular view that there is no Îsvara, in order to discourage the striving after a divine status (so common among Saints), or for some similar purpose. They would naturally think that if they, so far following the materialists, did not deny the existence of an active Îsvara, the acquisition of the discriminating knowledge (of the Sâmkhyas, between Prakriti and Purusha) would be impeded, because those who believe in an infinite, eternal and perfect Îsvara, have their thoughts entirely absorbed by this Îsvara (so that they might not attend to the essential doctrine of the Sâmkhyas). No attack is made anywhere on theism, so that the theistic doctrine of the Vedânta should be restricted to sacrificial and similar purposes only. But from passages like Mahâbh. XII, 1167: 'No knowledge is equal to that of the Sâmkhya, no power to that of the Yoga,' and again XII, 11198: 'Let there be no doubt, the knowledge of the Sâmkhya is considered the highest,' we should learn the excellence of the Sâmkhya knowledge as superior to other systems, though only with regard to that portion which treats of the distinction of Self and Prakriti, and not with regard to the portion that objects to an Îsvara. Furthermore from the consensus of Parâsara also and all other eminent authorities, we see that theism alone is absolutely true. And from Parâsara's Upa-purâna and similar works the truth of the Brahma-Mîmâmsâ in its chapter on the Îsvara is perfectly manifest. There we read :—

'In the systems of Akshapâda and Kanâda (Nyâya and Vaiseshika), in the Sâmkhya and in the Yoga, whatever portion is in conflict with the Veda, that has to be rejected by all to whom the Veda is the only law.'

'In the systems of *G*aimini and Vyâsa (in the Pûrva and Uttara-Mîmâmsâ) there is nothing in conflict with the Veda; for these two in their knowledge of the meaning of the Veda have by means of the Veda fully mastered the Veda.'

From other passages also the superior authority of the Brahma-Mîmâmsâ may be gathered, at least with regard to that portion which treats of Îsvara. Thus we read in Mahâbh. XII, 7663 seq. :—

'Manifold philosophical doctrines have been propounded by various teachers; but cling to that only which has been settled by arguments, by the Veda, and by the practice of good people.'

From this passage of the Mokshadharma also (XII, 7663), and on account of the practice of Parâsara and all eminent authorities, it follows that the proof of the existence of an Îsvara, as proclaimed by the Brahma-Mîmâmsâ, the Nyâya, Vaiseshika and other systems, is to be accepted as the strongest; and likewise because by passages in the Kûrma and other Purânas the ignorance of the Sâmkhyas with regard to an Îsvara has been clearly pronounced by

Nârâya*n*a and others; e.g. 'Take thy refuge with the beginningless and endless Brahman, whom the Sâ*m*khyas, though strong as Yogins, are unable to perceive.'

Besides, that Î*s*vara alone is the principal object of the Brahma-Mîmâ*m*sâ is proved by the very first words and by other indications. If then it had been refuted on that principal point, the whole philosophy (the Brahma-Mîmâ*m*sâ) would no longer be a means of right knowledge, according to the principle, mentioned before, that what a word chiefly aims at, that is its meaning. The chief aim of the Sâ*m*khya, on the contrary, is not the denial of an Î*s*vara, but the highest object to be obtained by the Self by means of the discrimination between body and Self which leads to it. Hence, though it be superseded in that part which treats of the denial of the Î*s*vara, it will remain as a means of right knowledge, and this once more according to the principle that what a word chiefly aims at, that is its purport. The Sâ*m*khya has therefore its proper sphere, and is vulnerable in that part only which treats of the denial of the Î*s*vara, the personal and active god.

Nor would it be right to say that in the Brahma-Mîmâ*m*sâ Î*s*vara may indeed be the principal object, but not its eternal lordship or godhead. For, as the objection raised in the Pûrvapaksha as to its (the Mîmâ*m*sâ's) allowing no weight to the other Sm*ri*tis cannot be sustained, it is clear that Î*s*vara can only be the object of the Brahma-Mîmâ*m*sâ, provided he is characterised by eternal lordship.

If it is said that the first Sûtra of the Brahma-Mîmâ*m*sâ does not say 'Now then a wish to know the highest Brahman,' and that therefore it does not by the word Brahman mean the Parabrahman, we must not on account of the Sâ*m*khya denial of an Î*s*vara suppose that the Vedânta and Yoga systems likewise refer only to an evolved Î*s*vara (a Kâryes*v*ara, a product of Prak*ri*ti), for in that case the whole string of Sûtras from II, 2, 1, directed against the Sâ*m*khya and showing that mindless matter, being incapable of creating, cannot be established by mere reasoning, would be absurd; for if the God of the Vedânta were a made God, or a product of matter, the Sâ*m*khyas would have been right in teaching an independent matter (Prak*ri*ti). Lastly, the eternal character of Î*s*vara is quite clear from such Yoga-Sûtras as I, 26, 'He (God) is the Guru even of the oldest sages, because he is not limited by time,' and likewise from Vyâsa's commentary on that Sûtra. It is clear therefore that as the Sâ*m*khya means to deny the common popular anthropomorphic view of Î*s*vara only, whether as a concession, or as a bold assertion, or, for some other reason, there exists no real contradiction between it, and the Brahma-Mîmâ*m*sâ, and the Yoga.

Such concessions are found in other authoritative works also, as, for instance, in the Vish*n*u-Purâ*n*a, I, 17, 83:—

'O Daitya, these various opinions have I declared for those who admit a difference (who are not yet monists), by making a concession (to dualism). Let this abstract of mine be listened to.'

Nay it is possible that in some accredited systems also opinions should have been put forward in contradiction with the Veda in order to shut out bad men from a knowledge of the truth. Such parts would of course not be means of right knowledge, but the other and principal parts only, which are in harmony with *S*ruti and Sm*ri*ti. Hence we see that in the Padma-Purâ*n*a fault is found with all systems except the Brahma-Mîmâ*m*sâ and Yoga. Here we see God (*S*iva) saying to Pârvatî :—

'Listen, O goddess, I shall in succession tell you the heretical theories by the mere hearing of which even sages lose their knowledge.

First of all, I myself have taught the *S*aiva, Pâsupata and other systems, and afterwards others have been promulgated by Brâhmans, who were filled by my powers. Ka*n*âda has promulgated the great Vai*s*eshika doctrine, Gautama the Nyâya, Kapila the Sâ*m*khya. The Brâhman *G*aimini has composed a very large work of atheistic character, the first of the two Mîmâ*m*sâs, which treat of the meaning of the Veda. Then, in order to destroy the demons, Dhisha*n*a (B*ri*haspati) propounded the altogether despicable *K*ârvâka system ; and Vish*n*u, under the disguise of Buddha, propounded the erroneous Bauddha system which teaches that people are to go naked, and should wear blue or other coloured garments, while I myself, O goddess, under the disguise of a Brâhman (i.e. of *S*a*m*kara) have taught in this Kali age the doctrine of illusion (Mâyâ) which is false and only a disguised Buddhism. It is spread far and wide in the world, and attributes a false meaning to the words of the Veda. In it it is said that all works should be relinquished, and after surrendering all works, complete inactivity is recommended.

I have taught in it the identity of the highest Self and the individual Self, and have represented the highest form of Brahman as entirely free from qualities; and this in order to destroy the whole world in this Kali age. This extensive, non-Vedic, deceptive doctrine has been propounded by me, as if it presented the true meaning of the Veda, in order that all living things might perish.'

All this and more has been explained by me in the commentary on the Brahma-Mîmâ*m*sâ, and it is wrong therefore to say of any of the admittedly orthodox systems of philosophy that it is not the means of right knowledge or that it is refuted by others. For in reality none of them is contradicted or refuted in what constitutes its own chief object.

But, if it be asked whether the Sâ*m*khya-philosophy has not likewise made a mere concession with regard to the multiplicity of souls, we answer decidedly, No. For on that point there is really no contradiction (between the two, Sâ*m*khya and Vedânta) because it is shown in the chapter which begins at Brahma-Sûtras II, 3, 43, and declares that the individual self is a part of the Highest Self, because the multiplicity is stated (in the Veda); that the Brahma-Mîmâ*m*sâ also recognises a multiplicity of Âtman. But that the individual souls, as conceived by the Sâ*m*khya, are Âtman is certainly denied by the Vedânta, for it follows from Sûtra IV, 1, 3: 'They know him and teach him as Âtman,' that to the Vedântins, from the standpoint of absolute truth, the highest soul only is Âtman. Nevertheless the Sâ*m*khya does not thereby lose its authoritative character, because it is not superseded by the Vedânta in what constitutes its own characteristic doctrine, namely that for the individual soul, the knowledge of its being different from everything else, constitutes the true means of liberation. There is no contradiction therefore, because the concepts of the manifold Âtman and of the one Âtman, so well known from Veda and tradition, can be fully reconciled according as we take an empirical or metaphysical view, as has been explained by ourselves in the *Commentary* on the Brahma-Mîmâ*m*sâ—*Sapienti sat.*"

I have given here this long extract from Vi*g*ñâna-Bhikshu, though I have to confess that in several places the thread of the argument is difficult to follow, even after the care bestowed on disentangling it by Professor Garbe. Still, even as it is, it will be useful, I hope, as a good specimen of the Indian way of carrying on a philosophical controversy. Nay, in spite of all that has been said against Vi*g*ñâna-Bhikshu, I cannot deny that to a certain extent he seems to me right in discerning a kind of unity behind the variety of the various philosophical systems, each being regarded as a step towards the highest and final truth. He certainly helps us to understand how it came to pass that the followers of systems which to our mind seem directly opposed to each other on very important points, managed to keep peace with each other and with the Veda, the highest authority in all matters religious, philosophical and moral. The idea that the largely accepted interpretation of the Vedânta-Sûtras by *S*a*m*kara was a perversion of the Veda and of Bâdarâya*n*a's Sûtras, not much better than Buddhism, nay that Buddhism was the work of Vish*n*u, intended for the destruction of unbelievers, is very extraordinary, and evidently of late origin. Nay, nothing seems to me to show better that these Purâ*n*as, in the form in which we possess them, are of recent origin, and certainly not the outcome of a period previous to the Renaissance of Sanskrit literature, than passages like those quoted by Vig*ñ*âna-Bhikshu, representing the gods of the modern Hindu pantheon as interfering with the ancient philosophy of India, and propounding views which they know to be erroneous with the intention of deceiving mankind. Whatever the age of our philosophical Sûtras may be, and some of them, in the form in which we possess them, are certainly more modern than our Purâ*n*as, yet the tradition or Paramparâ which they represent must be much older; and in trying to enter into the spirit of the Six Systems, we must implicitly trust to their guidance, without allowing ourselves to be disturbed by the fancies of later sects.

# INDEX.

THE END.